STUDIES IN THE EARLY HISTORY OF BRITAIN

General Editor: Nicholas Brooks

Scandinavian Scotland

Scandinavian Scotland

Barbara E. Crawford

Leicester University Press   1987

First published in 1987 by Leicester University Press
First published in 1987 in the United States of America
by Humanities Press, Inc., Atlantic Highlands, NJ 07716,
and also distributed by them in North America

Designed by Douglas Martin
Set in Linotron 202 Trump Medieval
by Wyvern Typesetting Limited, Bristol
Printed and bound in Great Britain by
The Bath Press, Avon

British Library Cataloguing in Publication Data

Crawford, Barbara E.
Scotland in the early Middle Ages. –
(Studies in the early history of Britain).
2 : Scandinavian Scotland
1. Scotland – History – To 1603
I. Title   II. Series
941.101   DA775

ISBN 0–7185–1197–2
ISBN 0–7185–1282–0 Pbk

Foreword

The aim of the *Studies in the Early History of Britain* is to promote works of the highest scholarship which open up virgin fields of study or which surmount the barriers of traditional academic disciplines. As interest in the origins of our society and culture grows whilst scholarship yet becomes ever more specialized inter-disciplinary studies are needed more urgently, not only by scholars but also by students and by laymen. The series will therefore include research monographs, works of synthesis and also collaborative studies of important themes by several scholars whose training and expertise has lain in different fields. Our knowledge of the early Middle Ages will always be limited and fragmentary, and progress will only be made if the work of the historian embraces that of the philologist, the archaeologist, the geographer, the numismatist, the art historian and the liturgist – to name only the most obvious. The need to cross and to remove academic frontiers also explains the extension of the geographical range from that of the previous *Studies in Early English History* to include the whole island of Britain. The change would have been welcomed by the editor of the earlier series, the late Professor H.P.R. Finberg, whose pioneering work helped to inspire, or to provoke, the interest of a new generation of early medievalists in the relations of Britons and Saxons. The approach of the new series is therefore deliberately wide-ranging and will seek to avoid being unduly insular. Early medieval Britain can only be understood in the context of contemporary developments in Ireland and on the Continent.

This volume is the third regional study to be published, but it changes the pattern established for Wales and the East Midlands. It did not seem desirable to commission a volume surveying the history and settlement of the whole of Scotland in the early Middle Ages. Yet no simple geographical or chronological division commended itself. When Dr Barbara Crawford agreed to undertake *Scandinavian Scotland*, the way forward became clear. The Viking impact upon Scotland, as on other parts of Britain, fluctuated; but Scandinavian rule in the north and west and in the Northern and Western Isles lasted far longer than elsewhere in Britain. Scholarly study has, therefore, been highly specialized, scattered in diverse publications and often torn by academic controversies. The need to bring different strands of scholarship together and make their problems accessible to the lay reader has long been apparent. Dr Crawford, who has faced these problems in her teaching and in her historical and archaeological researches, here proves the ideal guide. It is intended that the series' coverage of Scotland will be completed by Dr Anna Ritchie's sister volume on Pictish and Scottish Scotland.

Birmingham University, April 1986   N.P. Brooks

Contents

List of illustrations

Acknowledgments

This book has been a long time in writing. Many reasons account for this; not least the demands of University teaching, but also the nature of the subject itself. 'The Vikings' are an elusive phenomenon, and although very real in the popular imagination, exceedingly difficult to pin down through historical fact and archaeological artefact in the part of Britain covered by this book. Only the sum total of very different sources of evidence enables the researcher to grasp the reality behind the popular image of the Scottish Viking. Of necessity, therefore, I have had to learn how to use the tools of many different trades, as well as to range very widely over the whole geographical area of the Viking world in order to gain an understanding of the history and society of those Vikings who settled round the Scottish coasts. (See the recent reference to a common complaint among Viking scholars that by the time you have acquired sufficient knowledge to write a useful and reliable study of the Viking period in European history you are too old to hold a pen! – N. Lund, 'The Viking expansion as a European phenomenon' in *The Viking Age in Europe*, Council of Europe Course for Teachers, Oslo, August, 1986, p. 14.) In attempting to do this one lays oneself open to criticism from those specialists whose knowledge of their own discipline is far more profound than my own understanding. It is hoped that I have been rescued from most errors and confusion by the kindness of those friends and colleagues who have read chapters of this book and given me the benefit of their specialist knowledge. In particular I would like to mention Dr Per Andersen, Professor Geoffrey Barrow, Dr Ronald Cant, Dr Gillian Fellows-Jensen, Mr Aubrey Halford-MacLeod, Dr Lindsay MacGregor, Dr Christopher Morris, Mr Alan Small, Mr Brian Smith and Mr William Thomson. Thanks are also due to Professor Richard Bailey, Professor Donald Bullough, Mr Ian Fisher, Mr James Kenworthy and Dr Alan Werritty for help on particular points, and especially to Professor Donald Watt for reading the whole text and making many suggestions for clarification. But the book would never have been written at all without the invitation from Professor Nicholas Brooks, and his support, encouragement and trenchant criticism. Despite some notable differences of opinion, our friendship remains as firm as ever and I am very grateful for his help. The task of seeing it into print has been made so very much easier for me because of the efficiency and expertise of Susan Martin and the Leicester University Press, and of Nancy Wood at the St Andrews University Computer. Many drafts and corrections passed through her hands and re-appeared as miraculously clean print-out in a technological revolution beyond my comprehension. My thanks are due especially to her for all the hard work put in after hours and for her constant equability.

The two men in my life, who have lived with this book for years, have provided me with the confidence and spirit to finish it. We have all learnt much in the process, as well as enjoying to the full the Viking Isles of Scandinavian Scotland which form such an important part of our life together.

To the members of the Scottish Society for Northern Studies in whose stimulating and enjoyable company I have visited many of the places mentioned in this book

Introduction: Sources and Evidence

TERMINOLOGY

The title 'Scandinavian Scotland' is, like 'Roman Scotland', something of a contradiction in terms. 'Scotland' did not exist when the Romans attempted to incorporate northern Britain within their Empire. The kingdom of 'Scotland' was hardly in the making when the Scandinavian impact was first felt around the shores of Dál Riada and Pictland. Those parts of Albion which fell under the dominance of the Vikings, like the northernmost province of Cat and the archipelagos of the *Orcades* and *Hebudes*, were not to become part of the kingdom for centuries; three or four centuries in the case of Caithness and the Western Isles, six centuries in the case of Orkney and Shetland. But this title has been used for lack of a better one to describe those maritime and insular parts of north Britain which were settled and influenced by peoples speaking a Scandinavian tongue. Also included is the Isle of Man which only ever formed part of the Kingdom of Scotland for a very brief period, but which was an integral part of the Scottish–Scandinavian maritime milieu, controlled by the earls of Orkney at the height of their power in the late tenth and mid-eleventh centuries, and the seat of a line of kings who dominated the Hebrides thereafter. However, my coverage of the situation in the Isle of Man is incomplete; it is included primarily as a reference point for the archaeology and place-names of the Norse settlements round the Scottish coasts, being a particularly vital source of information and comparison as regards the many graves, sculptured stones and coin hoards which have been found in the island. These are worthy of far more attention and a much deeper analysis than it has been possible to give here.

The term 'Viking Scotland' has been avoided (although it might have helped the book to be a best-seller) because it is inapplicable to colonial settlements of farmers, and peculiarly inappropriate as far as Scotland is concerned, for the term 'Viking' was never used in contemporary sources of the pagan raiders around the Scottish coasts.[1] 'Scandinavian Scotland' is intended to be an umbrella term, bringing within its scope all parts of Scotland influenced by Scandinavian peoples, whether Norwegian, Danish or Irish-Norse, and all aspects relating to that influence – historical, social, literary, topographical, linguistic, archaeological and material – from the beginning of the raids in the late eighth century to the death of Earl Thorfinn the Mighty of Orkney which conveniently coincides with the Norman conquest of England. This is obviously a very diffuse theme, and the area covered is very wide. It has no territorial unity whatsoever, and the common link is singularly maritime – as will be explored in chapter 1. This reflects the nature of the Viking impact throughout Europe, which is widely spread, disparate and hard to quantify. But in one respect the Scandinavian settlement of Scotland resulted in a situation which made it different from any other Scandinavian settlement area; the islands off the Scottish coast were the only colonial settlement of inhabited lands over which the parent political authority of Norway came to exercise any control. This had long-term political repercussions, and the resulting close connections with the Scandinavian world were important in the history of the medieval Scottish kingdom.[2] For a few centuries the northern and western coasts of Scotland were a part of the Scandinavian world; for this reason alone the term 'Scandinavian Scotland' is justified.

The limitations of the word 'Viking' have been recognized by many writers: 'The association with piracy makes it something of a misnomer to call an entire period of Scandinavian history and civilisation the Viking Age, but it has proved too convenient to be abandoned'.[3] The origin of the word is obscure and many suggestions have been made as to its derivation.[4] But there is no doubt about its meaning in contemporary usage; Vikings were 'true professional pirates'[5] and the term is one of opprobrium. Modern usage of the term has, however, stretched it beyond its original connotation and it is now generally applied to all the populations of the northern countries during a far more extensive period. In fact the ninth and tenth centuries are universally known as 'The Viking Age' throughout northern Europe. However, if the Viking pirate abandoned his raiding/trading occupation and settled down as a farmer, he was no longer a true Viking.[6] An attempt will be made in this book to restrict the use of the word Viking in its narrower sense to those marauders who roamed the northern seas in the ninth century, and to apply the term 'Norse' to the settlers around the Scottish coasts and the culture which they brought with them.

As already noted, the northern marauders were never called 'Vikings' in the Scottish or Irish sources. The terms there used are *geinte* ('gentiles' or 'pagans') until the middle of the ninth century, with specific reference to their religion;[7] Danes, Northmen and *Lochlannaibh*[8] with reference to their origins; and *Gall* or foreigners, with variations of *Finn-Gall* (White Foreigners), *Dubh-Gall* (Black Foreigners) and *Gall-Gaedhil* (Foreign Gaels), all meaning something specific to the users, in an attempt to distinguish between the different groups of Northmen and Danes and those of mixed blood who moved in and out of Irish politics in the ninth century.[9]

SOURCE MATERIAL

All historians of the early Middle Ages have to learn to use a variety of evidence other than the purely historical. The inadequacy of written sources makes it necessary for historians to look to archaeology, place-names, numismatic material and stone sculpture for enlightenment about the society and culture they are studying. Nowhere is this more necessary than in the realm of Viking studies. In Scandinavia, the Viking period is regarded primarily as a prehistoric age in which all the major source material is archaeological.[10] This is not because the Vikings were illiterate, for they had their own script in the form of runes. But these have survived from the Viking period proper only as inscriptions on memorial stones: a valuable, but hardly a full source of historical information.[11] Not until the conversion to Christianity and the installation of a trained priestly caste conversant with the Latin alphabet and Roman methods of documentation did written sources of information in the Scandinavian countries begin to build up; and only in the twelfth century do these become an adequate source of information for historians to use. However, in other parts of Europe, the Viking Age is very much an historical period because Anglo-Saxon, Frankish and Irish societies were even then able to produce ample written sources: not only legal documents, but annals and chronicles of contemporary and past events. Moreover, much of this material is concerned with those same Northmen and Danes and their devastating effect on church and state alike in the different countries.

Documentary sources

We have always to remember that these written sources derive, not from the Vikings themselves, but from those who suffered from them. This point has been the lynchpin of the critical assessment of the significance and impact of the Vikings, and in particular the Danes in Anglo-Saxon England. Can we really rely on the accuracy of chroniclers who were determined to present the pagan raiders in the worst light because of the threat that they posed to the established Christian church and the teachings of that church?[12] As far as Scotland is concerned this problem is not particularly acute because there is no continuous contemporary national chronicle from the period of raiding and invasion like the *Anglo-Saxon Chronicle* in England. Irish chroniclers were, however, interested in the fate of Iona and give us a few vitally important facts about what was happening in Dál Riada and Pictland. When these come from the *Annals of Ulster* they are believed to be reliable, but another source of information, *Cogadh Gaedhel re Galliabh (The War of the Gael with the Gall)*, is a work of propaganda designed to glorify Brian Boru and the Dal Cais and written two and a half centuries after the event it describes.[13] Different versions of an indigenous *Scottish Chronicle* – some of the texts dating, however, from much later in the later Middle Ages – start to record events relating to Viking raids and attacks in the mid-ninth century.

Documentary sources do not survive from the Scandinavian parts of Scotland until the late twelfth or thirteenth centuries and in the Hebrides even post-date the handing of the Isles to Scotland in 1266. In fact, there does not exist a single contemporary document from the Western Isles during the whole of the Norse period. The Northern Isles are a great deal better off in many respects, and although there is no documentary material from the period covered in this book, we do at least possess one chronicle, written possibly in Orkney c.1200, which survives in a manuscript which was written in Orkney in the mid-fifteenth century, *Historia Norwegiae*.[14] Meagre though its information is about the history of the islands, it does appear to record genuine local tradition.[15] Information about happenings in the Orkney earldom and about settlers from the Hebrides who became the ancestors of prominent Icelandic families is woven into the rich corpus of Icelandic Saga material. This presents particular problems of its own for historians (see below, pp. 7–9), but some of the compilations by twelfth-century Icelandic historians, such as *Landnámabók (The Book of Settlements)*,[16] are recognized as being serious attempts to record the events of the colonization of Iceland which were remembered at that time, some of which relate to Vikings and settlers from the Scottish Isles. At the other end of the geographical spectrum, the relations of the Scandinavian kings of York and Dublin with Scotland are known only from English and Irish sources. These different historical traditions, of very uneven value, and widely divorced in time and space from Scandinavian Scotland, do not provide an easy corpus for the historian to interpret.

Because of the problems of interpreting these written sources, it is perhaps understandable (although hardly forgivable) that some archaeologists should regard the early Viking Age in Scotland as a 'document-hindered period'. Maybe it would be simpler to see the age as purely prehistoric,[17] but we have our written sources and we must use them; not only do they supply us with a partial chronological framework, they also provide us with a wealth of illuminating evidence about Norse society and culture which the dry bones of archaeology can rarely furnish. It has been cogently argued that the archaeologist who chooses to work in a historic period 'must recognise openly his dependence on historians',[18] and that the disciplinary barriers must be broken down between the archaeologist and historian. Most students of this period are trained in one discipline or the other, both of which require rather different approaches, one needing more 'scientific' aptitude than the other. Indeed, the gap between the two may be widening as archaeology becomes more technologically orientated; it is less easy now for an historian to master the archaeological material than it was two decades ago when F.T. Wainwright set a remarkable example in the field of Norse studies in both England and Scotland on how to synthesize different sources of evidence.[19]

Archaeological material

The glamour associated with archaeological discovery has fuelled great interest in the Vikings in the last 20 years, and it is the grave-finds and the settlement sites which are the basis of so many of the glossy books on the Vikings now filling the bookshops of Britain and Scandinavia. It certainly looks sometimes as if 'we depend in our study of Scandinavian Scotland almost entirely on archaeology' although it has to be 'largely interpreted in the light of later written sources'.[20] Here is another acknowledgment of the necessity of combining the two sources of information. Archaeology is a new science, and in Scandinavian Scotland there has been a settlement site to study only since the major excavations at Jarlshof c.1950 (resuming work started before the war) and their publication in 1956.[21] The random nature of the discovery of graves over the centuries and the poor preservation of grave-finds means that much of the material is worth little more than curiosity value. The very important and potentially significant Norse woman's grave from Perthshire was found so long ago that its exact location is very uncertain.[22] The study of the first Norse cemetery to be excavated in Scotland according to scientific methods of analysis is not yet complete or published.[23] Only in the last few years have the remarkable series of coin and silver hoards found throughout Britain in association with Viking raids and settlement been subjected to expert analysis, although they have excited interest for centuries.[24]

A new and potentially important branch of archaeology is environmental archaeology, which is concerned through the retrieval and microscopic examination of faunal and floral organisms to illuminate the living conditions of the people, their farming methods, their daily diet and their dire diseases. A start has been made on the laborious process of collecting and analysing this sort of material from several Norse and pre-Norse sites around the Bay of Birsay in Orkney.[25] All this new work is being done in the Northern Isles. Our understanding of Norse settlement in the Western Isles is virtually non-existent and will remain so until the site of Udal in North Uist is fully published.[26] The problems of locating suitable Norse sites for excavation have been discussed in relation to the Inner Hebrides.[27]

Despite the limitations of archaeological evidence, what little has been found or excavated tells us more about the domestic side of the Vikings' way of life than any of the historical sources, and unfolds another dimension to the picture of raiding and terror or the establishment of political structures. Strictly speaking, it is 'direct evidence only of practical skills, technological processes, aesthetic interests and physical sequences',[28] but this evidence also helps us to learn a great deal about the society under discussion, such as religious beliefs or relationships between peoples as well as the way man harvested corn and woman cooked food. However, there are big problems associated with the correct interpretation of this material, which is a matter for the expert investigator who understands what he is looking at, whether in the shape of a cooking pot, a heap of coins or a 'section' in the side of an excavation trench. Too often conclusions are based on limited material, or indeed the absence of material. Archaeological evidence is always incomplete and conclusions should therefore be tempered with caution. Problems of interpretation and chronology exist for the archaeologist as for the historian.[29]

Nonetheless, the potential of archaeology is unlimited, whereas the historical sources are finite: major archaeological discoveries may reasonably be expected, whereas substantial new written sources for our period are most unlikely to be discovered. What the existing documentary sources tell about the process of the Norse conquest of the Scottish islands can be retold in a few sentences: only archaeological examination of settlement sites can hope to add to that dim picture. What the written sources tell about the conversion of the Vikings is from a much later date and perhaps coloured by what later Norsemen thought had happened: only patient examination of graves and cemeteries may help us to understand something more about the process. Historians cannot afford to ignore the archaeological evidence, for it has become a major part of Norse studies.

Place-name studies

A third discipline, the study of place-names, has in recent years contributed a very great deal to Scandinavian studies throughout Britain. Toponymic evidence is a linguistic problem, but the historical information to be derived from place-names is exceedingly valuable. Historians are, therefore, increasingly looking to this body of evidence to provide them with answers to the how, where and why of settlement studies. However, only trained philologists can understand properly how the component parts of place-names have developed and the rules governing this development. Although 'the subject is not exceptionally difficult . . . it is full of pitfalls', and philologists are firmly convinced that untrained historians should not attempt to analyse the etymology of place-names without expert guidance.[30] The information which can be extracted from place-names about the nature of communities and tribal areas, the relationship of peoples and their administrative patterns, the growth and change of religion, personal nomenclature and the pattern and growth of settlement is so historically significant that historians are nonetheless deeply involved in the problems of place-name interpretation. This has been particularly so in England where the arguments of historians and linguists over the interpretation of Scandinavian place-names has dominated the field of Scandinavian studies for the last 15 years.[31] That debate shows what very far-reaching conclusions can be drawn from the pattern of place-names, about the nature of conquest by an incoming people with different speech, and about the relationship of the old with the new.

The whole study of place-names in Scotland lags far behind the situation in England. This is because of the very complex nature of the linguistic picture in Scotland, with, in particular, the existence of Gaelic names, which require specialized knowledge of a completely different language from either English or Norse/Danish. The pioneering work of Professor W. Nicolaisen – based on the researches of Hugh Marwick in Orkney[32] – revolutionized the study of Scandinavian settlement in Scotland. But there is a great need for this work to be furthered by more localized studies of place-names, particularly in Shetland and the Western Isles where we rely almost totally on place-names for evidence about Norse influence.[33]

The extent of Scandinavian place-names throughout Scotland is the surest indication of Scandinavian influence and provides us with *the* map of Scandinavian Scotland. Although names can change, particularly in the Gaelic-speaking areas where they can become almost unrecognizable to the untrained eye and ear, they do remain basically in form and content Scandinavian.[34] When recorded and mapped they give total coverage in a way that chance survival of archaeological finds will never do. Archaeological distribution maps distort reality because 'the gaps on them may have no significance'.[35] Odd finds of a Norse weapon tell us nothing beyond the fact that a Viking warrior may have passed that way. A scatter of Norse place-names, however, tell us quite clearly that there was a sufficiently permanent community of Scandinavian speakers established in the neighbourhood to impose their nomenclature on the local toponymy. Moreover, they offer a completely different aspect of Scandinavian activity, for these names are the names of farms and of farming activities for the most part, which were in the end the enduring imprint left by the Norse in Scandinavian Scotland. Or, in the case of coastal names which are scattered all round the Scottish shores we assume that they were impressed on the local nomenclature because of the dominance of the seas by the Vikings from the eighth to the eleventh centuries.

Saga literature

The historian of Scandinavian Scotland possesses one further source which, despite the problems of interpretation, can help us to have a better understanding of the Norse society of the colonies in the west than of any other society in Dark Age Scotland. This is the literature produced in medieval Iceland relating to the Viking Age, much of which has a bearing on the Norse societies in the Northern and Western Isles and which goes under the name of 'saga'. One of these, the saga of the Earls of Orkney (or *Jarls' Saga* as it will be referred to here) is specifically concerned with the history of the earls of Orkney from the late eighth until the end of the twelfth century.[36] Its twelfth-century section has been described as 'a brilliant portrayal in a living tongue with remarkable narrative power of the deeds and attitudes of all save the lowest in society' – of which any Scottish historian is rightly envious.[37] For the period up until the mid-eleventh century we have the problem of knowing how to treat a source which records tradition handed down by word of mouth and written down centuries later; but much use is made of it in the following chapters (in particular chapter 7, where its value as a source of information about Norse society in the islands is explored).

There are many different types of saga, some of them more 'historical' than others.[38] The Sagas of the Icelanders, or Family Sagas as they are sometimes called, and of which the *Saga of Burnt Njal* is the most famous, are a class of literature on their own. The saga writer took historical events and personages and turned them into dramatic entertainment by the addition of personal characteristics, clashes of personality and the influence of fate. They were written down long after the events they relate – many of the stories purportedly recording events of the time of the settlement of Iceland – and are no longer recognized as an accurate tradition which can be used by historians as a straight source of evidence about the past. The means by which these traditions were remembered and transmitted to generations of Icelanders before being written down is not known, although there are two schools of thought. 'Bookprose' theorists consider the sagas to be a primarily literary phenomenon which was created by individual authors and which sprang out of the cultural background of twelfth- and thirteenth-century Iceland, perhaps influenced to some extent by European writings coming into Iceland in this period. 'Freeprose' theorists think that the sagas are a written form of oral tradition and are therefore an accurate record of what happened long ago because these traditions were handed down faithfully over the centuries and were simply written down in the age of saga writing.[39]

These problems are also relevant – although not so obviously – as regards the more historical types of saga, which were not written primarily as works of literature, but as a record of the lives of the kings and great men. The most important of these is the remarkable compilation known as *Heimskringla*, or the *Lives of the Kings of Norway*, which was written by an Icelander, Snorri Sturlason, c.1225.[40] He was a learned, if rather worldly, member of a powerful Icelandic family who collected together an enormous amount of information relating to the poetry, history and mythology of a former age. He used earlier writings about the history of Iceland and earlier saga material about the kings, as well as the earls of Orkney, which he compiled into his own reconstruction of the past.[41] In this respect he is little different from any other medieval chronicler.

In one particular respect, however, Snorri is very different from most chroniclers, and provides historians with a valuable corpus of material which might otherwise never have survived into modern times: that is in his use of skaldic poetry. This had been composed by the court poets ('skalds') who were attached to the households of kings and great men for the purpose of recording their deeds, singing their praise, and lauding their prowess in battle. Most of it was composed during the lives of those men whose deeds were celebrated, and because of the complicated rules of alliteration and metre could not easily be altered, so that it was probably remembered very accurately – if sometimes misunderstood – over the period from the mid-ninth century to the age of saga writing. Moreover, as Snorri himself tells us in his preface:

> we rest the foundations of our story principally upon the songs which were sung in the presence of the chiefs themselves or their sons, and take all to be true that is found in such poems about their feats and battles: for although it be the fashion with scalds to praise most those in whose presence they are standing, yet no one would dare to relate to a chief what he, and all those who hear it, knew to be a false and imaginary, not a true account of his deeds: because that would be mockery, not praise.[42]

Whoever put together the disparate traditions about the earls of Orkney and wrote their saga (*Jarls' Saga* – and it was not Snorri Sturlason, although the author was probably closely associated with the intellectual centre at Oddi in southern Iceland, where Snorri was sent to be fostered[43]) – also used skaldic verses and wove his narrative about them. These include Earl Torf-Einar's own verse (and Earl Rognvald Kali's verse in the twelfth-century section of the saga). But of prime interest is the verse of the famous skald Arnor Thordarson, called *jarlaskáld* because he was patronized by both Earl Thorfinn Sigurdsson and his rival Earl Rognvald Brusisson, and was also related to one of them by marriage.[44] Arnor came from an aristocratic and wealthy Icelandic family and his own father was a gifted skald. He was of a peaceful disposition, and his dislike of the difficult situation when Thorfinn and Rognvald quarrel is expressed in his poetry:

> bad my lot will be, and
> bitter the test of friendship,
> if now, for war eager,
> the earls will fight each other[45]

Arnor followed Thorfinn in many of his battles and raids in Scotland and the Hebrides, and his poetry therefore reflects the quality of an eye-witness account, giving us a unique historical source for the reign of this most famous of the Orkney earls.[46]

If the historical sagas are woven around a core of skaldic verse, to what extent can we use the prose sections as a reliable basis for a historical framework? In the last half-century, Scandinavian historians have moved from a position of believing everything in the sagas to be an accurate record of their past to a position of not believing that anything in them is of much value for the historian.[47] Indeed this attitude of total scepticism has spread to such historical works as Ari Thorgilsson's *Íslendingabók* and the compilation on the settlers of Iceland called *Landnámabók*.[48] Historians have become very frightened of using this body of evidence and of being accused of writing 'saga history'. However, the school of Icelandic saga critics have shown how the historical sagas have to be treated like any other historical material; the researcher has to know how to sift in order to reach the basic factual evidence which can be grasped and used with confidence. As was said some years ago in a book which still remains a most comprehensive and stimulating study of the Viking Age: 'when the heaviest discount has been made on grounds of error, confusion, origin, transmission, invention, bias, propaganda, sources, influences, analogues, and dating ... a not too disappointing residue of acceptable material remains'.[49] One has to learn how to distinguish between the reasonable and incredible elements in the narrative; to be aware that information about persons and places may be reliable, whilst chronology and dates are probably not; to realize that dialogue is particularly liable to be literary invention; to appreciate that information about social customs of a past age is likely to be coloured by the saga writer's understanding of his own society, especially when this concerns the religion of his pagan ancestors which the church had been suppressing for centuries, elements of which may have survived to his own day as superstition and sorcery. This is not to follow the line of argument which would say that 'if there are no grounds for holding that a thing is unhistorical there are grounds for holding that it is historical'.[50] But it is to follow the latest comparative approach which sees many of the sources for the study of early medieval Europe as having similar inherent problems of interpretation and which urges a treatment of Scandinavian sources according to the same criteria.[51] All written sources are 'evidence only of a state of mind'[52] and the way to a better understanding of those sources is to appreciate the contemporary situation and psychology of the writer, whether he be a Bede, an Irish monk or an Icelandic literary craftsman interested in creating a work of entertainment. It is all 'historical' evidence and we have no right to reject any of it without sober consideration of its potential value.

One valuable feature of the last three sources of evidence – archaeological, place-name and literary – remains to be mentioned: their origin within the Norse world itself. Difficult though they may be to interpret, they do at least have the merit of being impartial evidence about the Scandinavian-speaking communities that settled around the Scottish coasts in the ninth century. Even if not free of the taint of being evidence of a 'state of mind' (even place-names), they are at least the state of mind of a Viking who gave a name to his farm, or of a skald or saga writer who knew and understood something of the society about which he was writing. The documentary sources which form the basis of chapter 2 are primarily the record of people who suffered at the hands of the Vikings or who were hostile to them. This point has been made already; the destructive aspect of Norse activity is therefore emphasized, and the early history of Scandinavian Scotland is primarily a record of violence and aggression. That this was initially the case is not much in doubt; but there was another side and a more peaceful one to the Viking picture, and the place-name and archaeological evidence do provide us with a view of the Norse in Scotland other than the traditional one.

METHODOLOGICAL FRAMEWORK

The above discussion of the sources is an important preliminary, for this book treats the history of early Scandinavian Scotland within a methodological framework. That is, the different source materials, an evaluation of them, and what we can learn about the Vikings in Scotland from them, form the basis of separate chapters. These are treated as the different frameworks essential for a study of this period which need to be understood on their own account, although they interlock one with the other to build up the whole picture of the Norse in Scotland from the ninth to the eleventh centuries. This is in some respects a rather ponderous approach to the subject, particularly at a time when the cry is all for more obvious liaison between scholars of different disciplines. However, the cautionary note expressed in a review of one historian's attempt to write an inter-disciplinary study of this period is timely: 'There is much talk these days of "interdisciplinary approaches", but the stress should be on the discipline as much as on the inter-.'[53] The need to consider and understand the different source materials is paramount; but they are, by their nature, so very different and conclusions drawn from them so disparate in their significance, that it is to some extent an artificial exercise to attempt a complete integration within the compass of separate thematic subject headings. As a place-name scholar has written, 'the disciplines of history, archaeology and philology must remain to some extent distinct', and it may unfortunately be true that 'Dr Wainwright's co-ordinating scholar is an ideal unlikely of attainment.'[54] Since the latter's remarkable attempts at synthesis were written, the disciplines have become more specialized and in some ways more separate, and these days there is not much room for the amateur linguist in the place-name field or the amateur archaeologist on the site. In truth, there does not appear sometimes to be much room for the historian who attempts to use all these sources of information in writing a comprehensive study of the period. It is certainly not axiomatic that only historians are able to handle a wide variety of source evidence, but they appear to be, in the main, the ones who are willing to try. Therefore, the following history aims to present the reader with the evidence for the Viking raids and settlements of Scandinavian-speaking peoples in Scotland in a series of framework chapters, which lay their emphasis in turn on the different sources and relevant techniques necessary for an understanding of the documentary, linguistic, archaeological and literary evidence. First of all, however, we must turn to the geographical framework within which these mobile invaders operated, and which is so basic to our appreciation of the Viking achievement.

1 The Geographical Framework

MARITIME ENVIRONMENT

The geographical framework of Scandinavian Scotland is maritime. Few of the events, and little of the culture outlined in the following chapters, were unaffected by the sea. Throughout the period covered the Northern and Western Isles and the northern and western Scottish coasts were controlled by a people whose outlook was seaward, whose way of life was dominated by the sea, and whose political structures were based on sea power. This introduced a very different political phenomenon into Dark Age Scotland, a thalassocracy, or naval state, which extended from a power base in the islands onto the neighbouring mainland coasts. The lines of communication between the Shetland islands at the northernmost point and the Isle of Man in the south were, however, too stretched and resources too few for this potential thalassocracy to become a permanent feature of the developing political structures in Scotland and north-west England.[1]

Sea communication

The importance of the sea, and the priorities of a people whose lives are dictated by it, are not easy for us to comprehend today, conditioned as most of us are by terrestrial ideas of society, politics and government. The maritime milieu of the North Sea and the Baltic is a totally different cultural environment from the land-based societies of central and western Europe. The latter were heirs of the Roman Empire, whose power was based on its network of roads and whose legions were the protectors and expanders of the land frontiers.[2] Eventually, these ideas of terrestrial empire spread to those parts of Europe which the legions never reached, mainly by means of conversion to Christianity and the teaching of the Church which everywhere relied on kings and princes of land-based states to protect it and further the work of conversion. To Scandinavian historians it appears that 'The Vikings were not merely defeated by Christ, but rather by an inland culture with Christian connotations.'[3]

The Scandinavian countries are a most notable example of those societies and states which use the sea as a means of communication. Although water is a frontier it is not a barrier, as mountains and forests are, but can be transcended by those with the means and become a link factor.[4] The Swedes forged their remarkable trading links across the Baltic and through the rivers of Russia in the Viking Age (see fig. 1), and were again to build up a great maritime empire in more recent centuries. The Danes live on a chain of islands linking the Jutland peninsula with the southern part of the Scanian peninsula and which they included in their area of influence right through the Middle Ages. Their

Figure 1. Scandinavia and the British Isles: places mentioned in the text.

colonial development in the Viking Age was across the North Sea and in the Middle Ages across the Baltic. The very name of 'Norway' indicates the maritime nature of the western Scandinavian kingdom; the country was merely the coastal hinterland to the very important sea routes up the west coast to the northern hunting grounds, the so-called 'North Way'. In the age of maritime cultural links, the southern part of Norway was sometimes dominated by Denmark from across the Skagerrak; the country was rarely united with the rest of the landmass of which it formed a part. The barriers to communication across the mountain ranges were far greater than the problems of crossing the North Sea. Norway's outlook was always seaward.

The radius of maritime contacts from Bergen in western Norway includes Shetland within the same diameter as Trondheim or the southern tip of Norway (see fig. 1). Orkney lies within the same range of sea-going contacts from Stavanger as southern Denmark. Given a good wind it might be possible to sail from Hordaland to Shetland in 24 hours. Of course, it would not be a voyage lightly undertaken in winter, but then neither was the sail round the headland of Stadt between Bergen and Trondheim, or round the tip of Jaeren, the most southerly point of Norway. In winter you stayed put wherever you happened to be. In summer, Shetland was perfectly accessible even without accurate knowledge of navigation, for being a long archipelago (70 miles from Muckle Flugga to Sumburgh Head) it did not require absolutely spot-on seamanship to make a landfall. In general, northern Viking voyages from western Norway probably started out by touching in at Shetland; most of the references to Shetland in the *Jarls' Saga* are of people calling in *en route* or of being storm-stayed there. The name of one of the approach waterways to Bergen – Hjaltefjord (ON *Hjaltland* = Shetland) – shows how important the Shetland link has been in the maritime history of western Norway. These islands were the gateway which took the northern Viking voyager to the centres of wealth and power in western Europe.

Another favourable factor when voyaging west from Norway was the prevailing direction of the winds. This was much to the advantage of those living on the eastern side of the North Sea, for the prevailing winds in spring are the easterlies, so that the Norwegian Vikings could sail west for their summer expeditions and return home in the autumn with the prevailing westerlies.[5] We forget too easily how not so very long ago man was utterly dependent on the state of wind and tide, and how indeed the change of wind has sometimes altered the course of history. The occasional mention in the sagas tells us about this aspect of man's dependence on the elements:

> Earl Rognvald and his men came to the conclusion that they ought to wait till the spring tide coincided with an easterly wind, for in those conditions it is virtually impossible to go between Westray and Mainland (Orkney), though with the wind easterly one can sail from Shetland to Westray.[6]

This factor makes it likely that prehistoric contact between Norway and North Britain started from the east; for with these winds it was unnecessary to have to spend the winter in strange territory, which most early sailors would have preferred to avoid.

Ships and seamanship

Viking skill in the art of navigation has been much discussed for, although the voyages around the seas of northern (and southern) Europe presuppose some sophisticated instruments for determining their ship's position, very little evidence for such instruments exists – either historical or archaeological.[7] Sailing directions that are mentioned in medieval sources are very generalized: to sail from Norway to Greenland one is told to sail north of Shetland 'so that you can just sight it in very clear weather' and so far south of the Faroe Islands 'that the sea appears half-way up the mountain slopes'.[8] At sea, the Vikings were unable to determine or check their ship's position by astronomical means since the observation methods possible were not accurate enough.[9] Obviously, however, they could hold a vessel on a line of latitude by practised observation of the sun and stars.[10] Perhaps they were less concerned about exact navigation than today's yachtsmen; and once in sight of land, coastal features were, as today, the main means of steering the right course. This is why the names of mountains, islands, headlands and rocks around the British coasts are strongly, and in many places totally, Scandinavian. In fact, 'sensible pilotage by eye and a good ship' were the most important factors in the success of the Viking voyages.[11]

The 'good ship' is a dramatic symbol of Viking culture, and thanks to remarkable archaeological discoveries in Scandinavia, we can appreciate the significance of these vessels in the Viking raids and voyages, and the techno-logical expertise which went into their construction.[12] Their ships gave the Vikings the advantage of surprise and were the secret of their mobility. In their campaigns in Anglo-Saxon England and in Frankia the mounted army and the sailing army were two units of one force.[13] The development of these vessels must have taken place throughout Scandinavia in the centuries before the Viking Age began, possibly as a result of the developing trade between western and northern Europe and a consequent growth in piracy.[14] Certainly some stimulus must lie behind the technical development of early craft into the superlative sailing vessels which have been uncovered in the grave mounds of Gokstad and Oseberg in Norway, and which stamp the Vikings and their culture with distinction in the history of Europe. The addition of a sail, the overlapping of the strakes (planks) bonded together with iron rivets (clinker-ing), the replacement of the flat keel plank with a T-shaped keel, the upward arching of the prow and the stern to strengthen the body of the ship, meant that long stretches of open water could be covered without rowing. The crew still acted as oarsmen but the oars were set lower and the rowports could be closed when the ship was under sail.[15] All these factors added up to important qualities which throw a good deal of light on the operations of the Norsemen. The vessels were exceptionally buoyant for riding over the waves; they were admirably adapted for rowing far upriver and for running up onto a beach so that the crew could jump onto dry land and be ready for fighting without having to swim. The vessel could also be drawn over an isthmus between two stretches of water.[16]

With advantages like that, the whole of the coast and all of the islands of western and northern Scotland provided an ideal and familiar playground for the Norsemen in search of plunder, trading opportunities or land. We have forgotten so much of the significance of ship transport; only those living in Scandinavian Scotland (and the few with sailing craft) now appreciate the importance of the right coastal waters for a life which revolved around sailing ships. But Scandinavian Scotland existed only within a network of transport by sea and water-borne cultural links. Place-names incorporating ON *skip* (= ship) are witness to the vital importance of their vessels in the lives of the Norse settlers around our northern and western coasts: for instance, Skippie Geo (ON *skipa-gjá* = ships' inlet) in Caithness and Orkney; Skipness in Argyll; Skiport (ship-fjord) in Uist; Port Sgibinis (ship-ness) in Tiree and Colonsay; Loch Long in Argyll was called *Skipa-fjörðr* by the Norse.[17] A few place-names actually include the Old Norse terms for particular kinds of vessels. Snek-kerem in Shetland may incorporate ON *snekkja* (= longship); Skudasund in Unst perhaps includes the name of a small general-purpose vessel known as *skúta*;[18] and Skennist in Papa Westray (Orkney) was in origin *skeiðarnaust*, the boat-noost (boat shelter above high tide line on a beach) where the fast long-ship (*skeið*) was drawn up.[19]

As these names show, different kinds of Viking craft were developed for different purposes. All would have been required in the new settlements: sturdy vessels for transporting whole families and their livestock; large, fast ships for warfare, trade and prestige travel; smaller boats with four, six or eight oars which could be manned by a family or group of neighbours for short sea-trips and fishing.[20] Very few of the boat graves found in Scotland have yielded any positive evidence of the type or size of boats used by the Vikings in their settlements; the boat from the grave at Balladoole in the Isle of Man measured 11m × 3m and was probably used for local fishing or trading trips.[21] Every settlement must have had its boat-house (ON *naust*); examples are gradually being recognized on the ground in the Northern Isles and recorded.[22] The paved and revetted ramp on the Brough of Birsay may have been designed to serve as a boat slip and if so would certainly have been fit for the finest earl's longship (see fig. 2).[23] It is probable that many others have disappeared due to the eroding coastline of many of the Scottish isles. Evidence of Viking seamanship and skill in boat-building has been found in the Western Isles; boat stems retrieved from a bog on the island of Eigg have close parallels in Norway and Denmark.[24] One of them, carved from a single piece of timber, has a V-shaped cross-section with six stepped edges on each side to which the strakes would be attached

Figure 2. Paved and revetted ramp on the Brough of Birsay, Orkney (photograph: author).
   Now abruptly eroded, this ramp must originally have sloped down to the beach, and may have been designed to serve as a boat slip. It leads up by the south side of the secular structures ('Sigurd's Hall'): see fig. 55.

with clinker nails (see fig. 3).[25] It compares very closely with a ship's stem piece found at Skuldelev, Denmark (wreck 3), which was from a lightly built cargo vessel c.13.5m in length and with a beam of c.3.2m.[26] Lying underneath a display case in the National Museum, one of the Eigg boat stems is not immediately recognizable for what it is: a testimony to the traditions of the Scandinavian north which were once alive in the Scottish islands, and which made this area a part of the Norwegian cultural milieu. Evidently a boat-builder on the island (but whether a specialist boat-builder or one of the island's farmers cannot be known) buried this very important part of his ship in a bog to season the wood.

Other remarkable and evocative memorials of the Viking ship culture were found at Jarlshof, Shetland. One is a lightly scratched representation of a rigged ship with high curving prow and stern; another is most probably a dragon's head prow (see fig. 4).[27] Both must have been common sights in West Voe and the pool of Virkie by Sumburgh Head in the ninth or tenth centuries. One of the few grave stones at Iona Abbey carved in a Scandinavian style has, on one face, a scene which includes a Viking ship with high stem and stern, and stepped gunwale (see fig. 5).[28] This is an early (probably tenth-century) predecessor to the more familiar late medieval war galleys carved on West Highland memorial slabs. But the most permanent memorial of Viking ship culture in the Hebrides is to be found in the number of Norse sea terms which were adopted into the Gaelic language.[29]

Maritime routes: Shetland to the Hebrides

Once across the stretch of open water between Norway and Shetland the Viking voyager could sail within sight of land all the way south-west to Ireland and the Irish Sea, which opened up southern Scotland, northern and midland England and the whole of Wales. He could continue further to western

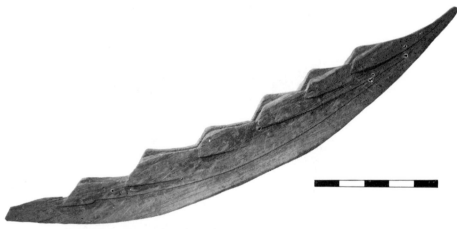

Figure 3. Boat-stem found in a bog on the island of Eigg, Inner Hebrides; ½m scale (Royal Museum of Scotland).
    Paralleled by many similar finds from Scandinavia, this remarkable discovery shows that the Norse settlers in the islands continued to build ships in the traditional manner.

0   8cm

0   3in

Figure 4. Drawings of ship and dragon's head from Jarlshof, Shetland (Royal Commission on Ancient Monuments, Scotland; Crown Copyright reserved).

Found in the midden surrounding the earliest Norse house at Jarlshof, it is difficult to give any precise date to these drawings, but they give a vivid impression of Viking ship culture. The masted ship (*a*) – with striped sail? – is of a more solid and sturdy type than the better-known longship; (*b*) is an unmistakable representation of a dragon's head, most probably a part of the ship's prow.

Figure 5. Ship-scene on a carved stone from Iona (Abbey Museum no. 49;
Royal Commission on Ancient Monuments, Scotland: Crown Copyright
reserved). Dimensions: 0.98m high × 0.08m thick × 0.42m wide at base.
     The lower part of the much-damaged shaft of a free-standing cross or
narrow cross-slab; for explanatory drawing see fig. 66.

England, western France and Spain and eventually into the Mediterranean Sea. Everybody prefers to sail within sight of land if possible and the Viking sailor was no exception. The chain of islands around the north and west coasts of Scotland are indeed a form of stepping-stones, and provide an ideal sailing route from Shetland down the western side of Scotland and Ireland of some 500 miles; a sort of extended coastline like the one with which the Norse Viking was entirely familiar at home. The route followed was much the same as that taken by *Odin's Raven*, the replica of a Viking ship which sailed from Trondheim to the Isle of Man in 1976 (see fig. 6); although it would have been safer to sail down the west side of Shetland in order to avoid the persistent sea fogs of the east side (see fig. 15), and the dangerous waters off the southern tip of Shetland, known as *dynrøst* (= roaring whirlpool) (see fig. 7). The latter is referred to in the saga sources, firstly when Earl Erlend of Orkney and Swein Asleifsson were sailing from Shetland to Orkney and 'they ran into dangerous tidal currents and fierce winds at Sumburgh Roost' which separated the ships,[30] and secondly, in 1248 when Harald Olavsson, King of Man, and his wife (the daughter of King Hakon of Norway) were drowned sailing from Norway back to Man: 'And it is the belief of most men that they were lost

Figure 6. The voyage of *Odin's Raven* from Norway to the Isle of Man (after A. Binns, *Viking Voyagers, Then and Now*, Heinemann, 1980).

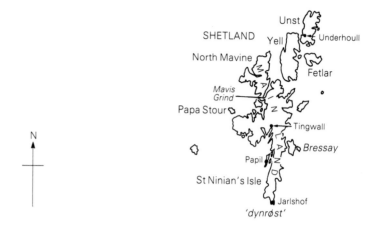

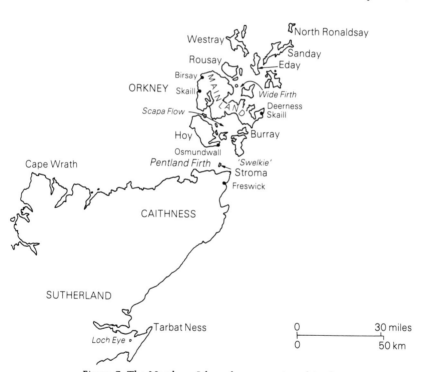

Figure 7. The Northern Isles: places mentioned in the text.

south of Shetland in *Dynrøst*; because wreckage of the ship was thrown up on Shetland from the south.[31]

Between Shetland and Orkney the island of Fair Isle (*Friðarey* in Old Norse sources) has always played an important role as a navigational aid, for its cliffs can be seen from both south Shetland and from North Ronaldsay, the most northerly of the Orkney Islands. It also had an important beacon, around the lighting of which several incidents in *Jarls' Saga* are woven. Reaching Orkney, the Viking voyager could either be guided round the heights of Noup Head on Westray down the western side of the archipelago and past the earldom site of Birsay to northern and western Scotland; or enter the sheltered, inland waters which lead from the north isles straight into Wide Firth and the isthmus at Scapa, where the later earldom centre of Kirkwall was established. Across the isthmus the almost-landlocked waters of Scapa Flow have provided a refuge for fleets throughout history, and they open out onto the Pentland Firth, the main shipping route around the northern coast of Britain. Fig. 9 below shows just how well placed the Orkney Islands are for any southward-moving colonial power with complete command of the sea: both the western and the eastern halves of Britain are fully accessible. It is not surprising therefore that the islands became the power base of the longest-lived and most independent of the west Norse dynasties.[32] It was from the Orkney viewpoint that the Hebrides were called *Suðreyjar* (the southern islands) and the earls' possessions on the mainland of Scotland beyond Caithness were called *Suðrland* (the southern land) (see fig. 7).

The Pentland Firth divided the two halves of the Orkney earls' dominions, but despite the treacherous nature of its currents and tides, it was no barrier to the political unity of Orkney and Caithness.[33] The name given to it by the Norse (*pettlands fjörðr* = Pictland's firth) may even date from well before the recognized beginning of the Viking Age c.800.[34] It clearly tells us that the north Scottish mainland and the Orkneys were very much the preserve of the Picts at the time of the early Viking exploratory voyages. The *Historia Norwegiae* also refers to the Pictland Sea 'so named by the inhabitants [of Orkney] because it divides the islands from Scotland',[35] the most dangerous part of which was 'the greatest of all whirlpools, which draws in and swallows down in the ebb the strongest ships and vomits and casts up their fragments in the flood'. This is the Swelkie (ON *svelgr* = whirlpool) near Stroma (see fig. 7), in which the ship of Earl Hakon of Lade, the powerful henchman of King Cnut, was most probably lost with all hands on returning to Norway from England in the autumn of 1029. As Snorri tells us:

> Some relate that the vessel was seen north of Caithness in the evening in a heavy storm, and the wind blowing out of the Pentland Firth. They who believe this report say the vessel drove out into the Swelkie; but with certainty people knew only that Earl Hakon was missing in the ocean, and nothing belonging to the ship ever came to land.[36]

Also in 1263, one of the ships returning to Norway after the Battle of Largs went down in the tidal race:

> And when they were sailing over the Pentland Firth, there was a great 'race' in the firth, and there a ship from Rygiafylk was lost, and all the men that were in her. John of Hestby was driven east along the firth, and it was a very near thing that he had not been driven into the Swelkie.[37]

Passing west through the Pentland Firth, the Viking ships had to round the headland of Cape Wrath (ON *hvarf* = turning point) for access to the northern Hebrides. This was – and is – an exposed and stormy stretch of open ocean with no shelter at all from the full blast of the Atlantic gales. If the Viking voyager was aiming for the southern Hebrides and Ireland, a far more direct route from Orkney leads down the eastern side of Caithness and through the Moray Firth to the Great Glen, that cleft dividing northern Scotland in half which has provided a relatively easy passage for man since prehistoric times (see fig. 8).[38] More recently, it had been 'the main communication route between Scottish Dál Riada and northern Pictland'[39] (see fig. 9 and fig. 17), and incidents in Adomnan's account of Columba's life took place by Loch Lochy and Loch Ness as the saint travelled between Iona and the territory of the Pictish King Brude.[40] Once Scottish Dál Riada and northern Pictland had been over-run and settled by the Norse, it seems self-evident that they would continue to use this 'great through route' if at all possible. The obstacles were stretches of terrain which interrupt the river and loch system of waterways, and unfriendly natives. However, before the Caledonian Canal was constructed, this route was navigable by small boats with only two or three short portages along the 70-mile length.[41] When the earls of Orkney expanded their power southwards and possessed some control over parts of Moray and Argyll, the ability to use the

Figure 8. The Great Glen from the air (Aerofilms Ltd).
  From just north of Fort William, at the south end of the Great Glen, this view looks up the almost continuous stretch of waterway via Loch Lochy and Loch Oich to Loch Ness in the distance.

N

Lewis
Eye
Peninsula
Harris
Tarbert
Udal
N.Uist
Moray Firth
Skye
Glen Elg
Great Glen
Barra
Rhum
Eigg
Coll
Ardnamurchan
Tiree
Firth of Lorne
Mull
Iona
Tarbert
Colonsay
Jura
Loch Long
Loch Lomond
Firth of Forth
Oronsay
Tarbert
Islay
Arran
Kintyre
Firth of Clyde
GALLOWAY
Loch Ryan
Luce Bay
Solway Firth
Isle of Man

0   50 miles
0   50 km

Figure 9. Western Scotland: places mentioned in the text.

Great Glen would be of much use when attempting to combine rule over their territories in northern Scotland and the southern Hebrides, and when carrying out their harrying raids in western Scotland and Ireland.[42] The struggle with the native dynasty in Moray which emerges quite clearly in the pages of *Jarls' Saga* may have been occasioned by the determined effort by the Norse conquerors to drive a route through the heart of Cenél Loairn territory. The settlement around the Firths of Easter Ross was probably stimulated by the need to exercise control over these waterways which lead towards the Great Glen. The Firth of Lorne and the sea lochs at the southern end may indeed have been the area known to the Norse as *Dalir* (= Dales) over which Earl Sigurd the Mighty is said to have exercised control.

Isthmuses and portages

The Vikings' ability to use narrow necks of land over which they dragged their boats in order to circumvent long sea routes is not to be underestimated. Wherever the Old Norse element *eid* can be traced in a place-name it is certain that the isthmus would have been used as a portage. The Gaelic equivalent is Tarbert (*tairm-bert* = an 'over-bringing').[43] The numbers of these names existing all over the Northern and Western Isles testify to the significance of such a geographical feature to a society in which ships and boats were basic to its way of life. In Shetland portages must have been particularly important due to the elongated formation of the archipelago and to the fact that all vessels traversing the routes from Norway to Britain and from Norway to the North Atlantic passed by Shetland, and very often, due to weather conditions, would have passed through. Aith (*Eid*) in the West Mainland, where the isthmus is two miles long and rises 100 feet above sea level was important enough to give its name to an assembly ('thing') district and a parish. Similarly the parish of North Mavine takes its name from the portage at Mavis Grind (ON *maf-eids grind* = the gate of the narrow isthmus) where a neck of land only a few yards wide enabled the voyager to pass from the sheltered waters of Sullom Voe across to the west coast of Shetland rather than round the exposed north Mainland. Another portage only a mile or so away called Brae derives its name from *breid-eid* (= a broad isthmus).[44] There are several other places in Shetland where the name and traditions firmly point to common use of such portages.[45] In Orkney the important isthmus at Scapa (*Skalp-eid* = isthmus of the divide/ship) has already been mentioned; Eday takes its name (*Eidey* = isthmus isle) from the very narrow crossing point in the middle of the seven-mile long island,[46] and there are many other places where the name tells us that a boat could be transported from one stretch of water to another.

Also in the Hebrides, there are many examples of useful portages, such as Tarbert in Harris providing access from one side of the Long Island to the other; and further north the Eye (*eid*) peninsula near Stornoway is probably named after the narrow beach joining it to Lewis (see fig. 9). Similarly Loch Eye near Tarbat, Easter Ross, probably retains an echo of the previous Norse name for the passage across that peninsula (fig. 7).[47] When Gaelicized, ON *eid* can take many strange forms.[48] Well-known incidents in the sagas took place at some of the portages in the west: at Tarbert in the Mull of Kintyre (known as *Satíris-eid* to the Norse), King Magnus Barelegs was drawn across the isthmus in a skiff with the rudder set and himself at the helm to claim Kintyre for Norway.[49] This may be picturesque legend about a famous king, but the interesting comment is made by the saga writer that this peninsula 'juts out from the west of Scotland, and the isthmus connecting it to the mainland is so narrow that ships are regularly hauled across'.[50] At Tarbert between Loch Long and Loch Lomond some of the Norwegian warships on King Hakon's expedition in 1263 were dragged across in order to ravage Loch Lomondside;[51] this is recounted in the contemporary account of the expedition in King Hakon's Saga which is a factual and sober record of the events of the king's reign. The ability of the Vikings to move overland with their boats in much more difficult terrain is evident from their campaigns in Ireland.[52] The evidence for such manoeuvrability in all these locations provides strong grounds for believing that passage through the Great Glen presented no insuperable topographical problems to Norsemen with ships.

Maritime routes: Hebrides to Man

The reason for King Magnus' journey across the Mull of Kintyre in 1097 was that the king of Scotland had agreed to 'let him have all the islands off the west coast which were separated by water navigable by a ship with the rudder set'.[53] The impracticalities of this arrangement which tried to distinguish the Scottish mainland from offshore islands must have been realized many times in a part of Scotland where it is sometimes difficult to tell whether land is mainland or island;[54] the saga tale of King Magnus' attempt to include Kintyre in his lot no doubt reflects a realization that to separate Kintyre from islands to which it is linked by water made no sense in politico-geographical terms. This must have been the case in many other parts of the western seaboard which were linked by water with the offshore islands but separated from the interior of the country by difficult and sometimes impassable terrain. The agreement of 1098 was a political settlement made according to the growing principles of 'terrestrial empire' which attempted to cut the maritime links created by the Norse in the west since the ninth century. The immediate political results were negligible except for the boundary of the diocese of the Isles: the spheres of control established by the sons of Somerled in the next century were over island groups and the nearest section of mainland coast.[55] One brief reference to a lost charter of resignation to the Scottish king tells us that Glenelg (opposite the Isle of Skye) had at one time belonged to the king of Man;[56] probably much more of the western littoral belonged to other powerful Celto-Scandinavian chieftains of the Isles.

The Western Isles and the neighbouring Scottish coast form one cultural zone, but Ardnamurchan Point divides the islands effectively into the northern and southern Hebrides; and this becomes a rough political division in the twelfth century with the domination of Somerled and his family in Argyll and the southern Hebrides.[57] In the earlier period, some of the earls of Orkney were strong enough to exercise some power in the Western Isles, although influence from Ireland and the Isle of Man was usually predominant. However, the extent of this dispersed island chain must always have made it very difficult for any one authority to exercise real political control; the islands formed 'groups of more or less independent communities under chiefs whose authority over their followers depended largely, in the early stages at least, on their success in raiding'.[58] Such chiefs would indeed exercise a 'fluctuating authority over a group of islands' linked together by naval power; but historical details of which groups formed which chieftainships are exceedingly sparse. We only possess a few names, such as Earl Gilli of Coll, who, as brother-in-law of Earl Sigurd of Orkney, and possibly his tribute collector, must have controlled a large part of the southern Hebrides.[59] The political situation was basically dictated by geographical circumstances, in which maritime units formed the foundation, refined by personal and family strengths. Even when the kingship of Man emerged as the dominating force throughout the Hebrides, the overlordship exercised would usually have been of a nominal nature, with a 'feudal' authority delegated to the established families in the islands.

In the southern Hebrides, *Ilasund* (the sound between Islay and Jura) was a sufficiently important navigational feature to be referred to in the twelfth-century Norse poem *Krákumál* as the route taken by the Danish fleet.[60] The open passage to the Irish Sea round the Mulls of Kintyre and Galloway may often have been avoided due to the very strong tidal race round these headlands and resort had to the Tarbert portage and the isthmus between Loch Ryan and Luce Bay.[61] Once in the Irish Sea, there were few navigational hazards to prevent Vikings with ships from dominating the surrounding littoral. The Isle of Man must always have provided a valuable staging post and refuge for the Viking voyagers, but it was not until the tenth century that it became the base of historically-recorded Norse chieftains.

Considering that Man is an island in what is virtually an inland sea, any authority, even nominal, which its rulers did come to exercise outside that sea over the rest of the Hebrides is rather remarkable and a testimony to the effectiveness of sea power. Its establishment as the headquarters of the kingship of the Isles was, however, comparatively slow to develop and resulted from the difficulties experienced by Vikings in Dublin and the other trading ports of Ireland and the demise of the kings of Dublin. Although the Norse raided and ravaged throughout Ireland, their permanent establishments were all coastal and estuarine. The kings of Dublin were really sea kings, and the extraordinary efforts to establish conjoint rule in York and Dublin in the tenth century are only explicable in terms of maritime superiority in the Irish Sea area and the fjords of northern England and southern Scotland (Humber, Tyne, Solway, Clyde, Forth). It has been argued that the main means of communication between York and Dublin was the sea route via the estuaries of Clyde and Forth, however indirect this may appear to the average land-based historian. This involves a sea journey in sheltered inland waters with an overland passage of twenty miles between the upper reaches of Clyde and Forth.[62] The problems involved in negotiating this stretch of land with ships, and the transport of men and goods across from one estuary to the other must, however, have been formidable.[63] The importance of penetrating this route may have been highly relevant to the activities of the Norsemen in Lowland Scotland in the late ninth and early tenth centuries.[64] It was possibly a more desirable way of transporting men and goods to Divlinstanes in York (the name of the wharf where presumably goods from Dublin were unloaded) than either sailing 600 miles round the north of Scotland (or via the Great Glen) or attempting to cross the Pennines on foot.

In the tenth century, the Irish Sea became a Celto-Norse lake. Influence from a mixed culture can be seen in all the coastal fringes of Ireland, south-west Scotland, north-west England and parts of the Welsh coast. In the centre of it all the Isle of Man became a repository of Norse culture and the most successful political settlement of all, maintaining Scandinavian links and with its kings subject to the Norwegian Crown for several centuries. Tenuous though those links may have been, on occasion they were strengthened by efforts from the Norwegian side, and were usually more acceptable to the rulers of Man than overlordship from Scotland or England.

PHYSICAL ENVIRONMENT

Maritime links and the importance of sea routes came first. But there is no doubt that a desire for good land *in the right coastal environment* was an important factor in the Viking's choice of settlement site. The islands off the northern and western coasts of Scotland provided an ideal combination of farming land with immediate access to and control of the waterways. The maintainance of a maritime way of life and the need for ease of communication by sea lasted for several generations. Eventually, different social strata developed with the growth of a farming class which had little interest in maintaining their boats for raiding or service in the earls' or kings' *leidang*.[65] This development is apparent primarily in those islands which were unique along the whole archipelago, the low-lying and fertile Orkney Islands with the adjoining north-eastern lands of the Scottish mainland. There the land was rich enough to support a farming population comfortably. Elsewhere the settler's descendants would be tempted to continue to supplement their living resources with raiding and trading expeditions.

It cannot be said often enough that the Norsemen must have been attracted by 'a physical environment very similar to that which they had left behind in south-western Norway'.[66] The west coasts of Scotland and Norway are unique in Europe for their geological formation: the combination of off-shore chains of islands, long sea-lochs and fjords penetrating the mainland with the steep and rugged mountains of the interior, make communication with the eastern territories difficult if not impossible. Both environments meant that a combination of fishing, pastoral farming and fowling were the main means of subsistence. The Norsemen found in the Scottish islands a home from home. There was greater variety of resources than along the Norwegian coast; some islands being far more fertile, some far less so. All of them provided a way of life which required little adaptation.

Geology and land resources

This variety is dictated by the big basic geological differences. These range from the ancient and intractable Lewisian gneisses of Lewis and Harris to the newer Old Red Sandstone in Orkney, much of Caithness, and a broad zone fringing the Moray Firth (the west side of which correlates closely with the distribution of Old Norse place-names in the same locality: see fig. 10). The hard rocks of the west make the Outer Hebrides one of the most barren landscapes in Scotland, providing hardly enough soil to cultivate – and in eastern Harris no soil whatsoever. As the chronicler of Man recorded in the thirteenth century when King Reginald gave his brother Olaf the island of Lewis as his estate:

> Lewis . . . is said to be more extensive than the other islands, but thinly peopled, because it is mountainous and rocky, and almost totally unfit for cultivation. The inhabitants live mostly by hunting and fishing. Olaf took possession of this island and dwelt there; living, however, very scantily.[67]

Needless to say, Olaf did not remain content with his brother's gift. However, this barren landscape is relieved by the strip of wind-blown shellsand which lines the western littoral and provides a fertile and easily tilled soil (Gaelic = *machair*), making the western side of the Outer Hebrides and some of the Inner Hebrides very attractive settlement areas. From the numbers of Old Norse place-names which cluster where the machair lies it was evidently appreciated by the Norse settlers for its arable potential (see fig. 10). Another notable geological feature of the Hebridean islands is the series of Tertiary igneous rocks which feature in Skye, Mull and Arran (see fig. 10), and which weather down easily to provide patches of good fertile soil in those islands. Outcrops of limestone where they occur provide green and lush vegetation; the most striking in Scandinavian Scotland is the limestone belt in the Mainland of Shetland, where some of the best land in those islands lies in Weisdale and Tingwall valleys (see fig. 10).

But the biggest contrast with the hard, old rocks of Shetland and the Outer Hebrides are the new sedimentary layers of Old Red Sandstone which make up the underlying geology of the whole of Orkney and Caithness. This easily weathered rock has formed a softly moulded landscape with some of the Orkney islands barely rising 20 metres above sea level. The well-drained and light soils which result are easily cultivated and have supported farming communities since the fourth millennium BC, as the remarkable series of prehistoric monuments in the islands prove. The Orkney archipelago and north-east Caithness form a settlement area unique in Scandinavian Scotland, which was the basis of the power and wealth of the family who ruled there from the ninth to the fifteenth century. Although the Orkney Islands are in general very different geologically from the northern group of islands which make up Shetland, there are outcrops of the same Old Red Sandstone in the latter (see fig. 10), which makes the landscape in Sandness in the West Mainland, and the eastern side of the South Mainland, similar to Orkney in appearance and in arable potential. The same rock outcrops in western Scotland only in parts of Kintyre (see fig. 10), and as the saga writer tells us: 'Kintyre is thought to be more valuable than the best of the Hebridean islands, though not as good as the Isle of Man.'[68] Here lies another reason, no doubt, why Magnus Barelegs was determined to include Kintyre among his Scottish colonies. He also attempted to ensure Norwegian superiority over the Isle of

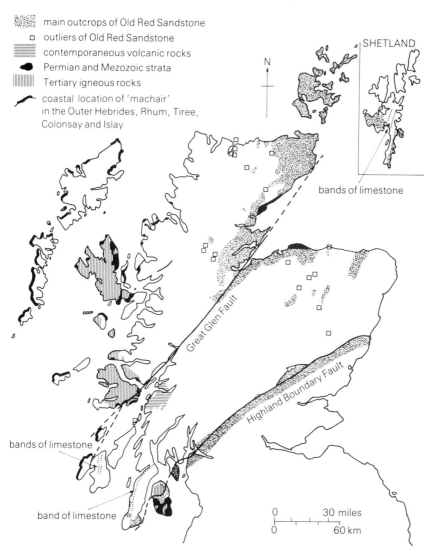

main outcrops of Old Red Sandstone

outliers of Old Red Sandstone

contemporaneous volcanic rocks

Permian and Mezozoic strata

Tertiary igneous rocks

coastal location of 'machair' in the Outer Hebrides, Rhum, Tiree, Colonsay and Islay

N

SHETLAND

bands of limestone

Great Glen Fault

Highland Boundary Fault

bands of limestone

band of limestone

0   30 miles

0   60 km

Figure 10. Geological features relevant to settlement in Scandinavian Scotland (after J.B. Sissons, *The Evolution of Scotland's Scenery*, Oliver & Boyd, 1967, fig. 7, and A.C. O'Dell and K. Walton, *The Highlands and Islands of Scotland*, Nelson, 1962).

Man, whose fertility, based on limestone and sandstone rocks, with a covering of glacial drift, did indeed make it a most desirable possession.

In general, the Norse settlers wished to farm those parts of western and northern Scotland which had been farmed by indigenous Iron Age populations. This may help to explain the absence of Norse settlement names along the west coast, for as can be seen from the map of Iron Age settlement zones (fig. 11), this was an area of patchy and localized settlement in the pre-Norse period.

☐ Highlands – sites rare

▨ Western Lowlands and Eastern Uplands – sites frequent

/// Eastern Lowlands – sites infrequent

0

0   50 miles

0   100 km

Figure 11. Iron Age settlement zones in Scotland (after H. Fairhurst, 'The geography of Scotland in prehistoric times', *Trans. Glasgow Arch. Soc.*, xiii, 1954, fig. 2).

Some economic comparisons

If the soil and land classification maps (fig. 12) are studied, it can be seen that in every respect the Orkney islands (except for Hoy) and north-east Caithness have qualities comparable with the Lowlands of Scotland, while Shetland and the Hebrides are significantly less favoured. Easter Ross and the firthlands

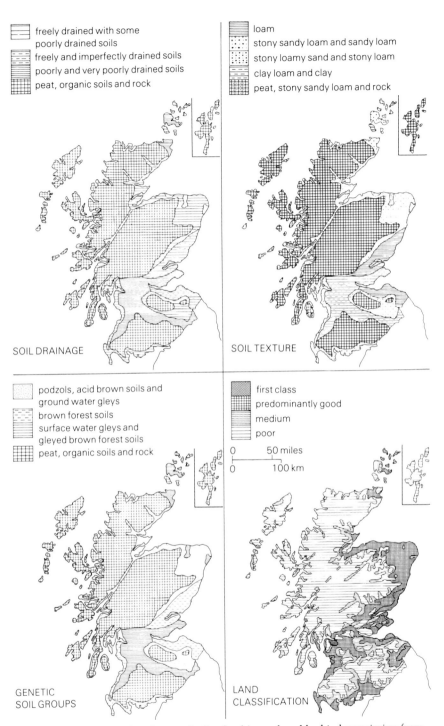

freely drained with some
poorly drained soils
freely and imperfectly drained soils
poorly and very poorly drained soils
peat, organic soils and rock

loam
stony sandy loam and sandy loam
stony loamy sand and stony loam
clay loam and clay
peat, stony sandy loam and rock

SOIL DRAINAGE

SOIL TEXTURE

podzols, acid brown soils and
ground water gleys
brown forest soils
surface water gleys and
gleyed brown forest soils
peat, organic soils and rock

first class
predominantly good
medium
poor

0   50 miles

0   100 km

GENETIC
SOIL GROUPS

LAND
CLASSIFICATION

Figure 12. Soil classification in Scotland (reproduced by kind permission from J.T. Coppock, *An Agricultural Atlas of Scotland*, John Donald, 1976, figs. 3–6).

round about, along with the coastal areas of Galloway, are the other parts of Scandinavian Scotland where grain grows well. The patches of better land throughout the Hebrides are rarely able to realize full arable potential because of the climatic factors. Average annual rainfall (fig. 13) is high throughout the Hebrides, although the western edges of the islands escape the worst of the

Figure 13. Average annual rainfall in Scotland (reproduced by kind permission from J.T. Coppock, *An Agricultural Atlas of Scotland*, John Donald, 1976, fig. 7).

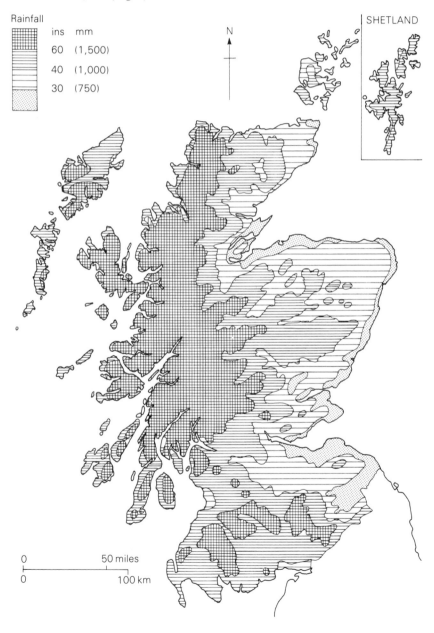

precipitation. Once more Orkney and Caithness are favourably situated, with the very tip of north-east Caithness and Easter Ross being in the driest band of the whole of Scotland. Nonetheless the comparatively low rainfall in Orkney and Caithness does not mean that drying of grain or hay is an easy process, for the moist Atlantic air carries a dampness which, with the wind and low summer temperatures, ensures that the growing and harvesting of crops is always difficult. The maps of the haymaking and barley harvest (fig. 14) show

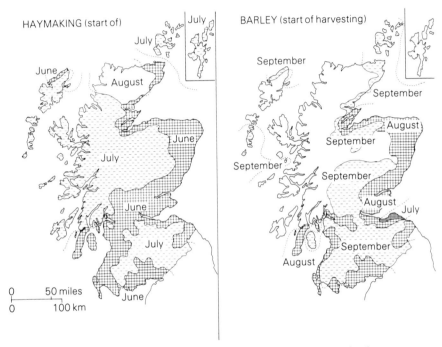

Figure 14. The start of haymaking and barley harvests in Scotland (reproduced by kind permission from J.T. Coppock, *An Agricultural Atlas of Scotland*, John Donald, 1976, figs. 14 and 15).

that Caithness is able to start the hay harvest in June, whereas July is the month for the haymaking season throughout the Northern and Western Isles (except, interestingly, for the Ness of Lewis and the Eye peninsula). Orkney, Caithness and parts of the Western Isles where barley is grown do not harvest until September. Galloway (and Kintyre) are both early in the hay and barley harvest season. The ability to harvest early means a far better chance of getting the grain into the barns dry. It was not uncommon in Orkney for the stooks to sit outside until blackened by the first frosts of winter. Even today, the Harvest Home in Orkney takes place in November.

Despite these difficulties, the climate and landscape of Orkney and north-east Caithness are, and always have been, far preferable to those of the rest of northern Scotland, and the Western Isles. Other favourability factors exist in the same areas, such as the excellent and easily-available sandstone flags for building. Man's preference for this environment is dramatically demonstrated by the evidence for very early neolithic farming settlement in several locations throughout the islands.[69] Grain-growing was probably an important feature of these early Orcadian societies, although proof of this in the archaeological record is not always easy to find. In the Norse period different kinds of cereal were grown, primarily oats and barley (*bere*).[70] The main taxes paid to the earl and the king of Norway in the fifteenth century were in malted barley and butter, reflecting the most important natural products of the Orkney Islands, whereas in Shetland they were paid in fish oil, butter and cloth, called 'wadmel' (ON *vaðmál* = a coarse woollen cloth produced in quantity throughout the North Atlantic islands). There is some evidence, however, that these commodities had replaced other, previous payments (in grain). Orkney malt had, no doubt, always been a highly valued product: *Jarls' Saga* describes Earl Rognvald Brusisson going to Papa Stronsay just before Christmas to collect malt for the Yule ale.[71] However, it was his rival Thorfinn who took the malt back to Kirkwall after he had put Rognvald to death.

Recent studies of Orkney prehistory conclude that 'The bulk of the palaeoenvironmental evidence points to the major landscape components of relief, climate, soil type and vegetation cover as having changed little since neolithic times.'[72] Perhaps the climate was slightly better in the Viking Age than today, for there was a period of climatic optimum in northern Europe from the ninth to the twelfth or thirteenth centuries.[73] If so, then it may have been possible for grain to be grown, dried and stored successfully without modern drying aids in the north Atlantic Viking settlements. No drying kilns have yet been recognized at early Norse settlement sites, and the late medieval house at Jarlshof provides the earliest excavated example of the round kiln so familiar from the older Orkney and south Shetland farms.[74] However, there must certainly have been more primitive ways of drying grain before the development of the round kiln, as on flat stones before the cooking hearth, which have been recognized at the Biggins, Papa Stour,[75] as well as at Norwegian sites.

Although in the seventeenth century the Hebridean farmer seems to have grown 'considerably more grain than was usual in Shetland',[76] we cannot be certain that such a contrast would have existed at an earlier date. All it is possible to say is that neither were able to produce grain as successfully as the Orkney farmer. Nonetheless, Shetland and the Hebrides must always have been a rich source of dairy products and skins and hides. We have no evidence of which commodities were paid in taxes in the Norse period from the Western Isles, only hearing about church tithes of butter and cheese in the thirteenth century.[77] In one important respect all the islands round the Scottish coasts had an advantage over the Viking homelands. The winter climate was mild enough for stock, in particular sheep, to be outwintered, which in Norway is possible only on the extreme coastal fringe. This cuts down a little on the need for large quantities of hay to be grown, or for the autumnal slaughtering of most of the stock, and enables the growth of wool and the manufacturing of cloth to be a major source of income. The small size of the native breed of sheep, cattle and horses, particularly well-known from the Northern Isles, but also probably similar in the Western Isles, made them more able to survive the rigours of the climate, and inadequate winter fodder.[78]

ABSENCE OF SETTLEMENT IN EASTERN SCOTLAND

The contrast between the physical environment of eastern England where the Danish Vikings settled and that of northern and western Scotland settled by the Norwegians certainly suggests that the different Scandinavian peoples tended to choose a farming environment that was similar to the one they left behind.[79] It was not simply the case that they made for the land which was nearer and more accessible, for both Danes and Norwegians are in evidence in raids all round the British Isles and Ireland. They had full mastery of the seas and coastal waters; as discussed above it is not unlikely that the Vikings used waterways further south in Scotland to obtain access from one coast to the other. Why then did they not attempt to settle along those waterways in southern Scotland? Were they content to take the poorer land of north and west simply because it was familiar and therefore more desirable? These are questions frequently asked, and they are not easy questions to answer.

Firstly, one should not ignore the scatter of place-names which show that there was a sparse but permanent Scandinavian presence in eastern Scotland.[80] Some of these are coastal, like the names of the two islands in the Firth of Forth, Fiddra and May; the former name of the harbour in Montrose – Stromnay; or of a sandbank in the Tay – Larick Scalp (ON? *leir-vík* = mud-bay). They are certainly given by maritime peoples in command of the waterways. Others are settlement names, such as Corbie (now lost) and Ravensby along the shores of the Tay, and Wedderbie and Sorbie further inland in Fife (see fig. 25). But there was quite clearly no large-scale settlement as in the islands and eastern England. Yet there was evidently a need for more land in the late ninth or early tenth centuries; this was the period when emigration took place from the Hebrides to the islands in the north Atlantic, and the period of the struggle to conquer north Scotland.[81] The most obvious area for further settlement was the interior of Ireland; that is, for a colonial movement from the trading ports of the Irish coast into the farming lands of Meath and Down. In fact, the Norse were pushed out of the coastal towns in the early tenth century and appear to have made attempts to win control in south-eastern Scotland.[82] The reason why they failed to do so must be the same as in Ireland: the leaders of the native population prevented them.

But that is only part of the explanation; there are very relevant geographical factors also. The sheltered and fertile lands of south-eastern Scotland, particularly around the estuaries of Forth and Tay, which would be the location most likely to appeal to Scandinavian settlers whose priorities were always for sheltered coastal waterways, are very cut off from any other area of Scandinavian settlement, whether in northern Scotland, or the Hebrides, or north-eastern England. Communities of Scandinavian speakers established around these waterways would not be in close or easy contact with other Viking settlements. Northwards it is a long sea journey around the 'inhospitable coasts' of Aberdeenshire and Banff to the Norse settlements of Easter Ross and Sutherland. This part of north-east Scotland is very exposed, with few rivers or sea inlets penetrating the land and giving shelter for shipping and with, moreover, the dangers of persistent sea fogs to boats navigating primarily by sight (fig. 15).[83] These factors presented an effective barrier to frequent maritime contact between northern and southern Scotland down the eastern side.[84]

less than 100 hours per annum
100-199 hours per annum
200-299 hours per annum
more than 299 hours per annum

N

0   50 miles

0   100 km

Figure 15. Frequency of coastal fog in Scotland (after F.E. Dixon, 'Fog on the mainland and coasts of Scotland', *Professional Notes*, no. 88, vol. VI, Air Ministry, London, 1939).

The sheltered and fertile lands of south-east Scotland also support a type of agriculture which was alien to the Norwegian Vikings. Once more we come back to the fact of national preference for an environment which was familiar. The Danish Vikings would no doubt have found the coastal farming lands of Fife, Perthshire and the Lothians very desirable, for they were looking for arable land which they could farm in the same way as they farmed in Jutland or Zealand. Eastern and midland England provided them with plenty of such arable land; although a few of this ethnic group probably eventually moved north, for those settlement names ending in -*bý* in south-eastern Scotland are perhaps most likely to have been coined by Danish settlers from eastern England, who used the element extensively.[85] The farmers of Sogn, Hordaland and Rogaland in western Norway who made up the bulk of the Norwegian emigrants to Scotland were pastoral farmers whose life-style was based on the raising of cattle and sheep with a little growing of oats or barley where possible. They lived in isolated farms, not in village communities. They could only have settled the arable lands of south-eastern Scotland if they had conquered the area with sufficient intensity to maintain a subject population who could farm the lands for them. Perhaps they chose not to do so when they were arriving in large numbers for the initial raids and possibly had the manpower; they were unable to do so when they tried to win control at a later date.

Figure 16. Scotland in the ninth and tenth centuries: places mentioned in the text.

2 The Chronological Framework: Part 1 c.800–954

RAIDING AND PIRACY

Dark Age Scotland was not unaccustomed to invasion. The Scots from Northern Ireland moved into the south-west c.500 and the Angles moved into British territory between the Tweed and the Forth during the following century. These were the outermost waves of the ferment of population movements which affected virtually the whole of Western Europe in the post-Roman era. From the long-term point of view, it is possible – and important – to see the succeeding Viking invasions of north and west Scotland (along with those of eastern England and the Irish coasts) as simply the last ripple of the Germanic barbarians' search for *lebensraum*.[1] However, the Nordic peoples' population movement has its own distinctive features, primarily the dominance of the waterways round the coasts of Britain and Europe which gave the Viking warbands a cohesion never possessed by earlier tribal invaders, and which contributed to their political and economic significance; an aspect which it is difficult fully to appreciate from scattered and disparate historical evidence. They also came from a different direction, and one which meant that the whole of the British Isles were exposed to their impact, not least the peoples of North Britain.

The first raids

The first thing one looks to the historical sources to provide is some indication of the beginning of the Viking Age in Scotland, and how this relates to the activities of the Nordic peoples throughout the rest of Britain and Europe. Considering the geographical factors discussed in chapter 1, it is evident that coastal Scotland must have felt the effects of the maritime expansion of the Vikings first of any of the coastal districts of Britain. All historians seem generally agreed that the Norwegians were on the move first, and as the isles of Scotland were on their route to the rich and populous parts of Europe we may suspect that raids, and perhaps some sort of pirate settlement, may have occurred in this maritime region already by the recorded date of the appearance of pagan raiders further south. One of the first raids on the English coast to be recorded, that on Portland in Dorset (between 789 and 802), may indeed have come from Hordaland on the west coast of Norway, which is where one of the English chroniclers understood them to have come from. But their route could have been via the west coast of Scotland and England and *east* along the Channel coast in search of merchandise, legally or illegally gained.[2] The first raid on the island of Lindisfarne (aimed at the shrine of St Cuthbert) in 793 is usually regarded as heralding the beginning of the Viking Age in Britain perhaps because historians 'find the pillaging of a monastery a more fitting opening than a slight but fatal misunderstanding with the customs' (such as the clash with the King's reeve at Portland).[3] The churchman Alcuin's much-quoted comment on this (or another early attack on Lindisfarne) – 'never before has such a terror appeared in Britain as we have now suffered from a pagan race, nor was it thought possible that such an inroad from the sea could be made'[4] – has suggested to most commentators that the attack came direct from Norway across the North Sea.[5] But the raid could equally well have been launched from the Northern Isles and these two raids on the English coast indicate a possible establishment of pirate bases in the Scottish Isles by the late eighth century. This is not to say, however, that these early raids were a by-product of settlement in the north.[6]

The dearth of sources from Scotland means that we are very badly informed about the first raids and seizure of lands or islands as raiding bases. The Irish monastic annals primarily record events down Scotland's west coast, and particularly the effect of raids on the community at Iona, which, as guardian of St Columba's shrine, was of particular interest to the Irish monks. The western seaboard of Scotland was regarded as one maritime region along with the north-western and north-eastern coasts of Ireland. The apocalyptic entry in the *Annals of Ulster s.a.* 794 – 'Devastation of all the islands of Britain by the gentiles'[7] – is the beginning of a dire catalogue of raiding and plunder which does not cease for the next half-century, and it is very remarkable how closely this ties in with the evidence of the first raids on England already mentioned. They may all have had a common origin or even have been carried out by the same raiders. But it was the Hebridean islands of Scotland and the coast of Ulster which bore the brunt of the attacks (according to the Irish sources): in 795 'The burning of Rathlin by the gentiles; and Skye was pillaged and devastated'; in 798 'The Hebrides and Ulster were plundered by Scandinavians (*Lochlannaibh*)'.[8] In 795 Iona was devastated as well as the monasteries of Inishmurray and Inishboffin, unprotected island communities, like Iona, down the west coast of Ireland, 'right in the path of southward bound vessels' (see figs. 16 and 17).[9] In 798 St Patrick's Island (off the east coast of Ireland) was burned by the gentiles 'and they took away tribute from the provinces, and Dochonna's shrine was broken by them and other great incursions [were made] by them, both in Ireland and Scotland.'[10] The litany continues and from the 790s to the 830s the raiding followed a clear pattern of 'hit and run affairs' by small and very mobile seaborne forces who were probably independent free-booters, attacking island and coastal monastic settlements, but with no certain raids recorded further than 20 miles inland in Ireland.[11] They gradually moved south until by 823 they had made a complete circuit of the Irish coast.

It is likely that these raids had been launched from somewhere nearer than western Norway, but it is surely not possible to go so far as to say that 'it is clear that the Orkneys and the Hebrides had been extensively settled by Norse fishermen and farming communities long before the Viking raids on the Irish coast.'[12] As a matter of fact the archaeological evidence does not permit such a conclusion to be made, and if it had been so then raids would probably have occurred earlier. The cumulative nature of the raids recorded in the late eighth century suggests that island or headland bases were being established by Norse

Figure 17. The abbey of Iona (Royal Commission on Ancient Monuments, Scotland: Crown Copyright reserved).

The later monastic buildings (restored) on the site of the Columban abbey, lying directly on the sailing route through the Hebrides. The Ross of Mull is in the middle distance, with Colonsay and the hills of Jura beyond.

pirates in the Northern Isles and the Hebrides at that time. But this is a very different matter from the permanent settlement of peaceful fishing and farming communities. The use of the Hebrides and Orkney as a base for piratical raids was well known in Icelandic tradition,[13] and this phase of *landnam* (land-taking) in the Scottish Isles may have gone on for a very long time. Its purpose was to provide bases for the Vikings' raiding activities rather than permanent settlements for agricultural exploitation (see below).[14]

We might be a little more definite on the matter of where the earliest raiders came from if we knew what the Irish monks meant when they used the term *Lochlannaibh* for the gentiles who attacked Ireland at this date (see the first entry for 798, quoted above). Translated as 'Scandinavians' the term is usually understood as referring to men from Norway (*Lochlann*), which indeed was the case at a later date.[15] But it has been suggested that in the first instance it meant the Hebrides or western Scotland,[16] although considering that the entry for 798 concerns the plundering of the Hebrides it is perhaps not likely that the two were then synonymous. As has been pointed out, the earlier form *Laithlind* suggests the use of the OI *lind* (pool), often used when referring to the estuarine bases of the Norse in Ireland. The first element could in that case be OI *loth/lath* (mud, mire; quagmire, marsh) and the whole name referring to an estuarine base of the gentiles in Gaelic-speaking Man or western Scotland.[17]

In conclusion, the historical sources give us sure evidence that the start of the Viking raids on western Scotland and Ireland was in the last decade of the eighth century. The total absence of documentary record from Scotland or Orkney means that we have no contemporary evidence whatsoever about the effect this population movement had on eastern Scotland or the Northern Isles. Later tradition certainly points, however, to the establishment of pirate bases in Orkney and Shetland, and their usefulness as winter lairs. These early raids were the precursor of the much more intensive raiding with political purposes, and the seizure of land for settlement purposes, which dominated the ninth century. The early raids were conducted by Norwegians only, for Danish participation starts a little later. Their purpose is the next point to be considered, and this is part of the vexed and contentious issue of the origins and causes of the whole Viking movement.

Origins and causes: raiders or traders?

For a phenomenon as widespread and diverse as that of Viking expansion, originating in Norway, Sweden and Denmark, one cannot expect to find a single cause, and in recent discussions of this problem the emphasis has been on the many and varied reasons involved in attempting to explain why the peoples of Scandinavia were impelled to move out of their homelands and impose themselves on their neighbours in the ninth century. However, the fact that *all* the peoples of Scandinavia – Danes, Swedes and Norwegians – were involved in this movement does suggest that there must be some common features in the nature of their economic or social development or in the stage of their relationship with western Europe which were responsible for this phenomenon. There is a long-standing explanation of over-population and land-shortage in Scandinavia, and it is very relevant in this connection to note that the arrival of the Norwegians off the shores of Britain a generation before their Danish cousins moved across the North Sea to England does suggest that the nature of the home environment may have played a part in stimulating their movement, first of all the northern peoples because agricultural resources were more limited in Norway than in Denmark.[18] Scandinavian historians have also thought that the inheritance system by which land was divided equally among all sons may have encouraged migration because it eventually produced too many farms which were insufficient for a family to live off.[19] Evidence for polygamy in the pagan societies of Scandinavia is likely also to provide a prime reason why the family units became too large for the land available.[20] A traditional explanation in Norway, based on Snorri Sturlason's account, is that the unifying activity of King Harald Finehair in the late ninth century impelled disruptive chieftains along the west coast to leave their homeland and move across the sea to lands where they could transfer their traditional social and political structures unimpeded: evidence for some sort of crisis in Scandinavian society has recently been restated, with emphasis on the dispossessed members of the royal dynasties being the important leaders of migrating warbands.[21]

But we are also being encouraged to look behind such factors, to the pre-existing contacts between Scandinavia and western Europe, stimulated by

trade, and to the important role which market forces played in the development of the wealth of Scandinavia and the confidence of the people to go out
and gain more wealth in the form of legally acquired, or illegally gained,
goods.[22] In the trading pattern of north Europe the natural products of the
northern lands – furs, walrus-ivory and ropes, amber from the Baltic – were all
highly valued commodities. The excavation of several trading centres in the
three Scandinavian countries[23] provides tangible evidence of this exchange of
goods. It probably stimulated a growth of wealth, which percolated through to
the general Scandinavian population, as witnessed by the grave-goods in the
pagan burials of the time. It seems that more and more of the population of the
Scandinavian north were becoming involved in the process of trading as the
eighth and ninth centuries progressed, and not all of them were as respectable
as the merchant Ottar who told King Alfred all about his mercantile resources
and the routes which he followed in the pursuit of his trading.[24] The growth of
piracy is attested as far as the Baltic is concerned.[25] It is these great trading
possibilities, and the need for traversing long stretches of water, which can be
seen as the stimulus behind the development of the ships of the northern
peoples in the century before the Viking Age.[26] All these factors lie behind the
Viking movement as a whole and they were steadily developing during the
centuries before the ships appeared off the coasts of Britain and Ireland.

Methods and purpose

How does Scotland fit into this picture of growing Scandinavian trade acting as
a stimulus to the superlative seamanship of the Vikings and their outward
movement from home in search of more wide-flung markets? First, there is the
question of what they were after, for the historical sources give no evidence
that the earliest arrivals were pursuing a peaceful trading course. Every entry
in the annals is of devastation and burning and pillaging and plundering. Is this
inflamed recording by monastic chroniclers who wish to put the marauders in
the worst possible light?[27] We should not doubt the horror of the impact of
these warlike peoples arriving out of the blue over the sea; nor were their
destructive raids entirely mindless. A significant piece of information is given
by the entry in the *Annals of Ulster s.a.*798 when the gentiles are said to have
'taken tribute from the provinces' and the shrine of the local saint was 'broken
by them' (see above, p. 40). This is the first mention of the classic piratical
technique of demanding protection money, which the Vikings were going to
perfect in all their dealings with the peoples of Europe. It was the most
satisfactory method of getting wealth – without having to pay for it, or fight for
it. The breaking of Dochonna's shrine was probably the means by which the
raiders acquired the precious objects and gold and silver which such shrines
incorporated; it is unlikely that they were destroying religious objects for
which they had no reverence through fury of pagan zeal. Their desire for and
acquisition of the beautiful reliquaries, shrines and mounts of book-covers
which filled the Celtic monasteries is attested by many finds of such metalwork in graves in Norway.[28] As has been pointed out recently, many of these
objects have been torn from their original mountings and re-used for secular
purposes. This makes it highly unlikely that they were acquired legitimately

through trade, as some Norwegian archaeologists have suggested, for no religious community would willingly allow their precious belongings, adorning the shrine of the saint of which they were guardians, to be given into pagan hands.[29]

The very process by which the raiders attempted to acquire such objects, and at what cost to the monastic guardians, is clearly described in a contemporary poem on the martyrdom of St Blathmac while attempting to protect the contents of the shrine of St Columba at Iona, an event dated in the *Annals of Ulster* to the year 825.[30] The poem was composed by Walafrid Strabo, abbot of Reichenau (838–849) in southern Germany, who undoubtedly got his information from Irish monks, many of whom were received at that monastery (see fig. 18). Blathmac, we are told, heard in advance of an impending attack on Iona, and determined to stand firm against the 'pagan horde of Danes'. He was celebrating Mass at the altar of the church when:

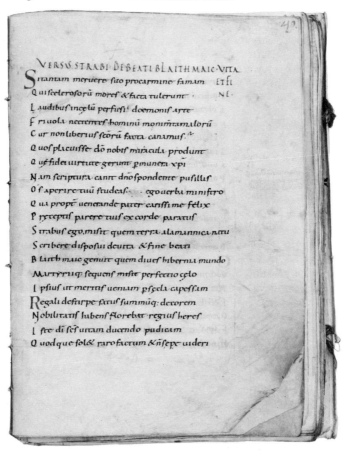

Figure 18. The opening stanzas of Walafrid Strabo's poem on the life and death of Blathmac, leader of the surviving monastic community on Iona (c.820–825). Strabo was abbot of Reichenau in south Germany (c.838–849). (Late ninth-century Codex in the Stiftstsbibliotek, St Gallen, Switzerland: MS 899, fol. 49r; reduced).

the violent cursed host came rushing through the open buildings, threatening cruel perils to the blessed men; and after slaying with mad savagery the rest of the associates, they approached the holy father, to compel him to give up the precious metals wherein lie the bones of St Columba; but [the monks] had lifted the shrine from its pediments, and had placed it in the earth, in a hollowed barrow, under a thick layer of turf ... This booty the Danes desired; but the saint remained with unarmed hand, and with unshaken purpose of mind, trained to stand against the foe, and to arouse the fight, and unused to yield.

So Blathmac won his martyr's crown, and this interesting account then adds the strange comment that 'what the fierce soldier could not purchase by gifts, he began to seek by wounds in the cold bowels of the earth'[31] suggesting that the intent had been to barter for the religious objects in some way. There has been some doubt over the translation of this particular passage[32] and the author was circumscribed by the metre of the poem and limited in his personal knowledge of the situation. Nevertheless he appears to have understood that the raiders may have attempted to offer money or goods in exchange for the precious objects they were seeking. But the monks would have been very unlikely to concur in such a transaction, and it would have been at the point when the raiders met resistance to their demands that such resistance had to be overcome. This was where the fine boundary between legal and illegal trading was over-stepped, and the Viking traders of recent history books and television series turn into the Viking raiders of yesteryear.

The evidence does suggest that the Vikings *were* resisted. The early raid on Jarrow in 794 was not entirely successful, for a combination of storms and attack by the local people seems to have decimated the raiding party.[33] The Scottish kingdom was in the long run very successful in defending itself against Viking attack, to judge at least from the sparsity of settlements apparently established in south Scotland. Even the martyr Blathmac whipped up opposition against the heathen, for he was an Irish prince who, according to Strabo, was 'trained to stand against the foe, and to arouse the fight, and unused to yield'. Perhaps we should interpret entries about the burning of Rathlin and the pillaging and devastation of Skye[34] as indicating some determined resistance by the island communities to the Vikings, rather than evidence of the latter's mindless violence. They were prepared to overcome all resistance to get what they wanted.

The 'quest for moveable wealth' was the dominating motif of Viking history,[35] and this quest took the form not only of direct plundering, but also of the 'more subtle exaction of tribute', and eventually the 'actual take-over of landed property';[36] all three aspects were practised in Scotland. Even plundering was a controlled exercise, for monasteries were not destroyed, but the surplus wealth of stock and provisions creamed off and the community left to re-establish itself so that it could be a source of exploitation on a future occasion.[37] Iona itself is recorded as having been attacked in 795, 802, and 806 (when 68 of the monks were killed), but the relics of St Columba were still being guarded there in 825, as we learn from the account of Blathmac's martyrdom. Nor can the relics have been discovered on that occasion, for in 829 they were taken to the mainland of Scotland.[38] Moreover, the Vikings learnt to raid monasteries on the great festivals of the church when thousands of people apparently gathered together, thus providing them with the opportunity to take captive and enslave large numbers of Irish and Scots.[39] There is nothing very mindless about such exploitation; even though it can be glossed by historians under cover of the respectable practice of 'trade', it was a policy of acquiring wealth coldly and ruthlessly put into practice.

Establishment of raiding bases

Such a life-style demanded manoeuvrability – which we know the Vikings had – as well as good knowledge of the geography and political circumstances of the societies they were marauding – which we can see they acquired. Throughout Europe they installed themselves on convenient and well-defended maritime points, such as headlands or islands, from which they could launch their attacks when local weather and political conditions allowed. In general, so far as we know, they do not appear to have launched piratical raids on merchant ships at sea, but to have attacked sea-borne wealth where it was most concentrated and convenient, that is in the merchant centres of western Europe or in the monasteries of Ireland and Scotland. So, suitably located islands were used as bases from which the Vikings could raid ports and prey upon nearby churches.[40] Off-shore islands anywhere were very convenient temporary or permanent bases, although few are as well documented as the Vestfold Vikings' settlement on the island of Noirmoutier at the mouth of the Loire.[41] However, archaeological evidence, such as that of a pagan grave on the Isle de Groix off Brittany, and place-name evidence of hundreds of islands, islets and holms round the coasts of England, Wales, Scotland and Ireland tell us that these places were known and much frequented by the sea-borne marauders.[42] In Ireland, Lambay island, north of Dublin, was one of the first places attacked in the late eighth century, and the sea lochs and estuaries around the coast formed raiding bases: some of these developed into trading towns in the tenth century.[43] The islands around the northern and western coasts of Scotland were eventually to become permanent Norse territory, but it may have taken some time for the Vikings to get a secure hold, establish complete possession and settle on the land. It depends very much on the numbers of the Celtic population in these islands and how well organized they were, and historians have differed in their conclusions about this. Entries in the Irish Annals about the pillaging and devastation of the Hebrides may suggest resistance from the native population; but no doubt some of the smaller islands would fall quickly under Viking control and serve as very useful raiding bases for sea-borne attacks on the monasteries of Scotland and Ireland.[44] Archaeological evidence bears this out.[45]

In the Northern Isles archaeological evidence for the state of the native population does not support the conclusion that the population of these islands 'had lost its organisation and power of resistance, and had perhaps also declined in numbers and in wealth'.[46] The existence of headland dykes in some of the Orkney islands can be interpreted as indicating that a process of 'ness-taking' (ON *nes-nám*) by the Vikings was a necessary preliminary to permanent conquest.[47] We do not know how long this process took, but it may have started before the first historical record of the raids in the late eighth century and continued perhaps until the establishment of the earldom in the second half of the ninth. It was well known in Icelandic tradition that the islands had been a haunt of pirates until cleared by Harald Finehair in the late ninth century, for Snorri Sturlason says that the Orkneys were 'peopled' then, before which they had been a 'Vikings' lair'.[48] This piratical phase need not have meant the immediate conquest and subjection of the Pictish population. Political control of the settlement was necessary before that was achieved. Establishment of pirate 'lairs' was part of the raiding phase of Viking activity and not part of the real process of colonization, settlement on the land by fishing and farming communities, which eventually took place.

SETTLEMENT IN THE WEST

When the real colonizing process got under way, the Vikings were never averse to mingling with the local population: they seem to have been well aware of the advantages of adopting the culture and authority of the societies they settled amongst. Thus in Ireland they appear from the evidence of mixed Norse-Irish names which are recorded in the Irish annals to have taken native wives – although the earliest of these names in fact suggests that the individual concerned had had a Gaelic father and a Norse mother, for his name was Godfrey MacFergus. He is said to have been lord of Oriel (in northern Ireland) and to have gone over to Scotland to help Kenneth MacAlpin in the year 836.[49] There are many problems associated with this entry in a late text, but there is nothing inherently impossible about the marriage of a Norse woman into an Irish princely family in the first decade of the ninth century.[50] By the middle of the century a recognizable group of warriors of mixed blood appear in the records as the *Gall-Gaedhil*, or the 'foreign Gael', the foreign element almost certainly being Norse. There is some doubt as to who exactly made up the Gaelic element, and the term may have varied in its meaning over the centuries, eventually perhaps acquiring a territorial connotation, if indeed it is the origin of the name of Galloway in south-west Scotland.[51] In the mid-ninth century it certainly is an ethnic designation, but whether referring to Irish who were renegades and supported the pagan invaders, or to Scots who had been fostered by Norsemen (as a late text describes them), is not entirely clear.[52] Their likely homeland can be seen as the Hebrides and south-west Scotland.[53] The leader of the *Gall-Gaedhil*, Ketil *Find* (White), who was defeated in Munster by two leaders of the Norse in Ireland in 857, has been identified with Ketil *Flat-nefr* (Flatneb) of the later sagas, the most famous of the early settlers in the Hebrides, although positive proof for this identification is lacking. Despite these problems of the exact identification of the *Gall-Gaedhil* and their leader Ketil *Find*, the conclusion that can be drawn from their appearance in the Irish sources is nonetheless certain: there must have been some integration and inter-marriage between Norse and Gael by the mid-ninth century for a mixed group of warriors to make such an impact on the Irish and for their existence to be recorded in the Annals. We should, however, be wary of the later unenviable reputation which these people acquired, and for which there is little contemporary evidence.[54]

Many traditions of the family of Ketil *Flat-nefr* survived in medieval Iceland, and although these sources associate Ketil's activities in the west with Harald Finehair's campaign at the end of the ninth century it is evident that his active career spanned the middle of the century (c.840–80).[55] Tradition consistently links Ketil's conquests with the Hebrides, although his daughter's marriage with Olaf, king of Dublin (see fig. 19), is an indication of the close connections which existed between the Norse settlers in the Isles and those in Ireland. There is also evidence that Ketil's family, many of whom moved on to Iceland in the second half of the ninth century, had come under strong influence from the Gaelic society of western Scotland,[56] notably in the matter of adoption of the Christian religion. This, of course, suggests that intermarriage must have taken place with the Christian Gaels in the Hebrides and that Ketil's rule over the Hebrides did not mean the annihilation or displacement of the native population. Indeed the emigration of Norse from the Hebrides to Iceland (and perhaps south-west Scotland) during the second half of the ninth century may indicate a period of native reaction at that time. Nonetheless the Norse imprint on the Hebrides was strong enough for them to become known as *Innsi Gall* (Islands of the Foreigners) at some point in the ninth century (although we cannot use the description of Godfrey MacFergus as *toiseach Innsi Gall* in 853 as a reliable indication that the term was in use in the middle of the century, for it may have been used anachronistically by the later annalist).[57]

Impact on Picto-Scottish conflict

The 836 entry concerning Godfrey MacFergus is probably as significant for the history of Scotland as is his mixed parentage for the question of intermarriage of Norse and Gael. In 836 it is said that he 'went over to Scotland to reinforce Dál Riada, at the bidding of Kenneth, Alpin's son',[58] which suggests that he was closely involved in the internal affairs of the Dalriadic Scots who were at this time in the process of expanding eastwards into Pictland. It is very probable that the impact of the Norse raids had had a devastating effect on the Scottish kingdom of Dál Riada, which had been a political force in Argyll and the Inner Hebrides since the sixth century. Although our historical knowledge of this kingdom amounts to little more than a list of kings and some battles, the dramatic events which can be perceived dimly unfolding in the ninth century are usually understood to have been motivated by the political upheavals resulting from the Norse raids and settlement of the islands.[59] For a start the 'long commune' between the peoples of Ulster and Argyll was disrupted, and the general overall result must have been a weakening of the political strength of the Dál Riada ruling family, which allowed Pictish influence from eastern Scotland to increase.[60] But in the end it was not the eastern Pictish kingdom which finally emerged – as one would have expected – as the dominant partner of a unified Picto-Scottish kingdom, rather it was the king of Dál Riada, Kenneth MacAlpin, who laid the foundation of the 'kingdom of the Scots'.[61] If his emergence really can be directly linked to Norse activity, then we may attribute to the Vikings a decisive role in the creation of the Scottish kingdom.

The historical sources suggest that the Scandinavian element was certainly involved in the internal struggle between Dál Riada and Pictland. In general the Norse were a very potent force in Irish politics by the 830s and 840s, when the mobile fighting force of *Gall-Gaedhil* was in the making. The first record of Norse presence in central Scotland is in the *Annals of Ulster s.a.* 839 when 'a battle was fought by the gentiles against the men of Fortriu' (the central Pictish province), and a large number fell in the engagement.[62] Scandinavian pagans may therefore have been involved in the process by which the Scots moved east against the Picts. Another, later, source (the *Chronicle of Huntingdon*), also suggests that Scandinavians played a part in the process by which Kenneth acquired dominance over the Picts. No doubt interpreting the situation with a certain simplicity, it attributes Kenneth's success to the fact that 'Danish pirates' had occupied the shores of Pictland and destroyed those Picts who defended their territory.[63] This may be no more than deduction from a knowledge of the same battle as that recorded in the *Annals of Ulster* for the year 839; for although the pirates are called 'Danes', this is not a reliable indication of the actual nationality of the invaders. There was a tendency on the part of English chroniclers to call all Scandinavian Vikings 'Danes' and this is no sure indication that the occupation was by Danes from England. It could just as likely have been a raid by Vikings from the Northern or Western Isles.

Conclusions about the part played by the Viking raiders in these significant years in the development of the kingdom of Scotland have to be tentative, when this is all the historical evidence that survives. It seems very likely that pressure from the Norse in the west did impel Dalriadic Scots eastward and helped to create the tension with the Picts which resulted in the surprising success of the Scots and the extraordinary demise of the Picts. It is also suggested by the sources that these same Vikings were more deeply involved in this situation by themselves creating hostilities with the men of Fortriu in the year 839, for their presence in central Scotland at that point can only have been for aggressive purposes. A recent assessment sees the Vikings as directly benefitting Kenneth MacAlpin in the realization of his political ambitions.[64]

Leaders and ambitions

One significant feature of the mid-ninth century is the emergence in the sources of named individuals who were leaders of the *Gall* in Ireland and Scotland. The first of these was the legendary Tuirgeis (ON Torgils) who brought 'a great and vast royal fleet' to the north of Ireland and about whom the only historical fact that can be relied upon is that he was drowned after capture by the Irish high-king Mael Sechnaill in 845.[65] He was followed by Olaf, 'son of the king of *Laithlinde*' (or *Lochlainn*), who came to Ireland in 853, and the Foreigners – or Norse – submitted to him, and tribute was given him by the Irish.[66] Whatever is meant by these 'royal' attributions the many references in the Irish sources to such high-born leaders of the Norse, and soon Danish, raiders does suggest that a new and significant phase of the Viking period in Ireland and Scotland had started. No longer does it appear to have been just a matter of raiding for the acquisition of available wealth wherever it might be obtained, but of permanent establishments for the regular extraction of tribute from the host country, as well as the pursuing of a lucrative trading business from well-placed and defended centres. We can also see the launching of more ambitious plans in the direction of political conquest of Scotland under the leadership of powerful individuals.

Viking activities in Ireland, England and Scotland became ever more closely related, for with the establishment of Olaf at Dublin in 853 the range of Viking activity in Ireland extended eastwards and eventually over the Irish Sea to include England and Scotland. The previous penetration of Ireland had been mainly from the west, with the Outer Hebrides providing the winter lairs which were such a useful base of attack, but 'the Irish Sea became henceforth the principal sphere of Viking activity rather than the Irish coasts'.[67] This eastward movement eventually linked up with the Danish presence in England, and it was probably at this date that the Isle of Man began to assume the importance it retained ever after in the history of the Norse settlements of the British Isles. Given this new direction it is not surprising that south Scotland also became part of the Viking sphere of activity. Late Irish tradition suggests that Olaf was married to a daughter of Kenneth MacAlpin, although there is also evidence for Olaf's marriage to a daughter of Aed Finlaith, the Irish high-king.[68] The *Chronicle of the Kings of Scotland* refers to a raid on Pictland by 'Danes' as far inland as Clunie and Dunkeld in Kenneth's reign,[69] but the first specific and well-recorded attack, led by Olaf of Dublin and Audgisl (possibly his brother), was not until the year 866, in the reign of Kenneth's son Constantine. The *Annals of Ulster* say that they raided 'all the land of the Picts and took hostages from them' and that they were leading a mixed band of 'The Foreigners of Ireland and Scotland', which suggests that Norse Vikings were well established in the Hebrides and Argyll by this date.[70] This may be the raid referred to in a late source (Duald MacFirbis' *Fragment s.a.*864) which tells of the destruction and devastation of Fortriu by Scandinavians (*Lochlannaibh*) who 'carried off many hostages with them as pledges of tribute', adding 'and they were paid tribute for a long time afterwards'.[71] After this raid Olaf resided in Pictland for a certain length of time, which was probably longer than the 11 weeks specified in the *Chronicle of the Kings of Scotland*, as there is no evidence of his activity in Ireland again until a raid in Armagh in 869. The impression given by these entries is that there was a serious attempt in the 860s to exploit the wealth of Pictland; the taking of hostages, as already mentioned, is the classic Norse method of enforcing compliance, and along with the demand for tribute shows that the treatment which Ireland had suffered for two generations or more was now being extended to southern Scotland. Olaf evidently had sufficient authority after his raid to remain for some time in charge of 'mopping-up' operations. The process of establishing a political presence was furthered in 870 when Olaf and his companion Ivar, 'two kings of the Northmen', besieged Dumbarton Rock for four months and destroyed and plundered it, an event which was recorded in many contemporary annals.[72] Dumbarton Rock was the citadel of the Britons of Strathclyde, a formidable natural fortress. Its capture was a remarkable achievement considering that the Vikings had not much experience of taking hill-forts at home in Scandinavia, or possibly in Ireland. Control of Dumbarton Rock, which commanded the entry up the Clyde from the west, gave the Vikings access to the heartland of Scotland. But the immediate result was that Olaf and Ivar captured a large number of English, Britons and Picts, whom they took back to

Dublin the next year in 200 ships, destined no doubt for the slave market. The absence of Scots from this list may suggest that Constantine MacKenneth was in collaboration with Olaf and Ivar against both the Picts and the Strathclyde Britons, thus continuing his father's policy of allying with the pagan Norse against traditional enemies.[73]

However obscure the political game of the Scots, it is not immediately obvious what the Northmen were up to either. Were they aiming for the total take-over of southern Scotland or was their policy in the south in some way related to the conquest of north Pictland by Thorstein the Red, son of Olaf of Dublin (see below)?[74] Such sustained and aggressive policies as we have seen Olaf and Ivar were pursuing in south Pictland were certainly directed towards penetration of the country, and it may be that the Irish-Norse were already realizing the importance of establishing a sea-route across the Scottish Lowlands by way of the headwaters of the Clyde and Forth estuaries (see fig. 16). According to Smyth this was certainly Norse policy in the tenth century.[75] In fact, the apparent quickening of Viking interest in southern Pictland in the 860s and 870s and the control of the main waterway into the Scottish Lowlands takes place at just the same time as the intensification of Danish attacks on eastern England which culminated in the arrival of the *micel here* ('Great Army') in the autumn of 865. It could therefore have been pursued in order to establish maritime contact with the Danish forces. If Ivar of the Irish Annals was the same as Ivar the Boneless who was traditionally associated with the attack on the city of York in 867,[76] such an identification would provide the personal link between eastern England and Ireland which may well have stimulated the forging of a maritime connection. Even if they cannot be proved to be one and the same person, it is not unlikely that the Norsemen of Dublin would want to establish a route through to the new and highly important theatre of Viking activity which was being established in north-east England at that time. Their knowledge of the sea and estuarine routes of the whole of northern England and southern Scotland would make this apparently indirect route the obvious one for them to use in a situation where they had not as yet penetrated the river valleys or mountain passes of north-west England. All of these reasons may lie behind the aggressive actions of Olaf and Ivar in southern Scotland in 866 and 870, among which the taking of Dumbarton on the Clyde gave them control of a key point in the western access by sea to the heart of Pictland. There was also the lucrative business of supplying slaves to the market at Dublin, which thrived on the exporting of Irish and Scottish slaves to the Islamic countries of the Mediterranean.[77] Indeed the development of this very important aspect of the Viking trade network in the west may date from Olaf and Ivar's highly successful campaigns in Pictland at this time. However, the death of Ivar 'king of the Northmen of all Ireland and Britain' in 873,[78] and the apparent withdrawal or death of Olaf about the same time, meant the decline of the strong leadership which such far-seeing and wide-ranging policies required.

KING HARALD FINEHAIR AND THE LATE NINTH CENTURY

With the death of these two leaders a new period in the history of the Viking attacks on Britain and Ireland is ushered in. A process of assimilation was taking place in Ireland,[79] as well as growing dissension amongst the Foreigners of Dublin. This enabled the native Irish kings to root out Viking bases around the coasts, culminating in the destruction of Dublin and the expulsion of the Dublin Norse in 902. During the last decades of the ninth century secondary migrations were taking place from Ireland to Iceland, to north-west England, and very possibly to south-west Scotland. This is also the period when the Scandinavian settlement of the Northern Isles begins to acquire some historical foundation and when the earldom of Orkney emerges as a political reality. It is in fact the period which medieval Scandinavian writers thought saw the beginnings of Norwegian settlement overseas as a result of the political ambitions of the Vestfold kings within Norway. Icelandic literature explains the emigration from Norway as being due to the unification of the petty kingdoms of Norway under Harald Finehair, whose family's power lay on the west side of Oslo fjord. This is the standard account in Snorri Sturlason's saga of Harald Finehair:

> In the discontent when King Harald seized on the lands of Norway, the out-countries of Iceland and the Faroe Isles were discovered and peopled. The Northmen had also a great resort to Shetland, and many men left Norway, flying the country on account of King Harald, and went on viking cruises into the West sea. In winter they were in the Orkney Islands and Hebrides but marauded in summer in Norway, and did great damage.[80]

In response to their depredations along the Norwegian coast, King Harald sailed on an expedition to Shetland, Orkney and the Hebrides where he plundered and slew many of these Vikings. He is said to have ravaged far and wide in Scotland, and reached the Isle of Man which had been abandoned by its people on hearing of his coming.[81]

However, the new critical approach to saga history has cast doubt on the account, as an explanation not only of the Norse settlement of the western lands, and of the far-reaching nature of King Harald's response, but also of the date of his final success over the west Norwegian Viking chieftains at the battle of Hafrsfjord in south-west Norway. In 1929, D.W. Hunter Marshall, whilst admitting that the question of the chronology of Harald's expeditions to the west 'is . . . rather an involved one', added that 'no-one denies that there was such an expedition'.[82] But that is precisely what some Norwegian historians have denied.[83] The statement of the author of *Flateyarbók* (a compilation of many sagas written down in the fourteenth century) that King Harald appropriated the land as far west as any later Norwegian king ever held sway gives us a clue as to what lay behind these exaggerated claims. The thirteenth-century writers were of course well aware that the kings of their own time laid claim to supremacy over all the 'skattlands' (tributary colonies) in the west. It was only natural that when writing of the events of four centuries earlier they should apply the thinking of their own time and interpret the skaldic claims for Harald's conquests in the west too widely.[84] There is, moreover, no record of any such royal Norwegian expedition in the Irish Annals, although other appearances of 'sons of Kings of Lochlann' are recorded. It has been suggested that the Olaf who arrived in Dublin in 853 and who is described as 'son of the King of Lochlann' in contemporary Irish sources, may have served as the prototype for the conquering Norwegian king, and that the tradition was later transferred by the saga writer to the better-known Harald Finehair.[85]

Creation of the earldom of Orkney

The account of King Harald's granting of the earldom of Orkney to his 'dearest friend' Rognvald of Møre has probably also been coloured by later thinking. The eldest son of Earl Rognvald is said to have been killed on the king's campaign in the west, and so in compensation Harald gave him the Orkney and Shetland Islands when he sailed back east. Rognvald transferred them to his brother Sigurd and King Harald confirmed the grant.[86] But was Harald in any position to be handing out territory which lay west-over-sea, when the situation regarding his control of the west coast of Norway was even in doubt?[87] In the medieval period the exact nature of the king's relationship with the earls of Orkney was a constant problem. Medieval writers simply did not know if the earls' ancestors had won the islands by force or whether they owed their position to a grant from the king, but in the political circumstances of their own time it was necessary to stress the latter. If, however, there is doubt about Harald's ability to lead an expedition west to the islands off the Scottish coast, then it is difficult to believe that he was in any position to give the islands of Orkney and Shetland to Rognvald of Møre as compensation for the death of his son, Ivar. There is a strong tradition linking the conquest of the Orkney islands with the family of Møre, and it may be that this conquest received some form of royal approbation, for the saga evidence suggests that friendly relations existed between Harald and Rognvald.[88] In such a situation it is hardly likely that Rognvald would have conquered in the west entirely without reference to his powerful royal ally.

Apart from the later stress on King Harald's role in the founding of the Orkney earldom there was apparently another tradition about the Møre family's conquest, which derives from sources more closely connected with the settlements in the west. One of these is the late Irish source (Duald MacFirbis' *Fragment*), which probably contains tradition handed down in Duald's family,[89] wherein the story is told – in a very saga-like way – of the expulsion from Norway of the eldest son of Halfdan, king of Lochlann, called Ronald (Ragnall), who came with his three sons to Orkney, and of the exploits of two of these sons in Spain, while Ronald and the youngest remained behind in Orkney.[90] The story is placed chronologically after the reference to the destruction and devastation of Fortriu by the Scandinavians (probably Olaf and Ivar's expedition of 866), and at about the time of the Danish conquest of York (867). Although the Ragnall in the tale has sometimes been identified with Ragnarr Lothbrok, the legendary Viking warrior,[91] commentators on the early history of Viking Orkney have interpreted the story as a garbled account of the conquest of Orkney by Rognvald of Møre,[92] even though it is placed chrono-logically earlier than Harald Finehair's time. This tradition also says that Ragnall was the son of King Halfdan, understood to be Halfdan the Black, father of Harald Finehair (interestingly the name of Rognvald of Møre's

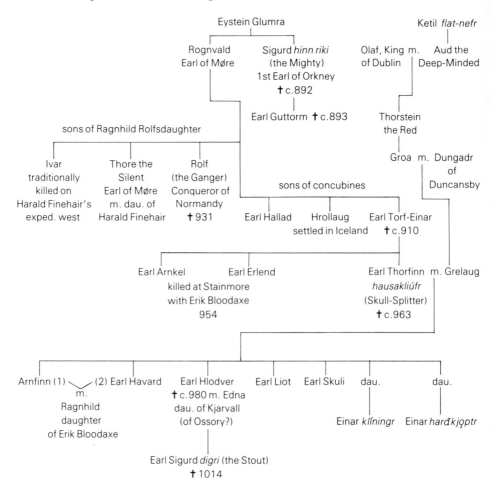

Figure 19. Genealogical tree: the sons of Rognvald of Møre and the line of the first earls of Orkney.

grandfather is given in one source as Halfdan, possibly a king of Valdres and Ringerike).[93] The theme of tension with the king and the loss of ancestral land (which was going to happen in the case of the Møre family), the numerous sons who were involved with their father in conquest in the west, and above all the association with Orkney (which is not often referred to in Irish sources), suggest strongly that this may derive from a tradition remembered in Ireland about the Møre family in Orkney and their conquest of the islands.

Another non-Icelandic source, *Historia Norvegiae*, possibly written in Orkney in the late twelfth century and recording local tradition, describes briefly but directly how 'certain pirates of the family of the most vigorous prince Ronald' crossed to Orkney in a great fleet, destroyed the native inhabitants utterly and subdued the islands.[94] These islands then provided them with 'safe winter seats' from where the conquerors were able to attack the English, Scots and Irish. Although this is said to have happened in the days of Harald Finehair the author makes no reference to that king being involved in the process of conquest at all; he implies that it was achieved entirely independently by the family of Rognvald.

Thus we have two traditions about the settlement of the Northern Isles and the establishment of the family of Møre over them. The official view of the Icelandic saga writers was that both had happened as a result of Harald Finehair's activity; the settlement because of his expulsion of the piratical elements from the west coast of Norway, and the political control because of his conquest of the Isles on a royal expedition and his grant of them to his close companion Rognvald of Møre in compensation for the loss of his son. The other tradition, possibly derived more closely from the Norse settlements in Britain, attributes the conquest of the islands entirely to Earl Rognvald and his sons, and this is the one usually preferred today. Even so, there is no doubt that the unifying Vestfold kings would be most unwilling to allow the Møre family to rule an island dominion independently and saga evidence suggests that the kings strove to get control. Indeed tension developed between Harald Finehair's family and the Møre dynasty, starting with the banishment of Rolf the Ganger and then the burning of Earl Rognvald in his house in Norway by Halfdan *Halegg*, son of King Harald, and continuing with the ghastly retribution taken upon Halfdan in Orkney by Rognvald's younger son Torf-Einar.[95] The verses, included in *Jarls' Saga*, and said to have been composed by Torf-Einar on this occasion, claim that a blow had been struck against King Harald himself, who mounted an expedition to Orkney in response. However, Torf-Einar remained earl of Orkney, and the conclusion to be drawn is that the king was unable to dislodge him: just as on later, better-recorded occasions, Harald's successors were unable to dislodge Torf-Einar's successors. The kings might be successful in curbing the Møre family's power in Norway (for the family died out there after the death of Torf-Einar's brother, Thore), but they were unable to prevent scions of this dynasty from re-establishing the family's power in the Scandinavian settlements overseas, in Orkney, Scotland, Normandy and Iceland (see fig. 19).

Problems of chronology

When we attempt to find a chronology for all this activity, we land in a quaking mass of uncertainty. According to the twelfth-century historian, Ari the Learned, Iceland was first settled in the year 870, the year of the murder of St Edmund in eastern England, and one of the powerful rulers referred to as ruling during the period of settlement was Earl Sigurd the Mighty of Orkney.[96] The Irish tradition of Ronald (Ragnall) and his sons arriving in Orkney (see p. 53 above) dates it vaguely to the time of the capture of the city of York by the Danes in 867. These two dates are as near as it is possible to get to a starting point for the earldom. How does this link up with the unifying activity of King Harald in Norway? Harald's victory over the piratical elements of western Norway is said by Snorri Sturlason to be the reason why many Vikings fled to Iceland and the Scottish Isles.[97] But the battle of Hafrsfjord is unlikely to have taken place as early as Iceland was colonized, for Harald can never have succeeded in unifying western Norway under himself by 870. Using a different system of reckoning, historians have argued that the battle of Hafrsfjord should really be dated nearer to 900, with recent opinion suggesting a date in the 880s.[98] Harald was in no position to lead conquering expeditions to the Scottish Isles in the period before he had won control over at least the south-western parts of Norway – which is what the victory at Hafrsfjord gave him.

However, strong traditions existed later in the Middle Ages about this king's campaigns in western waters, and the account of his second expedition to Orkney, to avenge the death of his son Halfdan, is more plausible than the supposed earlier expedition; it is also chronologically more acceptable, taking place during the rule of Earl Rognvald's son Torf-Einar (c.895). A skaldic reference to King Harald plundering in Scotland afterwards can perhaps be linked with the recorded destruction of Dunnottar by 'gentiles' at some date between the years 889 and 900.[99] An attack on this major eastern Scottish stronghold (see fig. 16) by 'gentiles' is an unusual event in this period (when Scottish records do exist), and presupposes a large and well-organized army and fleet to take such a magnificently defensible site. No other known Viking leader was roaming around the British Isles in this period who could have had such force in readiness; it may be that this is indeed a reference to an attack by King Harald, ensuing from an expedition to Orkney at the end of the century.

In conclusion, we can see that, although later Icelandic tradition very likely lays too great a stress on the role of King Harald in the initiation of the Norse overseas movement and the creation of the earldom of Orkney, yet he was remembered as being a most dominant figure in the stirring events of the late ninth century.[100] The growth of a unified kingship in Norway, as in the other Scandinavian countries, was doubtless a very important factor in the population upheaval and social changes that were taking place. It can indeed be regarded as both a cause and an effect of Viking activity.[101]

The conquest of Orkney and northern Scotland

Turning next to the process of conquest and settlement of Orkney, we find that the earls' own saga (*Jarls' Saga*) is of little use, and the impression given is that the earls have complete control of the islands from the start. Recorded battles with the natives all take place in northern Scotland. The only historical evidence to give us any hint as to how Earl Rognvald and his family won the islands comes from the twelfth-century *History of Norway* (*Historia Norwegiae*) which refers in sweeping terms to the native inhabitants of Orkney – called the 'Peti' and the 'Papae' – being destroyed utterly by members of Rognvald's family.[102] This appears to be a valuable piece of information, but it stands alone, without another shred of evidence to support it; and it tells us only what twelfth-century tradition believed had happened in the process by which the earls acquired political control of the islands. Moreover, we can hardly expect that no clash had occurred until the time of Earl Rognvald and his sons. These islands had formed pirate lairs since the late eighth century, and until the establishing of control by the earls must have been subject to different Viking chieftains for half a century or more, though this was of no interest to the authors of *Jarls' Saga* or *Historia Norwegiae*. However, it seems likely that strong control by one family was imperative for actual colonization and settlement of the land to take place. For without the creation of peaceful conditions, the removal of piratical elements and the subjection of the remaining natives, the establishment of farms with Norse names and the tilling of the soil by the Norse farmers who also flooded into these new lands at this time would not have been possible. This was as true in Orkney and Shetland as in the Hebrides and Man. It needed the establishment of a powerful dynasty like the Møre family in Orkney or Ketil *Flat-nefr* at an earlier date in the Hebrides for permanent colonization to take place and for roots to be put down into the soil.

The process by which land was wrested from the Celts can in fact be viewed more clearly in northern Scotland than in either Orkney or the Hebrides. This phase involved the first of the earls to be lauded in *Jarls' Saga*, Sigurd the Mighty, brother of Earl Rognvald, to whom King Harald is supposed to have given Orkney and Shetland. But no-one granted him the right to Caithness and Sutherland; this area and Moray and Ross were conquered in an heroic way by Sigurd himself and a grandson of Ketil *Flat-nefr*, Thorstein the Red, two of the most famous warriors of the Viking Age. It was a deliberate partnership, combining the resources of these two powerful leaders apparently for the purpose of extending Norse control across the northern half of the mainland of Scotland. It may be that opportunities for gain in Ireland and the Hebrides were coming to an end, and that the Norse in the west were experiencing difficulties at this time.[103] If Thorstein the Red, grandson of Ketil Flatneb, was not finding it easy to maintain his family's position in the Hebrides, he was easily able to move into Moray and Ross which were quite accessible from the west, particularly via the Great Glen (see figs. 8 and 16). The Møre family, having consolidated their position in Orkney, must have regarded the neighbouring parts of north Scotland across the Pentland Firth as their rightful preserve. Thorstein and Sigurd may therefore have focussed their attention on different parts of northern Scotland, but they created a partnership which was famous in Icelandic tradition, for their campaigns are recorded in many different saga sources,[104] which all tell of their conquests of Caithness and Sutherland, Moray and Ross. The *Book of Settlements* (*Landnámabók*) gives Thorstein the greater role, actually saying that he was king over the territories conquered, but that he died in battle.[105] It seems likely that the *Chronicle of the Kings of Scotland* is referring to Sigurd and Thorstein's campaigns when it records that the 'Northmen wasted Pictland' during the reign of Donald, son of Constantine (889–900).[106] If so, it substantiates to some extent *Landnámabók*'s statement that the two of them won 'more than half Scotland'.[107] Snorri, however, says very specifically that they 'subdued Caithness and all Sutherland, as far as Ekkialsbakki'.[108] This last name is interpreted as referring to the banks of the River Oykell which runs into the Dornoch Firth, and is very much the traditional boundary of the southern part of the province of Caithness, or 'Sutherland' as it was known to the Norsemen (see fig. 16). But place-names suggest that some form of territorial control was also won south of the River Oykell, in Easter Ross, during the ninth or tenth centuries.[109] *Jarls' Saga* gives the tantalizing and unspecific information that Sigurd built a fort 'in the south of Moray', which has been tentatively identified – without any archaeological verification – with the Dark Age fort of Burghead on the north coast of Moray.[110]

From what can be gleaned from the sources it seems that the battle for the control of this part of Scotland was hard-won. We know nothing of the native military organization of these northern provinces of Pictland, although it has been suggested that the use of new names for the 'mormaers', the military leaders of provinces, in this period, suggests new divisions, which probably were established as a response to the need for defensive measures against the Vikings.[111] The survival of the names of some of these local leaders in Icelandic tradition certainly tells us that they were formidable opponents of the Norse, and in the case of Dungadr of Duncansby, well enough established to retain his position – in the very north of Caithness – and to ally with Thorstein through marriage (see fig. 19).[112] Maelbrigte 'Tooth' was 'an earl of the Scots' or mormaer of a province, perhaps Moray, with whom Earl Sigurd was forced to have a peace meeting, presumably to arrange the terms of a truce. According to saga tradition, this peace meeting broke down, and legend adds that despite Sigurd's victory in the ensuing hostilities he was poisoned by the tooth sticking out of Maelbrigte's severed head, hanging from his saddlebow.[113] (Some form of deceit by the Scots was also remembered as playing a part in Thorstein's death.) Sigurd's burial place is said to lie on the banks of the Oykell, suggesting that he met his death while engaged in conquering this frontier area. The place-name 'Sigurd's howe' (Sidera or Cyder Hall) on the north side of the Dornoch Firth (which is the estuary of the Oykell) provides what appears to be remarkable corroborative toponymic evidence for the location of Sigurd the Mighty's burial place (see figs. 16 and 20).[114] Snorri adds the comment to his statement about the deaths of Sigurd and his son Guttorm – who died childless after a year's rule over those parts: 'after that many vikings settled in the lands, [both] Danes and Norwegians'.[115] Evidently the deaths of strong leaders, who were not replaced by strong earls, simply allowed the raiding to start again; and 'the farmers brought their injuries before Earl Hallad' (son of Rognvald of Møre) who took over the earldom from Guttorm, but who was unable to restore control, whereupon he gave up the earldom and sailed back home to Norway, which 'made him a laughing-stock' (see fig. 19).[116]

NORSE STRUGGLE FOR POLITICAL CONTROL: THE TENTH CENTURY

The early tenth century saw disruption in the whole Irish Sea province and the expulsion of the Northmen and probably Danes from Dublin and north Ireland can be interpreted as the impetus leading to the evident settlement of Cumbria, coastal Lancashire and the northern shores of the Solway Firth by Scandinavian speakers. Much of this process is glimpsed only through the place-names of the regions concerned. However, many of these settlements may be attributed to Hebridean-Scots rather than Hiberno (Irish)-Norse,[117] particularly if the Hebrides and surrounding Scottish coasts had become over-populated during the preceding century. Certainly the movement of Ketil's family from the Hebrides slightly earlier indicates that some political develop-ment had taken place to cause the dispersal of such a powerful family; and it is not unlikely that some of these displaced Hebridean-Scots would have clung to the shores of Britain rather than venturing over the Atlantic to Iceland.

Renewed attack on Scotland

There are indications from the sources that the leaders of the Dublin-Norse tried hard to penetrate the heartland of Scotland after their expulsion. They raided Dunkeld in 903 but were faced by a defending army the next year when a great battle took place in Fortriu and Ivar II, grandson of Ivar the Boneless, was killed.[118] A king of the Picts is said to have fallen in battle the same year fighting against the two grandsons of Ivar and another Norse leader called Catol (Ketil).[119] Can we see this attack as a renewal of the earlier attempts by Olaf and Ivar in the 860s? Circumstances were rather different from what they had then been, for in 903 and 904 the Irish-Norse were wanting a permanent base, having lost their foothold in Ireland. Presumably they wanted a trading base from which to maintain their interrupted links with York. But considering the success story of the Danes in various English kingdoms there is every reason for thinking that they may have been quite seriously intentioned about political control. If these campaigns *were* a serious bid for conquest, then the Norse leaders found the Scottish kingdom too well defended for them, and they failed to establish any form of political control. The king who has been given credit for this achievement is Constantine II (900–943).[120]

During the second decade of the tenth century another grandson of Ivar,

Figure 20. The farm of Sidera or Cyder Hall on the north side of the Dornoch Firth, estuary of the River Oykell in Easter Ross (photograph: author).
  The thirteenth-century form of the name was *Syvardhoch* (= 'Sigurd's howe' or burial-mound). The traditional site of the burial-mound of Earl Sigurd 'the Mighty' (†c.892) lies 0.8km north-west of the farm.

Ragnall, tried to re-create a kingdom for himself in Northumbria. His ambitions touched Scotland also, for fear of the situation probably drove King Constantine to make a mutual treaty of support with Æthelflæd, the sister of Edward the Elder, who was the main organizer of the defences of English Mercia against the Danes and Norse.[121] This may have been in 914 and afterwards Strathclyde was plundered, probably by Ragnall. He led further expeditions to Scotland, that of 918 being well substantiated by the account in the *Annals of Ulster*,[122] and culminating in a battle as far south as the River Tyne.[123] It was probably fear of Ragnall and his Norsemen that dictated the submission of Constantine, king of the Scots, and of Donald, king of Strathclyde, to Edward, king of the Anglo-Saxons, in 920. It may well be that this was an anti-Norse coalition, which the West-Saxon annalist expressed in terms of Edward's political success. Certainly Ragnall's seizure of York in 919 had made him a very powerful figure indeed, and even though he did submit to Edward in 920, this submission may have been due to his recognition of the circumscribed position he was in when the powers both to north and south were united against him.[124]

The more usual political development was, however, for the king of Dublin-York and the king of Scots to ally (as has been seen may have been the case in the previous century).[125] Such alliances were made or unmade according to the current balance of power, and with the accession of Athelstan to the Anglo-Saxon throne there arrived a ruler who came nearer than any other before him to conquering the whole of the British mainland. In face of this threatened overwhelming political hegemony the northern kings banded together to preserve their independence, and this alliance culminated in the clash with Athelstan at *Brunanburh* in the year 937. Only three years before, Athelstan had invaded Scotland, when his fleet sailed as far as Caithness and his land army reached Dunnottar.[126] The threat was clear enough and Constantine II, king of Scots, Olaf Guthfrithsson of Dublin (determined to win back York) and Owain of Strathclyde joined ranks to put an end to Athelstan's expansionist plans. But this remarkable alliance came to nothing at the famous battle of *Brunanburh* whose location remains unproven.[127]

The kings of Dublin-York were a political element taken very seriously in the courts of North Britain at this time. They had political ambitions which affected both the kings of Scots and kings of the English, and it was important therefore that they should be emasculated by alliance and assimilation. We know that they formed an element at the court of Athelstan and it seems very likely that they were also drawn into the court of the Scottish kings. There is good evidence that Olaf Guthfrithsson of Dublin was married to a daughter of King Constantine II,[128] and there are likely to have been other marriage alliances from the appearance of some Scandinavian names in the Scottish royal family during this period, such as Olaf, son of Indulf – which is itself probably Danish –[129] as well as the nickname given to Olaf's brother (Culen) of 'Ring' (ON *hringr* = 'ring-giver', the bestower of silver rings). If indeed the Forth-Clyde route was an important means of access from Dublin to York, then good relations with the Scots must have been of paramount importance to the kings of Dublin.[130] Certainly the kings of Dublin were an established part of the political *status quo* in North Britain in the first half of the tenth century.

Erik Bloodaxe: 947–954

Another period of marauding and disturbance in North Britain was stirred up by the attempt of Erik 'Bloodaxe' to win control of York in the middle of the tenth century. He was the favourite son of Harald Finehair who should have been content with establishing himself and consolidating his father's political gains in Norway; but, faced with opposition from his brother Hakon, he saw better prospects for his personal position in the British Isles. His career tells us very clearly that control of the Scandinavian settlements in Britain and Ireland was envisaged as an ambition worthy of members of the Norwegian king's family, who still had to be exceedingly experienced raiders of the northern seas in order to maintain their following and therefore their political authority. For the first – and only – time the disparate areas settled by the Norse around Britain were drawn together under one controlling authority. Evidence is scanty, but there is for a start no doubt about the importance the Orkneys were to play in this political bid as a base from which operations were launched. As was to happen centuries later when another Norwegian king was powerful enough to lead an expedition to the west, it was the Orkneys which were seen as the vital and important geographical base that they are, giving access to west or east side of the British Isles.[131] For a power-seeker who had ambitions in northern England, where the kingdom of York was by now a legitimate goal for any Norse claimant, these islands were a most important spring-board from which to launch operations and draw resources. This completely changed the east-west axis established by the link-up between Dublin and York, replacing it with a north-south alliance based on York and the Isles.[132]

On departing from Norway, Erik seems to have gone first to Orkney (c.947), where the joint earls of Orkney, Arnkel and Erlend, sons of Torf-Einar, accompanied him on his further voyaging.[133] This was a pattern repeated on later royal expeditions, and suggests that the earls were considered duty-bound to follow a Norwegian king who was pursuing ambitions further south in the British Isles; certainly they forfeited their power in the islands when a king was in control there. Erik also established himself over the Hebrides either straight away or after he fled from York c.948; 'and there were many vikings and war-kings there, and they joined the army of King Eric',[134] as Snorri tantalizingly tells us. However, he did not succeed in dominating the Scandinavian towns of Ireland, and the king of Dublin, Olaf Cuaran, was one of his bitterest rivals. Nor can the king of Scots have relished the raids which were carried out on his lands, while the Anglo-Saxon king, Eadred, exacted fierce reprisals on the Northumbrians for taking Erik as their king.[135] It was not possible for an outside adventurer to maintain himself in this position, with no allies among the neighbouring political authorities, however well supported by the earls and war-kings of the Scottish Isles. Such an affront to the established order – which the Vikings had caused many times during the previous centuries – was no longer tolerated, and Erik's brief period of power ended in bloodshed on the lonely place called Stainmore (on the Yorkshire-Westmorland border) in 954; the spot is perhaps commemorated by a stone called the Reycross/Rerecross and certainly commemorated in the poem *Eiríksmál* which describes Odin in Valhalla waiting to give Erik and the five kings who fell with him a heroes' welcome.[136] The two earls of Orkney, Arnkel and Erlend, died with him, and it was to Orkney that Erik's wife, Gunnhild, fled with her children after the news of his death was brought to her, with all the wealth that had been gathered together in England, in taxes and booty.[137] They 'subdued the Isles' even though the powerful Thorfinn 'Skull-Splitter' was earl, and they may have remained in control of the islands for some years if the record of raids mentioned in 962 can be plausibly linked with them.[138]

The rule of this last pagan Viking from the north marks the end of an era. Despite some evidence that Erik had been converted, the event does not seem to have made much of a mark on his life-style,[139] although the adoption of Christianity was becoming recognized as a prerequisite for kingship rule after the West European fashion. The final breaking of the links between Dublin and York meant that Scotland was no longer involved in the ambitious projects of the kings of Dublin-York who needed passage through the heartland of the Scottish kingdom in order to maintain sea-borne traffic between the two halves of their trading empire.

Concluding this early part of the history of Scandinavian Scotland, the scanty written sources suggest that the impact of Norse raids and settlement on North Britain was immediately significant. Scandinavian control in Argyll seems to have started a chain reaction by the 830s and 840s when the leaders of Dál Riada, perhaps with the help of Norse elements in the mixed society of the Hebrides and west Scotland, embarked on an aggressive movement eastwards. On later occasions – in the 860s, the early tenth century and the 940s and 950s – the leaders of the Irish-Norse seem to have made sustained attempts to win some control in the heartland of Pictland. If this was not a desire for political control then perhaps they were motivated by the need to have territorial control of the waterways of Clyde and Forth for commercial purposes. They did not, however, succeed in the former, and we have no real proof that they succeeded in the latter. The young Scottish kingdom in any case maintained its integrity, and this should be regarded as a great success story. How this was achieved will never be fully known, except that the kingdom was not overrun militarily and the kings evidently made judicious alliances with the leaders of the Irish-Norse, to judge from the record of marriages and the appearance of Scandinavian names in the Scottish royal family. The Scandinavian connection may indeed have helped the nascent Scottish dynasty to establish itself as the rulers of Lowland Scotland and to aspire to hegemony over parts of Albion which might have been more difficult to assimilate otherwise;[140] while the generally disturbed conditions allowed the Scottish kings to extend their control into Cumbria and Northumbria.[141]

While this political struggle was going on in the heartland of the Picts and the Scots, the coastal fringes of North Britain were heavily influenced by an immigration of Scandinavian-speaking peoples. By the mid-tenth century the whole of the Northern and Western Isles were Norse colonial settlements, and a war of conquest was embarked upon against native chieftains in the north Scottish mainland. The distant parts of North Britain had become firmly part of the Scandinavian world in the ninth and tenth centuries.

3 The Chronological Framework: Part 2 c.975–1065

THE AGE OF THE EARLS

In the late tenth century, we enter into a new period in the history of Scandinavian Scotland, when the earls of Orkney become the most important political figures of the Norse colonies in the west. The 'second' Viking Age started in which the raiding had a more political purpose and the kings of Denmark and Norway directed their fleets towards the conquest of Anglo-Saxon England.[1] There was no place in this Viking age for the old-style 'war band' under individual chieftains raiding monasteries for wealth and looking for lands to settle. The Norse in Ireland had become thoroughly integrated into Irish politics and such control as they had exercised over the Hebrides in the preceding period was probably declining.[2] Into this vacuum stepped the earls of Orkney, and the late tenth century saw the expansion of the northern earldom, when it became an established power around the coasts of Scotland and also, if we are to believe the sagas, within the Scottish kingdom as well.

The political situation in Orkney and North Scotland

The descendants of Rognvald of Møre had by the late tenth century been established as earls in Orkney and probably also in Shetland for over a century; and apart from periods when kings of Norway or members of their families attempted to establish a claim to authority, the earls had had sole possession of this rich, strategically important archipelago. It is likely that they soon established an efficient administration of estate farming and tax collection, although our evidence for this is all from a later date (see below, pp. 82–6). But the main weakness of the earls' power, a factor which the kings of Norway were to make much of, was soon in evidence: the rivalry of different sons, and other descendants of previous earls, in claiming their share of the family lands and authority. The five sons of Thorfinn Torf-Einarsson *hausakliúfr* (Skull-Splitter) were all active in pursuing power and conquest in northern Scotland, as were two grandsons by daughters, Einar *klíningr* (Buttered-Bread) and Einar *harðkjǫptr* (Hard-chaps) (see fig. 19 above). Even at this date (late tenth century) any male descendant of an earl, whether through the male or female line, could claim land and authority in the earldom. The story of Ragnhild (daughter of Erik Bloodaxe and Gunnhild) who was reputedly married to three of Earl Thorfinn's sons, scheming with claimants to the earldom, is an excellent theme for the saga writer,[3] who was making the most of probably fragmentary traditions about a powerful woman in the earldom at the time, but also indirectly tells us of the hard reality of rivalry in the dynasty at this date (977 x 991).

Of Thorfinn's five sons, one of them, Skuli, looked to the 'king of Scots' for support for his claim and a grant of authority, evidently over Caithness.[4] At a later date the kings of Scotland certainly claimed overlordship of Caithness and the right to grant the earldom to a member of the earldom family. Whether the kings of Scots were in any position in the late tenth century to make such a grant to Skuli is, however, exceedingly uncertain. It is possible that by the 'king of Scots' the saga writer meant the ruler of Moray, and was referring to the political authority immediately to the south of the earls' domain, on the analogy of the title *Rí Alban*, king of Alban (Scotland), given by the Irish annalists to the rulers of Moray.[5] In general, however, the impression given in this section of *Jarls' Saga* – and other Icelandic sagas – is of a bitter struggle between the Orkney earls and the rulers or 'jarls' of Moray for control of Caithness. If the late ninth-century conquest of northern Scotland by Thorstein the Red and Sigurd the Mighty had indeed led to permanent colonies in Caithness and along the coastal areas of Sutherland,[6] then the late tenth-century struggle may have been a result of aggression from the Scottish side in an attempt to regain control of the northernmost province of the Scottish mainland.

It is clear that the Norse settlement had not removed all the native aristocracy from Caithness, for Thorfinn Skull-Splitter married Grelaug, the daughter of the native earl Dungadr (who had himself married Groa, the daughter of Thorstein the Red: see fig. 19); diplomatic marriages which signify some sort of settlement between a native chieftain and the Norse conquerors of northern Scotland. If Dungadr's property is commemorated in the place-name Duncansby,[7] on the north-east tip of Caithness, looking across the Pentland Firth to Orkney (see fig. 16), then this native family must have continued to reside in an exposed area after Norse settlement had taken place all round about. Two marriages between the most powerful level of Norse incomer and native ruler in the tenth century show how important this native house was, and how necessary it was for the earls to ally with it. Neither of these marriages are mentioned in *Jarls' Saga*, although they were well-enough known among the saga writers of thirteenth-century Iceland.[8]

If a *modus vivendi* had thus been reached with the native ruler of Caithness, this was not the case with the powerful rulers of the province of Moray, for according to *Jarls' Saga* both Liot Thorfinnsson and his nephew Sigurd Hlodversson fought separate battles at Skitten Mire in Caithness with an Earl MacBeth and an Earl Finnlaech, both of whom were apparently rulers of Moray.[9] If there really were two separate battles, both as hard-fought as the saga suggests (Liot dying from his wounds after the first one) and both fought as far north as Wick, we get an impression that the earls of Orkney were very hard-pressed indeed in this period in Caithness. Sigurd Hlodversson *digri* ('the Stout') was, however, 'powerful enough to defend Caithness against the Scots';[10] it is also said that he married a daughter of King Malcolm of Scotland. It is possible that this may have been a daughter of Malcolm II (1005–1034) and that the earl of Caithness and the king of Scots were allying against a mutual enemy – the ruler of Moray[11] – although it has been suggested that the saga writer is again calling a Scottish mormaer 'king of Scots' and it was a daughter of a mormaer of Moray or even Argyll that Sigurd married.[12]

EARL SIGURD II 'THE STOUT' (c.985–1014)

If Earl Sigurd II was indeed in alliance with Malcolm II, king of Scots, this is an important development in the history of the earldom and tells us that an earl of Orkney was powerful enough to be considered a worthwhile ally by the Scots, as the Irish-Norse had been in the tenth century. Sigurd was a 'mighty chief, with wide dominions', who harried in the Hebrides, in Scotland and in Ireland, the writer of *Jarls' Saga* tells us.[13] But did he really lay all western Scotland under his sway? Did he levy tribute from the Hebrides and the Isle of Man and from possessions in Ireland? Did he indeed 'force' Malcolm to accept his alliance and relationship by marriage as has been claimed?[14] The *Jarls' Saga* says nothing so specific about the nature of any of his conquests, although it has to be said that the author of the saga is surprisingly ill-informed about Earl Sigurd, who was otherwise well known to Icelandic saga writers.[15] Some of the events retold in the Family Sagas are situated in the Orkneys of Sigurd's time, and he is the first Orkney earl in whose honour a laudatory poem is known to have been written (by the skald Gunnlaug Ormstunga), but which unfortunately does not survive.[16] It is from the Family Sagas that information is derived about Sigurd's conquests in the west, about his tax-collections in the Hebrides and Man, and about his relationship with Earl Gilli of the Hebrides, his brother-in-law. Can we accept such detail without corroborative evidence?

The extent of Earl Sigurd's dominions

In *Njal's Saga* it is said that Earl Sigurd 'owned this dominion in Scotland: Ross and Moray, Sutherland and the Dales'.[17] This last place has been interpreted as referring to the valleys of the western seaboard[18] from which the conclusion can be drawn that Sigurd had control of Argyll. It is indeed true that later in the *Jarls' Saga* the name *Dalir* ('dales') is used of the chieftain Somerled's realm, where Argyll is undoubtedly meant,[19] but the name is also used of that part of Caithness which includes the river valleys running down towards the Pentland Firth, where Skuli and Liot had met in battle not long before,[20] and it could have been these 'Dales' which were remembered as forming part of Sigurd's dominion.[21] In this instance the saga writer's knowledge may have been on a more localized scale than has been appreciated by commentators. The sense of the passage in *Njal's Saga* suggests this: 'Ross and Moray' are linked together, and then 'Sutherland and the Dales', an unlikely conjunction if indeed 'the Dales' were Argyll. Later evidence suggests that the Dales of Caithness and Sutherland were considered to be separate areas from Caithness proper. Indeed the name Caithness may initially have been applied only to Duncansby Head, becoming more extensive in its application as the Scandinavian settlement grew.[22] Why is Caithness itself not mentioned in the list of Sigurd's dominions in *Njal's Saga*? Because it was considered to be such an integral part of the Orkney dominions?[23] Or, conversely, because it was *not* part of the Orkney earl's dominions at that particular point? The author of *Njal's Saga* immediately continues by describing the battle of 'Dungal's Peak', probably the same as the second battle of Skitten Mire in *Jarls' Saga*, in which the Norse are fighting hard to get control of Duncansby. As already suggested it would appear that a native family had continued to keep their position in this north-east corner, and according to *Njal's Saga* the chieftain there was then called Moddan. Even though there had been inter-marriage with the Norse earls, tension erupted, and the location of Skitten (just west of Wick: see fig. 16) for the two battles of *Skíða Mýrr* between Orkney earls and 'Scots earls' certainly suggests a frontier area between conflicting powers. *Njal's Saga* also gives interesting information about some sort of clash between 'Earl Melsnati' (evidently a native leader) and Earl Sigurd's brother-in-law, Havard, in Freswick, which lies just south of Duncansby, and evidently part of the same area of tension between Norse and native.[24] These indications suggest that Caithness proper, the north-east corner, was in fact *not* part of Sigurd's dominions at the time of the battle of Dungal's Peak in *Njal's Saga*. If so, the coupling of Sutherland and the Dales together, the areas to the south and the west of Caithness proper as part of Sigurd's dominion, makes good sense in the context of the saga writer's story; in which case we have to look for other evidence that Sigurd had power in Argyll, down the western seaboard of Scotland.

The sagas mention that Sigurd was active in the Hebrides and Man, and the Irish annals record a great deal of disturbance in the area in the years 986, 987 and 989.[25] Dál Riada was raided by Danes (*Danair*: probably meaning simply 'pirates') and Iona was plundered; in 987 Danes fought a battle off Man against the 'son of Harald' while in 989 Godfrey, Harald's son, king of the Hebrides, was killed by the men of Dál Riada. In *Njal's Saga* it is remembered that Earl Sigurd and his followers, the sons of Njal, fought with Godfrey, called the king of Man, and defeated him.[26] Although we cannot be sure who exactly is meant by these Danes of the Irish sources nor even the 'men of Dál Riada', it does look as if Irish and Icelandic traditions can be linked together to show that the perpetrators of trouble in the Hebrides and the victor in a battle with some local Norse kinglet of Man and the Isles were Earl Sigurd and his followers. What evidence is there for the nature of the power that Earl Sigurd apparently won in the Hebrides and Man? According to *Eyrbyggia Saga* he laid a tax on the inhabited lands of Man[27] which was collected by his men, while the earl returned to Orkney. This was evidently some kind of tribute, which does not necessarily indicate a permanent establishment of Orcadian rule. As far as the Hebrides are concerned tradition as recorded in *Njal's Saga* suggests that Earl Sigurd ruled through a tributary earl called Gilli, who resided in either Coll or Colonsay and who was drawn into the earl's family circle by marriage to Sigurd's sister.[28] Such a marriage would have given Earl Sigurd some authority in the area. Whether one can also believe the tradition that Earl Hakon of Lade (Norway) received tribute from Sigurd for holding the Hebrides is less certain.[29] Despite older historians' belief that the Western Isles were tributary to the kings of Norway from the early centuries, the first firm historical evidence for any form of payment by the kings of Man to the Norwegian Crown is not until the mid-twelfth century.[30]

The evidence that we have suggests that there was a struggle for power in Hebridean waters in the 980s, and saga tradition remembered that Sigurd was the victor. He certainly must have had at his command a formidable fleet of warships for his participation some years later in the battle of Clontarf to have been so important (see below). What about his successes on the mainland of

Scotland? His resistance to the rulers of Moray in Caithness turned into a triumphant conquest of their own dominion if we are to believe the listing of Ross and Moray by the author of *Njal's Saga*. Ross in this period comprised the present-day Easter Ross – the firths and river valleys between Inverness and Dornoch. The Norse place-names of this area certainly confirm that it was strongly influenced by Scandinavian presence, and Sigurd's control here is highly likely. Moray was a much larger province stretching across the northern half of Pictland from the Spey valley in the east to north Argyll in the west, and there is no toponymic evidence that the Norse ever had permanent settlements in this area. However, control of access to the Great Glen was probably an important consideration for ease of communication between the Moray Firth and the west coast. There is some evidence that the kings of Scots in the late tenth or early eleventh century were strong enough to impose their overlordship on the men of Moray,[31] an unusual development which may reflect the help of the earl of Orkney in pressurizing the rulers of Moray from the north. If so, an obvious choice of person to whom the king of Scots might have committed the province would have been Earl Sigurd, for their close relationship is reflected in the supposed marriage of King Malcolm's daughter to the earl. This is no more than a conjecture to explain the statement in *Njal's Saga* that Sigurd had dominion in Moray. But the saga's assertion may indeed lend some colour to the belief that King Malcolm, if not 'pushed' into a marriage alliance with the earl, saw it as a useful means of tying into his family the one counter-balancing power in the north of Scotland to the rivals of the MacAlpin dynasty (*Cenél nGabráin*) – the rulers of Moray (*Cenél Loairn*).

Figure 21. Genealogical tree: sons and grandsons of Earl Sigurd 'the Stout'.

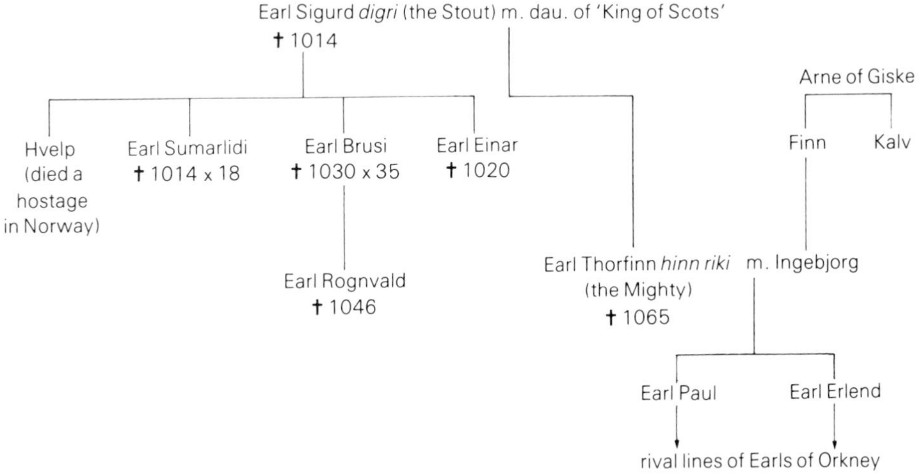

The battle of Clontarf

The final piece of evidence that Earl Sigurd was indeed the most powerful figure in Scandinavian Scotland in the early eleventh century, and a great warrior with large resources of men, supplies and ships at his disposal, comes from the multiplicity of traditions regarding his participation in, and death at, the battle of Clontarf. Previous earls are not recorded as having had any interest in Irish affairs, but Sigurd's mother was Edna (Eithne), the daughter of an Irish King Kjarvall (Cearball),[32] so that Sigurd's family links with Ireland were strong, and it was to Sigurd that King Sitric of Dublin is said to have looked for support in the war that was being waged against the Norsemen in Ireland. A strong Icelandic tradition records that Sitric visited Sigurd in Orkney, and the rewards promised to Sigurd for joining in the coalition against Brian Boru, king of Munster, were said to be 'the kingship of Ireland' and Brian's widow (Sitric's mother) in marriage.[33] The account of the ensuing battle in *Jarls' Saga* is factual and surprisingly brief, considering that this was a most famous event in northern history; its chronology is also mistaken, saying that it took place five years after the Battle of Svoldur (i.e.1005), for there is no doubt that the battle of Clontarf took place in 1014.[34] From a late Irish source we have a list of the wild foreigners who are supposed to have come with Sigurd to fight at Clontarf: the Foreigners of the Orkney and Shetland islands, from Man and from Skye, and from Lewis; from Kintyre and from Argyll (as well as from Brittany and Cornwall).[35] Although modern historians do not accord to the battle of Clontarf the significance which it very soon acquired in Irish history and legend,[36] the gathering of Norsemen from the Norse settlements of Scotland and Ireland to defend the independence of the coastal trading centres from the domination of Brian and his Munstermen has an apocalyptic quality about it. His victory surely does mark the end of an era; an era in which the raids and settlements of the Norse had made a new world of the islands and coasts around Scotland and Ireland – linked together by the western water-ways, in which territorial limitations played little part. That Earl Sigurd was able to gather together a force from this scattered community of islands testifies to the creation of some sort of maritime dominion, united by the common interest of defending Norse influence in Ireland – however diluted that may have become during the two centuries since the Norse first mingled and fought and entered into the turbulent world of Irish-Gaelic society. Earl Sigurd's death at the battle with the famous raven banner wrapped around him[37] is a symbol of the end of this era in the history of the Scandinavian settlements of Scotland. It also represents a very great defeat for the Orkney earldom,[38] for Sigurd was certainly hoping to extend his dominion from the Hebrides to Ireland.

The conversion of Earl Sigurd by Olaf Tryggvesson

Just as older writers used to see the battle of Clontarf as a clash of the 'old and new faiths',[39] so was the saga account of Sigurd's supposed conversion by Olaf Tryggvesson of Norway accorded great importance in the process of christianization of the pagan settlers of Orkney. More recently, however, this event has been interpreted as being less relevant, because of the growing belief that the pagan settlers may have come under Christian influence much earlier.[40] We are here approaching a most important event in the history of Scandinavian Scotland, the conversion of the Vikings who had so disrupted the life of the Christian communities they raided and settled amongst. The change of faith is a turning-point in the whole Scandinavian world, for it is probably true to say that conversion signalled the end of the Viking Age in that some of its results, such as the decline of a slave-based society, radically changed the economy of the Scandinavian peoples.[41] As the eleventh-century writer Adam of Bremen smugly put it, 'Since accepting Christianity . . . imbued with better teachings, they [the Norwegians in particular] have already learnt to be content with their poverty, indeed to disperse what they had gathered, not as before to gather what had been dispersed.'[42] The interpretation of the Viking Age which plays down the pagan aspect of the raiding element, suggesting that the Northmen were quickly assimilated, and that adoption of the Christian religion took place more by osmosis than by active conversion methods, has most recently been countered by persuasive arguments that such an interpretation is simply ignoring the more violent aspects of the Viking way of life.[43] How ought the historical evidence for the enforced conversion of Sigurd and the people in his earldom to be interpreted as a basis for our understanding of the state of the pagan religion during the Viking Age, its decline, and the spread of Christianity among the Norse settlers in the Northern Isles?

The nature of such historical evidence is, of course, partial, and coloured by later thinking and prejudices. Once conversion was complete it was part of church policy to wipe out any symbol of paganism, so that deliberate obliteration makes it exceedingly difficult to know anything about that religion or its survival. Moreover, later medieval writings tended to attribute a whole conversion process to particular individuals, and in the case of Norway, to the proselytizing kings Olaf Tryggvesson (996–1000) and Olaf Haraldsson (1016–1030), the Saint. To compare the Icelandic saga accounts of Olaf Tryggvesson's life with Saxo Grammaticus' and Adam of Bremen's assessments of his religious position is to understand how the historical sources are affected by the standpoint of the compiler. The Icelandic saga writers interpret him as the zealous protagonist of the new faith whose actions were accomplished in an almost legendary way; he was indeed the 'stuff legends are made of'.[44] In Saxo Grammaticus' *Historia Danica*, Olaf is presented as stupid, brutal, and untrustworthy,[45] while Adam, who was writing from the point of view of the church of Hamburg-Bremen, which had not had control over Olaf's supposed missionary activities (he had been converted under the aegis of the Anglo-Saxon church) was exceedingly sceptical about the kind of Christianity that he had endorsed: 'some relate that Olaf had been a Christian, some that he had forsaken Christianity, all affirm that he was skilled in divination . . . he was also given to the practice of the magic art and supported as his household companions all the magicians with whom that land was over-run.'[46] But the legends triumphed and eventually Olaf Tryggvesson was credited with the initial christianization of Norway, Iceland, Greenland, Faroe and the Northern Isles.

As far as Orkney is concerned the story of Olaf Tryggvesson's encounter with Earl Sigurd at Osmundwall (in south Hoy) in the year 995 is preserved in many sources.[47] The two are said to have met when Olaf was returning to Norway via the Pentland Firth after his well-documented raids on England in the company of King Svein Forkbeard. He had been baptized the year previously when King Æthelred stood as sponsor for him.[48] He was therefore a nominal Christian, but also an exceedingly active ruler, so the likelihood is high that he might have attempted to impose his authority on the independent earl in the Orkney islands while sailing past. Part of such an imposition of his authority would be to oversee the conversion of the earl in imitation of the ceremony he himself had lately undergone at the court of King Æthelred. The circumstances are likely and the account itself very probably does enshrine the memory of an actual meeting when Earl Sigurd was forced into some sort of submission; certainly its association with a particular place lends the story an air of authenticity. But the additional details recorded in different accounts are no doubt highly coloured: the threat of immediate death to the earl if he refused baptism (*Heimskringla*);[49] the earl's prevarication and attempt to avoid conversion (Theoderic's *History*, written in Norway in the late twelfth century);[50] the apparently immediate and widespread success of the christianization of the islands (*Jarls' Saga*).[51] As far as the king was concerned the temporal submission of the earl was no doubt just as valuable an achievement as his conversion; the taking of the earl's son as hostage for his good and loyal behaviour was an inevitable part of such royal visits to the earldom.

No doubt too much has been made of the whole famous incident; but the fault for that lies with historians rather than with the saga writers. If it 'is not easy to accept the high significance attributed to it in the sagas',[52] this is really because too much has been expected of the sagas as historical sources in the past. The significance of the event to the saga writer was the dramatic nature of the confrontation between these two famous leaders of the Viking West. He was not particularly concerned with the exact effect this enforced baptism had on the actual state of the religious beliefs of the islanders, although no doubt assuming that the change of religion of the powerful earl of Orkney was a significant matter for the lands he ruled. And it probably was. If we reject this piece of information about the conversion of Earl Sigurd as a historical source we are left with very little evidence of any kind that can be used to throw light on the stages of conversion of the Norse settlers. The archaeology of grave-goods can tell us something about the decline of pagan beliefs in the islands but it does not tell us much about the adoption of the new religion, Christianity.[53]

The likely fact that the ruler of Orkney was baptized in 995 was in itself bound to be of some significance for the state of the Christian religion in the islands, for a process of proper conversion would then at least have been allowed to get under way. One version of *Olaf's Saga* says that Olaf Tryggvesson left priests behind in the islands 'to instruct the people'.[54] The real adoption of the new religion would be carried through only by decades of contact with practising Christians and by the work of preaching, baptizing, missionary clergy who had the support of the secular authorities in providing back-up when compulsion or retribution were required, and in providing funds for the building of churches. Such a programme was established with the support and encouragement of Sigurd's son Thorfinn, as discussed below, but it was possibly initiated as a result of Sigurd's formal acknowledgment of the new religion. Previous earls had come under the influence of Christianity: Sigurd's mother and grandmother must have been Christian, as also was his wife, all of them coming from Christian societies. But contact of that kind alone was probably not enough for either the earls or the Norse settlers to adopt the new religion. True conversion was a process requiring more sustained effort and a much longer period of time than has been generally appreciated. Seen against this background the formal conversion of the earl at Osmound-wall in 995 and the toleration and probable encouragement of Christian teaching within his earldom thereafter surely remains a crucial episode in the history of northern Scotland.

EARL THORFINN II 'THE MIGHTY'

Although we are left with many uncertainties about how Earl Sigurd expanded his power south and west and about the manner of his conversion, we do have more solid evidence to go on for both political and ecclesiastical matters during the reign of his son, Thorfinn. First of all it is relevant to note what *Jarls' Saga* says about the division of Sigurd's territory on his death in 1014. He left four sons, three by his first marriage and one, Thorfinn, by his union with the daughter of the 'king of Scots' (see fig. 21). Thorfinn was only five when Sigurd was killed at Clontarf and apparently lived at his grandfather's court in Scotland. The saga says that Thorfinn was given Caithness and Sutherland by his grandfather King Malcolm along with the title of 'earl', and counsellors were appointed to govern that land with him.[55] It is stressed thereafter that Thorfinn benefited much from the support of the king of Scots. The other three sons divided Sigurd's realm between them, possibly the first time that the earldom had been so divided.[56] One of them, Einar, is recorded as warring in Ireland, Scotland and Wales, suffering a crushing defeat in Ireland with heavy loss of life,[57] and there is no evidence that he had any sway in the Hebrides. The disastrous defeat at Clontarf had evidently meant the collapse of the earls' control in the west.

After the death of another half-brother, Sumarlidi, Thorfinn claimed his share of the Orkneys, a claim which was resisted by Einar, who said that Caithness and Sutherland were larger than a third of the Isles. Even when he got his third of Orkney, Thorfinn continued to live in Caithness, and Duncansby is said to have been his residence during his later struggle to retain Caithness. This had probably been the seat of the native family mentioned earlier but it is evident that by Thorfinn's time it had passed into the hands of the Norse earls. It is also evident that other claims to Caithness were still alive, for the early part of the account of Thorfinn's rule in *Jarls' Saga* is largely concerned with his struggle to retain Caithness.

Conflict in North Scotland: Karl Hundison

That struggle involved in particular a mysterious individual called 'Karl Hundison' who appears in Thorfinn's saga as a powerful Scottish ruler. This seems to be a continuation of the war which had been waged since the end of the ninth century by the Orkney earls against the rulers of Moray.[58] The identity of Karl Hundison has exercised the minds of many commentators on this period of Scottish history and the description of him in the saga as successor to the Scottish realm after King Malcolm has suggested that it must have been Malcolm II's grandson, Duncan, under the guise of some name by which the Norsemen knew him.[59] But there are problems of chronology,[60] as well as of geography, for it is unlikely that at this date the king of Scots would have been fighting lengthy campaigns in the north of Scotland. The important role of the rulers of Moray as rivals for the control of Caithness is certainly relevant here, and since one of those rulers – MacBeth – also became king of Scots then the identification of Karl Hundison with the famous usurper of the Scottish throne seems likely.[61] The name 'Karl' could possibly be an opprobrious epithet ('churl') applied by allies of the family of Malcolm II to the usurper,[62] whilst the name Hundi (ON = dog), had also been the name given to Earl Sigurd's opponent at the battle of 'Dungal's Peak' in *Njal's Saga*. If, as seems likely, Hundi can be identified with the Earl *Finnleikr* of the *Jarls' Saga* version of the battle (located at Skitten Mire – see above, p. 65), then the 'son of Hundi' (Karl) can also be identified with the 'son of Findlaech', whom we know from other sources was certainly MacBeth.[63] The name 'Karl' given to the Scottish king in the Norse sources is a contemporary one enshrined in Arnor Jarlaskald's skaldic verses about Thorfinn's victories which form the basis of this section of *Jarls' Saga*.[64]

Campaigns south and west

Karl Hundison/MacBeth must have waged a successful campaign in Thorfinn's home territory, for the chief (said to be Karl's nephew) whom he wished to set over Caithness was able to move north to Caithness with an army and base himself in Thurso (not securely enough, however, to defend himself against a surprise attack by Thorkell *Fóstri*, Thorfinn's right-hand man).[65] But the only battles we hear about in *Jarls' Saga* are all victories for the Norsemen, the most famous being the sea battle of Deerness, off Orkney, and the battle at Torfness, 'in the south of the Broad Firth', probably Tarbat Ness at the entrance to the Dornoch Firth, and described as 'south off Oykell' in the skaldic poem[66] (the river Oykell still formed an important geographical feature: see figs. 16 and 22). They were famous victories for Thorfinn, although we must not forget that there may have been other encounters less favourable to him which were not lauded in skaldic verse. As a result of these victories some expansion of Thorfinn's realm southwards from Caithness and Sutherland in his father's footsteps is likely to have taken place. If Thorfinn started his warrior's career before the age of 15 (as is said in one of the skaldic verses), then he was probably engaged in a struggle with Karl Hundison from the mid-1020s through the 1030s. Indeed, MacBeth's assumption of the Scottish throne after 1040 and his involvement in wars in the southern half of his new kingdom and on the southern frontier probably left something of a vacuum in the northern territories which Thorfinn was then able to fill. It is in the context of Scottish history that the saga's claim that Thorfinn marched through much of Scotland conquering the land as far south as Fife and laying the region under his rule has to be considered.[67] It is presumably on the basis of this tradition that the epilogue on Thorfinn's rule claims that he won for himself nine Scottish earldoms.[68] This number is really meaningless as we have no idea what constituted a Scottish earldom in the eyes of the Icelandic saga writer, and his wild estimate of Thorfinn's rule as being 70 years long does not encourage

Figure 22. Tarbat Ness, Easter Ross (Aerofilms Ltd).

This headland is likely to be 'Torfness', where Earl Thorfinn 'the Mighty' met 'Karl Hundison' (MacBeth?) in battle (1030 × 1035). The victory of the former allowed the consolidation of Norse settlement around the shores of the Dornoch and Cromarty Firths (seen in the background).

A keen sword at Tarbatness
Reddened the wolf's fare.
The young Prince wielded it –
It was a Monday.
Their swords sang there,
South off Oykell.
There fought with Scotland's King
Our valiant lord. (Arnor Jarlaskald, trans. Taylor *OS*, p. 167)

confidence in the reliability of his numbers. But it is very likely that the powerful earl of Orkney who commanded a formidable naval force would be closely involved in the struggle between the Scottish royal dynasty and the mormaers of Moray. As a valuable ally of the former against the latter, Thorfinn may well have participated in campaigns in southern Scotland and been given rewards in the form of control of territory or earldoms. The best piece of evidence that the Scottish kings of the line of Dunkeld did consider the Norse earls to be valuable allies is the fact that Malcolm III Canmore's first wife was Ingebjorg, said in *Jarls' Saga* to be Thorfinn's widow, but sometimes thought to have been his daughter.[69]

The second stage of Earl Thorfinn's career was, like his father's, devoted to expansion down the western seaboard towards Ireland. This was in company with his nephew, Rognvald Brusisson, who was well known to the Icelandic saga writers as the associate of St Olaf and Magnus the Good, and who survived both the battle of Stiklestad (1030) and years of exile in Russia before returning to Norway and deciding to claim his father's share of the earldom of Orkney. Since Einar's murder (1020) and the death of Brusi (1030 x 1035) Thorfinn had held all the Orkneys without any rival. He seems to have been seeking to extend his power to the west, for we are told in the saga that when Rognvald sailed for Orkney (1037 × 1038) Thorfinn 'was having a great deal of trouble with the Hebrideans and the Irish'.[70] It was, of course, nearly 30 years since Earl Sigurd's involvement in the west, and during the intervening period Sitric Silkbeard, king of Dublin, had ruled the area with the probable support of King Cnut from England.[71] But the abdication of King Sitric in 1035 provided an opportunity for Thorfinn to attempt to reassert Orcadian dominion. Irish support for the Scots, or forces of Karl Hundison, is attested to by skaldic verse about the battle of Torfness, and Karl's nephew, Moddan, is similarly said to have sent for an army from Ireland;[72] this is an element not noted otherwise in the accounts of the battles of the period, and it suggests Irish antagonism to the revival of earldom power in the west which Thorfinn's successes in the east threatened. The *Jarls' Saga* tells us generally that Thorfinn and Rognvald 'raided in the Hebrides, in Ireland, and over a wide area in the west of Scotland'[73] and more specifically that they fought a fierce battle at *Vatsfjǫrdr* (identified as Loch Watten on the west coast of Skye, but possibly located further south).[74] The Isle of Man is nowhere listed specifically as one of Thorfinn's conquests, although control of it is to some extent pre-supposed by his famous raid on England in the year 1042, which is located only 'south of Man', in Arnor Jarlaskald's poem.[75] We have no evidence about the internal situation in Man before Godred Crovan established his dynasty in the island by conquest c.1079. If the situation in Dublin after Sitric's abdication was uncertain, then Man would be even more open to outside control, and the evidence of hoards of silver treasure which had been buried in the ground suggests that the island was in an unsettled state.[76] For his great pillaging raid on England, Thorfinn is said to have drawn men from the Orkneys and Caithness, and large forces from Scotland and Ireland and from the Hebrides flocked to join him.[77] It was evidently the large numbers of different peoples in Thorfinn's train which so impressed contemporaries and was remembered for posterity. He was widely known as a successful war-lord who could offer those in his service promises of wealth in the form of battle-spoils and booty.[78]

The extent of Earl Thorfinn's dominions

However, the saga eulogy assesses Thorfinn's success in even more concrete terms. Besides the nine earldoms in Scotland that he is said to have won for himself it was firmly believed that he had control of 'all the Hebrides and a large realm in Ireland'.[79] If this were really the case it is rather surprising that Thorfinn is not mentioned in any Irish sources; one suspects that what was remembered as a process of conquest by the Icelandic saga-writer was to the Irish only a case of traditional raiding by the *Gall*. Nonetheless, Thorfinn apparently did raid and plunder more widely than any of his predecessors, for we have the skald's record that his earl fought battles in England, even though the abstruse verses give us so little specific information.[80] Arnor's final eulogy of his hero gives us the contemporary view of the extent of Thorfinn's dominion in the west:

> Unto Thorfinn, ravens' feeder,
> Armies had to yield obedience
> From Thussasker right on to Dublin
> Truth I tell, as is recorded.[81]

This has been interpreted rather differently, depending on where 'Thussasker' is supposed to lie. Older commentators thought that it referred to some outlying skerries off south-east Ireland, known as the Tuscar Rocks, and that Thorfinn's conquests in Ireland are being remembered, the extent of which is 'doubtless exaggerated'.[82] But it is more likely that the skald was referring to the whole area of Thorfinn's realm and that 'Thussasker' would lie on the northern perimeter of his dominions, as Dublin lay on the southern. We should probably look to the far north for the location of 'Thussasker', for exactly the same name is used in *Hacon's Saga* in the thirteenth century when King Alexander of Scotland is represented as being determined to win back the Scandinavian lands off Scotland as far east as 'Thussa-sker'.[83] In both sources these rocks seem to be the recognized limit of Norse control, and that must have included Shetland.[84] There are no skerries called 'Thussa sker' or Tuscar around Shetland today; but the traditional name of some fishing grounds off North Unst was 'de Tussek',[85] which is a possible pointer to the former existence of a very similar name for skerries in that locality, exactly the place where outlying rocks (such as the Muckle Flugga group) would be well known to Norse mariners as the first indication of the islands in the western sea.[86]

The extension of Thorfinn's power over Shetland seems to have been regarded as a matter of conquest. Throughout *Jarls' Saga* Shetland is usually referred to as a port of call *en route* between Orkney and Norway with little mention of any political control exercised there by the earls. A contemporary poem about King Olaf the Saint, by Ottar the Black, says specifically that the Shetlanders were subject to him.[87] Later, Rognvald Brusisson, sailing west after seeking help from St Olaf's successor, Magnus, against Earl Thorfinn, is said to have gathered forces in Shetland on his way; this may imply that Shetland belonged to the Norwegian king and had been granted out to Rognvald. Certainly Rognvald is called 'lord of the Shetlanders'.[88] Thorfinn would have been able to bring Shetland in under his own rule after Rognvald's defeat, and when Snorri discusses the extent of Thorfinn's dominion he says that 'he had under him Orkney, Shetland and the Hebrides besides very great possessions in Scotland and Ireland'.[89] It would seem clear then that Thorfinn's dominion was traditionally known to have covered the Northern and Western Isles as far north as Shetland and as far south as the Irish Sea, including most probably the Isle of Man – the old traditional route ploughed in the past by the keels of many of his ancestors' ships.

Thorfinn's relationship with King Olaf Haraldsson

The relations of the earls of Orkney with the Norwegian kings form one of the main themes in the history of the earldom through the Middle Ages. The problems of knowing how much control the early kings had exercised over the settlement of Orkney and the establishment of earldom power have already been discussed.[90] By the mid-eleventh century we have arrived at a period when the historical sources should provide us with a little clearer information. Olaf Haraldsson was a king of Norway who can be regarded as a national figurehead, and even though that status is one that developed only posthumously along with his sanctity, the accumulation of evidence suggests that King Olaf united most of southern, eastern and western Norway under his political and ecclesiastical hegemony which lasted from 1015 to 1030. It is highly likely that in this process some attempt would have been made to exert more regular political control over the earldom in the west.[91]

The division of the earldom amongst the sons of Earl Sigurd provided an opportunity for the king; both Brusi and Thorfinn are said to have sought Olaf's help in gaining what they claimed was their rightful due, but he decided to keep Earl Einar Sigurdsson's third of the earldom in compensation for Einar's murder of Eyvind Urushorn, the king's close companion. Some highly interesting chapters in *Jarls' Saga* give full details of the visits paid by Earls Brusi and Thorfinn to King Olaf and the settlement reached between the king and the earls.[92] The fact that these two earls did submit to Olaf is corroborated by a rare entry in the Icelandic Annals (which have very little information to offer about Orkney in the eleventh century generally) under the year 1021: 'Earl Thorfinn and earl Brusi, Sigurd's sons, gave the Orkneys into the power of King Olaf.'[93] The saga fills in these sparse details with a reconstruction of their visit, of the conversations that took place during it, and of the arrangements which were made at it. The plausibility of the scene, and historical discussions of the relationship of previous Orkney earls and their Norwegian overlords, merely tell us that the thirteenth-century saga writer knew his Orkney traditions and the recurring factors which did indeed come to the fore on occasions during the thirteenth century when the kings and earls fought or negotiated from their related positions of strength. These were the matter of submission and of overlordship; the problem of dual allegiance and the threat of the earls looking to the kings of Scots as an alternative source of support; the Norwegian kings' use of hostages; and their general aim of attempting to turn the Orkney earls into royal officials bound to them by oaths of homage, and returning tribute to them on a regular basis. We have to take relative matters into consideration when assessing the value of passages in *Jarls' Saga* which refer to the eleventh century, matters such as the strength of the kings concerned and their recorded relationships with other chieftains, and the numbers of heirs in the earldom striving to get their due inheritance – always a source of weakness for the earldom and of strength to the kings. King Olaf was a skilled practitioner of 'divide and rule' with regard to his powerful *stormenn* in Norway[94] and would doubtless have taken advantage of rivalry between the earls in Orkney. Moreover, at the time when Brusi and Thorfinn sought a settlement with Olaf, Thorfinn can only have been still a boy, although it is likely that he would indeed have challenged his brother at an early age for a share of the islands. We can probably accept therefore the information in the saga that Olaf gave both earls a third each of the islands, keeping one third himself, which he then handed out to Earl Brusi to govern for him; certainly the retention of the young Rognvald Brusisson as a hostage, a well-known practice in Icelandic saga tradition, was the prime method of ensuring the loyalty and good behaviour of an earl (as Olaf Tryggvesson had taken Sigurd Hlodversson's son at the end of the previous century). But King Olaf did not neglect to tie the young Thorfinn into his courtly circle either; it can only have been with his approval, and very likely at his instigation, that Thorfinn was married to Ingebjorg, the daughter of Finn Arnesson of Giske, a family strong in support of Olaf Haraldsson and used by him to counter the power of the Lade earls in the Trøndelag.[95] It was during these years, before Olaf was ousted by Cnut of Denmark and England, that Thorfinn would have married, and there is no indication in any source that he ever had any wife other than Ingebjorg.

Thorfinn's quarrel with Rognvald Brusisson

The upheavals in the Norwegian kingdom which followed the fall of King Olaf at Stiklestad in 1030 probably coincided with Thorfinn's struggle with Karl Hundison/MacBeth and his efforts to extend his realm in Scotland. When Olaf's son, Magnus the Good, came to the throne (1035) he was unlikely to make any special effort to come to terms with Thorfinn, for Rognvald Brusisson was his close follower. Rognvald had followed Olaf Haraldsson into exile in 1028, returning to Norway and fighting alongside him at the battle of Stiklestad in 1030. He sought refuge thereafter at the court of Yaroslav of Novgorod along with Magnus, accompanying him back to Norway when he returned as the new king.[96] Rognvald was very much a king's man and well placed to be entrusted with his uncle Einar's much-disputed third of the earldom, along with his own inherited third from his father. This division of the earldom was not a cause of trouble for some years after Rognvald's arrival in Orkney (1037 x 1038), for he and Thorfinn allied together in the process of re-asserting control over the Hebrides, and very successfully fought many battles together. However, this situation did not last, and the trouble seems to have arisen from the fact that Thorfinn provided a refuge for one of the king's enemies, Kalv Arnesson, who fled to Orkney after a breach with King Magnus probably engineered by one of the other great chieftains, Einar Tambarsk-jelve.[97] Kalv was the only one of the powerful family of Arnmødlings who had not been faithful to St Olaf but fought against him at Stiklestad, and he and Rognvald Brusisson were not therefore the closest of companions. Kalv and Thorfinn were, however, closely allied by marriage, for Thorfinn was married to the daughter of Kalv's brother, Finn (see fig. 21), which no doubt was the reason why Kalv fled to Orkney in the late 1030s.

Kalv's stay was probably crucial to the development of Thorfinn's career, for there seems little doubt that he was the cause of the deterioration in Rognvald's and Thorfinn's relationship, and according to the saga it was the expense of maintaining Kalv which caused Thorfinn to raise the matter of Einar's third of the islands once again, for 'Kalv had a large following of his own, and this was a source of considerable expense to the Earl.'[98] He demanded the return of Einar's third from Rognvald, and this resulted in the final breach between the two former comrades-in-arms, with Rognvald receiving a great deal of support from King Magnus in the quarrel. The two earls came to blows in the naval battle off *Raudabjorg*, and the situation is sketched in two verses, one skald showing how the decision of Kalv Arnesson to fight on Thorfinn's side was crucial for the outcome of the battle, and the other, Arnor Jarlaskald, grieving that his two patrons had come to blows, for 'awkward our choice when Earls are eager to fight'.[99] The battle was not of course the end of the struggle between the two earls and it was not until Rognvald had been murdered on Papa Stronsay and King Magnus had died (1047) shortly afterwards that Earl Thorfinn was finally certain of his position in the islands.

The accession of Harald Hardrada to the throne of Norway probably meant an easing of the situation in several ways: Kalv Arnesson was given permission to return to Norway and took up his possessions and his position as *lendmann* (king's man) again; Harald took as his wife or concubine a member of the Arnmødling family and was therefore related to both Kalv and Thorfinn by marriage. Harald in general allowed his *stormenn* freedom of action so long as their ambition did not threaten his own.[100] The saga certainly gives the impression that Thorfinn's relations with King Harald were very cordial, informing us that he visited the king in Norway on his own initiative. This brief account of their meeting is just as valuable a piece of historical information as the much fuller account of Thorfinn's meeting with King Magnus after the murder of Earl Rognvald, which for all its detail and dramatic dialogue tells us no more than that the earl and king did not part on very good terms.[101]

Assessment of Thorfinn's position

Thorfinn's visit to King Harald was part of his great European tour which took place c.1050, culminating in his audience with the Pope where he obtained absolution from all his sins. This tour sets the stamp on Earl Thorfinn's 'foreign policy' and brings him up to the rank of a leading Scandinavian ruler. Despite his half-Scottish origin and his early links with the Scottish royal court, Thorfinn was a powerful figure in the Scandinavian world. His relationship with the different kings of Norway may have been chequered, but the saga evidence is quite clear that he visited three Norwegian kings, and on several occasions. This is not suggested of any earl prior to Thorfinn and Brusi. Previous recorded contacts with the Norwegian kings had been in the western lands only: Sigurd Hlodversson under some compulsion at Osmundwall, Arnkell and Erlend in Erik Bloodaxe's train during his career in the British Isles; Sigurd 'the Mighty' and Torf-Einar at home in Orkney during Harald

Finehair's supposed visits to the west. The Sigurdssons' visits to Norway, combined with the reliable tradition of Thorfinn's marriage to Ingebjorg Finn Arnesson's daughter tell us that the links between the earldom and the home country were being strengthened. The three earls prior to Thorfinn had all taken wives from the western land: Sigurd from Scotland, Hlodver from Ireland, and Thorfinn Skull-Splitter from the native dynasty in Caithness. Certainly three of Hlodver's brothers were traditionally remembered as having been married to the wicked Ragnhild, daughter of Erik Bloodaxe, but we cannot be entirely sure what grain of truth lies behind the literary accretions of this chapter in *Jarls' Saga*.

Thorfinn's visits to the kings in Norway suggest a real growth of royal authority, which was able to exercise some influence in the western lands by means other than royal visitations. This was primarily by supporting a rival earl such as Rognvald Brusisson, who was so closely associated with the kings of Norway that he fought at the side of St Olaf and went into exile with his son. Rognvald was later remembered in the earldom family as having been 'the most able of all the Earls of Orkney', although Snorri Sturlason was to use similar terms about Thorfinn, who 'has been the ablest earl of these islands, and has had the greatest dominion of all the Orkney earls'.[102] Nonetheless, in order to maintain some sort of control over an area stretching from Ireland to Shetland, Thorfinn had to keep on good relations with the political authorities to whom he was certainly obliged to accord some form of recognition. Thus the problems inherent in the nature of the medieval Orkney earldom are already apparent; it was by this period the dual earldom which it was to remain almost without break to the end of its existence. As earl of Caithness (Thorfinn is specifically said to have been given the realm of Caithness and Sutherland with the title of 'earl' by his grandfather), he was subject to a king in Scotland, and as earl of the islands (perhaps including the Sudreys although they are never mentioned in the saga as having been granted by the king) he was subject to a king in Norway. Such a position may have had its advantages, for an astute earl could play off one overlord against another. Indeed, we see the beginnings of that in the alleged but somewhat anachronistic reply that Thorfinn is said to have made to King Olaf that he could not do him homage 'for I am already an earl of the King of Scots, and a vassal of his'.[103] But increasingly as the Middle Ages progressed this position was to be full of disadvantages, as the kings of Norway and Scotland increased their actual power over their territorial possessions rather than simply having theoretical authority over individual earls.[104]

ESTABLISHMENT OF ADMINISTRATIVE STRUCTURES

The plan of Earl Thorfinn 'the Mighty' to create a realm stretching from Shetland to Man under one political and ecclesiastical authority marks a peak of ambition in the history of the Scandinavian settlements in Scotland. When we are told that after his European tour Thorfinn settled down in Birsay (West Mainland of Orkney) and 'devoted all his time to the government of his people and country and to the making of new laws',[105] we have a very significant indication that he was attempting to create some sort of governmental structures; which, if so, suggests that he was well in the forefront of eleventh-century political development. Prime among these structures was the organization of an ecclesiastical framework for the ministry of a Christian priesthood.

Founding of the Orkney bishopric

Earl Thorfinn is primarily credited with the establishment of a bishopric in the islands and with the building of the first documented church in Orkney. This was a very significant development in the christianization of the Norse population of the Northern Isles, and the real conversion of the Norse in Orkney can be said to belong to the reign of Earl Thorfinn.[106] The Vikings had, of course, had some contacts with Christianity since the beginning of the Viking Age, and there is evidence that they could be brought into a semi-official relationship with the Christian Church by the process of 'primsigning', a blessing (but not baptism) which enabled them to trade with Christians.[107] In most areas this half-way house was probably regarded as no more than a convenience, and would by no means lead to full conversion and baptism later. Christ might be added to the pantheon of pagan gods, but the forsaking of all heathen worship and deep-rooted pagan customs may have taken many centuries. There is evidence that some of the earliest settlers in the Hebrides had been influenced by Irish Christianity and that they had taken their beliefs with them to Iceland.[108] But the situation in the Hebrides was very different from the Northern Isles where, as will be discussed, influence from existing Christian centres was less marked.[109] Moreover, political control was less easily exercised over the Hebridean islands. In Orkney the earl's role was crucial: he and his hird (ON *hirð* = military following) dominated society, and what they practised in the way of religious observances would be followed by the remaining Norse settlers. Despite Sigurd's official conversion, we have strong traditions, as discussed above, that he died holding the magical raven banner at Clontarf – the raven being closely associated with Odin. A few years after his death, somewhat unsatisfactory reports of the state of Christianity in the Orkneys and other Atlantic islands are said to have been received by King Olaf in Norway;[110] it was probably during this period that the archbishops of York started to appoint missionary bishops to Orkney.[111]

From the age of five, the young Thorfinn Sigurdsson was under the protection of his grandfather and probably lived for a while in the Christian atmosphere of the royal court in Scotland. This presumably made him more than just a nominal Christian, even if it did not change his early life-style much from that pursued by his pagan ancestors. The adoption of a Christian name for his eldest son, Paul – the first Christian name used in the earldom line – is good evidence for Thorfinn's Christian upbringing. Once he was free of any rivals, and assured of his control of the islands (c.1048), then he set out on his famous journey to Rome where he visited the pope, seeking the remission of his sins; after which he is said to have 'finished with piracy'. In the latter years of his rule he built a 'magnificent church' at Birsay, his main seat of residence, called Christ's Kirk, where the first bishops were based.[112]

The historian is fortunate in having independent evidence to corroborate the saga traditions about this new and significant development. About the year 1070 Adam of Bremen wrote his history of the archbishops of Hamburg-Bremen, who claimed responsibility for the conversion of the whole of Scandinavia. He records what he had heard about the pagan north, and above all he gives almost contemporary information about the first bishops sent out by the archbishops of Hamburg over the whole Atlantic area. They were sent, he tells us, in response to a request by the peoples of Iceland, Greenland, and the Orkneys, who had sent legates or messengers asking the archbishop to appoint preachers in those areas.[113] This had been in the time of Archbishop Adalbert of Hamburg (1042–1072), during which period Earl Thorfinn had travelled to Rome via Denmark and Germany. It is therefore possible that the 'legate' from the Orkney islands had been Thorfinn himself, who can hardly have avoided passing through Hamburg on his way from Denmark to Rome. Adam also says that the first bishop appointed by Adalbert to the Orkneys was called Thorolf, and that his appointment was 'by order of the Pope'.[114] Since Adalbert's episcopal consecrations were normally independent actions, this may confirm that Thorolf's election was a result of Thorfinn's visit to Rome. Indeed the fact that this bishop had a Norse name is also a possible indication of the earl's influence over the appointment, for there were very few trained clerics from the Scandinavian world at this early date, so we may guess that some relation or close associate of the earl had been given the position; the earls always liked to have bishops over whom they could exercise some influence. Finally, Adam says that Thorolf was appointed *in civitatem Blasconam*[115] ('to the city of Blascona'), meaning that his episcopal seat in the Orkneys was at a place which Adam understood to be called 'Blascona', or which he has latinized as 'Blascona'. Given the strong saga tradition that Thorfinn built Christ Kirk at Birsay, which was the first seat of the bishops in the Orkneys we simply have to assume that Blascona was Adam's reading of the name 'Birsay' which he did not understand. There is no other place-name in the Orkneys which remotely resembles it. Adam of Bremen's account of the appointment of Bishop Thorolf therefore provides supporting historical evidence to corroborate the saga information about the date of the establishment of the episcopal seat in Orkney and of the place where it was established.

Ecclesiastical context

It is interesting to compare this achievement with the establishment of bishoprics in other parts of the Norse world. Missionary bishops had probably been in Iceland since the 1020s, and fairly soon became associated with Skalholt, which was the first episcopal see.[116] Christ Church Cathedral was founded in Dublin by the Norse king Sitric Silkbeard, also after a pilgrimage to Rome c.1028.[117] In Norway the process of political unification went hand in hand with christianization, and the bishops were therefore mobile for longer, accompanying the kings as members of their hird as they moved around the country. It was not until the late eleventh century that episcopal churches (dedicated to Christ) appear in Trondheim and Bergen based within the perimeters of the *kongs gard*, the royal residence.[118] The dedication to Christ was usual for the first episcopal churches, as at Birsay and Dublin, following

English and Roman precedents. As a modern ruler of a Christian realm, Thorfinn was therefore well to the fore in the Scandinavian lands in seeking a bishop for his earldom in the 1050s and building an episcopal church near his own residence. This close physical relationship of ruler's palace and bishop's church is a feature of all the early bishoprics in territories where there was a powerful ruler,[119] and establishes the importance of favourable political authorities being in charge. Bishops would not have been able to exist within these territories, or go about the process of establishing churches, implanting a clergy and seeing to the conversion of the people without the piety and goodwill of the local ruler. They would, moreover, require endowments in order to survive, in a period before tithes could be instituted for the maintainance of a church. It seems highly likely that it was right at the beginning that the Orcadian bishops were given the lands in Birsay which they possessed later in the Middle Ages, and which the earls must have possessed there in the eleventh century.[120]

Thorolf was a hird bishop who would probably have travelled round with the earl and have exercised his episcopal functions throughout the different parts of Thorfinn's dominions. Shetland was always included in the bishopric of Orkney, and whereas Caithness was to get its own Scottish bishop in the mid-twelfth century, it seems very likely that before then they, too, would have been subject to the earl's bishop from the north.[121] The only evidence that can be adduced for the Hebrides in this period is all very indefinite: the last bishop on Iona occurs in the late tenth century, while the first of the bishops of Man who received the bishop's seat there (*episcopalem suscepit cathedram*) was Hamond (a Manxman) in the days of Godred Crovan, i.e. after his conquest of Man in 1079.[122] However, two earlier bishops, about whom the medieval compiler of the list of the bishops of Man knew nothing except that they were called Roolwer and William, may be identifiable with known bishops of Orkney, particularly the first one whose name appears to be a medieval variant of ON 'Rolf', and therefore either the same as Thorolf, Earl Thorfinn's bishop already mentioned[123] or Radulf, bishop of Orkney in the 1070s.[124] Indeed if Earl Thorfinn exercised any political control in Man and the Hebrides then, we could expect his bishop to have exercised some spiritual authority there, too.

Laws, tribute and administration

The creation of a new church and the firm establishment of a new religion necessitated changes in customary laws (which we are told Earl Thorfinn made). The situation is very similar to that in Norway where we have the contemporary example of a lawmaker in King Olaf, long revered as the maker of good laws, for 'St Olaf's Law' was the ideal of fair and traditional laws which became the rallying cry later in the Middle Ages against any arbitrary attempt to alter established custom. His renown as a lawgiver can be traced back almost to his own time, but when details of his laws are looked for, only the joint declaration on church matters with the missionary Bishop Grimkell can be certainly associated with the saintly king.[125] Thorfinn may have had the power to create new secular law in the earldom, although it seems more likely that, as with St Olaf, he was involved in the imposition of church law. The weighty hand of the secular ruler would have been required to assist the bishop's authority in making many changes in customary practice: in social customs of birth, marriage, burial and inheritance, as well as in the kindred's choice of marriage partner; in pagan customs such as the eating of horseflesh, sacrifices and ancestor worship. All we are told in the saga, however, is that Thorfinn made changes in the customary laws.[126]

As regards the government of his dominions, the uncorroborated saga evidence suggests that Thorfinn and his father imposed some form of tribute on those parts of Scotland and the Hebrides which they conquered. They may have used relatives or reliable members of the hird to help them exercise control in the Hebrides, such as Earl Gilli of Coll, Thorfinn's uncle by marriage, and Kalv Arnesson whom Thorfinn sent to the Hebrides 'to make sure of his authority there'.[127] Thorfinn and Sigurd before him are both said to have been able to muster forces from the Hebrides and Scotland. But on what sort of basis could such a tax and military levy system be organized? There is evidence of an assessment system for men and money which covered the Northern Isles and the north and west mainland of Scotland, the Hebrides and Man; but there are many problems concerned with analysing such material.

If we look first at the earls' administrative system in Orkney we can appreciate that it was composed of several elements. Primarily, there were the earls' own landed estates from which they derived sustenance for their families and retinues, and which they must have possessed from the early days of the earldom.[128] These 'mensal' estates which supplied their own table were later called 'bordlands' and these were supposed to be inalienable, and were also free of tax burdens.[129] The remainder of their estates were later known as 'auld earldom' and were used for endowing members of the family or rewarding their closest followers. Further, within Orkney there is some evidence that the earls established a system of administrative farms of military character known in Norway, and called 'Huseby' farms. The system had possibly been introduced into Norway from Sweden at an early date by members of the Yngling dynasty; certainly it was known in Sweden, where there are about 70 'Huseby' place-names, as well as in Denmark, where there are only about eight. Norway itself has about 45, and Orkney three or four still surviving. In Sweden the system of food renders for the kings organized round these 'Huseby' farms may be as old as the seventh or eighth centuries, and associated with the cult of the pagan god, Ullr. They are traditionally said to have been established in western Norway by Harald Finehair[130] and were possibly introduced by him into North Møre and Romsdal, where Earl Rognvald of Møre may have been involved in their organization. The suggestion has been made that a similar system was introduced by Earl Rognvald or one of his family in Orkney after their conquest of the islands.[131] In fact, the existence of six 'huseby' districts in Orkney has been postulated, which is just the same number as in North Møre and Romsdal. They all centred on earldom farms, three or four of which still have the name Houseby-Husabae (ON *húsabýr* = house farm; see fig. 23), and which could have formed administrative centres for the collection of tax (ON *skattr*) and organization of the naval levy in surrounding districts of 35 or 36 ouncelands (see below). Some rather similar place-names existed in Shetland, but whether on such a regular basis that they indicate the same kind of

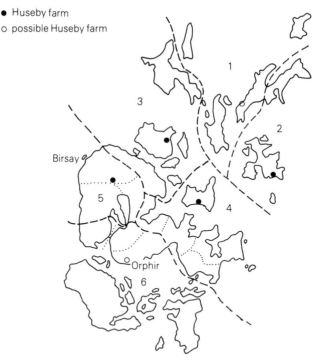

● Huseby farm
○ possible Huseby farm

Figure 23. (left) Orkney Huseby farms and *(right)* Manx sheadings (after A. Steinnes, 'The "Houseby" system in Orkney', *Scottish Historical Rev.*, xxxviii, 1959, and B.R.S. and E.M. Megaw, 'The Norse heritage in the Isle of Man', in *The Early Christian Cultures of North West Europe*, ed. B. Dickens and C. Fox, Cambridge University Press, 1950).

administrative system is not clear. No such system in the Hebrides has yet been elucidated, although the Isle of Man was divided into six administrative districts called *sheadings* (ON = *séttungr*, a sixth part; see fig. 23), which were composed of a similar number of land divisions ('treens'). The 'huseby' name does not, however, exist in Man, and it is not known whether the earls of Orkney had any estates in the Hebrides and Man during their period of control. We only know that the later kings of Man and the Isles were well-endowed with estates in Man, and in the Isles, where the island of Islay seems to have formed an important estate centre.[132]

Another place-name of significance in administrative history is 'herad' (ON *héraḍ*), which is an early district division in south-east Norway, associated with the legal structure of public courts or 'things' (ON *þing*). This name can be recognized in the West Mainland of Orkney (Harray), close by the earldom base at Birsay (called *Birgisheraḍ* in *Jarls' Saga*); in the name 'de Herra' in three places in Shetland;[133] and in the name Harris (G. *Na Hearradh*) in the Outer Isles, which is also found in Rhum and Islay in the Inner Hebrides, and possibly in Dumfriesshire.[134] These are apparently the remaining traces of a different or complementary administrative structure.

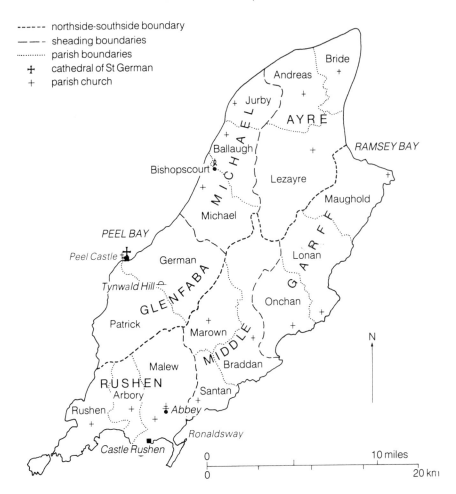

Assessment for tax and defence

Turning to the naval levy system, we come to the most difficult, but potentially most exciting, aspect of the earldom administration. Clearly, there was a
system of assessment both for taxation purposes and for naval defence. The
late medieval Orkney rentals give us full information as to the tax system but
there are no contemporary fiscal or military records from the period under
discussion. However, we have glimpses from the saga text of a fully-fledged
system of defence whose intricacies of organization can only be guessed at.
The naval levy, without which no earl of Orkney could hope to maintain a
vestige of power within or without the islands, could certainly raise a
minimum of 15 or 16 ships from Orkney and 5 or 6 from Caithness – and
probably more.[135] There is good historical evidence that in the eleventh
century would-be conquerors around the shores of Britain were able to raise –
presumably hire – a naval fleet from Orkney for the pursuing of their own

political ambitions, just as the kings of the Isles were leaders or providers of warships at a slightly later period.[136] In 1058 Magnus Haraldsson, son of the Norwegian king, used Orkney ships in his attack on the west of England:[137] in 1066, 17 ships from Orkney joined Earl Tostig in his famous enterprise of that year.[138] In the late eleventh century Gruffydd, king of North Wales, is said to have collected 24 warships from the Orkneys for a raid on South Wales.[139] So long as there were maritime adventurers and Scandinavian claimants around, then the Orkney islands formed an exceedingly important recruiting-ground for fighting-men and ships – as well as a very useful retreat in case of ill-success.

How was this fleet raised? From Norway there is evidence of very sophisticated arrangements for the naval levy called in ON *leiðangr*. This name does not appear to have been used in Orkney, although in the late Shetland rentals there is a payment called 'leanger', and the word passed into Irish as a loan-word meaning naval forces or a fleet.[140] The 'leidang' system in Norway, as it can be understood from later sources, was a system imposed on the coastland districts of the west and south for the provision and manning of a longship or warship. Districts called *skipreiður* were responsible for the building of a ship, which might be a 20- or 25-seater (i.e. 25 benches on both sides). Smaller areas, groups of farms called *manngjerden* in the west and *lide* in the Oslo fjord, were responsible for the providing and equipping with weapons and food of one warrior for the vessel.[141] Opinions vary as to when the system reached such a high degree of organization, for although there was evidently some kind of military levy far back in the Viking Age, it does not seem possible that the kings' authority was wide-ranging enough to impose such a regularized arrangement as the 'leidang' throughout the western and southern areas much before AD 1000.[142] The provisioning of the 'leidang' formed the basis of the later taxation system known as 'skatt' (*borð-leiðangr*), when the food renders were converted into monetary payments at the end of the twelfth century.

Ouncelands and pennylands

As far as the Norse colonies in the west are concerned, there are traces of a similar levy system but one with some very basic differences from the Norwegian stereotype. Whereas the Norwegian system of manning was closely tied up with the judicial structure of 'thing' districts and numbers required to attend the assemblies, in the islands in the west it appears to have been based on a system of territorial divisions called ouncelands and penny-lands, which have no parallel in Norway. These were valuation units for the imposition of 'skatt' and from the names would appear to have always been associated with tax or render of some kind; 'The term [ounceland, or 'eyris-land' in Orkney] must have originally denoted land in respect of which an eyrir or ounce of money had to be paid.'[143] These territorial divisions are best understood in Orkney, where they continued to form the basis of a taxation system into modern times. But they are traceable in Shetland and all round the Scottish coast from Caithness to Galloway and throughout the Hebrides as far south as Man (see fig. 24).[144] Wherever Norse place-names exist (except apparently in Ross) ouncelands or pennylands also occur and are a marker of

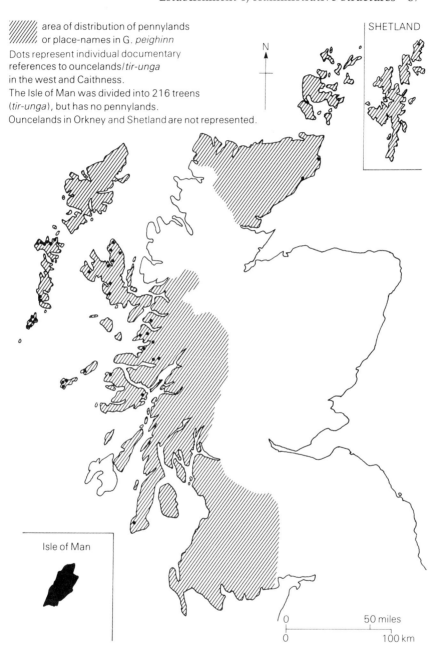

area of distribution of pennylands
or place-names in G. *peighinn*

Dots represent individual documentary
references to ouncelands/*tir-unga*
in the west and Caithness.
The Isle of Man was divided into 216 treens
(*tir-unga*), but has no pennylands.
Ouncelands in Orkney and Shetland are not represented.

SHETLAND

N

Isle of Man

0   50 miles
0   100 km

Figure 24. Distribution of ouncelands and pennylands (based on work done by A. Easson and M. Bangor-Jones).

Scandinavian influence of some kind. In the west, the Gaelic equivalent to ounceland was *tir-unga* (= 'land-ounce') in the Hebrides and in Man *treen*, a name which has been interpreted as deriving from *tir-unga*.[145] This unit was divided into quarters, called quarterlands in Man but 'skattlands' in Orkney, which can perhaps be related to the Norwegian *manngjerden* and *lide*, the area required to furnish one warrior for the levy.[146] Pennylands have a slightly different coverage; the name is widespread in south-west Scotland (where ouncelands do not occur),[147] and they exist throughout mainland Argyll and further north as far as Glenelg, whereas ouncelands are traceable on the west Scottish mainland only in Ardgour, Garmoran and Knapdale. But pennylands are missing entirely from Islay and from the Isle of Man.[148] This suggests that the two units may not have been contemporaneous in their imposition over this very extensive area, nor were they necessarily imposed for the same purpose.

Interest in this problem has been focussed mainly on the significance of the land divisions as a basis for a naval levy system, although the unstressed assumption has been that the ounceland was 'established as a basic unit for Norse taxation' by Harald Finehair.[149] Doubtful though that assumption may be, it does look as if these units must have been associated with an assessment system for taxation from the start, even though they may also have been utilized for a naval defence levy. The division of the ounceland into four 'skattlands' in Orkney, for instance, provides an incontrovertible link with a taxation system (ON *skattr* = tax),[150] and it can be worked out that 216 ounces of silver were due from the whole earldom, which would probably be paid in the form of rings of gold or silver (*baugar*), whole or hacked.[151] This at least was the theory, but, as in the later Middle Ages, it is highly improbable that such income would regularly get past the earl and be paid direct to the king in Norway.

The name 'ounceland' suggests the use of silver bullion, whilst 'pennyland' denotes the use of coinage. That difference in itself shows that the two assessments cannot easily be related, and moreover the well-known fact that the ounceland was divided into a different number of pennylands in the Northern Isles and in the Hebrides strengthens the suspicion that the imposition of the pennyland system was not a uniform procedure and must have related to different factors in the north and in the west. In Orkney and Caithness the ounceland was always divided into 18 pennylands but in the Hebrides it was mostly divided into 20 pennylands, except in a few places like North Uist where the division may have been on a duodecimal basis. It seems likely that the assessments in north and west were made at different times and according to some different criteria. Yet, the territorial divisions of ounceland and pennyland are used throughout Scandinavian Scotland, and for this there must be some historical reason.

Origins of the tax and naval system

As these land divisions are unknown in Norway it is no use looking to the home country for enlightenment as to their use and origin. It has, therefore, been suggested that the assessment system in the Northern and Western Isles must have been based on pre-Norse administrative divisions, and that the ounceland was related to the measure of land called a 'davoch' which is known primarily from eastern Scotland, although an Irish word in origin.[152] Certainly, in late Hebridean sources, the davoch is an equivalent to *tir-unga* (ounce-land), but it is never used in Orkney or north-east Caithness; in south Caithness and Sutherland the relationship between davoch and pennyland is fixed at six pennylands.[153] It is exceedingly difficult to be certain that any association between davochs and ouncelands/pennylands dates back to a period when the incoming Norse might have utilized the administrative system which they found in the lands they settled. Because there is no evidence of any similar assessment system in Norway or Iceland, it has been doubted whether an ounceland assessment could have been introduced by the Vikings.[154] But they were accustomed to weighing bullion in units of marks, ounces and 'ertogs',[155] so there seems no reason to doubt their ability to use the ounce as the basis of an assessment system from the earliest days of political control in the Northern and Western Isles. They might, however, have adopted and developed a tax system based on the ounce which appears to have existed at that time in Ireland.[156] The amount of hack silver found in hoards and the weighing scales found in Viking graves afford striking evidence from the ninth and tenth centuries for the use of precious metal for its intrinsic value rather than in coined form among the Viking communities around the coasts of Britain, particularly in Scotland.[157]

As regards the problem of naval assessment, it has been rightly pointed out that both the Picts and Dalriadic Scots had navies, and must have had some method of raising them; it is known that in Dál Riada 20 houses were grouped together for the purpose of furnishing a vessel. It may be that the later pennyland was based on the previous Dalriadic 'house' system, and that the 20-penny ounceland in the Hebrides related to that Dalriadic grouping for naval requirements.[158] But this theory does not help to explain the use of the penny, and some adjustment would have to have been done in the matter of the size of ships and numbers of rowers, for the Dalriadan vessel would appear to have been smaller than the Viking warship of 25 benches.[159] The Vikings in general were adept at using whatever administrative systems they found in the countries they settled if these suited their purposes, and there may well be elements of the ounceland and pennyland system which have pre-Norse roots; but the appearance of that system throughout the area ruled or influenced by the Norse around the Scottish coasts is a very clear indication that much of it was imposed by them, or even by one particular ruler, using relatively sophisticated assessment techniques, based on units valued according to ounces and pennies.

When looking for suitable political and geographical circumstances for the establishment of such an assessment system then surely Orkney and Caithness provide the right starting point. In this location tight political control was exercised by powerful earls who controlled a fertile collection of islands and territory which made up their earldom, where access was never restricted by difficult terrain, or – within Orkney – by wide stretches of open water. This is an ideal environment for the development of a sophisticated assessment system, controlled by a hierarchical society which culminated in the most powerful political figure in the Viking settlements overseas. Any historian who has discussed the question of the imposition of the ounceland system over the whole area of Norse-colonized Scotland has looked for a single political authority powerful enough to have been able to introduce it. If we reject Harald Finehair, by virtue of rejecting the evidence for his conquest of the settlements overseas, then we have to look to the earls of Orkney. The Møre family's control of the islands was firm enough from at least the days of Torf-Einar for an administrative structure to be imposed by them on their earldom, but on Caithness and Sutherland hardly before the days of Earl Hlodver or even Sigurd Hlodversson (late tenth century). Then an assessment system could have been extended to the Hebrides and western mainland of Scotland during the period of Sigurd's or his son Thorfinn's conquest of the Hebrides and Argyll in the early eleventh century. Is it possible, therefore, to say that wherever the system of territorial divisions based on the ounce can be traced this is an indication of the exercise of some regular political control by the northern earls, Sigurd and Thorfinn? It is known that ouncelands existed on the western mainland in Ardgour, Sunart, Garmoran and possibly Knapdale and Kintyre (see fig. 24),[160] but this evidence is entirely due to chance survival of documentary sources. Earls, whose authority was based on sea power, would most probably have controlled all those parts of the western mainland which had social and geographical links with the off-shore islands.[161] The existence of ouncelands in these mainland territories can probably be used as evidence in support of the view that Sigurd and Thorfinn did indeed include the western mainland of Scotland in their dominions, and attempted to impose a system of assessment there for the purpose of raising taxes and a naval levy.

The question of pennylands appears, however, to be quite another matter. The variation in the number of pennylands to the ounceland does not suggest that this was imposed by a single political authority, although the standard 18-penny divisions of Orkney and Caithness is clearly related to the control which the earls had over these two areas. Conversely, the evident *absence* of pennylands from the Isle of Man and Islay may contain a clue as to the purpose of this denomination, for both these islands were closely connected with the later kings of Man, being administrative centres, and possibly largely royal demesne estates. The use of a monetary unit ('penny') suggests that this fiscal structure of pennylands may have had its origins in the south of the area, where influence from Dublin was all-important, for the kings of Dublin started to coin money in the tenth century, basing their coinage, moreover, on the Anglo-Saxon penny.[162] The name pennyland (G. *peighinn*) also suggests that the territorial division was first utilized as a taxation unit, but the association with a naval or military levy is clearly apparent from later medieval evidence: for instance, two named pennylands had to provide one man each for the hostings of Argyll 'as was customary'.[163]

It is not at all clear when the pennyland unit was fitted into the ounceland system or to what extent it relates to a pre-existing naval assessment. The stronger Gaelic imprint in the West is always significant and in this respect it is worth stressing that both the ounceland and pennyland are known there primarily in their Gaelic form. Moreover, the element *peighinn* (penny) is a marked feature of the toponymy of western Scotland and Galloway – in contrast to northern Scotland where the place-name Pennyland occurs rarely, and only in Caithness. Why is this so and how did it come about? Does it suggest the imposition of an administrative structure by outside political control or is it evidence for later administrative reorganization? The use of the term in Galloway may indeed point to a later extension of a pennyland system of land division, for it can hardly relate to either the administration of the earls of Orkney or of the kings of Man and the Isles. In the north we are on safer ground where the 18-penny ounceland in Orkney, Shetland and Caithness suggests a more certain Scandinavian structure because it relates to a duodecimal method of calculation which was followed in Scandinavia.[164] If this method can also be shown to be the basis of a territorial assessment in parts of the Outer Hebrides this would fit in with the evidence of a stronger Scandinavian imprint in these islands,[165] and might provide some dating bracket for the pennyland imposition in this area.

The whole complex problem will remain unclear until we have greater elucidation of territorial divisions in the west Highlands, and of the monetary and commercial basis of the Viking trade in the British Isles. The above lines of enquiry serve to emphasize that the tax and levy system was not as uniform as the impression given by the names for these territorial units. The indications are that the earls of Orkney from early times had a taxation system in the Northern Isles which they imposed on the west when they had enough military control as a result of their period of conquest in the late tenth and first half of the eleventh centuries. This taxation system was intimately bound up with a naval levy system, a situation rather different from Norway where the 'leidang' only formed the basis for a taxation system in the twelfth century.[166] Such precocious development in the Norse settlements overseas must have been one of the main reasons why the kings of Norway were so determined to dominate the earls and derive some benefit themselves from Norse control of land in Orkney and the Hebrides. This development may have been stimulated by the pre-existence in the colonial areas of native systems of taxation or boat levies. It may also have been stimulated by the growth of a wealthy trading structure in the islands and waterways controlled by the Vikings which enabled the earls to derive an income from settlements which were not only agricultural but also had commercial value.[167]

4 The Linguistic Framework: Place-Names and Settlement

The names borne today by towns, villages and farms, by hills, rivers and other natural features of the landscape are, at first acquaintance, an unlikely source of great knowledge about Scandinavian Scotland. But if it were not for this rich material and the work of place-name scholars in analysing it our understanding of the impact of the Norse on Scotland would be largely defective. Norse place-names have a recognizable character whether topographical like Laxdale (ON *laxár-dalr* = 'salmon-river valley'), Seaforth (ON *sjá-fjörðr* = 'sea inlet'), Flotta/Flodday (ON *flat-ey* = 'flat island'); or habitative, like Grimista (ON *Grims-staðir* = pers. name 'Grim' + 'farm'), Melbost (ON *melr-bólstaðr* = 'sandhill-farm' or 'links-stead'), Crosby (ON *cross býr* = 'cross farm'). Such names can give evidence of, and help our understanding of, the pattern, nature and extent of settlement by peoples of Scandinavian extraction.[1]

PROBLEMS AND THEORIES

As far as Scotland is concerned the recognition of Scandinavian place-names is in some places relatively easy and in others much more difficult. It is rather a different problem from the recognition of Scandinavian place-names in England where the blending of two similar Germanic languages, English and Norse, has taken place. The Celtic languages of Scotland and Norse did not blend; a mixed dialect did not, as far as we know, ever emerge, although a few Norse words have become permanent loans in Gaelic. The speech of the northern Picts in the Northern Isles did not survive at all, so that the language there became a Norse dialect until overtaken by Scots during the sixteenth to eighteenth centuries. This was also the case in north-east Caithness and a clear-cut boundary was established in this province between areas of Norse speech and Gaelic – which spread throughout the rest of northern Scotland during the Middle Ages. In the Western Isles Gaelic made a total revival and also spread through all areas of former Norse speech. There is therefore a distinct difference between the Northern Isles and north-east Caithness where the 'Norn' dialect of Old Norse continued to be spoken for many centuries, and the Western Isles where Gaelic supplanted Norse probably soon after the decline of Norwegian political power in the thirteenth century, if not before. Then there is south-west Scotland which is a quite different linguistic province where English entered into the picture much earlier. This diverse development has affected the body of Scandinavian place-name evidence and created three if not four distinct linguistic regions (see fig. 25): (1) that of the Northern Isles and north-east Caithness which is almost purely Scandinavian; (2) that of Sutherland, Easter Ross, the Western Isles and the western seaboard

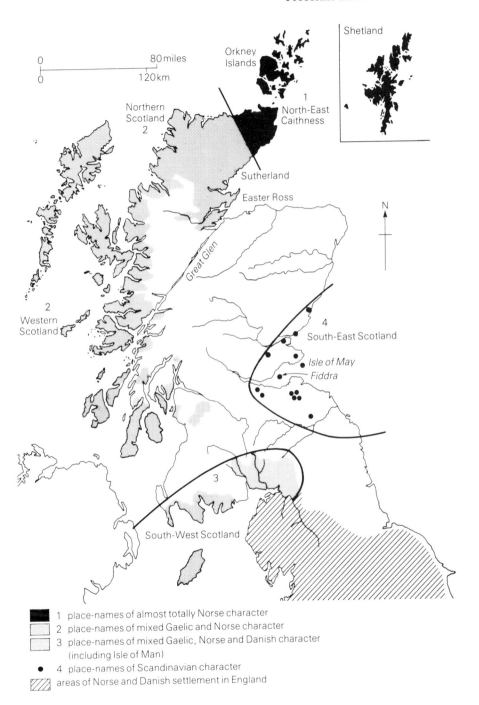

Figure 25. The linguistic regions of Scandinavian Scotland.

where original Norse place-names have been adopted by Gaelic speakers whose linguistic influence has sometimes made Scandinavian names almost unrecognizable even to the linguists; (3) a south-west province which has to be studied in relation to the Scandinavian place-names of north-west England, with, in the western parts, a possible Gaelic admixture which derived from one or more of the Gaelic-speaking areas around the Irish Sea; and finally (4) south-eastern Scotland, where there is only a scatter of Scandinavian place-names which, however, have somewhat different characteristics.[2]

This diverse body of material presents many different problems, and yet Scandinavian place-names in Scotland have not been so intensively studied as those of England in recent years. In England, research was stimulated by an historical debate about the numbers of Viking warriors and settlers that arrived in England in the ninth century. It has been doubted whether the hundreds of Scandinavian village names of eastern England really represented settlement by Danish peasant farmers or whether they might represent Danish overlordship of villages which were still farmed by the native English. Can, in fact, *numbers* of place-names be used as an index to the *numbers* of settlers? Or do 'habitative' names which are formed with personal names only indicate that the estate was owned at some time by a lord of that name? – a theory which place-name experts are very unwilling to accept. The controversy between the historians and the linguists over the nature and density of Danish settlement in England still goes on, and has reached a very detailed level.[3]

Details of the debate do not concern us here, but the principles do. That is, what conclusions can one draw from the pattern of place-names about the density of settlement of peoples of Norse extraction, and about their relationship with the native population of the colonized area? Does a Norse place-name tell us that the settlement was farmed by a Viking himself, or could it mean that the native farmer now acknowledged a Viking lord who gave a new name to that settlement? In addition we have the problem in western Scotland of knowing how to interpret a situation which is complicated by the Gaelic language and Celtic revival. This is mirrored in the Isle of Man where there is also uncertainty about what place-names signify in a mixed linguistic environment, and work has been done which is very relevant to the western seaboard of Scotland.[4] The earlier historical information from the Isle of Man gives a better insight into the relationship of Norse and Gaelic than can be gleaned from the Scottish islands or from Caithness, so that the conclusions made about the situation there have to be borne in mind and used as comparative material when the impact of the Norse on western Scotland is being assessed.

SURVEY OF LINGUISTIC REGIONS

Northern Isles and north mainland

In surveying the Norse place-names of Scotland, it is natural to start with the Northern Isles where the vast majority of place-names are of Scandinavian origin.[5] Even although it is clear that the impact of the Norse was overwhelming there the almost total absence of pre-Norse place-names is rather surprising, since elsewhere it is known that Scandinavian speakers took over part of the existing nomenclature. This led some older Scandinavian archaeologists to formulate the theory that the islands were empty when the Norse arrived or at least only thinly inhabited.[6] But in recent years, archaeologists have demonstrated that there was a flourishing Pictish culture in the islands in the centuries before, and probably at the time of, the Scandinavian arrival.

Across the Pentland Firth is another area of dense Scandinavian settlement according to place-name evidence; the arable lands of eastern Caithness. As the terrain changes from arable culture to pastoral farming in the interior of Caithness the proportion of Celtic place-names increases and the line of

Figure 26. Norse and Gaelic settlement names in Caithness (after W.F.H. Nicolaisen, 'Scandinavians and Celts in Caithness: the place-name evidence', in *Caithness: A Cultural Crossroads*, ed. J. Baldwin, Scottish Society for Northern Studies and Edina Press, 1982, fig. 5.1).

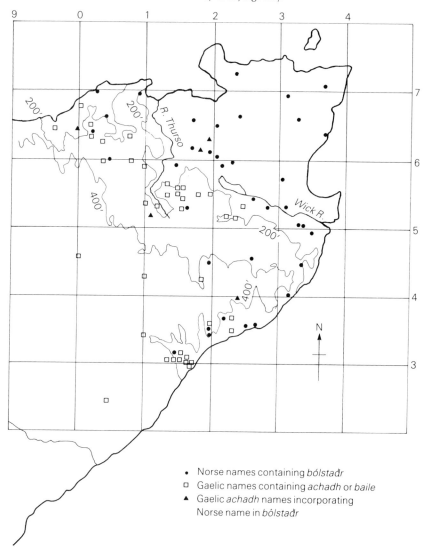

- Norse names containing *bólstaðr*
- ☐ Gaelic names containing *achadh* or *baile*
- ▲ Gaelic *achadh* names incorporating Norse name in *bólstaðr*

demarcation between these and Norse place-names may indicate confrontation between the two cultures (see fig. 26).[7] This is unlikely to have been a result of expulsion of the native population to the hillier area but must indicate a later spread of Gaelic speakers into what had been a completely Norse-speaking province.[8] We are here meeting the first of the problems associated with the relationship of Celt and Norseman. Down the east coast of Sutherland Celtic and Scandinavian names are now intermingled, with the Norse settlements evidently thinning out towards the Moray Firth. Dingwall (ON *þing-völlr* = 'assembly-field') is a remarkable survival of a significant administrative place-name so far south which must reflect the organizational activity of a community of Norse speakers settled around the Cromarty Firth in the wake of the recorded conquests of the earls in the late ninth and the eleventh centuries (see fig. 16).[9] No Scandinavian name has been recognized south of Beauly but the Norse farm-names of the good arable lands of Cromarty and Easter Ross are a sign that the Vikings were once politically dominant here even though they may have been a numerical minority. Scattered Norse names up the valleys of the interior may be some evidence for movement through the valleys to the west coast.[10]

Western Isles and west mainland

On the western seaboard of Scotland the relationship of Norse and Celtic names is even more complex. Here there was a later spread of the Gaelic language over what had once been a predominantly Norse-speaking area. It is not known when this happened because of the total lack of documentary material, and it is impossible to make any firm statements about exactly how it happened. It is not even known for sure what branch of the Celtic languages was spoken in the area before the Norse invasion; whether Gaelic-speaking peoples survived the Norse settlement; or whether the language died out and only spread through the Isles again after the collapse of Norwegian political authority in 1266. There appears to be a general consensus among place-name specialists that none of the Celtic place-names in the Western Isles can be proved to be of pre-Norse origin,[11] and as far as Lewis is concerned 'most or all non-Norse names have a post-Norse character.'[12] Lewis is, however, rather a special case for it has been intensively studied and some definite statistics are available about the village names and the dialect of this most northerly of the Hebridean islands (which may not be typical of the archipelago as a whole). There appears to be no doubt that Norse settlement in Lewis was extensive, and that the Norse language was dominant there during a considerable period.[13] In fact, of 126 village names in Lewis, 99 are purely Scandinavian and a further 9 contain Norse elements. The later acceptance of the Gaelic language by a previously Norse-speaking population has left its impressions on the intonational pattern of Lewis Gaelic, although surprisingly rather few actual Norse loan-words have been recognized in the dialect.[14] It seems likely that cultural influences from the Scandinavian north could have helped to keep the Norse language alive longer in the northernmost of the Hebrides.[15] There were also strong links between the Outer Hebrides and the Isle of Man which was the political centre of Norse power in the islands. After the seizure of the southern Hebrides by the sons of Somerled in the twelfth century, Lewis and the Northern Hebrides continued to be ruled from Man, and ruled sometimes by a member of the royal house until the handing-over of the Hebrides to Scotland in 1266.

That Gaelic came late and incompletely to the Outer Hebrides is suggested by the almost total absence of names incorporating Gaelic *-achadh* (=field), which never replaced the equivalent Norse term *gard*, gaelicized as *gearraidh*. The absence of such a basic Gaelic word from many parts of the Hebrides 'makes the Western Isles almost look like the Northern Isles in terms of intensive Scandinavianisation'.[16] Very strong Norse influence on coastal and sea terms has been recognized in islands where the maritime element was most important economically, in particular Lewis, Uist and Tiree.[17] But the total coverage of this area by Gaelic speech has changed many Norse place-name elements almost unrecognizably. For instance, the island of Sanday, off the north-western Scottish coast, which still had its unaspirated – that is, its Norse – form in 1386 has since then become Handa due to aspiration in the Gaelic, whereas Old Norse *Hábólstaðr* (= 'high farm') in some environments has turned into *Tabost*.[18]

A clear difference can be detected between the Northern and the Southern Hebrides, where the influence from Ireland and mainland Scotland was greater. The incidence of Norse place-names decreases from a 'very large percentage in Skye to a rather low one in Arran'.[19] These two extremes illustrate the importance of connexions with neighbouring communities, for north Skye is in easy contact with Lewis across the Minch, where Norse remained the dominant language for a longer time than anywhere else in the Hebrides; and Arran lies close to populous parts of Gaelic-speaking Scotland. In between these two the picture is very mixed and not in any way closely researched, so that conclusions are difficult to draw. The most southerly of the Hebrides – Man – has a remarkable number of surviving Scandinavian place-names, as will be seen. In fact, Norse place-names are found in *all* the Hebridean islands and it should be noted that all quoted figures of the proportion of Norse settlement-names to Gaelic are considerably higher than the proportion of Scandinavian to English names in those areas of England where Viking settlement was most dense.[20] This suggests that the incoming Norse rejected native place-names and that even when Gaelic spread again during the post-Norse period the Gaelic speakers continued to use many of the Norse settlement-names unchanged while others became gaelicized. Although the date at which the Gaelic farm-name element *-baile* spread in Scotland is a matter of debate, the fact that some of them in the Western Isles have a Norse specific (descriptive element) *after* the Gaelic generic (defining word for settlement or geographical feature) proves that those at least were coined in the post-Norse period.[21] Others may have replaced earlier Norse names, a process which is suspected in Man and the Southern Hebrides, but very difficult to prove.[22] Hard and fast conclusions cannot be reached, but the Western Isles may once have been as wholly Norse in their settlement nomenclature as the Northern Isles; it may only have been during the Middle Ages that the resurgent Gaelic influence altered the place-name picture. The strength of Gaelic varied according to the degree of influence from the mainland of Scotland; one measure of that influence may be seen in the contraction of the final element in the Norse farm-name -*bólstaðr*, so that names ending in -*bol, -pool, -bo* such as Eriboll, Ullapool and Embo perhaps represent settlement where Gaelic influence was strongest while those ending in -*bost, -bus*, such as Carbost, Canabus, where it was weakest.[23]

On the western mainland there is a scatter of Scandinavian place-names from Sutherland to Galloway; those from Ayrshire northwards belong with the Norse settlement in the Isles, whilst those in Galloway and the south-west form a separate linguistic province. Very few of these names north of the Clyde are such as to suggest permanent Norse settlement and only six examples of the Old Norse element -*bólstaðr* occur down the west coast from Cape Wrath to the Clyde. This is in strong contrast to the Old Norse element -*dalr* (=valley), which is thickly scattered throughout the same area, but which as a topographical name (that is, a name referring to a natural feature) is not a conclusive indication of Norse settlement, although suggesting strong Norse influence. It has therefore been argued that such names may have been given by Norse speakers perhaps as a result of hunting or raiding, or of using these mainland areas for summer grazing. Any map of Scandinavian Scotland which includes the western littoral is claimed therefore to be misleading in not distinguishing between areas of primary Norse settlement and areas coming under Norse influence only.[24] However, even if the latter areas were still farmed by indigenous inhabitants (and it should be noted that there are in any case very few Gaelic *baile* farm names along the whole west coast, particularly north of Loch Long) they must certainly have come under the control of Norse-speaking settlers in the Isles.[25] The channels and sounds separating the islands from the mainland were a means of linking the communities, easily traversed by Scandinavian settlers who were such highly skilled sailors. In western Norway, the communities along the shores and at the heads of the fjords form one geographical grouping with the nearest islands and are completely cut off from the interior of the country; similarly, to a less extreme extent, the western littoral of Scotland and the closer off-shore islands are one geographical unit which in any period form one cultural zone. The grouping of Norse place-names around Largs in Ayrshire were probably, for instance, an offspring of Norse settlement in the Cumbraes or Arran.[26] It seems likely that the farm-names of Scandinavian origin north of the Clyde are few in number because there were few suitable settlement sites for Norse colonists rather than being due to any failure to take land or exercise political control over pre-existing farmers in the area.[27]

South-west Scotland and south-east Scotland

In linguistic regions 3 and 4, we meet place-names of Scandinavian type which point to links with the Danish settlements of northern and eastern England. Galloway and south-west Scotland were also open to linguistic influence from the Gaelic-speaking world so that the resulting place-name pattern is of a particularly complex mixture. Just as the Irish Sea was no barrier, neither was the Solway Firth a political boundary for most of the early Middle Ages, but rather it allowed easy communication between dwellers on either shore (as can be seen from sculptural influences).[28] A northerly movement of settlers from

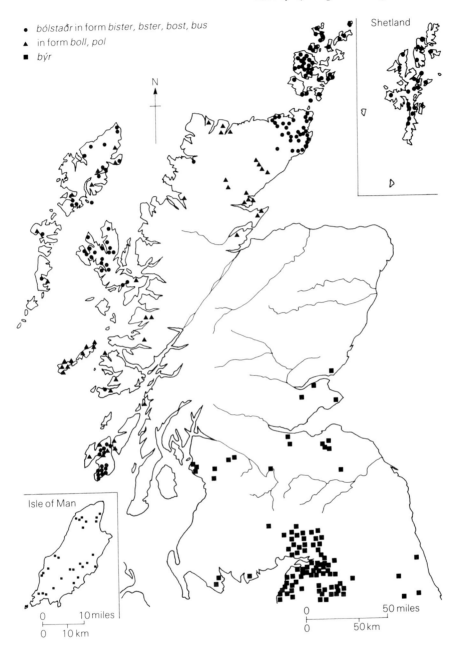

- • *bólstaðr* in form *bister, bster, bost, bus*
- ▲ in form *boll, pol*
- ■ *býr*

Shetland

N

Isle of Man

0   10 miles

0   10 km

0   50 miles

0   50 km

Figure 27. The distribution of place-names in *-bólstaðr* in western and northern Scotland and *-býr* in southern Scotland, northern England and the Isle of Man (after W.F.H. Nicolaisen, *Scottish Place-Names*, Batsford, 1976, maps 7 and 9, and G. Fellows-Jensen,'Scandinavian settlement in Man', in *The Viking Age in the Isle of Man, Ninth Viking Congress*, 1983, fig. 3).

the north Danelaw into Dumfriesshire and the Carlisle plain seems to be evident from the place-name element *-býr* (farm) which is particularly common in north Cumbria and eastern Dumfriesshire, clustering at the head of the Solway Firth (see fig. 27).[29]

The name Galloway is generally thought to be derived from *Gall-Gaedhil*, indicating that this part of Scotland was settled in the tenth century by those of that name who were of mixed Norse-Gaelic birth and speech.[30] This bi-cultural situation has been considered responsible for a type of place-name occurring in Galloway, the so-called 'inversion compounds': Germanic compound names whose elements show Celtic not Germanic word-order. The most common examples are the names beginning with *Kirk-* (ON *Kirkja* = church) in which the saint's name follows the word for church rather than preceding it (e.g. Kirkoswald). The distribution of these names covers Galloway and Carrick, being particularly located in coastal districts or up easily accessible river valleys, and they are essentially a south-west Scottish feature with a few outliers over the border in England.[31] They are thought to derive from a Gaelic linguistic background, which may have been Irish or Manx, Hebridean, or simply a result of Scandinavian speakers mingling with native Gaelic speakers.[32] However, a recent discussion of these *Kirk*-compound place-names in Galloway and Carrick casts doubt on whether they can be regarded as evidence of *Gall-Gaedhil* influence at all, suggesting instead that the *Kirk-* element was a late change from an older English *Church-*.[33] In which case, Scandinavian settlement in Galloway as evidenced by place-names would be confined to a 'fairly large district west and north of Kirkcudbright . . . and a rather smaller district in Wigtownshire' (see fig. 25),[34] which may not necessarily be a result of *Gall-Gaedhil* settlement at all. In the absence of any written account about the Scandinavian settlement in this part of Scotland, the linguistic information has to be treated with circumspection, and is capable of several differing interpretations. One thing is clear; this corner of Scotland where the native population was still British, was open to influence from many different parts of the Scandinavian and Gaelic world (as well as Anglian), so that the place-name pattern is bound to reflect the ethnic complexity.

In south-eastern Scotland, the linguistic background was primarily Anglian[35] and positive evidence for additional Scandinavian settlements here is sparser than the dots on the place-name map suggest. These are mostly farm-names, ending once again in *-býr* and scattered through the Lothians, Berwick-shire and on the Tay estuary, such as Begbie, Corbie and Ravensby. But there are, in addition, several place-names in which a Scandinavian personal name combines with an English generic, such as Bonnington (ON personal name 'Bondi' + OE *-tun*), and the well-known Corstorphine where the Old Norse personal name Torfinn combines with Gaelic *crois* ('crossing') in a Gaelic word-order.[36] Despite the Scandinavian look which these names give to the Scottish Lowlands, it is highly unlikely that the settler with the Scandinavian name was still speaking Old Norse even though he was of Scandinavian extraction. The English and Gaelic generic suggests otherwise. The *-býr* names are more certain evidence of settlers of Scandinavian speech and, along with the hogback grave monuments of southern Scotland, seem to testify to links with north-eastern England rather than the Northern or Western Isles.[37].

RELATIONS WITH PREVIOUS INHABITANTS

From this survey of the total incidence of Scandinavian place-names in Scotland, it has been seen how important place-names are as a source of evidence for Scandinavian influence, which may be historically undocumented or else archaeologically unrecognizable. To understand the relations that the Scandinavian settlers established with native Picts, Scots, Britons and Angles in the different regions of Scotland involves the weighing of different types of evidence; the linguistic material is far more significant in its distribution than the handful of settlement sites that have been excavated or the scanty written sources which throw scarcely any light upon this thorny problem.

The Northern Isles

The apparent rejection of names which the settlers found on their arrival in the Northern and Western Isles is uncharacteristic, and it is easy to draw the unwarranted conclusion that therefore the native population did not survive. It has been said that 'in terms of comparative models and of common sense' such an absence of linguistic survivals must represent 'total expulsion, extinction, or complete cultural de-characterisation of a most improbable kind'.[38] A study of the -staðir names in Shetland has concluded, however, that they bear no relationship to broch sites near which the existing population was probably living,[39] and that therefore the Norse do not appear to have taken over the best land, but to have settled alongside the native Picts who remained in possession. Nonetheless, the whole body of place-name evidence from Orkney and Shetland tells us that any native survivors did not exercise enough influence to pass on their names for settlements or the features of the surrounding countryside. Evidently they were not the dominant linguistic group and did not form part of the governing class. The clear deduction from this evidence is that contact between native-speaker and incomer was 'minimal' and 'of such a nature that already existing names were not easily passed on',[40] and it is certainly easiest to explain the lack of contact in terms of the military conquest and subjection of much of the native population. But it has always to be remembered that there *are* names in the Northern Isles which are not easily explicable in terms of the Scandinavian languages (of which 'treb' for the pre-Norse dykes which run across Sanday and North Ronaldsay is a well-known example.[41]) However, the scarcity of such survivals in the Northern Isles is considered by linguists to be more remarkable than those few that have been identified. The general conclusion from the place-name evidence is that the language of the native inhabitants of the Northern Isles must have been quickly dominated and submerged by that of the new class of Viking settlers.

The Western Isles

It is not possible to reach such a conclusion about the situation in the Western Isles where the re-emergence of the Gaelic language has made the linguistic development so much more complex. Moreover, the literary and historical evidence gives us some positive indications that there *was* a mingling process with native Gaelic speakers.[42] If this mingling took the form of marriage with local women, through whom native culture and personal names would survive, it would not automatically mean, however, that existing place-names would be retained. It seems that Scandinavians in England were more likely to reject names of individual farms and dispersed settlements and retain the names of nucleated settlements, which are unlikely to have existed in the Isles.[43]

Turning again to the situation in Lewis, which has been closely studied, it is noticeable that a high proportion of the present-day village-names of Lewis are Norse, but that the percentages are much less where natural features are concerned. This has suggested that 'the moors and hills were chiefly the domain of a subjugated Celtic-speaking class whose tasks were, among other things, to attend to the shielings, the sheep, and the peat-bogs, activities in which it was necessary to know the names of topographical features'.[44] A similar social situation may have existed in Skye,[45] but this marked contrast between different types of place-names becomes less as one moves southwards through the Hebrides. The numbers of *-bólstaðr* farm-names in islands such as Coll, Tiree, western Mull and Islay (see fig. 27) surely indicate firm and long-lasting Norse control here along the important sea-route. In the Southern Hebrides Gaelic place-names *either* survived in greater number *or* ousted Norse place-names in a post-Norse period of revival. As always the exact location is all-important; it is impossible to describe the relationship between Norse and Gaelic speakers in the Hebrides as a whole when it probably differed from one island to another, so much are islands cultural entities.

Comparable problems have arisen over the place-names of the Isle of Man, which have been used to prove the dominance of one language or another in a fully bilingual situation.[46] The numbers of Norse place-names seem to indicate considerable Scandinavian settlement on the soil, perhaps to the detriment of any surviving Gaelic-speaking class. It certainly seems unlikely that the numbers of Scandinavian place-names could have been imposed by warrior lords alone and the numbers of Norse speakers must have been numerous enough to be able to impose their names on the local nomenclature and thus make them permanent features on the toponymical map. But if Man was for a time overwhelmingly Norse in speech, as has been claimed,[47] this situation is unlikely to have lasted for long, when influence from Ireland must have always been important. A bilingual situation must quickly have developed when Norse was probably 'the language of the *thing* and of tribunals and taxation, while proto-Manx was the language of the pillow, kitchen and farm':[48] a situation comparable to that in Lewis in the Northern Hebrides, which was, as already mentioned, closely connected with the political centre of the kingdom of the Isles.

The close association of the Gaelic section of the population with pastoral farming activities is also suggested by the adoption of the Gaelic *airigh* (= shieling) into their language by many Scandinavian communities around the British Isles, and even as far away as the Faroe Islands.[49] It seems likely that the word has a Scottish origin rather than an Irish one, but it is still not clear why the Norse found this place-name element so useful, nor how their use of it differed from their own names for upland summer pastures.[50] The surviving Gaelic speakers in a mixed cultural situation were probably, however, so closely associated with the upland areas (as in Caithness) that the term which they used passed into the current speech of the Norse settlers nearby – and beyond.

SETTLEMENT TOPONYMY

Place-name studies can also help to tell us how the incomers set about naming their newly acquired lands in the west. As the Vikings appear to have rejected the place-names which they found on their arrival in the Isles (excepting some island names which will be discussed later), they had therefore to draw on their stock of place-names from their homeland for the naming of their new settlements. These peoples had a rich vocabulary of topographical and maritime terms which were ideally suited for naming coastal and settlement features in an environment which was in so many respects similar to the one they had come from. Many of the Scottish names of Scandinavian origin have identical equivalents in Norway, such as Lerwick (ON *leir-vík* = 'mud bay'), Laxay (ON *lax-á* = 'salmon river'), Oronsay (ON *Ørfiris-ey* = 'tidal island'),[51] and these names were transferred whole to topographical situations identical to places which had been left behind. It is also possible that some names were transferred commemoratively to remind the settlers of well-known places back home, although this was not such a notable feature of Viking colonization as of later colonial movements.

A few names contain elements which seem to have already passed out of the general name-giving vocabulary by the time of the Viking Age, such as *-heimr* (= 'home') and *-vin* (= 'field'). Sulem/Sullom in Shetland is perhaps the best-known one, denoting an original *sol-heimr* (sun-homestead), a very popular name in Norway, that also occurs in Iceland, even though *-heimr* does not seem to have been used to coin new names in the colonies generally. The element *-vin* appears as a generic in Lyking in Orkney and possibly Levna in Shetland, both deriving from *leik-vin* (play-ground or sports-field) and probably having some social or ritual significance to the community. Such names may have been brought over from Norway as whole names, having some particular association for the colonist, rather than as an apt topographical description in the current language of the new settlement. They cannot be used as evidence that settlement had taken place in the Northern Isles before the Viking Age proper.[52]

Geographical names

In general the settlers simply drew upon their current language to give names to the geographical features of the islands they sailed amongst and to the farms they established there. Features such as headlands, rocks, bays, sounds, harbours, tidal streams, were of course likely to be given names first as they were so important for navigation, and we must assume that the Norse were familiar with the waterways of the Scottish coast long before they attempted to settle on the land. The fact that the vast majority of islands have Norse names ending in *-ay, -øy* (or *-a* in the Western Isles), most headlands end in Norse *-nes* (Gaelicized to *-nish*), most rocks end in ON *-sker* (Gaelicized to *-sgeir*), and many hills end in Norse *-fjall* (Gaelicized to *-val*) – whereas most other natural features have Gaelic names in the west – testifies to the importance of these features to the Vikings. Their names obliterated all previous nomenclature and remained in use in the west during the post-Norse Gaelic revival.

A significant exception to this generalization concerns the names of some of the most important islands or island groups: Orkney and perhaps Shetland, with Unst, Fetlar and Yell; Uist, Skye and Canna in the Northern Hebrides; Tiree, Muck, Islay, Arran and Bute in the Southern Hebrides. All of these names have caused a great deal of trouble to linguists, for they are all pre-Norse names and some may even be pre-Celtic.[53] Their adoption by the Vikings points to some cultural intercourse with the peoples of these islands or their neighbours. It is probably significant that they are all islands which are important for navigational purposes on the sea-routes from Norway round the Scottish coast, just as in Norway itself there are some obscure island names along the main waterways which formed important travellers' reference points.[54] These names became assimilated into the Norse place-nomenclature, and the islands failed to receive new names when actually settled by the Norse.

Farm-names

Coming to the process of settlement and establishment of farming communities, geographical common sense has to be our main guide when looking for the localities most likely to have been suitable for primary settlement.[55] Easily defended locations must have been valued in the early stages of settlement such as the long, extended headlands of Tresness, Elsness, Lopness and Spurness on the northernmost Orkney island of Sanday, which were probably seized by early Viking raiders and became their first bases. Similarly, the peninsulas of north Skye – Duirinish, Trotternish and Vaternish – would form important early settlement areas, controlling the sea passage (the Minch) between the Outer and Inner Hebrides (see fig. 30). Names derived from such important topographical features would probably be the first to be given to the Viking settlements. Research in other areas has suggested that names describing natural features are among those first given by settlers.[56] Unfortunately it is impossible to use such names to date the progress of settlement in any area.[57]

It is also impossible to say how large the original land-holdings might have been. But they would very soon have become divided as families flourished and multiplied in a favourable colonial situation. The division of such a primary unit resulted in two or more secondary units which would have acquired new names, and the original (possibly topographical) name may well have become obliterated, or applied only to its topographical feature.[58] There followed a continuous process of separation of parcels of land from the primary settlement which came to form independent units with their own names (see fig. 46). Several of the place-name elements used by Scandinavian speaking peoples for their settlements have already been mentioned, such as -býr, -bólstaðr and -staðir. It is possible to give rough chronological time-spans to certain generics (we have seen that the elements -vin and -heimr had gone out of fashion by the Viking period). There has been an attempt to give a relative chronology to those others which were fashionable at the time when the Scottish Isles were being colonized. Basically this means giving dates to different farm-names, categorizing which were the earliest and which belong to the period of expansion and division of settlement.[59] This method is, however, fraught with difficulties.

The element -boer/-býr (usually surviving as -bi, -by) has been shown to be important in Scandinavian place-names in south Scotland: there are comparatively few in number in the Northern or Western Isles but where they exist they are nonetheless regarded in Orkney as denoting primary Norse settlements, 'or at least the core of such settlements, and as such they must be ranked highest of all in the scale of ancestral dignity'.[60] Next in line of antiquity have been listed the Orkney farm-names with the final elements -land, -bólstaðr, -garth and -skaill, all denoting farming settlements of some kind; -staðir, which usually occurs in Orkney names today as -sta, -stay, or -ston was seen as being apart from the main chronological sequence but secondary in some way. The last in the line are -qvi (usually -quoy) and -setr/-saetr, both coming to mean farm, but originally peripheral, probably pastoral establishments dependent on a main farm. When this Orkney sequence was adapted by W.F. Nicolaisen and extended to Shetland and the Western Isles -býr was omitted from the scheme as being such a variable and long-lasting element that it could not be used to point to 'original settlements' (see below).[61] -Staðir was included in its place as it is a very common element for independent and original farms in other parts of Scandinavia and although there are problems about interpreting its exact status, it was a 'fashionable' place-name element when the settlement of the Scottish Isles was taking place. Despite its rather peculiar distribution in Orkney (nearly all -staðir farms being clustered in the West Mainland), in the rest of the Scottish Isles it seems to have been very important in the place-name picture. The current distribution maps for Scandinavian settlement in Scotland therefore omit -býr and include -staðir, along with -bólstaðr, and -setr, as well as -dalr (-dale) for a non-habitative name, to point a contrast with the actual settlement picture (although see doubts expressed above about this interpretation of -dalr).

Theory of chronological sequence

Nicolaisen's distribution maps have become the classic exposition of the extent and development of Norse settlement in the Scottish Isles. When he plotted all the names ending in the elements listed above a pattern appeared to emerge. The most limited geographical range of names was said to be those ending in -staðir, of which there were 37 in Shetland, 25 in Orkney and 25 in the Hebrides.[62] Significantly perhaps, only one appears in Caithness, which was probably settled from Orkney during a secondary phase of settlement. However, the 12 -staðir names in the Isle of Man were not included in this distribution (see fig. 28). Next in order of range came -setr/-saetr,[63] of which

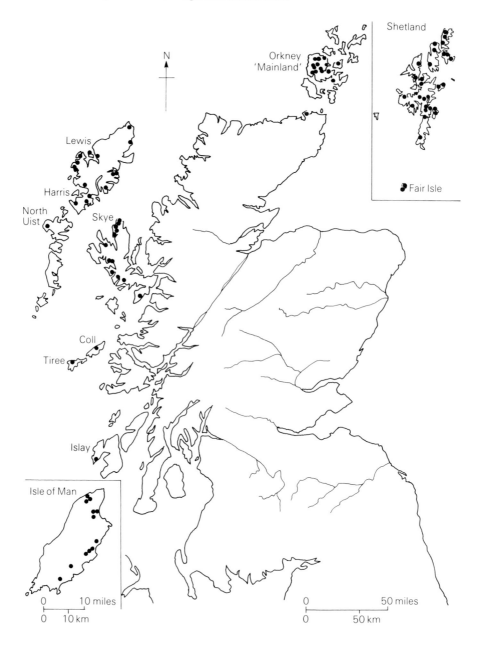

Figure 28. The distribution of place-names in *-stadir* in Scotland and the Isle of Man (after W.F.H. Nicolaisen, *Scottish Place-Names*, Batsford, 1976, map 5, and G. Fellows-Jensen, 'Scandinavian settlement in Man', in *The Viking Age in the Isle of Man, Ninth Viking Congress*, 1983, fig. 2).

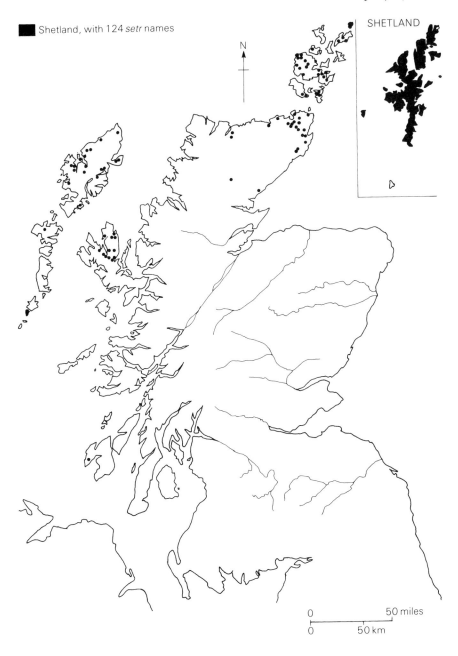

Shetland, with 124 *setr* names

N

SHETLAND

0   50 miles

0   50 km

Figure 29. The distribution of names in *-setr* in Scotland (after W.F.H.
Nicolaisen, *Scottish Place-Names*, Batsford, 1976, map 6).

there are so many in Shetland that they cannot be plotted individually on the place-name map; plentiful distribution in Caithness, as well as Orkney; a scatter in the Hebrides (where it is generally Gaelicized to -*shader*) similar to that of -*stadir*. The -*side* place-names of Sutherland were omitted from Nicolaisen's maps although they are another variant of an original -*setr*/-*saetr* (see fig. 29).[64] He argued that there are 'cogent reasons' for seeing -*setr* as the next name-forming element after -*stadir*, and that the maps of these two elements must show 'a gradual progressive spreading of settlement in this order'.[65] Then comes -*bólstadr* (see fig. 27), a common name-forming element throughout the period of Norse settlement, which has the widest distribution of all, covering the whole of Caithness, Sutherland and Easter Ross with sporadic distribution down the western seaboard, and throughout the Inner and Outer Hebrides.[66] This distribution is said to delineate the definitive map of Norse settlement in the Northern and Western Isles and on the adjacent mainland.[67]

The premise that 'differences in geographical scatter really mean distinction in time' leads to the conclusion that the different distribution of these name-forming elements gives us approximate dates for the spread of Norse settlement throughout Scotland.[68] Firstly the -*stadir* names are said to represent settlement within the first generation or two of the Vikings leaving Norway and taking land in the west, which suggests the date 850 as a general average for the foundation of the -*stadir* farms.[69] But, as noted, Nicolaisen's distribution map of -*stadir* names does not include those examples in the Isle of Man which extends this element beyond the most restricted limit accorded to it in the geographical sequence. Moreover, the fact that -*stadir* names are common in Iceland shows that this name element remained productive until after the settlement of Iceland in the late ninth century.[70] Next in this chronological sequence came the -*setr* names which are said to post-date 850, but pre-date 900 because there are very few -*setr* place-names in Iceland, the colonization of which started c.870.[71] However, the absence of -*setr* names from Man and Iceland may be explained by other reasons and in the case of Man the survival of an equivalent Gaelic word for shieling (*airigh*) is possibly sufficient explanation.[72] The premise that the near-absence of -*setr* farm names in Iceland means that the word had dropped out of use by the date of the settlement of Iceland has been questioned. Alternative explanations suggest that conditions may not have been suitable in some way for the application of the element -*setr*.[73] The rigid chronological sequencing of these place-name elements does not seem necessary or realistic.[74]

-*setr* names

If the generic -*setr* is looked at in closer detail there is first the difficulty of distinguishing between the two names -*setr*, 'dwelling-place', and -*saetr*, which generally denotes a shieling. Although in Norway it is normally possible to distinguish between the two, this is not the case in the Scottish Isles. It is probable that both originally denoted shielings or out-fields, and that when a pastoral establishment became a permanent farm another form had to be devised to denote the summer pastures. It is not at all clear that both forms were in use in the colonies, and early recorded forms of such place-names in Shetland as Bragister, Brouster, Scarvister and Neddister show that they are all -*saetr* names,[75] although there is no means of telling this from the modern form of the name. The large numbers of these names in Shetland require some explanation and they have been defined by a Shetland place-name authority as 'very early secondary settlements which began as pasturage farms, either in the outfield or between the main tuns',[76] which suggests that the reason is likely to be associated with the largely pastoral nature of the economy in those islands.[77] It certainly is dangerous to suggest that they were all formed between

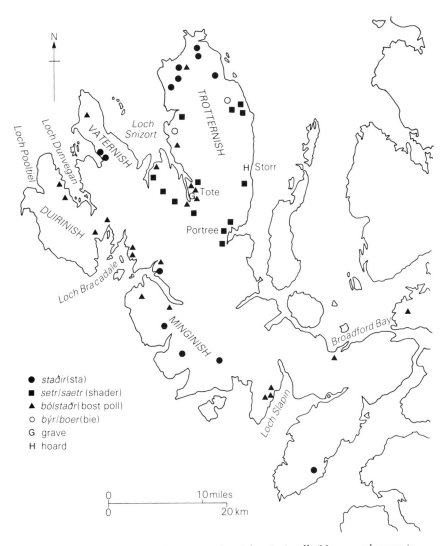

Figure 30. Norse settlement in Skye (after A. Small, 'Norse settlement in Skye', in 'Les Vikings et leur civilisation', ed. R. Boyer, *Bibliothèque Artique et Antartique*, V, 1976, fig. 2).

880 and 900 simply because of the absence of this element from Iceland; this would point to an exceedingly quick rise in the birth-rate in one generation of Shetlanders! In fact, it looks as if -*setr* went on being used as a name-forming element for a very long time in Shetland; the name Mangaster (*Magnusar-setr*, from the personal name Magnus) is very unlikely to have been coined before the mid-eleventh century when the name became popular.[78] Improvements on the commons in Shetland were called 'setter-lands' as late as the eighteenth century.[79] The appearance or absence of the element -*setr* in the Scottish islands cannot therefore be used to indicate the date of particular settlements. Its distribution here must reflect either a difference in local economic conditions, or a difference of nomenclature for summer pastures.[80] Absence of the element from most of the Inner Hebrides (including Man) does not therefore suggest that some of these islands were not settled by Scandinavians until after 900 – a proposition which is inherently unlikely as they were highly desirable bases for Vikings, controlling as they do the sea route from Norway to Ireland.

Instead of placing -*setr* names in a tidy chronological sequence between -*staðir* and -*bólstaðr* names, we should look for the many geographical and social variants which have to be taken into account in reaching an understanding of the chronological development of settlement patterns and place-nomenclature within a particular locality.[81] Local studies provide a far more realistic insight into the geographical situation and place-name distribution of Norse-speaking communities or islands. A survey of the place-names of Skye shows the dangers of rigidly following the -*staðir*, -*setr*, -*bólstaðr* chronology. The distribution of -*setr* names in the island has been interpreted according to this theory; that is, as indicating extension of the original Norse settlement southwards from -*staðir* farms in north Trotternish towards Portree (see fig. 30).[82] The -*setr* names should, however, be interpreted rather as evidence of internal expansion into peripheral, often inland, pastoral areas around earlier farms, usually primary settlements at the head of bays (see fig. 10). Their distribution suggests that they are secondary to such farms, some of them -*bólstaðr* farms, and thus evidence of *consolidation* of settlement in several favourable locations of north Skye.[83] Moreover, other -*staðir* names exist in southern Skye, showing that early Norse settlement was not confined to the Trotternish peninsula (see fig. 30).[84] Mistaken conclusions have also followed from a similar analysis of the Norse place-names of Islay, where the all-important topographical names have been left out.[85]

bólstaðr names

-*bólstaðr* names are also evidence of an expansion of settlement, but by division of a primary Norse farm, for they normally remained central to the settlement area, and not peripheral like -*setr*/-*saetr* names (see fig. 50). The first element in -*bólstaðr* derives from ON -*ból*, meaning a 'lot' or 'portion' and in Norway, it was probably a division of the homefield.[86] Similarly in the Scottish islands division of older, bigger units is exactly what one should be thinking of with respect to -*bólstaðr* farms.[87] In Orkney it can be seen from their location and valuations that they were large and well-established farms at an early period.[88] But even though they are highly valued that does not prevent them from having been a division of an original farm; it merely reflects the high valuation of some Orkney land. In Shetland they are said to be on average half the size of -*staðir* farms,[89] which certainly suggests that they are secondary to -*staðir* farms there. If we return to the place-name map of Skye (see fig. 30), it can be seen that there is a cluster of three -*bólstaðr* names on the shore of Loch Slapin which might indicate divisions of an earlier farm. Such a farm would probably have lost its original name when subdivided.

It is noticeable that in the Northern Isles the specific first element frequently indicates compass direction to distinguish the divided farm from neighbouring -*bólstaðr* farms. One has only to look at the two examples of an Easterbister and Westerbister in Orkney (Holm and South Walls) to understand that they are by nature secondary divisions of an earlier undivided farm: 'The conjunction of the two half-urislands Easter and Westerbister (in South Walls) is fairly clear evidence of an earlier undivided urisland settlement.'[90] But the evidence is not always as clear as that; an Easterbuster existed on the island of Papa Stour in Shetland in the seventeenth century, but this name has disappeared and is probably represented by the collection of crofts now called East Biggins or East Tun. The existence of an Easterbuster in the seventeenth century presupposes a Westerbuster, or at least a western division of an earlier undivided farm.[91] There is indeed a settlement to the west of East Tun, called Biggins, but no record exists of it ever having been called Westerbuster (although 'Biggins' is certainly not an original settlement name). Here then we have one recorded but lost -*bólstaðr* place-name, and one presupposed one, neither of which will ever make the place-names statistics. How many more like that may there have been? A lot more work at a local level has to be done before we can be sure that the distribution maps give a fair representation of the Norse place-name picture. The evidence of the many changes which have taken place in farm names in Papa Stour over the centuries shows that the picture is often likely to be defective.

Indeed, in one very important respect the place-name maps of the Norse settlement of Scotland are entirely defective, and that is because they do not include what are now recognized as being some of the earliest and most important farms of all: those with topographical names.[92] In Iceland some of the largest and oldest farms had names ending in -*dalr*, -*ness*, -*fell* and -*eyri*, as well as simplex topographical names like Foss, Holm and Tongue.[93] This was also the case in Orkney, where they have been called 'old seaboard tunships' which 'have undoubtedly to be classed among the very earliest settlements'.[94] Of the 15 Orkney farm-names recorded in the *Orkneyinga Saga*, there are only 3 habitative names proper (all -*staðir* names), while the other 12 bear originally topographical names, 7 of which end in -*ness*.[95] The significance of these names in Orkney is appreciated, but whether important early farms were given such names in Northern Scotland or the Western Isles is unknown, for no-one has studied these areas with this in mind.

boer and *býr* names

Names ending in *boer*/-*býr* are also missing from the distribution maps of Scandinavian names in Northern and Western Scotland, although the element is recognized as having been both important and long-lived elsewhere. Numbers are few in Orkney, but some have a particular significance, like the Huseby farms.⁹⁶ -*býr* names may have disappeared in other places due to the early division of the oldest farms and the bestowal of new names on the component parts. In Scandinavia, however, recent research has suggested that *boer*/-*býr* may have been used as a secondary element itself when an older name for a primary farm had been extended in use to denote a parish or larger area.⁹⁷ Some of the Shetland *boer*/-*býr* names may also be the result of this kind of development. At Sandness in West Mainland there is a Melby (*medalboer*, middle farm) and Norby (*nordr-boer*, north farm) close together and both evidently divisions of an earlier farm. At Levenwick in South Mainland, Everby (*øfra-boer*, upper farm) and Netherby (*nedr-boer*, lower farm) imply a similar division. It has been suggested that as far as such names in Orkney are concerned they may indicate division of an early large *boer*/-*býr* farm⁹⁸, whereas in Shetland *boer*/-*býr* names might have been used for the first time when old coastal farms with topographical names were divided up, as Sandness and Levenwick cited above. The former became the parish name also, and was still used to define the taxable area in the first Shetland Rental (c.1500) rather than Melby or Norby. Melby was certainly in existence at that time, however, for in 1509 the farm was described as 'Medalboe a Sandnese',⁹⁹ but interestingly with the topographical name included and still obviously important – as indeed it is today. Everby and Netherby are at a later date called Everpund and Nethertun,¹⁰⁰ showing that in Shetland *boer*/-*býr* was not so important and rigid a place-name element that it could not be interchanged with alternative forms.

There are many problems connected with the use of *boer*/-*býr* in the Northern and Western Isles which have yet to be resolved. One of them is the absence of any Kirkaby names in Orkney, an appellatival name given to a settlement with a church, and very common in the English Danelaw. It has been suggested that its absence from Orkney may have been due to the decline of the use of *boer*/-*býr* by the traditional date of the conversion of the Norse in the Northern Isles, so that a settlement which had a church would have used some other element than the old-fashioned *boer*/-*býr* to describe their church-farm.¹⁰¹ The favourite combination in Orkney is in fact Kirbister = *kirkju-bólstadr*. The Danes in the Danelaw however certainly gave names in *kirkju-bý* to settlements in which they found a church, perhaps even before their own conversion.¹⁰² But it does not appear that the Norse in the Northern Isles designated an existing church settlement thus. It may be that the pre-Norse ecclesiastical establishments in the Danelaw and the Northern Isles were entirely different, and that there was not the type of settlement in the Isles to which the Norse could apply the term *kirkju-bý*. Whatever religious establishments they did find were given a name incorporating *papar* (= priests). This was either an -*ay* name referring to the whole island where the Norse found these Celtic priests, or sometimes Papil, supposed to be derived from *papar-býl/ból*, suggesting a priests' portion of some kind. By the time the Norse were giving the name *kirkju-bólstadr* to settlements with a church in Orkney it was to settlements which Norse colonizers had themselves established and must therefore date from a time after they had been converted so thoroughly that they were founding their own family chapels. According to what has been said above about *-bólstaðr* place-names, this must have been during a secondary rather than a primary phase of settlement and is likely also to have been at a stage after the official conversion of the earl and the leading families in the late tenth century.[103] As has been convincingly shown by a local historian with an unrivalled knowledge of the Orkney landscape, many of these Kirbister farms were peripheral in a tunship area, only one of them became a parish church later, and they 'were not in general the seats of the most influential local families, whose private churches usually became the parish churches'.[104] This may suggest that they signify a stage in the conversion of the Norse when the new faith was becoming more firmly established and the building of a family chapel had spread to a wider section of society; a very different conclusion from that drawn about the *early* date of Kirbister farms in Orkney and the evidence they were once thought to provide for Christian Norsemen in the Isles long before the official conversion.[105]

Another distinction which place-name scholars have noted about the *boer/-býr* names in the Northern and Western Isles is that very few of them have a personal name as the first element (which is also the case in Iceland). This is in strong contrast to the Danelaw and north-west England. It has been suggested that as far as Orkney is concerned the absence of such names may indicate a more gradual development and exploitation of agricultural potential.[106] It is very difficult to know how the rate of colonization proceeded in the various parts of the Norse colonies, and the place-names are our main evidence for it. Geographical situation and political direction must obviously have both been very relevant – and both have been suggested as important in explaining the *boer/-býr* and *-staðir* names in the Isle of Man.[107]

-staðir names

Turning finally to the important early *-staðir* names again (see fig. 28), we find a bewildering variety of different interpretations have been given. The geographical explanation for *-staðir* names is that they had a non-habitative significance, meaning 'fields in meadowland', which suits the situation in the north of the Isle of Man, and in the West Mainland of Orkney where most of the Orcadian *-staðir* farms are found.[108] Yet if one looks to Iceland *-staðir* names seem to have been used to describe secondary settlements dependent on an old farm with a geographical name. That they are secondary in Orkney and the Isle of Man, too, certainly seems to be indicated by the frequent combination of the generic with a personal name. The incorporation of a personal name in a place-name suggests a secondary holding carved out of a larger unit. Political direction from above has, of course, always to be borne in mind when considering the colonization pattern of Orkney and Man, for powerful rulers like the earls of Orkney and kings of Man must have exercised some control over the settlement and colonization of the islands. For this reason the *-staðir* farms of the West Mainland have also been seen as the settlements of followers of the earl whose political centre was close by at Birsay.[109]

This is unlikely to be the explanation for the *-staðir* farms in Shetland, which are in any case much more widely distributed than the Orkney examples. But are they primary or secondary farms? The study of *-staðir* farms in relationship to the brochs of Shetland already mentioned (see above, p. 101) sees them as primary Norse settlements.[110] However, if they were mostly secondary in Shetland, too, as in Iceland and Orkney, then the conclusions drawn about the survival of the native population in the brochs would be invalidated. It would not be unlikely for primary Norse settlement sites to be given topographical names, or indeed a name incorporating the word *borg* (ON for broch) of which there are many in Shetland.[111] The evidence from Jarlshof, where an early Norse farm was established in the shadow of a broch is difficult to argue away, and we have no idea what the name of that farm was (see fig. 43).

In general it would appear that the use of *-staðir* and *-bólstaðr* in the Isles took the place of the use of *-bý* in England. This may merely reflect the difference in origin of the settlers in the two regions, or it may reflect the differing geographical conditions in the islands from eastern England, or it may reflect a different date for the place-naming of these disparate parts of Scandinavian Britain. Whatever it reflects, it shows us that the situation in one part of the Scandinavian colonial world cannot necessarily be used to interpret the place-names of another, where geographical and social conditions may have engendered a different type of nomenclature, or use in a different way.

This discussion illustrates some of the complexities of interpreting the place-names of Scandinavian Scotland, as well as showing what an important branch of Norse studies they form. The whole subject inter-relates with the economy of the new settlements and provides evidence of continued population growth; this even engendered a further class of farm-name, in which the second element was *-hús* (= 'house'), *-skaill* ('hall' or, conversely, a more lowly type of dwelling), and *stofa* (= 'heated wooden room'), derived from the particular type of dwelling-house in the farm division.[112] It can be concluded that secondary elements which, according to most interpretations, include *-staðir*, *-bólstaðr*, *-setr* and perhaps even *-boer/-býr* names (as well as the *-land* and *-garth* names which may be associated with a secondary wave of immigration[113]), may have masked the earliest farm-names in the majority of instances. No map of these place-names, or of any group of them, is therefore a map of primary Norse settlement, but only of expansion in the following decades or centuries. This does not matter too much, if field-workers are aware that the earliest sites of a primary farm must lie somewhere in the vicinity of these names. What does matter is that these elements alone should not be treated as giving a definitive picture of the growth of Norse settlement or of the pattern of land-taking throughout Scandinavian Scotland, for if they were, mistaken conclusions would be likely to emerge. The main requirement is a series of detailed surveys on a localized basis taking into account the historical position, the geographical location, and *all* the place-names available for study before a picture of settlement and expansion in that one community or location can be clarified; only when numbers of such studies have been undertaken will conclusions of a more widespread nature be justified.

Linguistic origins

There is finally one other aspect of this study of place-names which is relevant to our survey and that is whether they can be used to indicate the part of

Norway from where the settlers had come. It is always assumed that the settlers in the Northern and Western Isles were Norwegian, and that would appear to be a justified assumption from the evidence of place-names. There is no doubt that Danish Vikings were familiar with the area, that they clashed with Norwegians in the Isles,[114] and that the earls had to struggle with Danish elements in their earldom;[115] but typical Danish place-names such as *-thorpe* (= 'secondary, outlying settlement') are very rare and this suggests that Danish involvement in the settlement of the Isles was indeed minimal. Instead the place-names reflect what is, of course, indicated by all other sources, that the settlers came from the western littoral of the Norwegian coast. They point in particular to the coastal districts north of Bergen (Sogn and Fjordane) and south of Trondheim (Møre and South Trøndelag).[116] This conclusion has been derived from the evidence of the frequency of distribution of the element *-bólstaðr* in Norway, and *-setr* names, which are particularly common in Møre, where the historical link with the earldom family is very relevant. The distribution of *-land* names has also been considered significant for they are particularly noticeable in the very south of Norway (Jaeren and Agder) as well as appearing in Orkney and Shetland.[117] Linguistic evidence may be a little misleading, for although the Shetland dialect has also been claimed to derive from West-Agder, Rogaland and South Hordaland,[118] it is difficult to be certain whether the nineteenth-century dialect forms are a good guide to how the Shetlanders spoke in the tenth century. South Hordaland was indeed the area which had closest links with Shetland in the post-medieval period when there was a thriving timber trade between this part of Norway and the islands in the west; such mercantile and social intercourse, which went on until the eighteenth century, is likely to have influenced the dialect in the islands. Archaeological finds add another dimension to this question of the derivation of the settlers,[119] and the general conclusion would seem to be that the whole of the west coast of Norway from Trondheim southwards probably provided the bulk of the men and women who sailed west over sea in search for new land and new homes.

5 The Archaeological Framework: Part 1 Settlement and Economy

The Vikings in Scotland disrupted, raided and in some areas settled amongst societies by no means backward politically, culturally or in their economic development. The Picts of north and east Scotland are no longer the archaeological 'problem' they once were thought to be.[1] Advances in excavation and in aerial photography are now providing a great deal more evidence about the density and quality of settlement sites which can be attributed to the dwellers in north and east Scotland in the post-Roman period. In Orkney, the availability of building stone enabled the pre-Norse population to build houses and other structures which have survived remarkably well and much is being learnt from excavations about their society and culture.[2] Although there is still a lack of archaeological evidence about the indigenous population in the northern Hebrides at the time of the Norse invasions, the growing trend among archaeologists appears to be a recognition that this formed part of the Pictish cultural area.[3] Further south in Dál Riada, Scottish settlement is recorded archaeologically at several impressive fortress sites, and the great Christian monastic centre at Iona formed an important cultural missionary power-house for these people and their religion. What is the material evidence for the impact of the Vikings on these societies and can the new settlers be recognized in the archaeological record as bringing with them a distinctive cultural tradition and way of life?

GRAVES

The graves of the pagan Norsemen primarily mark the incomers out as distinctive in their culture and beliefs and they provide a remarkable body of evidence about the life-style of the peoples of Scandinavia prior to their conversion in the late tenth century.[4] The pagan Norse graves of Scotland are of exceptional importance as a source of evidence for material culture in a period when the native population had long foregone the practice of burying grave-goods with their dead; it is a tragedy that so many were discovered and excavated before there was any understanding of scientific methods of recording or preservation.

Distribution

The distribution of Norse graves 'conforms in general to the distribution of Scandinavian place-names',[5] which is not surprising as they are similarly evidence of Norse settlement – at least when found in sufficient number (see

Figure 31. Pagan graves in Scotland and the Isle of Man (prepared for publication in new edition of *Historical Atlas of Scotland*).

fig. 31). They are of course a far less complete guide to settlement than place-names because of the chance nature of survival or discovery.[6] But where there is some disparity between numbers of place-names and occurrence of grave-finds explanations have to be looked for. The few finds from south-west Scotland may be an indication that Scandinavian-speaking settlers in this region had abandoned their pagan ways of burying goods with the dead when they established their settlements along the shores of the Solway Firth and up the river valleys; the one certain pagan grave in the area was found in a churchyard in Kirkcudbright.[7] The movement into this area may have been connected with the period of difficulty experienced by the Norse in Ireland during the early tenth century, by which time the *Gall-Gaedhil* had come under strong Christian influence.[8] North of the Clyde, the west coast and sea lochs form an area where few Viking settlements were established (from the absence of habitative elements in the nomenclature[9]), but where the topographical names of Norse origin reflect a great deal of Norse influence. The few grave-finds from this coastal zone similarly indicate an absence of permanent settlements which probably had a lot to do with the quality of the land. Even in the more densely settled north Scottish mainland grave-finds conform remarkably closely with the location of the best arable land – in north-east Caithness and the Dornoch area of Sutherland (see fig. 31). Geographical considerations are possibly also relevant to the distribution of pagan graves in the Northern Isles, for only two certain pagan graves have been found in Shetland[10] whereas the much larger number of graves in Orkney includes two cemeteries at Westness (Rousay) and Pierowall (Westray).[11] This disparity can be hardly due entirely to chance discovery and suggests that the rich arable lands of Orkney supported a much larger and wealthier population than Shetland, although there may also be other factors influencing this distribution.[12] Chance finds of Norse objects in the rest of Scotland are probably evidence of the death and burial of warriors on raids, although the grave of a Norse woman found near Perth suggests that pagan communities may have settled in this area, which links up with the Scandinavian place-names around the Tay (see fig. 32).[13]

Apart from the evidence of Norse presence of one kind or another, what else can these graves tell us? A great deal about the nature of the people and their society, along with an indication of the date of the Norse invasions and settlements. The vital information they give about the length of time that pagan beliefs persisted and the nature of those beliefs will be discussed in chapter 6 below.

Dating of raids and settlements

Estimates of the date of the Norse settlement of the Northern and Western Isles have fluctuated.[14] The historical evidence shows conclusively, however, that the raids were having an impact around the coasts of Britain and Ireland in the last decade of the eighth century, from which it can be deduced that pirate settlements had been established in the Northern and Western Isles by then. Evidence of individuals with mixed parentage in the fourth decade of the ninth century suggests some mingling of Norse and Celt in the early decades of the

Figure 32. 'Tortoise' brooches from female graves in Lewis and near Errol in Perthshire (a: Perth Museum and Art Gallery, photograph: John Watt; b: Museum nan Eilean, Stornoway, Lewis).

These pairs of very similar bronze brooches were found in completely different parts of Scandinavian Scotland, and testify to the death and burial of pagan Norse women on (a) the north bank of the Tay estuary (said to have been found in the late eighteenth century near Errol, Perthshire) and (b) at Valtos on the west coast of the Isle of Lewis, Outer Hebrides.

It is the most common type of early Viking period brooch and dates from the late eighth to late ninth centuries. The circular bronze brooch from the Valtos grave is of Celtic manufacture, as is the pin from a pennanular brooch found very near the site of the original find.

ninth century, and certainly by the middle of the century when the *Gall-Gaedhil* appear in the historical record. Turning to the archaeological evidence, we have first of all the problem of dating Norse graves, which has been done primarily on the typology of objects found within the grave – that is, the style of a sword or an axe, the shape of a brooch, the pattern on a metal plate. This is now recognized to be a rather unreliable method of dating the burial of the individual concerned, not only because of the uncertainty regarding changing styles and techniques, but also because of the real possibility that the brooch might have been inherited from a grandmother and the sword from an ancestor and thus be very much older than the date of its interment. The likelihood that some of these precious possessions might be heirlooms renders this method of dating the deposition of grave-goods highly uncertain: the Westness brooch, for example, was probably over a century old when it was buried (see fig. 33).[15] Indeed, the axe which was used to carve the runes when a party of Crusaders broke into the prehistoric tomb of Maes Howe in Orkney in the twelfth century had belonged to the rune-writer's great-great-great-grandfather.[16] The majority of graves are most likely to be of ninth-century date, although a few objects appear to be of eighth-century date – a

Figure 33. Grave-goods from a female grave at Westness, Rousay, Orkney (Royal Museum of Scotland).

Apart from the famous Celtic brooch (*middle right*: length 17.4cm, width 6cm), the woman's possessions included the usual pair of 'tortoise' brooches (one illustrated) and a necklace of 40 variegated beads (*centre*) which was probably strung between the two brooches across her breast. Other objects from her adornment were the two bronze strap-ends (*right of necklace*) and the usual comb, found in the majority of female, and male, pagan graves. In addition, this grave included objects associated with the important women's craft of clothmaking: two iron heckles (one illustrated, *top right*), shears (*bottom left*), a plaque of whalebone (*left of necklace*) perhaps used in pressing seams or working leather, and an iron weaving-sword (not shown) for beating down the weft on the loom. In addition there was the blade of a sickle (*top left*) and, next to it, a small bone tool for use in making some textile, perhaps French knitting.

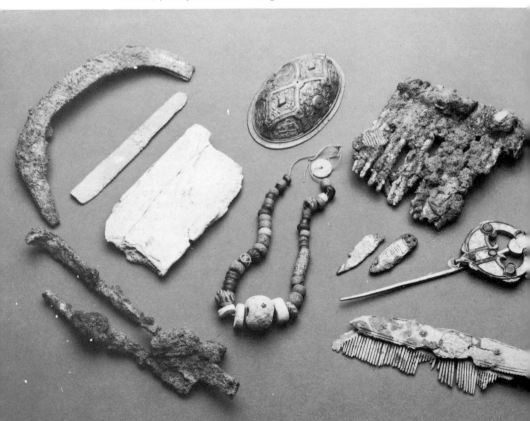

spear-head from Skaill (from which it has been concluded that there may have been settlement in Orkney in the eighth century[17]); a shield-boss and sword from a grave at Lamlash, Arran;[18] and a sword from a grave at Pierowall, Westray.[19] However, the presence of such eighth-century objects does not prove that the burials took place in the eighth century, for we do not know for how long these grave-goods might have been handed down in families. The occasional inclusion of coins among grave-goods may help to date a grave far more closely. Thus the grave excavated at Buckquoy could be dated from a coin of 940–6 to the second half of the tenth century,[20] but the other grave-goods would never have suggested a date as late as the tenth century. Until this particular discovery, it had been thought that very few Scottish Viking graves were likely to date from the tenth century,[21] and it confirms that typology provides a treacherous guide to dating, suggesting also that the pagan period may have been more lengthy in some places than was once thought.

Nowadays, skeletons can be subjected to the scientific method of dating organic materials by measuring their reduced carbon-14 content; but such dates have a margin of error of ±70 years for our period. That is perhaps little better than human error over typology. Thus the recent excavation of a probable Viking burial at Machrins on the island of Colonsay in the Inner Hebrides has produced a carbon-14 estimation of 780 ±70 years – suggesting that eighth-century interments might indeed exist.[22] This island has produced many other grave-finds in the past and was evidently a favoured resort of early raiders and settlers, lying directly on the sailing route through the Inner Hebrides. Graves found at Machrins come from around an area known, perhaps significantly, as Cnoc nan Gall (Hillock of the Foreigners).

The nature of Norse settlements

The grave from Machrins mentioned above had probably been the interment of a woman, although the upper half of the grave had been so disturbed that any brooches or personal adornment which might have been buried with the body had not survived. This grave did not, therefore, possess a pair of the oval ('tortoise') brooches, which are a diagnostic feature of Norse women's graves throughout Norway and the settlements, and provide incontrovertible proof that the Vikings took their wives and daughters overseas with them.[23] These brooches can be placed in a ninth- or tenth-century dating bracket, becoming more elaborate in the later part of the period.[24] There is frequently a third brooch in Norse women's graves, one which is usually based on West European design, and in Scotland of typical pennanular Celtic type, sometimes of great beauty and rarity like the Westness brooch (see fig. 33) or the circular bronze brooch found at Valtos in Lewis (see fig. 32).[25] The graves of wealthier women usually contained utensils, tools and other domestic equipment which they would have used in their daily life around the home, such as the set of cloth-making equipment in one of the Westness graves (see fig. 33).[26] The evidence for the presence of women in the Norse settlements overseas (and from early in the raiding phase, to judge from the Machrins grave) suggests that we are dealing with a colonizing movement. That is, family units were established on certain islands, possession of which had been secured from an early date, and it

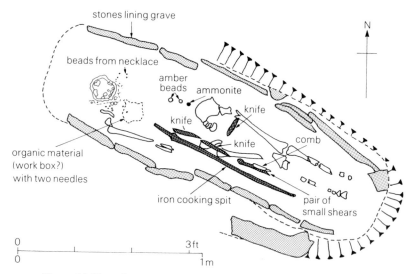

Figure 34. Plan of pagan woman's grave at Peel, Isle of Man (after D.J. Freke, *Peel Castle Excavation Second Interim Report, 1984* (1985), fig. 5a, with additional information kindly supplied by the author).

was not just a movement of landless younger sons. The only exception to this picture is in the Isle of Man, where no pagan Viking woman's grave has yet been recognized, for even though an equipped woman's grave has been recently excavated on St Patrick's Isle at Peel, the lack of any distinctive 'tortoise' brooches suggests that she may have been native rather than Norse (see fig. 34).[27] The very impressive and richly-equipped chieftains' graves which have been excavated on the Isle of Man and on some of the other islands such as Eigg have suggested that the occupation of the Hebrides by the Vikings may have been of rather a different order from the settlement further north (see below) (fig. 35a and b).[28]

Can archaeology provide any support for the evidence of the annals and sagas that Scandinavian expansion in Scotland was founded upon a prolonged period of raiding and piracy?[29] The equipment of the men's graves, which contain a weapon, either sword, spear, axe and shield, or combination of these, is sufficient witness to the important part fighting and the martial arts had played in these men's lives throughout the pagan period.[30] So long as the colonists continued to bury these objects with their dead, we must assume that such equipment had been of significance in the lives of the settlers. No study has attempted to suggest that emphasis on weapons declines in tenth-century graves. However, if direct evidence of their raids is looked for in the archaeological record, it is very difficult to find. No settlement site yet excavated shows signs of burning at the native-Norse interface. Even at Iona, which is on record as having been destroyed on several occasions, it is impossible to prove whether burned layers are a result of Norse attack or domestic conflagration.[31]

It has been said of the Norse colonists that 'they may have been warrior-adventurers at heart ... but their chief interest was in the acquisition and

Figure 35. (above) Sword-hilt (Royal Museum of Scotland) and *(below)* plan of grave-mounds on the island of Eigg, Inner Hebrides (based on drawing by N. MacPherson, 'Notes on antiquities from the island of Eigg', *PSAS*, xii, 1876–8, 590ff).

The magnificent bronze sword-hilt was found in one of three burials on Eigg; it dates from the early Viking period (late eighth–late ninth centuries); length 18.4cm. The plans show two of the burial mounds, all of which contained richly furnished Viking warrior graves. They may have been re-used prehistoric cairns.

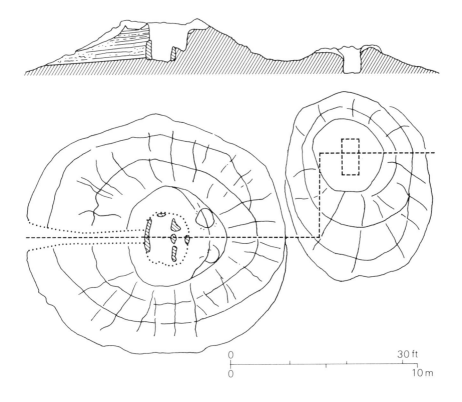

Figure 36. Views of Village Bay, St Kilda (photographs: Commander E.F. Spragge).

Village Bay is on Hirta (ON *?hjǫrtir* = stags), the main island of the St Kilda group, which lies 40 miles west of North Uist, Outer Hebrides. Although all structural remains visible today are of a later period, the Norse settlement is likely to have been in the location of Village Bay.

cultivation of land.'[32] The tools found in the graves certainly attest to another, more peaceful, side of the emigrants' way of life. Indeed the evidence for settlement by Norse colonists in that remotest of the Hebridean islands, St Kilda,[33] brings into sharp focus the need for land which must have impelled Norse men and women to seek out such an inhospitable location for their new home (see fig. 36). These remarkable emigrants used tools either for the business of farming the lands they settled or of carrying on some profession such as that of smith, for both agricultural implements and smithying tools have been found in men's graves (see fig. 37). If weapons and tools are found in the same grave then both can be understood to have been of importance to the dead owner. Here it may be possible to distinguish between the graves of the Orkney settlers and those in the West, particularly on Man, where few recognizable agricultural implements have been found, and the overwhelming impression of the excavated Manx graves is of a warrior caste.[34] This distinction between the Orkney grave material and the Hebridean was strongly emphasized by a Norwegian archaeologist who argued that the Orkney settlers were only 'peaceful, peasant colonists'.[35] It is very difficult to quantify such scattered and often poorly preserved material, but the grave-finds from the Inner Hebrides do appear to represent an aristocratic class of Norsemen who had taken up residence in the ninth century.[36] The Orkney material appears to be more broadly based, and extensive in time.

Figure 37. Weapons and smithying tools from a pagan male grave at Ballinaby, Islay, South Hebrides (Royal Museum of Scotland).
   The mixture of weapons (sword, axe-heads, shield-boss and mounting for handle – *top, middle*) and smithying-tools (blunt-ended hammer, forge-tongs, *bottom*, and possible fragment of iron cauldron handle, *top left*) illustrate the diversity of the Viking settlers' way of life.

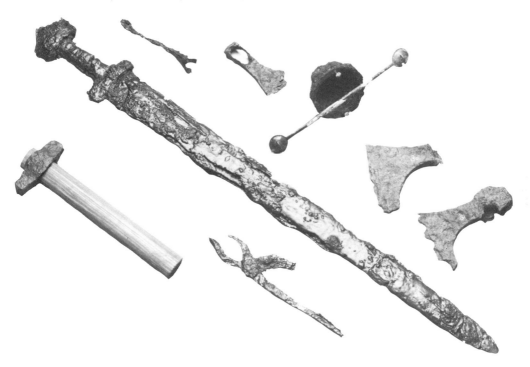

What about the role of the Viking as trader? Can the grave-material help our understanding of this aspect of his life-style? Unfortunately, we have no means of knowing how goods of foreign provenance and in particular 'insular' items (that is, those of Celtic origin) came to be in the possession of the dead settler or of his cousins at home in Norway. The fine pieces of gold and silver which may once have adorned the shrines of the holy saints, or the books and ecclesiastical objects of the monks who guarded those shrines could never have been acquired legitimately. But on the other hand, the Celtic brooches and ring-headed pins appear to have become a normal part of the Vikings' dress adornment very quickly, suggesting patronage of native craftsmen and legal purchase.[37] There are fewer objects of Celtic provenance in the Orkney graves than in the graves of Norway, from which it has been deduced that the Vikings liked to have some souvenir of their western voyage to take back home.[38] In this respect there appears to be another contrast between Orkney and the west, for the graves from the Hebrides, and particularly Man, have produced Celtic material showing strong connections with Irish and Scottish culture, which may well have resulted from inter-marriage or trade. Nonetheless beautiful objects of Irish/Scottish manufacture like the Westness pin must also have been highly valued in Orkney. If the graves of the early earls and their closest followers could be found in Orkney then the disparity with the Hebridean material in the matter of objects of Celtic workmanship might not be so obvious.

Another contrast between the grave material in the west and the north is worth noting; that is the presence in western graves of weighing scales. These were used for weighing precious metals – gold or silver – in exact quantities and are a very important feature of grave furniture of the Viking Age.[39]It is usually supposed that the weighing was done as part of a trading transaction and that, for instance, the man whose scales and weights form part of the impressive Kiloran Bay grave equipment, found on the island of Colonsay, was a Norse merchant.[40] But he also possessed a sword, an axe, a shield and a spear and arrowheads (see fig. 38). Was he, therefore, an armed merchant, preparing to defend himself while on his trading voyages around the British Isles? If, however, the presence of weights and scales were regarded as the essential equipment of the warrior chief who needed to weigh out precious metals when distributing booty to his followers,[41] then this grave would begin to look more like the final resting-place of a Viking chieftain who had based himself on this favoured island of the Inner Hebrides from where he carried out his raiding and 'trading' activities. Such alternative explanations which can be put forward illustrate some of the inherent difficulties of interpreting archaeological material.

But whatever the true interpretation, the infrequency of such discoveries in Orkney, in contrast to the number found in the Hebrides,[42] further suggests a broad difference in the nature of the Norse establishments in the Northern and Western Isles. The Orkneys were dominated by the earls and their following – chieftains indeed – who controlled the body of Norse settlers. But the bulk of the settlers took over the rich farming lands of the Pictish population which provided them with sufficient resources (and slave labour) to allow them to live primarily as landowners. The earls continued to require military service which would have necessitated the settlers' maintainance of military equip-

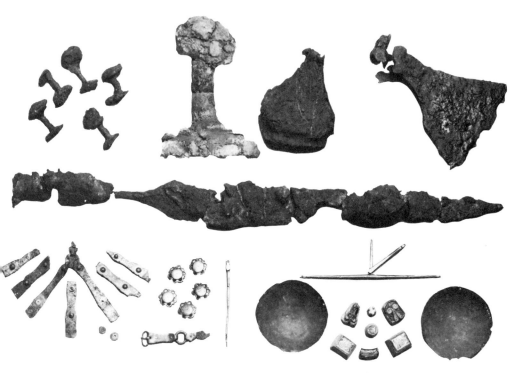

Figure 38. Some of the grave-goods from a richly equipped male grave at Kiloran Bay, Colonsay, South Hebrides (Royal Museum of Scotland).

The man was buried in a boat (rivets, *top left*) and his horse was sacrificed for interment with him (bronze harness-mounting, *bottom left*). The full complement of weapons included sword, spear, axe, shield (boss, *second from right, top*) and arrowheads (not illustrated). Among his other possessions were Anglo-Saxon coins (mid-ninth century) and the fine set of bronze scales, balance-beam and small leaden weights (*bottom right*) – the latter ornamented with scraps of Celtic or Anglo-Saxon metalwork, two of which are decorated with enamel; for discussion of the use for such sets of scales see p. 126 above.

ment and continuation of practice training for war expeditions or reprisal raids. These relics of war accompanied them in their graves along with agricultural implements. In the Hebrides, trade and raiding were probably more fundamental to the success of the Norse settlers in an environment which could not support large numbers of farmers and which it was difficult for one family to dominate politically. Involvement in the lucrative trading world of the Norse in Ireland was therefore very important to the Hebridean settlers, some of whom formed themselves into the renegade band which went under the name of *Gall-Gaedhil*.[43] They prospered in the turbulent Norse-Irish world until a revival of Irish solidarity forced them out of the Hebrides to look for emptier spaces in the North Atlantic.[44] The archaeological material found in graves of the Western and Northern Isles is a broad indicator of the rather different nature and status of the Gaelicized petty chieftains of the west as compared with the Norse farmers of Orkney.

HOARDS

Although our knowledge of Viking trade in the Scandinavian settlements of the ninth century is limited to what can be gleaned from grave material, this is supplemented from the tenth century onwards by the remarkable evidence of silver hoards. The practice of hoarding coins and bullion is well known from Scandinavia, and this method of protecting your valuables was also used in the west as *Jarls' Saga* tells us: 'People were now so very much afraid of him [Swein Asleifsson] in the Hebrides, that they buried all their movable property in the earth or under heaps of stones.'[45] Recent studies of the silver hoards of Scotland and Ireland, and of the Isle of Man (with the associated numismatic research), have revolutionized our knowledge of this aspect of Norse studies.[46] Moreover, these hoards may relate to military or political events, for as the above extract suggests, in times of danger or uncertainty, people buried their treasured valuables in the ground.[47] Even so, it is not absolutely clear that peaks of hoarding activity must be associated with political disturbance, although it may be tempting to look to the known political circumstances for guidance as to the reason for the deposition of coin hoards. It is not unlikely that valuables were buried at any time for safe-keeping and dug up only when required. In which case the numbers of hoards could be an indication of periods of maximum wealth, and perhaps, active trading.[48] However, failure to recover buried wealth does suggest (as is normally the interpretation of the St Ninian's Isle hoard[49]) a situation of unrest.

Hoards buried by the Vikings are nearly always recognizable because they include coins of many countries, ingots of a particular shape, ornaments with distinctive Viking Age art styles, and, above all, 'hack silver' (cut-up fragments of ingots and ornaments) and 'ring-money' (silver rings which served as a form of currency among the Norse settlers of Scotland). In fact, Viking hoards are distinctive by the eclectic nature of their contents; they include silver in any shape or form and sometimes in huge amounts. The largest and finest hoard to be found in Scotland is from the Bay of Skaill, in Orkney, which probably weighed about 8kg – similar in size to the largest Viking Age silver hoards found in Scandinavia.[50] It included over 100 items, with rather few coins among them, the most famous objects being the magnificent 'ball-type' brooches of which there were at least 16 (see fig. 39).[51]

Distribution

The Scottish material is only one part of the whole west Norse pattern of hoard deposition, and the disparity between the numbers and types of hoards found in Ireland and in Scotland tells us that the economic situation in the two areas must have been very different (see fig. 40). The Norse colonies in Scotland may not have been so wealthy as the trading ports in Ireland; nonetheless in comparison with the rest of Scotland the Scandinavian settlements had the greatest wealth in the tenth and early eleventh centuries and even had a type of currency in the form of ring-money.[52] Out of a total of about 40 known Scottish hoards, 31 of them have a Scandinavian character (i.e. including hack silver, rings or ingots). The great majority of these are scattered throughout the

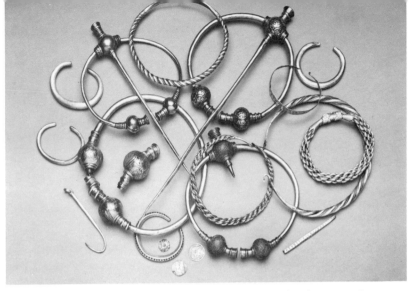

Figure 39. Selection of objects from the Skaill hoard, Orkney (Royal Museum of Scotland).

Some of the silver arm-rings, brooches, necklets and coins which form part of the impressive hoard found at Skaill, West Mainland, Orkney, in the middle of the nineteenth century, and which was deposited around the middle of the tenth century. The small wrist- or arm-rings (*upper left, upper right and bottom*) are examples of silver 'ring-money'; see pp. 133–4 below. Diameter of thistle-brooch (*top right*) 16cm.

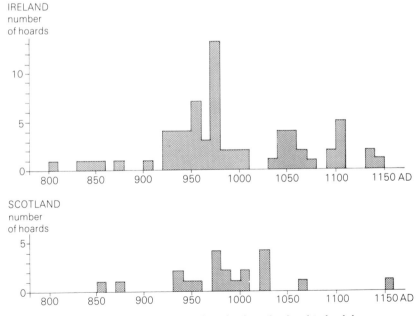

Figure 40. Deposition of silver coin-hoards of Scotland and Ireland, by decades (c.800–1170) (after J. Graham-Campbell, 'Viking-Age silver and gold hoards from Scotland', *PSAS*, cvii, 1975–6, fig. 2).

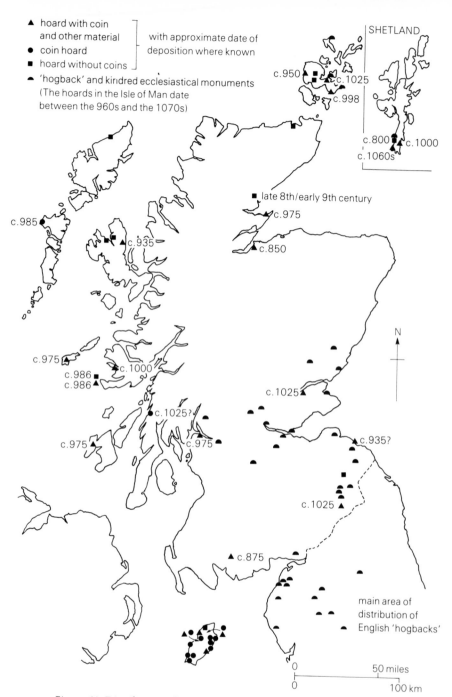

Figure 41. Distribution of Scottish silver hoards and hogback tombstones (prepared for publication in new edition of *Historical Atlas of Scotland*, after J. Graham-Campbell, 'Viking-Age silver and gold hoards from Scotland', *PSAS*, cvii, 1975–6; idem, 'The Viking-age hoards of the Isle of Man', in *The Viking Age in the Isle of Man*, Ninth Viking Congress, 1983; and J.T. Lang, 'Hogback monuments in Scotland', *PSAS*, cv, 1972–4).

islands and coastal areas known from other evidence to have been settled by the Norse, while there are an additional 20 hoards from the Isle of Man. They provide tangible evidence of economic activity along the coastal routes and waterways and give further coherence to the discrete political units of Norse Scotland (see fig. 41).

The few hoards found in non-Scandinavian parts of Scotland which are of Scandinavian type were most probably hidden by Vikings passing through those parts of Scotland. They can therefore be used as evidence of the movements of Scandinavians through southern Scotland which are recorded in the historical sources. The Talnotrie hoard (Kirkcudbrightshire) is one of the few clearly definable Viking hoards of the ninth century found anywhere in Britain.[53] It has been specifically associated with the campaigns of Ivar the Boneless in 870–1 when Dumbarton was captured, or perhaps with Halfdan's ravaging amongst the Picts and Strathclyde Britons of 874–5. The Gordon hoard (Berwickshire) can be linked with the plundering of Lowland Scotland by Irish-Norse after they were expelled from Dublin in 902.[54] The Jedburgh and Lindores hoards dated to c.1025 have been associated with the activities of King Cnut in Scotland (although there seems no reason why the Lindores hoard at any rate might not relate to the conquests of Earl Thorfinn which are supposed to have reached as far south as Fife). Even the native hoards, that is Pictish hoards of ninth-century date, can be linked up with Viking activity for they provide evidence of disturbance resulting probably from fear of plunder; most probably in the case of the St Ninian's Isle treasure (Shetland) and the Rogart hoard (Sutherland); possibly also in the case of the Croy hoard (Inverness-shire).[55] If the Vikings were prone to hiding their silver in troubled times, it is likely that so also were the natives when the Vikings were about.

In this context, it is relevant to mention some stray items found in Scotland of Celtic manufacture but with runic inscriptions on them, from which we know that the lost object had at one time been in the possession of someone of Norse speech. The most famous of these is the Hunterston brooch,[56] found near Largs in Ayrshire (fig. 42a); and the most enigmatic, the bronze crescent-shaped plate found near Monifieth on the Tay estuary (now lost: fig. 42b).[57] The former fits perfectly into the mixed Norse-Celtic world of Western Scotland, for the owner had the Celtic name Melbrigda (scratched in Norse runes); the latter object, of Pictish manufacture, had apparently been owned by a Norseman called Grimketil. Both provide tangible evidence of the interpenetration of Norse and Celtic worlds in localities where the Scandinavian presence is proven but faint.

Dating

A comparison of the chronology of the deposition of the coin-hoards of Scotland and Ireland brings out strongly the importance of the period from the mid-tenth to the early eleventh centuries. The small number of ninth-century hoards must indicate that little silver was in circulation at that time.[58] It cannot be taken as indicating peaceful times, when the historical record proves otherwise. The sudden increase in the use of silver is a tenth-century phenomenon. The number of hoards found in Ireland dated to the period

Figure 42. Runic inscriptions on (*a*) the Hunterston brooch and (*b*) the Monifieth plate (drawings from J. Anderson, *Scotland in Early Christian Times*, 1881, figs. 3 and 34).

The Hunterston brooch (diameter 122mm) is one of the most elaborate and largest of the famous Celtic brooches, and possibly also the earliest known (?AD 700). It was therefore of considerable age when lost, and an heirloom no doubt when acquired by 'Melbrigða' whose name was scratched in Norse runes round the hoop (reverse) in the tenth century.

The enigmatic bronze crescent-shaped plate (diameter 114mm), found at the Laws, Monifieth, on the Tay estuary in the eighteenth century but now lost, is decorated with typical Pictish designs, the V-rod symbol on one face and double-disc and Z-rod symbols on the other (not shown). It came into the hand of a (Norse) Viking whose name (?Grimketil) was scratched in runes on the bottom left border. He probably acquired – and lost – it in the Pictish heartland around the river Tay, further evidence for Viking movement along the coastal waters of south-east Scotland.

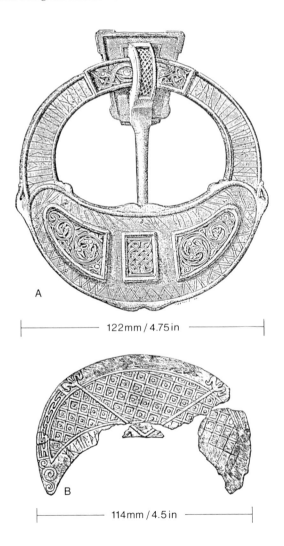

A

|———— 122mm / 4.75in ————|

B

|———— 114mm / 4.5in ————|

c.920–1010 dramatically demonstrates the importance of the new trading establishments founded by the Norse around the Irish coasts, but the Scottish evidence also shows a similar change in the same period, although on a far smaller scale.[59] Likewise in the Isle of Man there are hardly any coin-hoards until the second half of the tenth century when a number were deposited.[60] This proliferation of hoards, as well as the beginnings of a Hiberno-Manx coinage (which was possibly minted in the Isle of Man) is evidence of an increased amount of commercial activity in the island in the late tenth and throughout the eleventh centuries.[61] The development of this coinage in the eleventh century has also suggested closer ties between Man and Ireland, and the breaking of links with the earldom of Orkney.[62]

The quantity of hoards deposited in Scandinavian Scotland in the period 975–1025 coincides with the period when Earl Sigurd was extending his sway over the Hebrides, and including the aftermath of the battle of Clontarf. The disruption after the battle in which so many political leaders were killed is well illustrated by events in *Njal's Saga*; Flosi was with Earl Gilli in the Hebrides when they heard news of the battle from Hrafn the Red, and Flosi decided to sail south, so 'the earl told him to do as he wished; he gave Flosi a ship, and anything else they needed, as well as *a load of silver*' (my italics).[63] In uncertain circumstances such as these it is understandable that large amounts of silver would come to be buried in the ground, and sometimes not be collected again by the recipients or owners. A hoard found near the Abbey in Iona has been associated with a recorded raid on the island in 986.[64] In the case of the Caldale hoard found near Kirkwall and dated to c.1025 we can look to the political situation in the earldom during the rule of Earl Einar (1013–1024), when 'many were the men of mark who fled [from their lands] in the Orkneys'[65] through his tyranny. This might well be the occasion when a Norseman's worldly wealth would be secreted in the ground to be safe from the grasping earl, and this particular hoard was actually located in the part of the island thought to have been the 'trithing' (third division) belonging to Earl Einar.[66] Thereafter there are very few hoards in Orkney or West Scotland to suggest continuing disturbance during the period when Earls Thorfinn and Rognvald Brusisson were establishing their power in north and west, although the decades in which the greatest number of hoards were deposited in the Isle of Man are the 1030s and 1040s.[67] Can this be seen as evidence for the struggle by Thorfinn and Rognvald to assert Orcadian control in the Irish Sea in the period after the abdication of King Sitric of Dublin in 1035?[68] We have to remember the warning that it is 'often dangerous to try and fit the dates of the deposition of coin hoards into the historical record'.[69]

Ring-money

In one particular respect the Scottish hoards of the late tenth and early eleventh centuries are exceedingly significant, and that is for the inclusion among the hack silver and coins of examples of 'ring-money'. These silver rings which were probably worn as adornment on the arm or wrist (see fig. 39) also appear to have been used as a form of currency in Scotland from the mid-tenth until at least the mid-eleventh century; they relate to the ounce of 24 grams.[70] Examples of these arm-rings are known also in Norway, but their distribution has suggested that they were manufactured in Scotland by the Viking colonists.[71] They were being used at a time when the Norse in Ireland were not only using coins, but also minting them. The incidence of such rings in hoards in the Isle of Man indicates that they may have been used as a form of currency there too, suggesting continued contacts between Man and Norse Scotland during the eleventh century.[72] New hoards may change the known distribution of ring-money and make new explanations necessary. There is, however, a possibility that ring-money was linked with the assessment system based on the ounce, found in the Northern and Western Isles.[73] The fact that the use of this ring-currency spans the period when the Orkney earls were at the height of their power in the north and west suggests that it was they who had the political authority to introduce such a standardized metal currency in the earldom.

Certainly this type of non-coined currency seems to have kept out the Hiberno-Norse coins of Ireland for there is a total absence of eleventh-century Hiberno-Norse coins from Scottish hoards[74] (though such coins may, of course, have been melted down and converted into ring-money).[75] The kings of Dublin started minting their own coinage in 997 and their coinage was strongly influenced by Anglo-Saxon example. The 'ring-money' was also a state currency but of a quite different type. The Norse traders in Ireland similarly had used an arm-ring type of currency, at an earlier date, but this was probably originally of Danish manufacture, although developed in Ireland.[76] When this Hiberno-Norse ring-money was abandoned by the Norse traders in Ireland, ring-money of a different type went on being used in the Irish Sea area, possibly manufactured by the Norse in Scotland. Hoard evidence suggests it was used right through the period of Earl Thorfinn's rule. Its existence points to an economic and trading system in the north which had no need of coins and which was independent to some extent of the Irish trading world.

Trade

It has been claimed on the basis of the Scottish hoard material that 'overseas trade, other than in basic commodities, did not play a central part in the economic life of the Norse settlers in Scotland.'[77] Yet the amount of silver which was circulating in Norse Scotland, even if not in coined form, testifies to the wealth of these communities. It could have been acquired from the Isle of Man where silver occurs in considerable quantities. But the settlements around the coasts of north and west Scotland were geographically very well placed to control and benefit financially from the trade which passed along that route to and from Dublin.[78] This chain of islands and sea lanes provided mariners with the sort of extended coastline with which they were very familiar in Norway, and an easily navigable way to reach Britain and the Irish Sea. It continued to be the route used by settlers or their descendants when they were waving the trader's flag. The exhortation by the chieftain Brynjolv of Urland to his son Bjorn in *Egil's Saga* to go south to Dublin is frequently quoted in books on the Vikings; what is not always mentioned is that Bjorn wanted a longship to go a-viking but that his father would only give him a merchant-ship 'and wares withal' for a trading expedition.[79] It can be predicted what these wares would have been: walrus ivory, furs or hides, from which ship's cables could be made; timber, dried fish and fish products such as oil; iron, whetstones or soapstone vessels; maybe antlers for the manufacture of combs or birds' feathers for eiderdowns. The excavations at Dublin have shown what an important entrepôt it was for trade, as well as being a large manufacturing centre.[80]

There is no evidence that any such urban complex existed in the Northern or Western Isles as early as the founding of Dublin, although Kirkwall may have functioned as a market long before it is first mentioned in *Jarls' Saga* in connection with events in 1047.[81] It is certainly likely that there were trading stations in Orkney, of which Pierowall in Westray, where a substantial number of pagan graves has been uncovered, may have been one.[82] Considering its geographical situation and natural harbour (it is called Hǫfn [haven] in the *Jarls' Saga*) Pierowall would have been a useful port of call for ships sailing down the west side of the Orkney Islands, which was probably the preferred sailing route.[83] The Northern Isles were at the crossing of the trade route from Dublin to Norway with the route from Britain to the North Atlantic, and are likely to have provided important refuge points and revictualling stops in the many sheltered harbours and sounds. Their nodal position made them the obvious place for merchants to take on fresh supplies or to sell cargo; it would also enable the earls to exact some form of toll from merchant ships – if not plundering them – while they passed.[84] Given the grain production of Orkney also (possibly surplus to local needs in most years) then the islands had a valuable export for less fertile parts of the Norse world. We hear incidentally about such trade from a thirteenth-century saga which tells of the quarrel between an Orcadian, Thorkell Walrus, and Snorri Sturlason with whom Thorkell spent the winter in Iceland. The two quarrelled over the price of flour which Thorkell had brought in his ship from Orkney.[85] When traded to Norway, such a cargo would be exchanged in particular for timber, for which there is written evidence from the later Middle Ages.[86] If trading of this kind had taken place in earlier centuries, it would help to explain the amassing of the sort of wealth in Orkney which is evident from the Burray and Skaill hoards (1.9kg and 7–8kg respectively). The wealth of the sea was probably also exploited, as initial research at Freswick in Caithness is beginning to reveal.[87]

The number of hoards found in the Western Isles also indicates a comparable prosperity, and one which is likely to have derived more from passing trade than from agriculture. That the later Manx kings could exact a well-regulated toll is illustrated in a saga account of the journey of Gudmund, bishop-elect of Holar in 1207, in a merchant ship from Iceland to Norway, when the ship was blown off course and landed in the Outer Hebrides. The king's bailiff claimed land-dues 'according as the laws of the Hebrides required', which were 100 lengths of wadmell (cloth) for each man in the ship (or a monetary equivalent).[88] Comments on the 'irregular and ill-organised trade of the Western area'[89] in comparison with the eastern Viking world are perhaps unjustly deprecating about the effectiveness of the trading and commercial methods practised in the west.

Trade apart, however, the main source of wealth in Scandinavian Scotland in the period 975–1025 was probably the rewards of service with earls who still maintained conquering and raiding life-styles. Earl Sigurd and his sons strove continuously to exercise political control in the West and in Ireland. This process was pursued by initial raiding which compelled local communities to submit to demands for tribute, and which probably helped to syphon off some of the surplus wealth of farmers and townsmen alike. Exchanged or looted, this wealth was then transferred back to the Northern Isles and helped to improve the standard of living of the earl, his family and following, as well as seeping down through society as a whole. No wonder the great war-leader's praise was sung by his skald and his memory cherished by his people.

SETTLEMENTS

A completely different but expanding category of archaeological evidence relates to living conditions in the Scandinavian colonies: namely what has been uncovered during the excavation of settlement sites. Only rarely can such settlement be linked with the historical record, although the temptation to do so sometimes produces controversial results. It is the best source of information about the routine circumstances of the life of the ordinary Viking and his family; and about the social and economic changes that occurred in the Norse settlements from their beginning through to the twelfth century and beyond. We can look to this material for some enlightenment on how the Norse settlers replaced the indigenous population in the islands (or on the Scottish mainland) and of the relationship between them. Information gained from the excavation of house sites in the British Isles and the other islands in the North Atlantic is of immense importance for Norwegian archaeologists, who look to them for an understanding of the dwellings of their ancestors in the absence of such excavated sites in Norway. Yet the number of excavated – and published – Norse sites in Scotland still remains scarcely more than one dozen, representing only a minute fraction of those settlements once established throughout the north and west of Scotland and numbering many thousands. Size, building materials, wealth and living conditions would have varied enormously among these different units, and the fragmentary picture we have so far acquired may be in many respects unrepresentative.

The sites at present available for study are scattered throughout Scandinavian Scotland. In southern Shetland we have the fully excavated and published site of Jarlshof, which has therefore served as the type-site of Norse settlement archaeology (see fig. 43).[90] On the northernmost Shetland island of Unst is the much smaller site of Underhoull which provides a contrasting picture as a poorer and less successful farming establishment,[91] and the later Norse house at Sandwick.[92] On the island of Papa Stour, off the western Mainland of Shetland – where the kings of Norway had an estate and a farm in the thirteenth century – the disturbed remains of a Norse house have been excavated in a location which has been continuously settled up to the present day.[93] In Orkney most attention has been focussed on the supposed earldom residence on the Brough of Birsay[94] and on the pattern of settlements around the whole of the Bay of Birsay.[95] In this locality is the site of Buckquoy, which although half destroyed by erosion is especially important because it provides some evidence about the succession of the Norse from the Picts.[96] Other very

Figure 43. Jarlshof, Shetland: an aerial view of the whole archaeological site (Royal Commission on Ancient Monuments, Scotland: Crown Copyright reserved).

The Norse long-houses lie on the landward slope of the mound formed by the ruins of prehistoric and Iron Age structures; the circular shape of the surviving broch wall can be seen under the west corner of the seventeenth-century laird's house (given the name 'Jarlshof' by Sir Walter Scott). This photograph illustrates dramatically the Norse settlers' choice of previous settlement sites on which to locate their own houses. Norse House I, dating from the earliest period of settlement (ninth century) and distinguished by a floor-covering of white sand, can be seen lying in a NW–SE alignment; the later Norse houses lie at right-angles to it.

promising sites in Orkney, such as Skaill in Deerness, Tuquoy on Westray and Pool on Sanday, are still in the process of excavation or publication.[97] In Caithness, a partly excavated site at Freswick is at present being re-examined,[98] while in the Western Isles the multi-period site at the Udal, North Uist, will provide a wealth of information on aspects of Norse and pre-Norse settlement archaeology when it is fully published.[99] The present under-researched situation in the Hebrides is illumined a little by two sites in South Uist and Bute[100] and by evidence from the Isle of Man.[101]

Defensive sites

Among the many sites which have been excavated in the Isle of Man are a series of promontory forts which suggest that Norse raiders or settlers used such locations, in some cases succeeding pre-Norse usage.[102] Careful excavation at Vowlan fort, Ramsay, showed that five rectangular wooden houses had been constructed and then reconstructed within a short space of time, although clear dating evidence for these is absent.[103] In two particular respects the picture drawn from excavated sites in other parts of Scandinavian Scotland may be defective: there may have been a great deal more construction in wood than is now recognizable on the sandy sites of the Northern Isles. There may also have been a period when defensible sites on promontories formed the usual base for the Vikings, before farming settlements proper could be established. A 'ness-taking' phase in the Northern Isles is very likely and the whole problem of the use of fortification by the Norse needs examining. It is not enough to accord to the Norse the initiative in the building of stone castles in Scotland in the twelfth century yet to suggest there was no need of any fortification to their farms at an earlier date.[104] Earlier defensive structures may simply not have been recognized, and if the situation demanded them the Norse would have adapted local examples to their own use, as they did in other spheres. The lack of stone castles in the homeland of Norway is irrelevant to what the colonists could learn about fortification in the west; the political and military situation in Norway was not conducive to the building of defensive structures at this time. However, there were fortifications in Pictland and Dál Riada with which the Norse would become very familiar during the early centuries of raiding in the west.[105] Their ability to besiege such defensive positions has already been commented on; excavations at Dumbarton Rock have produced evidence which gives probable archaeological support to the record of the taking of 'Alt Clut' by Olaf and Ivar, the two kings of the Northmen in 870 (or to the occurrence of some other onslaught on this stronghold by a Viking force).[106]

We should not, therefore, be too surprised that the excavation at Udal in North Uist is said to have produced evidence of a fort built probably during the first decade of Norse occupation at the site (mid-ninth century). Its dimensions have not yet been published, although it has been described as small, sub-rectangular and 'built of massive stone walling set in turf and based on a substantial foundation trench packed with a rubble core of stones and turf',[107] perhaps not too dissimilar to the twelfth-century Cubbie Roo's Castle still to be seen on the island of Wyre in Orkney.[108] Its existence is said to have been short-lived, from which one can conclude that the circumstances in which defence was required must also have been short-lived. It is not clear of course whether those circumstances of defence were required against the native population, or against fellow-Vikings. However, the archaeological discovery of an early Norse fortification means that saga references to the building of forts like Earl Sigurd the Mighty's fort 'in the south of Moray'[109] must certainly be taken seriously, rather than being dismissed as anachronisms of the saga-writer.

Domestic Norse settlement and the question of continuity

Some preliminary Norse settlement may have been of a defensive kind. On the other hand, all the early settlement sites examined so far in the Northern Isles are of apparently peaceful communities. This introduces the historical problem of the relationship between the incoming Norse and the indigenous Celtic population. We have already seen that the pagan graves in the Northern Isles are broadly different from those in the west and indicate a farming establishment with little evidence of trading contacts. Nonetheless the Orkney farmer maintained his weapons throughout the pagan period. This does not suggest that he was only a 'peaceful peasant'.[110] How did he relate to the Picts whom he doubtless found in this land when he arrived?

Looked at in a wider sphere this problem is a perennial feature of academic arguments concerning the historical situation where invaders dominate a native population. What was the process involved in the ousting of one culture by another? How much survived of the indigenous culture? What was the relationship of the incomers and the natives? These are questions which have to be asked, whether it is of the Anglo-Saxons arriving in Britain in the fifth century or of the Normans arriving in Anglo-Saxon England in the eleventh century, or of the Scots arriving in Pictland in the ninth century. Interpreters of these situations usually adopt one of two lines: either the 'Continuity' approach or the 'Big Bang' theory. That is, the survival of the native population and its culture is considered to be significant in the new society which arose out of the ashes of the old, or else the domination of the military elite which arrived and subjugated the natives is regarded as complete and the death of the indigenous culture follows. Very often interpretation rests on the personal inclination and preferences – and perhaps even national and political preferences – of the individual interpreting the evidence. The Vikings in particular have aroused passionate debates of this kind because they came into contact with established populations in many places throughout Europe where they settled and to varying extents influenced the local social patterns. There are arguments about the impact of the Swedish Rus on the development of Russian society (where the nationalist element is strongly to the fore[111]). There has in recent years been a most stimulating controversy about the impact of the Danes on the settlement pattern of Eastern England.[112] Similarly in Ireland the nature of the settlement of the Norse and the influence they and their raids had on the economy of the country as a significant factor in social change have been interpreted in widely different ways.[113] These arguments have all been about countries where the native language survived and the admixture was with a recognizably strong local population.

If we turn to the excavated settlement sites of the Northern Isles, there would appear to be a sufficient number from which some generalized conclusions could be drawn about the way incoming Norse settlers related to the pre-existing population. At Jarlshof, the Norse houses are situated on the landward slope away from the pre-Norse structures, the broch and associated wheel-houses (see fig. 43); but it is not possible to say whether the native site was abandoned at the time of the Viking raids or long before the Norse settled there.[114] At Underhoull the Iron Age structures lie directly under the Norse house, but the excavator concluded that the site 'had been deserted for some considerable time before re-occupation by the Vikings'.[115] In Orkney the re-investigation of the complex site on the Brough of Birsay does not yet allow any firm conclusions to be made as to the relationship of Norse and Pictish cultural horizons. This apparently important centre of Pictish ecclesiastical and secular activity was taken over by the Norse; at one side of the site there is direct succession of Norse buildings to pre-Norse structures although the central part of the settlement still awaits full investigation.[116] Another major Pictish site at Skaill in Deerness suggests a 'regression in material culture' once Norse occupation is in evidence, with 'the sense of a clean break' between Pictish and Norse horizons.[117] At Buckquoy, near the Brough of Birsay, excavation has exposed a site where a probable Norse structure replaced a Pictish 'figure-of-eight' house and there was 'a break in temporal continuity' of perhaps half a century between the two.[118] Turning to the Hebrides, only the site at Udal in North Uist has also produced close association of a Norse house with pre-Norse 'ventral' houses, where the situation is described as showing 'direct and unambiguous interaction between indigenous settlement of long-standing and Norse settlers' which indicates Norse colonization 'totally obliterative in terms of local material culture'.[119] Apparently similar arch-aeological circumstances at these last two sites have, nonetheless, led to very different conclusions about the relationship of Norse and native, suggesting that the local population was obliterated at Udal but survived to influence the newcomers at Buckquoy. The one safe conclusion that can be drawn is that there 'would appear to have been a distinct preference on the part of Norse immigrants for settling on old occupation sites',[120] which strengthens the argument against the theory that the early Norse settlers in Shetland avoided the sites of brochs (pre-Norse defensive structures with a long period of occupancy in the Iron Age).[121] If there is indeed continuity of settlement site, one is entitled to ask what happened to the old occupiers when the newcomers settled on or near their homes?

Building styles and the Norse house

Some of them no doubt did survive. But hardly, it appears, living their old way of life. The most striking archaeological evidence for a changed social and ethnic situation is the dramatic difference in building styles between the rather elegant cellular type of pre-Norse houses found at Buckquoy and Udal, as well as in a post-broch building at Gurness,[122] and the rectilinear houses which superseded them at all three sites. Anyone who has stood in the middle of the immensely long and rather straggling Norse farmhouses at Jarlshof, the oldest of which measures an amazing 21.3m in length (see fig. 44) is in no doubt that they are in the presence of a very different cultural tradition from anything excavated in the Northern Isles from an earlier period. The conjunction of the two different types of building tradition is seen in dramatic juxtaposition at the Braaid, Marown, in the Isle of Man, where long rectangular houses of apparent Norse style are found close to the remains of a circular dwelling, which is presumed to be of native Celtic construction (see fig. 45).[123] It may be possible to see slightly varying types of house structure among the Picts, the circular and the axial, the latter of which is tending towards the sub-rectangular;[124] but these buildings and the techniques of roofing required are still quite distinct from the Norse longhouses which succeeded them (see fig. 46). Apart from the house plan, there are major differences in construction technique; the pre-Norse houses have a distinctive use of horizontal masonry and upright slabs[125] whereas the walls of Norse houses are constructed of horizontal slabs alone, sometimes in association with turf facing. The cells of the figure-of-eight houses may have had stone corbelled roofs; Norse houses are usually considered to have had turf roofs supported by a double row of wooden posts.[126]

Figure 44. The interior of Norse House I at Jarlshof (photographs: author).
Looking towards the dwelling end (*a*) from near the original east gable wall, the later cross-walls can be seen dividing the ninth-century hall-house up into separate rooms. In (*b*) the view is towards the east and with the later extension (see fig. 46b) which probably served as a byre (although cattle stalls are missing, as is a central drain). The centre hearth lay between and just beyond the two side-benches.

A

B

Figure 45. Aerial view of the settlement site at Braaid, Isle of Man (photograph by courtesy of The Manx Museum and National Trust).

A round-house of apparent Celtic type lies close to two rectangular structures, the left one of which, with its bowed walls, may have been a dwelling-house and the right one a byre. These latter are in the Norse tradition of rectangular building but of exceptional size, particularly in view of the upland location. Excavation produced little dating evidence.

The rooms of the Pictish houses are divided by slab-lined piers reminiscent of the older traditions in aisled roundhouses or wheelhouses;[127] this technique is certainly not used in recognized Norse house-forms. There is nothing here to indicate any direct influence from the native building styles on Norse houses. The suggestion that lateral benches may have been adopted by the Norse from native design has not yet been fully explored.[128] In the light of present evidence it would appear that the Norse settlers in the Northern and Western Isles brought their own building style with them, and there is no reason to think that they were influenced by the native house-building tradition in any way. If surviving natives continued to live in their own style of houses these are unlikely to be found on the high-status and prestigious sites which have been subjected to archaeological investigation.

In the coastal parts of western Norway where the immigrants came from stone was – and still is – used as a building material, although excavations have shown that this was in conjunction with wood-lined walls in houses of the Viking and pre-Viking period.[129] The settlers would certainly have been quite familiar with stone construction, but it is probable that they continued to use wood in the building of their houses in the colonies. Acquiring the raw material can have been no great problem; it was available on the mainland of Scotland and could also have been brought from Norway by the emigrants. The acquisition of wood in the equally treeless Faroe Islands has never prevented the continuation of the tradition of building in wood there, in strong contrast to post-medieval development in the Scottish Isles. It is now recognized in Faroe that rows of stones just within the long walls of Norse houses are

Figure 46. Plans of (*a*) the last Pictish house at Buckquoy, Orkney (House 4, eighth-century) and (*b*) the earliest Norse house at Jarlshof, Shetland (House I, period I = early ninth century) (after A. Ritchie, 'Excavation of Pictish and Viking age farm-steads at Buckquoy, Orkney', *PSAS*, cviii, 1976–7, fig. 27, and J.R.C. Hamilton, *Excavations at Jarlshof*, 1956, fig. 52).

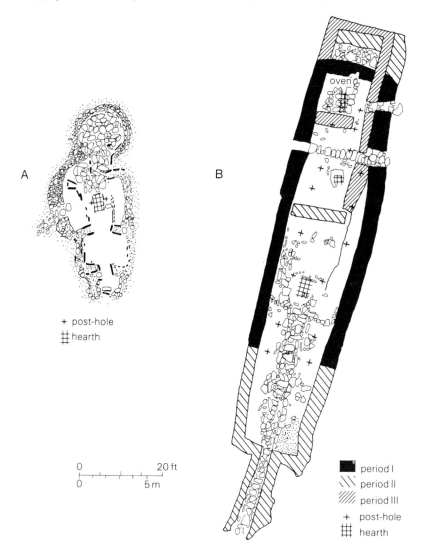

A

B

+ post-hole
╫ hearth

0   20 ft
0   5 m

■ period I
╲╲ period II
▨ period III
+ post-hole
╫ hearth

probably sills for wooden panelling which lined the walls; a later development was to rest the roof timbers on this wall panelling and thus do away with the need for inconvenient timber uprights in the centre of the house.[130] It is time that Norse houses in Scotland were re-examined with the possibility in mind that more wood may have been used in their construction than has been realized. The sandy conditions prevailing on most Norse sites yet excavated in

Figure 47. Wooden floor in Norse house at the Biggins, Papa Stour, Shetland; 60cm scale (photograph: author).

Although such a floor is highly unusual in Norse archaeology in Scotland, this survival shows that wood was a material which could be used by the Norse settlers in the Northern Isles for sophisticated furnishing and house construction in the traditional Scandinavian way.

Scotland leave little if any traces of wooden structures, and wooden artefacts have rarely survived. Where anaerobic conditions do occur as at the Biggins in Papa Stour, Shetland, wood can be found, and a wooden floor dating from the late tenth or early eleventh century has been uncovered (fig. 47).[131] It is probable that the limited quality of wood available to the pre-Norse population in the islands had dictated the length of the roof-ridge in their houses (4m over the main living-hall at Buckquoy).[132] Because the Norse had access to far stronger and straighter timbers which they could bring with them, they were able to construct houses of greater length. It seems likely that, in house construction at least, the Norse would be able to continue building in styles that were traditional to them.

This view is reinforced by comparison with houses excavated in the other Norse colonies in the North Atlantic where there was no native population to exercise any influence on the Norse settlers or their building styles. Houses of the Viking period in Faroe range from 14m to 20m in length and from 4.5m to about 6m in width.[133] These particular examples have bowed sides which in Scandinavia are considered a diagnostic feature of early Norse houses;[134] they can also be recognized both in the early houses on the upper slope of the Brough of Birsay (see fig. 48) and the wide curving walls of the boat-shaped hall at the Braaid (Isle of Man) (see fig. 45).[135] The earliest sites in Iceland are remarkably similar,[136] although in the ensuing centuries the Icelandic house was to develop several distinctive features which were an adaptation to the climatic conditions. The early Norse colonial houses in Faroe and Iceland were not long-houses, in that they did not have the animals housed under the same roof

Figure 48. Early Norse house on the upper slope, Brough of Birsay, Orkney (photograph: author).
The rounded ends and slightly bowed sides are typical of an early style of Norse house-plan in the settlements, sometimes called 'boat-shaped'.

as the human population.[137] Nor did the first house at Jarlshof, and it is not clear how soon the byre was added on at one end.[138] These earliest colonial houses consisted therefore of a main open living area, with a long-hearth (*langeldr*) in the middle, and, in the case of House I at Jarlshof, a cooking area in the *eldhus* (kitchen) end possibly separated from the living area by a partition wall (see fig. 46b).[139] Along both side walls can normally be found traces of the low benches which were used to sleep on and where tables may have been set for eating. This undivided dwelling-house was called the *skali* (= hall) and it appears to have been built throughout the Norse world for several centuries – even though it was not particularly suited to north Atlantic climatic conditions, which suggests that it held a strongly symbolic significance for the Viking emigrants.[140] Only after the end of our period did the partitioning of the *skali* take place along with the construction of a new type of timbered living-room, the *stofa*.[141] In all these developments, houses of the Norse period so far excavated in the Northern Isles give the impression of being in the mainstream of a cultural tradition which was transplanted in all the North Atlantic colonies settled by the Vikings.

Artefacts and the question of integration

If the evidence so far discussed suggests a clean sweep when the Vikings came to the Scottish Isles, recent studies of small finds from excavations at Birsay point in rather a different direction; that is, of some continuity of native material culture into Norse archaeological levels. Bone pins and combs of a type found in pre-Norse Pictish house sites have also been recovered from the middle Norse farmstead at Buckquoy, from which evidence the excavator has drawn the conclusion that 'there can be no doubt that some form of social integration between Pict and Norseman existed at least in the ninth century and probably into the tenth'.[142] Similarly, finds of Pictish-style bone objects and pottery from the nearby Brough of Birsay show that 'elements of native culture still persisted locally' into the early Norse period.[143] The settlement mound of Saevar Howe, also on Birsay Bay, gives evidence of Pictish occupation yielding to Norse, with a hint of overlap in the use of bone pins, which again suggested to the excavator 'a certain degree of integration'.[144] This evidence raises the possibility of an entirely different interpretation of Norse settlement involving significant mingling with the Pictish population in the Northern Isles. By contrast, at the site of Udal in North Uist, there are big differences between the Norse and the pre-Norse levels, in metalwork, in the

Figure 49. Examples of ring-headed bronze pins found in different parts of Scandinavian Scotland (1–5 reproduced by kind permission from T. Fanning, 'Some aspects of the bronze ringed pin in Scotland', in *From the Stone Age to the 'Forty-Five*, ed. A. O'Connor and D.V. Clarke, John Donald, 1983; 6 from A. Ritchie, 'Excavations of Pictish and Viking age farm-steads at Buckquoy, Orkney', *PSAS*, cviii, 1976–7).
 This Celtic type of dress-pin was adopted by the Norse and transferred to all their settlements in the North Atlantic, and variants were developed in Scandinavia.

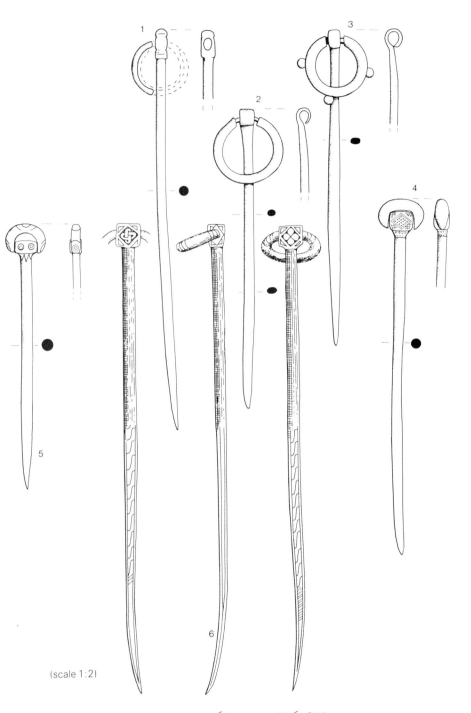

(scale 1:2)

1 spiral-ringed, baluster-headed pin, Á Cheardach Mhór, S.Uist
2 plain-ringed, loop-headed pin, Ballinaby, Islay
3 knob-ringed pin, Carn-nan-Bharraich, Oronsay, Argyll
4 kidney-ringed pin, Boreray, Harris
5 stirrup-ringed pin, Jarlshof, Shetland
6 ring-pin (3 views) from Buckquoy, Orkney

production of combs and in the making of pottery.[145] Some degree of native survival in an important corner of the Orkney Mainland is suggested; but what sort of social integration does the continued use of bone pins and combs imply?

There is no doubt whatsoever that the incoming Norse were inclined to adopt Celtic taste in jewellery and personal adornment. It has already been noted that the Norse women took over Celtic-style brooches. Another remarkable feature of many Norse sites and graves in the North Atlantic is the widespread occurrence of a Celtic type of ring-headed bronze pin (see fig. 49). This may have been adopted during the tenth century, and one of the earliest datable examples is from the tenth-century grave at Buckquoy.[146] Recent discussion of the magnificent silver 'thistle brooches' suggests that their origin was in an Irish prototype, although the style was elaborated by Norse settlers somewhere in the west before being transmitted back to Norway and copied there.[147] There was much in native Celtic ornament which the Norse men and women evidently admired and were ready to adopt. Although some of the finer examples of jewellery were probably made in Irish workshops and disseminated through trade, there may also have been more local centres of production in the Northern and Western Isles, where native craftsmen continued to work under Norse control and patronage producing objects like the bone pins and combs found in Norse levels at the sites in Birsay.

It is clear from excavations on the Brough that the Norse were acquiring goods from a variety of sources, so there would be no reason why bone pins and combs manufactured by neighbouring communities – within Orkney or further afield across the Pentland Firth – should not be among them.[148] These finds provide no evidence, however, that Picts were still living *in situ*, and the cessation of any bronze working on the Brough suggests that they were not. The house remains of indisputable Norse form are the strongest material evidence for the change of population in these localities, and any surviving Picts were probably living on the fringes of society both metaphorically and physically. Archaeology as yet provides no indication of their status in social circumstances where other evidence suggests that the incomers were politically dominant.[149]

Moreover, at Skaill, the overall impression from excavations is that 'the coming of the Vikings caused in some respects a regression in material culture which lasted for the best part of 200 years'.[150] This seems surprising, for the site is likely to have been the home of Thorkell *Fóstri*, Earl Thorfinn's close follower, and a most favoured and desirable settlement area. But Skaill has not yet produced an early Norse house of any size or wealth. The structural remains of the Pictish period, the products of their native potters, and the bronze pins of their metalworkers suggest a developed and more refined economy than that which evidently succeeded it. The lack of continuity in such traditions and the subsequent decline in material culture seems also to be reflected at Pool in Sanday, currently under excavation.[151] We are not being presented with consistent evidence that the flourishing native culture survived to influence the incomers in any significant way. Conclusions about 'considerable integration' between Norse and native therefore seem inappropriate in the present circumstances of archaeological knowledge.[152]

ECONOMY OF THE NORSE SETTLEMENTS

If ethnic continuity is in doubt in the Northern Isles, what of the economy? Did the Vikings bring new ways of making a living, new methods of farming to these islands? Did they have to adapt their traditional way of life to new colonial circumstances? A particular value of the growing number of excavations which have taken place in the Northern Isles in recent years has been in the expansion of information concerning the economic basis of Norse settlement and environmental economy. Prior to these, next to nothing was known about the diet or the husbandry practised by the Viking settlers. Knowledge of these aspects has increased greatly and will go on increasing as scientific methods of analysis become more sophisticated and methods of information retrieval more reliable.

Location and development

The majority of Norse settlements were maritime, and the sea has certainly exercised a dominating influence on their history and economy.[153] Of all the favourability factors listed in attempts to construct a hypothetical model for a typical Norse settlement, access to the sea by a suitable harbour or sheltered beaching ground has been considered of prime importance.[154] However, in the areas where such surveys have been carried out – Shetland/Faroe and different locations in the Hebrides – there is very little farming land which is *not* close to the sea. The Orkney landscape presents a rather different picture and the model here may not be exactly the same.[155] The Huseby site in Birsay, for instance, which was probably an early earldom administrative farm, was situated on the shore of an inland loch a few miles from the sea.[156] Even in Shetland, the most important administrative site in the Norse period was at Tingwall, also on an inland loch a few miles from the sea, and in a limestone valley which is one of the best farming areas in Shetland. Both these locations must have been valued because of the fertility of the land, with immediate access to the sea being apparently of secondary importance. Easily tilled, well-drained soil with potential for grain cultivation was therefore the prime requirement for primary settlement. An adjacent grazing area, an adequate supply of fresh water, abundant fuel and building material were naturally also important. Locations with these requirements had also been valued by the previous inhabitants of the islands: this suggests that conflict between the two peoples would have been inevitable and theories of amiable co-existence or the avoidance of native sites by the incoming Norse are hard to maintain.[157]

The settlement landscape as seen today in the Northern and Western Isles has in some places been completely altered by dramatic growth in population and the reorganization of the farming communities.[158] Nonetheless, the high proportion of crofts and farms which have Norse names in the Northern Isles and the Outer Hebrides suggests that they were established in the Viking (or late Norse) period. In Shetland, it may be possible to recognize the original Norse settlements from the areas of common grazing known today as 'scattalds'.[159] By the time of historical record, these areas were shared by several farms which all paid tax or 'scat' together, but the scattald is given the name of one of the farms – usually the most important, and presumably the primary Norse farm.[160] Over the centuries that farm had most probably grown into a clustered settlement and separate new farms had been founded within the original cultivable area. These would be given one of the secondary names such as -*bólstaðr*, -*setr/saetr*, -*land* or -*gardr*, already discussed (see fig. 50).[161] These units themselves could subdivide and the resulting new farms were often given -*hús* (=house) names with directional prefixes: North-/South-; Inner-/Outer-; Upper-/Lower-. The whole settlement unit (township or scattald) would then be a legal and economic entity, taxed together and sharing privileges such as rights to common grazing, to use of seaweed from the foreshore, to collection of sea-birds and their eggs from the cliffs, to digging of fuel from the peat-banks, and to use of the driftwood found in the bays and the voes.[162] The scattalds relate closely to the ounceland divisions, suggesting that they are as old, if not older, than the imposition of a taxation system which probably dates to the early centuries of the earldom.

The way in which an original farm expanded can be traced archaeologically

Figure 50. Schematic plan of Orkney or Shetland township.

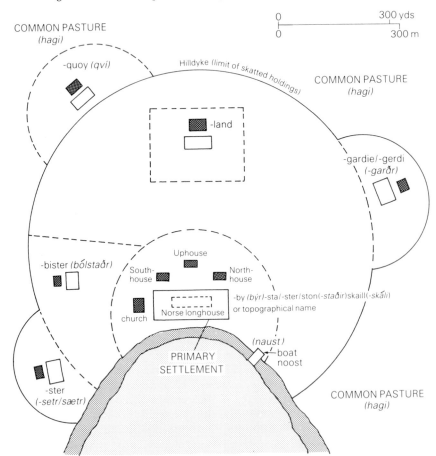

at Jarlshof where a second house had been built by the mid-ninth century, and a third one in the tenth century.[163] This is no more than the normal growth of a family unit would demand and Jarlshof need not be regarded as 'atypical' in its development.[164] Most of the other sites excavated in the Northern Isles have been unsuccessful settlements in that they have been abandoned at an earlier or later date (and for that reason could more easily be excavated). Underhoull never grew larger than the single farmstead which has been excavated, and it is likely that in the eleventh century the inhabitants moved to a new farm nearer the shore.[165] Successful settlements could eventually grow into nucleated villages, known in many places in Orkney and Shetland today as 'Biggins', a name probably the same as the Faroese *bygð* (with definite article *bygðin* = the village).[166] Such places are still the centres of settlement today in the wider unit called a township and therefore seldom available for excavation. Settlement studies pursued in Orkney and Shetland[167] have helped to elucidate the development of the township from the primary Norse farm; but in the Western Isles, research lags far behind, so that we cannot yet fully understand the early medieval basis to the later settlement pattern.[168]

Farming and other means of subsistence

The Norse settlements around the coasts and islands of Scandinavian Scotland were farming communities, although throughout the period with which we are concerned it is likely that raiding was also 'an essential feature of the economy'.[169] A site like Jarlshof gives clear evidence of an economy that was based on agricultural activity. The byres, for instance, are an important feature of the building layout. Recent archaeological investigation of Norse sites in Orkney has produced bone and plant material confirming that the farming was both arable and pastoral. Barley and oats were the main cereals, but the proportion of arable to pastoral cultivation varied widely throughout the area.[170] Examination of the bone material from Buckquoy has shown that there was little difference between the stock raised – and eaten – in the Pictish and Norse periods. The proportion throughout the occupation of the site was about 50 per cent cattle, 30 per cent sheep and 20 per cent pig. Fish was not a dominant element in the diet, and although apparently more important as a source of food to the Norse than to the Picts at Buckquoy, no difference existed at the site of Saevar Howe in the same locality.[171] In the less fertile parts of the Northern and Western Isles fish and shellfish must have been a very important food resource, and there is some evidence to suggest that fish became more important at Jarlshof and Underhoull in the period after the initial settlement phase, perhaps as population increased.[172] The Northern Isles are unlikely to have supported many herds of deer or boar for hunting, and the saga tells us very clearly that 'The earls used to go over to Caithness every summer, hunting red deer and reindeer in the woods there'.[173] In the Hebrides, the island of Jura (*dýr-a* = Deer Island) was obviously so named for its hunting potential.[174] At Buckquoy the hunting of mammals 'played little part in the economy',[175] but the Norse farmers here may not have been of the social strata to join in comital hunting expeditions. They did, however, hunt wild sea-birds, a feature of the economy of all the Atlantic islands until very recently,[176] as it is still in the Faroe Islands. For an illuminating glimpse of the traditional economy of the more pastoral parts of the Atlantic islands one need only visit the Faroe Islands, where so much of the life of the people is still devoted to the traditional methods of farming and food-collecting – including the slaughter of the whale – in contrast to the Scottish islands where the economy of the Norse settlement has been smothered under centuries of landlord improvement.

These Norse farms were basically self-sufficient units. Later evidence tells us that they produced a surplus of natural products: these were malt and butter in Orkney but in Shetland taxes were paid in fish oil, butter and cloth ('wadmel'). Evidence of weaving on all excavated sites and weaving tools found in some women's graves show the importance of woollen products in the economy. Spindle-whorls and loom-weights are found in quantity on house sites, although the wooden parts of the upright loom which would have been used have not survived. Linen was also certainly woven, for seeds of cultivated flax have been found recently at sites in Orkney and Lewis,[177] confirming that the smooth, domed glass objects found in Norse women's graves and known as linen-smoothers must have been used for finishing off the cloth.[178]

In one respect Shetland produced a marketable natural product which the wealthier Orkney islands did not possess: soapstone or steatite, the soft rock which can be worked as a building stone but which was also made into utensils by the Norse in all their Atlantic colonies. Evidence of intensive quarrying near Cunningsburgh shows that this site was an important production centre of soapstone artefacts, as were several other places in the Shetland islands.[179] It is highly probable that such a valuable commodity would be exported from Shetland, especially when steatite outcrops are rather few in the rest of Britain. Soapstone was the basic raw material for the manufacture of household goods such as cooking-pots, baking-plates, oil-lamps, spindle-whorls, gaming-pieces, fishing and loom-weights (see fig. 51). It withstood heating on the fire and therefore made the production of pottery less important to these northern Norse communities. Although the finds assemblage from Jarlshof and other sites suggests that steatite fulfilled the need for cooking vessels in the early centuries of occupation, some Norse sites *were* using pottery of a very crude kind.[180] Soapstone vessels were evidently in demand in other parts of the Norse world, for pieces have been found at York and Dublin,[181] but whether made from Shetland or Norwegian steatite has not yet been determined.

Evidence for any metal-working or smelting at any of the excavated Norse sites is very slight and in no way compares with the remains of a large bronze-casting workshop found in the Pictish levels on the Brough of Birsay.[182] This apparent absence of metal-working may, however, be a misleading impression, for the silver ring-money discussed above (pp. 133–4) is thought to have been manufactured somewhere in the Norse settlements of Scotland. An industrial site, probably dating from the Norse period, has been recorded near the earldom residence at Orphir on the south coast of the Orkney Mainland.[183]

In most of the examples yet discussed, the Norse were simply exploiting the natural wealth of the land which they were colonizing. It is hardly surprising if they carried on the economy of the previous population for they, too, utilized what resources were available to them. In one major respect only did the islands differ from the Norse homelands in western Norway. The lack of timber, even if it did not noticeably affect their house-building techniques,

Figure 51. Examples of steatite (soapstone) domestic objects found in Norse levels at Jarlshof, Shetland (Royal Commission on Ancient Monuments, Scotland; Crown Copyright reserved).
   Handled vessel on left: diameter of bowl 20cm; scoop or ladle on right: diameter of bowl 7cm; hanging lamp 19 × 11.4cm.

must have affected their method of heating their houses and cooking their food, for they cannot have had sufficient wood available to use freely as fuel. However, there was an alternative in the peat mosses of the Northern and Western Isles of Scotland. Here the Norsemen may have had to learn from the natives the method of cutting and drying peat for fuel. Some folk-memory of this process might be supposed to lie behind the nickname 'Torf-Einar' ('Peat-Einar') by which the youngest son of Earl Rognvald is known in *Jarls' Saga*. He is said to have been the first man to learn how to cut turf from the bogs for fuel – at Torfness in Scotland.[184] This attempt to explain the earl's nickname by associating it with the supposed eponym, Torfness, is doubtless entirely fictional. The art of cutting peat must have been learnt by the Norse before Torf-Einar's rule in the late ninth century, for the need for fuel existed from the earliest days of settlement. However, the saga writer may well have heard that the earliest Norsemen in Orkney had to learn how to cut peat.

   It seems possible that this change of fuel may have dictated a change in the style of cooking, which is reflected in the different types of hearth used in the colonial houses. The long-fire (ON *langeldr*) was replaced by a shorter hearth which was perhaps more suited to the burning of mounds of peat turves rather than pieces of wood. Another type of hearth, a square stone-lined pit, was also constructed, although less often, the only examples in Scotland so far being one found in the earliest levels of the Norse house at The Biggins, Papa Stour, Shetland,[185] and a square sunk hearth in Room VI of the early Norse building on the Brough of Birsay (fig. 52).[186] An oblong paved box in House I at Jarlshof was more clearly used as an oven (fig. 53).[187] These changes may be evidence of adaptations to the lack of wood available in the islands and the need to conserve heat more carefully in the cooking process. However, much remains to be learnt about this and related aspects of the Norse domestic economy.

Figure 52. Paved room (Room VI) in lower Norse horizon, Brough of Birsay, Orkney (photograph: author).

The quality of the paving, walling, bench structures and covered drains or flue (visible in front of bench on further side), together with the sunken hearth, mark this fragment of a building as exceptional in Norse archaeology. Unfortunately the erosion to which this site has been subject (note flagstones on beach in background, some 7m below) means that the function and purpose of this room may never be fully understood.

Figure 53. Fireplace in Norse House I, Jarlshof (photograph: author).

This is of a distinctive type, different from the usual open Norse hearth and known Pictish examples. The long hearth with large stones down each side at the front of the picture was probably used for heating stones which were then transferred to the oven at the back, which measures 78.7cm × 58.3cm × 38.1cm deep. Food, wrapped in a moisturizing material (hay or seaweed) would be baked among the stones.

SECULAR STRUCTURES ON THE BROUGH OF BIRSAY

The concentration of excavations in particular localities of Orkney is beginning to demonstrate that the settlement pattern in densely settled areas in the
Norse period was exceedingly complex. In Birsay, where the Birsay Bay project
has focussed on several sites (see fig. 54),[188] as well as in the Bay of Skaill,[189]
excavation has shown that the location of individual homesteads and farms
has been constantly changing in response to growing population numbers and
other social factors, as well as possible geographical ones. An understanding of
these developments requires a multi-disciplinary approach with the interpretation of farm-name sequences[190] as well as knowledge of the social and
political background.

In Birsay, this last element can never be forgotten. Somewhere in the locality
lived the earls of Orkney from at least the mid-eleventh century[191] and very
probably from the foundation of the earldom in the late-ninth century.

Figure 54. Excavated archaeological sites on the Bay of Birsay (after C.D.
Morris, 'The Vikings in the British Isles', in *The Vikings*, ed. R.T. Farrell,
Phillimore, 1982, fig. 6).

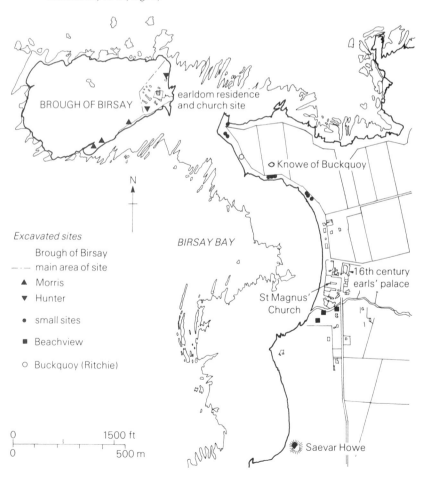

Although we have no specific indication from the historical sources as to the exact location of Earl Thorfinn's residence in Birsay – the name as given in *Jarls' Saga (Birgisheradᵗ)* covers the two parishes of Birsay and Harray (*heradᵗ*) – it is most likely to have been near to the only coastal section of these parishes, on the good lands around Birsay Bay. The remains of high-status buildings dated to the eleventh century uncovered on the tidal island called the Brough of Birsay were identified by one of the excavators as Earl Sigurd's and Earl Thorfinn's Halls (see fig. 55).[192] The location of an immediately adjacent ruined church gave this identification some substance, for this was interpreted as the church which Earl Thorfinn built for the bishop whom he installed in his earldom.[193] The secular buildings must indeed have been the residence of powerful and wealthy Norse chieftains, for they display a degree of sophistication unmatched by any other houses excavated in the Norse settlements. Although incomplete, they contrast well with the simpler Norse houses of more traditional construction – with bowed walls and side benches – which lie on the upper slope (fig. 48).[194] If indeed the earls did settle here they were probably following the example of their Pictish predecessors, for the Brough was an important pre-Norse settlement and not unlikely to have been the seat of a military leader such as the one depicted on the carved symbol stone which was found, broken, in the graveyard.[195] The truncated remains of some of the large Norse houses recently excavated at the north-east cliff edge seem to relate closely to the site of previous native structures, which had however been dismantled.[196]

Unfortunately the whole of the secular complex of buildings east of the church has been drastically truncated by marine erosion (see fig. 70), although enough remains for the visitor to be able to appreciate the scale and quality of the building and the architectural conception of the whole.[197] The main focus of interest is Room VI, which has walls of carefully cut stones and a well-paved floor (an unusual feature in Norse houses) around a large central fire-pit (fig. 52). A stone dais or bench raised above the floor is set round the walls, along two sides of which run a channel connected with a pit outside the room. This has been variously interpreted as drains leading into a sump or heating ducts leading from a fire-pit.[198] A complex and sophisticated series of lined and covered drains percolate across the paved court outside. We certainly have here a fragment of some domestic living quarters and, if the ducts can be shown to be part of a heating system, Room VI may even be the remains of a bath-house, although that identification was reserved by the excavator for the strange Room VII, built into an earlier dwelling, and divided into compartments by upright slabs.[199] Bath-houses, or saunas, are a well-known feature of Scandinavian societies, and their existence in Norse times is attested by many saga references.[200] Recognition of such structures on the ground is much more difficult, although their existence has been postulated – not without controversy – at Freswick, Jarlshof, and more recently, at Skaill.[201] The stone-covered benches uncovered at Skaill and Birsay, the former with hollow interior filled with peat ash and the latter beside a possible flue structure, suggest a similar function: this can hardly be connected with a normal central heating system for the benches at Birsay surrounding the large fire pit (1.22m × 1.07m) are only a metre in front of it.

Although inadequately described in print by the excavators and the layout of

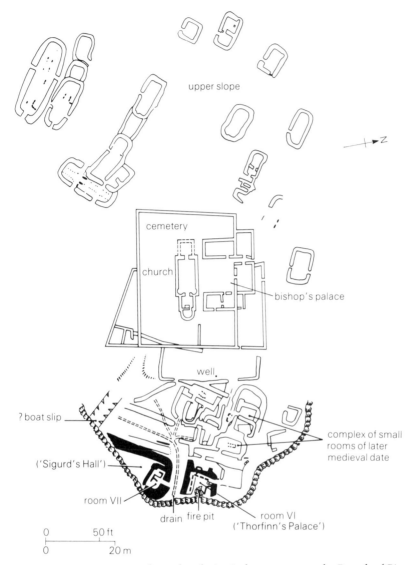

upper slope

cemetery

church

bishop's palace

well

? boat slip

complex of small
rooms of later
medieval date

('Sigurd's Hall')

room VII

drain fire pit

room VI
('Thorfinn's Palace')

0   50 ft
0   20 m

Figure 55. Norse secular and ecclesiastical structures on the Brough of Birsay
(after J. Hunter and C.D. Morris, 'Recent excavations at the Brough of Birsay'
Eighth Viking Congress, 1981, fig. 2).

the buildings imperfectly understood, the impression gained of the structures
that remain on the Brough of Birsay is of an establishment which far exceeds
any other Norse site in complexity and elaboration. The size of the long hall
('Sigurd's Hall'), the skilful masonry, the sophistication of the heating and
drainage systems, the paved courts or 'passages', all expose dramatically to
view a fragment of the domestic circumstances of the wealthiest section of the

Norse community in the Scottish Isles. When interpreting these remains it has to be remembered that the likely builders were widely-travelled men, who had contacts with rich and cultured courts in northern Europe, with the kings of Norway and Scotland and, in Earl Thorfinn's case, with the Anglo-Danish kings in England and Denmark, and the imperial and papal courts. It would be hardly surprising if such contacts influenced their own domestic circumstances. We have, of course, no concept of the decoration or furnishings which would have adorned their residential quarters, although the magnificent equipment found in the Norwegian ship burials as well as the later saga descriptions can give us a most vivid comparison of the standards of luxury enjoyed by the wealthiest section of Norwegian society. It can hardly be imagined that the circumstances of the powerful earls of Orkney would have been much poorer. What has already been uncovered by excavation shows that the social and economic situation in Birsay is likely to be untypical of the majority of Norse settlements in Scotland. Elsewhere in the Northern Isles, we do not find Norse communities with a similar degree of sophistication in their domestic circumstances. Society in the locality of Birsay was dominated by the most powerful dynasty of all the Norse families in the west and without a doubt the area would have been economically directed and organized for the maintainance and support of the earls and their followers.

6 The Archaeological Framework: Part 2 Conversion and the Organization of Christianity

The Vikings came to a Christian country. The monks and missionaries of the Celtic church had spread their religion to the Northern and Western Isles during the sixth and seventh centuries.[1] Although Iona's influence dominated the Hebrides, it was only one of several Irish monastic centres which are known about from the many carved stones at church sites in the islands. Despite the complete absence of historical references to similar monastic centres in the Northern Isles and the north Scottish mainland, surviving archaeological material points towards recognizable places of Christian worship, particularly in Shetland, where the carved stones from both Papil and St Ninian's Isle form a notable collection: the remains of five corner-post shrines from these two sites have been described as a 'remarkable assemblage of ecclesiastical stone monuments, unparalleled in either Britain or Ireland'.[2] In the eighth century, influence from Northumbria and the Pictish church (and thus Roman Christianity) was also probably relevant in the north.

The Viking raids on these centres of wealth all round the British and Irish coasts, and the Norse settlements along the Scottish coasts where these communities were founded – often in ideal locations for the sea-faring raiders – must have meant the collapse of a Christian literary culture and the dispersal of an educated priesthood, even although Iona survived and probably continued to be a source of teaching and perhaps conversion. The Vikings brought new religious beliefs with them, manifested most clearly in their burial practices.

FROM PAGAN GODS TO CHRIST

Graves: pagan belief and custom

Religious beliefs are an important part of a people's distinctive culture. We have already seen that the pagan graves add a great deal to our knowledge of the Viking way of life. What can they tell us about the Viking way of death and the nature of pagan religious beliefs? It is clear that there must have been a strong belief in a life after death. Inhumation and cremation were both practised in Scandinavia, although the latter is extremely rare or else unrecognized in the colonies overseas.[3] Furnishing the dead with goods was a very important feature of the pagan ritual, and was presumably to equip for the afterlife; as these goods were weapons and tools in the case of a man, and domestic implements for a woman, this suggests that the life after death was supposed to be not very different from life on earth. There was, no doubt, also concern by the surviving members of the family that the dead should be seen off in fitting style, both for the purpose of keeping up appearances in front of the neighbours and to make sure that the dead would be in the best company in the next world.[4] There was also very probably a fear that the dishonoured dead might return to haunt the living.[5] Some sort of journey was apparently expected for the dead man or woman, and this seems to be the idea associated with the not uncommon practice of boat burial. None of the Scottish boat graves come anywhere near the magnificence of the famous ship graves of Norway;[6] indeed, often the only surviving traces of a possible vessel are numbers of rivets.[7] But in the whole corpus of known graves in Scotland and Man, a significant number may have included a boat; two most exciting boat graves have recently been excavated in the cemetery at Westness (Rousay).[8] The difficulties of replacing these vessels in the treeless islands off the north and west coast of Scotland sharpens one's appreciation of the importance this ritual must have had for these people, and what a significant symbol of their way of life the boat

Figure 56. Female burial with grave-goods from the cemetery at Westness, Rousay, Orkney; 1m scale (by kind permission of Dr Sigrid Kaland, University Museum, Bergen).

This cemetery, discovered after a richly equipped female grave was found in 1963 (see fig. 33) is composed of pagan graves, and burials without any grave-goods. The ninth-century burial illustrated is contained in an oval stone-lined grave, the stones perhaps serving the purpose of revetting the sides of the grave in the soft, sandy soil of the coastal locality. The skeleton was buried with legs bent, the skull shows signs of trepanation. A comb can be seen below the right arm and a sickle below the head. There were also spinning whorls and a bronze pennanular brooch by the right leg.

was. The dead were also provided with animals to accompany them, both horses and dogs, and at the well-excavated sites of Balladoole and Ballateare in the Isle of Man a cremated layer of bones of many different animals was recognized covering the graves, presumably the residue of a sacrificial offering to the dead man or the gods.[9] At these same sites examples of human sacrifices were also found; at Ballateare a wife or perhaps a female slave had been chosen to accompany her lord to the next world and had been executed by a slash to the skull.[10]

Traces of post-holes found on top of the mounds covering some of the burials in Man have shown that wooden or stone markers had been raised, doubtless to commemorate the dead. Stone surrounds to graves have sometimes been recorded, either rectangular or oval, and most notably in sandy sites of the Hebrides or Orkney (fig. 56).[11] The presence of prehistoric monuments in Scotland meant of course that the Norsemen could avail themselves of mounds and stones quite easily for marking out the graves of their dead. Although there is a lot of confusion in many of the old reports of excavations about the siting of burials in artificially created mounds[12] there is no doubt that in a great many cases the desire to create a prominent memorial for the dead was of paramount importance. This custom is probably to be regarded as integral to the staking out of a land claim by the first generation of settlers in a new colony, for the possession of family lands and the practice of ancestor-worship were closely related in pagan societies.[13] Once more the situation in the Isle of Man provides more than a hint of the social significance of these matters; in the parish of Jurby, six out of eight 'quarterland' farms have their own prominent burial mound 'as if each of the original land-takers had been laid to rest singly, with full pagan ritual, at or near the highest point of his own lands'.[14] Burial in undifferentiated graves in family groups must have sufficed for many communities: at the only pagan burial grounds really qualifying for the term cemetery, at Pierowall (Westray) and Westness (Rousay) in Orkney and at Reay in Caithness, the graves were all sited in a low-lying, coastal location.[15]

There was a wide range of burial practice; for example, in the orientation of the graves no general rule can be said to have been observed.[16] There is little direct evidence of the funeral ceremonies involved, although later literary sources give us a vivid picture of these occasions. Icelandic tradition remembered that on the death of Aud the Deep-Minded feasting continued for three days before she died and three days afterwards.[17] The cremated layer of animal bones on the Manx graves may have been connected with such funeral feasting. The excavation of the grave at Cronk Moar (Isle of Man), gives us further basic details: from the puparia of blow-flies found in the cloth in which the body was wrapped it can be estimated that interment did not take place until three weeks after death;[18] although the reasons which lay behind such a delay are not, of course, known.

Graves: Christian influences

The predominance of inhumation may have been a result of conformity to practices existing among the Christian population of the Scottish islands and mainland, as also may the use of stone-lined rectangular cists for pagan burials.[19] The richly furnished grave from Kiloran Bay, Colonsay, has a feature suggesting clear Christian influence. Two of the stone slabs surrounding the grave enclosure had scratched on them representations of a cross (see fig. 57).[20] In other respects this burial is similar to pagan burials in Norway, including the presence of a horse's skeleton which was buried with its master, as well as the boat of the Viking seafarer. But it is quite evident that the individual, or his family or following, had been influenced by Christian beliefs to the extent that they felt impelled to add the symbol of Christianity amidst the pagan ritual. This is a most important piece of evidence for a very early stage in the conversion process; a tentative adding of the Christian cross by peoples who nonetheless were still burying their dead in the customary way. There is some

Figure 57. Stone slabs with crosses from the richly equipped grave at Kiloran Bay, Colonsay, South Hebrides; see fig. 38 (Royal Museum of Scotland).
Two of the stone slabs surrounding the ship burial, one at the east end and the other at the west, were marked with rough but clear representations of a cross. These would appear to be deliberate Christian emblems added to a pagan burial, and illustrate the mixed beliefs of the Hebridean warrior class of the ninth century.

rather uncertain dating evidence for this burial; Anglo-Saxon coins were found (after the excavation, but apparently having formed part of the original grave deposit) which may have been used as decoration for some time after their date of minting in the first half of the ninth century.[21] During the second half of the ninth century, the *Gall-Gaedhil* were active as a formidable fighting force in western Scotland and Ireland; perhaps the warrior buried in the Kiloran Bay grave was one of such a group, and if so, then the pagan and foreign element would appear to have been the dominant characteristic of the breed at that time. Of course the literary evidence of Ketil Flatneb's family, closely associated with the Hebrides at the same period, suggests that such people could also be deeply influenced by Christianity.[22]

Influence by Christianity and the rate of progress towards conversion is a very difficult thing indeed to monitor. The graves themselves are so disparate and difficult to date that only the very broadest generalizations about the progress of conversion of the Norse settlers to Christianity can be drawn from them (see below, p. 169).[23] The decline in the numbers of tenth-century pagan graves discovered can tell us only that pagan beliefs were changing, but not how, when and why the Christian religion was adopted. Pagan burials in Christian churchyards have been found in many parts of Scandinavian Britain, but what do they tell us? Certainly in the Isle of Man, so many of these finds have been made that a prolonged phase during which the pagan incomers half-adopted religious practices of the native Christians may be indicated (fig. 31).[24] This is generally how such finds are interpreted, but not all of the sites are known to have been existing Christian graveyards; so it is possible that pagan Norse cemeteries were later turned into Christian graveyards, ultimately becoming the sites of parish churches.[25] The most dramatic – and most puzzling – illustration of the rapid use of an existing Christian graveyard by pagan Norsemen is the excavated boat-grave at Balladoole in the Isle of Man which was placed on the top of long-cist Christian burials, destroying some of them in the process (fig. 58). How is this situation to be interpreted? The excavator thought it was an example of the 'slighting' of the Christian graves by pagans;[26] but it may be that the juxtaposition of the two was entirely co-incidental, and that the prominent site was regarded by the incomers as simply a suitable place for the burial of one of their number.[27] It seems unlikely that the destruction of the existing graves was a deliberate slight to the native population, but on the other hand it does suggest a total disregard for the recent dead, which might be thought uncharacteristic of superstitious pagans. They do not in this instance seem to have been seeking out a Christian cemetery for its religious associations. The recent excavation of pagan burials alongside Christian interments in a cemetery on St Patrick's Isle, Peel, Isle of Man, is giving us even more evidence of the mixed situation which existed in the island.[28]

There are no such dramatic examples known from Scotland; the only proven pagan burial yet found in a Christian churchyard is that from St Andrew's, Kirkcudbright.[29] This paucity of evidence is all the more surprising in a context in which the chances of such discoveries are favourable, for digging is a constant activity in graveyards. Although the axe found in a churchyard at Whiteness, Shetland,[30] has been interpreted as an example of a burial by Scandinavians who had accepted Christianity but who laid a weapon with the

Figure 58. Early Christian lintel grave overlain by the stone surround of a Norse boat burial at Balladoole, Isle of Man (photograph by courtesy of The Manx Museum and National Trust).

dead 'as a last gesture of respect to old pagan practices',[31] it is safer to regard it as no more than a stray find.

Christian survival

Having seen the problems that such archaeological evidence presents, it is important to ask what sort of Christian church was established in northern and western Scotland at the time of the Viking raids, and in what ways it might have influenced those raiders and settlers who came into contact with it.

The priests of the Celtic church must have been a powerful and well-established class in the native societies of the Scottish islands. We also have contemporary record of the amazing voyages of Irish hermits to uninhabited islands further north in the Atlantic. The Irishman Dicuil, writing at the Carolingian court c.825, says that after 100 years the hermits had abandoned their refuges in these islands because of the depredations of northern pirates.[32]

The Christian grave-stones found in the Faroes may date from this period and provide further evidence of the voyages of Celtic monks. Later historical evidence tells us that the Irish priests also reached Iceland, since the remains of Celtic priests' equipment were found by the Norsemen settled there.[33] In all these areas the Norsemen used the name *papar* when referring to these people, a name apparently derived by them from an Irish word for priest or hermit. The impact made on the early Norse raiders and settlers by these priests is demonstrated by the number of place-names which they applied incorporating the element 'papa' in northern and western Scotland – at least 27, with possible examples in Cumberland and the Isle of Man (see fig. 59).[34] It is noticeable that these names are concentrated in the areas of densest Norse settlement – Orkney, Shetland, Caithness and the northern Hebrides; they do not appear in Ross, Sutherland or the southern Hebrides. Traditions about the *papar* in Orkney (along with the Picts) as being an important part of the native population in the islands survived the Norse settlement and were still current in the late twelfth or thirteenth centuries (see below).

Some of the places incorporating this name, such as Papil (*Papabýl* = 'priests' dwellings') on West Burra, Shetland, were evidently important

Figure 59. Papar names in Scotland (after A. MacDonald, 'Papar' names in North and West Scotland, BAR 37, 1977).

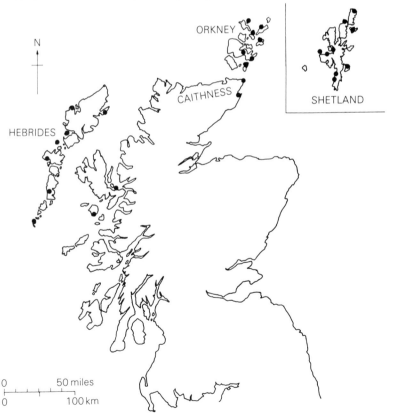

monastic centres from the early Christian sculpture which has been found there. One notable fact (commented on by the author of *Historia Norwegiae*) is the number of islands called Papay/Pabbay (*papar-øy* = priests' island) – eight in the Outer Hebrides alone. It is not clear what should be deduced from this nomenclature about the kind of priestly establishments which existed at these places or their survival. Because some of the islands are small and marginal it has been suggested that they were eremitical communities.[35] But what is marginal today has not always been so: many of these islands are exceedingly fertile and can support large populations. Both the Lewis and the Harris Pabbays were from time to time the residence of the MacLeod chiefs.[36] Papa Stour, Shetland, was the seat of powerful Norwegian officials in the Middle Ages and supported a population of several hundred in the nineteenth century.[37] It seems unlikely, therefore, that such islands were devoted entirely to the support of small numbers of hermits but probable that tribal-monastic communities would have served the needs of local secular society.[38] Certainly, the dominant place of the *papar* on these islands must have been forcibly impressed on the Norse for them to give a name derived directly from the priestly inhabitants, and for that name to become permanent. Moreover, the *papar* were remembered later (as recorded in the *Historia Norvegiae*) as having worn white robes and having books associated with them[39] which, if not a later antiquarian reconstruction, suggests that these figures survived the initial phase of raids and settlement. Can we deduce from this that the *papar* themselves remained in possession through the early Viking period? As far as archaeological evidence goes, it may be significant that no pagan graves have yet been found on any island or near any location bearing a *papar* name, while a study of the place-names of Papa Westray suggested to Marwick that the *papar* may have been left undisturbed, as he found no examples of early Norse settlement names on the island.[40] Such negative evidence may point towards an unexpected tolerance from the Vikings for the priests of the Christian religion.

Such tolerance might have allowed the persistence and transmission of Christian beliefs in some of the islands, and another feature which points in the direction of continuity of Christian tradition is the eventual re-use of some of the earlier church sites by the Norse when they had themselves adopted the Christian religion. In a few places, like St Ninian's Isle in Shetland, the twelfth-century ecclesiastical building has been proved by excavation to be located right on top of the early Christian church.[41] At the Brough of Birsay, Orkney, the Norse church was built in a location where there had also been an important early Christian site.[42] Excavation around the medieval church on the Brough of Deerness, East Mainland, Orkney, has not as yet produced positive evidence that it also is located on a pre-Norse ecclesiastical site as had been previously assumed.[43] But the Norse certainly did re-use some – perhaps important – former Christian church sites when they themselves built churches; what we cannot know for certain is whether the early churches survived and there had been continuous worship at these sites through the settlement period. Re-use of them does not necessarily mean that there had.[44] Memory of previous sites of Christian churches could persist through a pagan period as is seen in Iceland, where the farm-name Kirkjubaer commemorated either a former establishment of *papar* or the religion of the Christian settler,

Ketil the Foolish, even though the Celtic priests vanished and Christian beliefs disappeared for well over 100 years.[45]

Equally problematical are the church-dedications to early Celtic saints in parts of the Northern Isles, and especially in the Western Isles. Some of these do point in the direction of persistence of Christian traditions in certain areas, and that itself could suggest the survival of a Christian population. In the case of St Ninian on Shetland no such conclusion can be reached, since the form in which the name survives does not suggest that it is an ancient survival.[46] But St Triduana and St Boniface on – significantly – Papa Westray, and St Colme on the Brough of Birsay (probably to be associated with a Pictish saint of Buchan rather than the great Columba) were all early saints whose names are unlikely to have been invoked by the later Norse Christians without the stimulus of local tradition.[47] In the Western Isles the dedications are almost overwhelmingly Irish and stem from the early missionary phase of the church – Columba, Maelrubha, Bride, Moluag, and German in the Isle of Man. It seems unlikely, however, that all these medieval sites of churches and chapels were of pre-Norse origin, and their distribution in relation to Norse 'settlement areas' and their architectural similarity to early Norse chapels in the Northern Isles suggests that they should be related primarily to the era of post-conversion church-building by the Norse.[48] The Norse had no saints of their own until the eleventh century, and after conversion were likely therefore to adopt the locally-revered holy men. There are, however, dedications to St Olaf at Gress on Lewis and St Clement at Rodel on Harris, both popular saints among the Norwegians and Danes at home. They are further indications of the stronger Scandinavian imprint in the Outer Hebrides than in the Inner.

The situation in the Isle of Man is particularly interesting and there appears to be a relationship between chapel sites and land divisions similar to that in Orkney, in that most 'treens' have their own 'keeil' or chapel.[49] But whether these were oratories of the early Christian period taken over by the Norse or whether they were erected after the Norse had been converted has not yet been resolved.[50] In some places, as at Maughold, where there was an important early Christian centre, it can be assumed that the small chapels must have been associated with the Celtic organization. But this does not mean that such chapels are all of pre-Norse foundation. The conclusion that many of them 'although inspired by Celtic usage, were no less an integral part of Manx-Viking culture than . . . the cross-slabs with runes'[51] is still reasonable, but it is not improbable that when selecting sites for their chapels the Christian Norse would have chosen places known to have been venerated by an earlier Christian population.

The question of conversion

What does this evidence add up to? Can it help us to form a conclusion as to the manner and date of the conversion of the Norse when they settled in the Northern and Western Isles? The application of the Papa place-names may suggest some toleration on the part of the Vikings for the Celtic priests, but the evidence of early Christian dedications is very uncertain ground on which to draw any firm conclusions. The 'continuity of resort' to older sites of worship is perhaps what would be expected when pagan settlers eventually adopted the God of the previous population.[52] This rather intangible evidence may suggest the survival of strands of Christian belief and tradition which were probably thicker in some places than others. The Southern Hebrides were, of course, close to the influence emanating from the spiritual centre of Iona, which after a century of eclipse 'survived the Viking storm to become a shrine for Scottish Vikings of the late tenth and eleventh centuries'.[53] But even the powerhouse of Columban Christianity had seen its members scattered and its relics moved, before it regrouped its forces and, with a possibly greater emphasis on episcopal organization, made a come-back from the middle of the tenth century.[54]

Was there any such religious centre of Celtic Christianity in the Northern Isles – on the edge of the world of the Columban church and far removed from the Christian communities of both Ireland and southern Scotland? The impressive archaeological material at two early Christian sites in Shetland has already been mentioned. However, the total absence of any historical record of any monastic centre makes it doubtful whether the Celtic church in the Northern Isles had the organization, structure and headship which was necessary to organize any systematic programme of resistance to paganism, let alone a programme of conversion. This is not to say that the incoming Norse had an inbuilt hostile attitude to Christianity. The incorporation of the *papar* element in place-names suggests otherwise, and it is a common feature of most Viking settlements that they rapidly adopted the culture and religion of the societies that they settled amongst. But in Ireland, England and Normandy the Vikings were settling in close conjunction with societies organized with political and ecclesiastical structures which survived their arrival, and which were – at any rate in the case of Wessex and France – determined to convert these peoples at the earliest opportunity. In the Northern Isles, however, the most determined proponent of the assimilation theory would find it hard to argue that the ecclesiastical and political structures of the Pictish population survived to that degree, and we know of no Pictish Alfred near enough to Orkney to be able to insist on the baptism of the leader of the Norse invaders. The *papar* may have been left to continue their lives of worship for some while, but their communities would find it difficult to thrive in the new and very changed social conditions caused by the Norse settlement and, as in Iceland, they must eventually have dispersed leaving their distinctive possessions behind them for, according to the *Historia Norvegiae*, it was deduced 'from . . . the writings of their books abandoned there' (on an island called Papay) that they were 'Africans, adhering to Judaism'.[55]

Particularly in Orkney, the Norse leaders were members of a very powerful dynasty of jarls whose links with the home country and the kings of Norway remained strong enough throughout the tenth century to keep them in line with the religious practices of the home country. Their cultural contacts were not so much with Christianized Ireland as with pagan Norway, and not until the kings of Norway were converted would the earls of Orkney be likely to submit fully to the influence of Christianity. So the enforced conversion of Earl Sigurd by the newly-converted Olaf Triggvesson in 995 is, as has already been argued[56] likely to have been an important event in the islanders' change from pagan worship to the Christian religion.

Returning to the evidence of the pagan graves, we find that an increasing number are now being dated to the tenth century, which also suggests a more extended period of paganism than was considered likely a few years ago; then it was thought that there were very few tenth-century graves and that paganism was dying out by 900.[57] When the known grave-material from around the Bay of Birsay and the cemetery at Westness, Rousay, has been fully analysed it will be possible to build up a clearer picture of the extent of the pagan period. But it may be significant that two of the three single graves recently dated to the tenth century in Orkney were found at Buckquoy, close to the earls' supposed residence on the Brough of Birsay.[58] If the earls had been Christian during this period it is highly unlikely that such interments would have taken place right on the doorstep of the political centre of the earldom. These finds strengthen the conclusion that pagan practices were continuing in Orkney through the tenth century and only ceased when the political leader accepted the new religion. Of course, Christian influence must also have been at work among the population by that date, and the long-cist cemetery found at Saevar Howe, also on Birsay Bay, has been established as tenth-century – or possibly later.[59] If it is indeed a Norse Christian cemetery – and grave-finds were almost totally absent – then it is surprising (but perhaps significant) that it does not appear to have been an early Christian chapel site (despite the finding of a Celtic handbell), nor did it ever become a medieval ecclesiastical site.

All this new evidence comes, however, from Orkney; the numbers of pagan graves in Shetland are still only two in number, with an extraordinary lack of any proven male graves at all. Along with some stone sculpture which will be discussed next, this may suggest that Shetland was influenced rather earlier by Christianity than Orkney. Being far less immediately under the control of the earls – and in the early period perhaps entirely free of earldom control – there may have been a greater freedom of choice in the matter, resulting perhaps in more direct influence from the surviving Pictish population or ecclesiastics. Such an interpretation is entirely at variance with Wainwright's conviction that 'Christian influences were stronger in Orkney than in Shetland.'[60]

CARVED STONE MONUMENTS

Shetland

Evidence of a different kind may provide more tangible proof of the survival of a Christian population in Shetland into a period after Norse settlement had taken place. Such a conclusion has been based on sculptured crosses from Shetland for, unlike the corpus of Christian Pictish sculpture in Orkney which ceases at the end of the eighth century, carved stones apparently continued to be produced in Shetland after the historical date for Norse raids and settlement.[61] The most significant of these stones is from Bressay (fig. 60), sculptured in the style of earlier stones such as a one-sided cross slab from Papil in West Burra but with a late Pictish ogam inscription along the edges which appears to incorporate the Scandinavian word for 'daughter' as well as the Gaelic words for 'cross' (also adopted into the Scandinavian languages) and for 'son' (fig. 61).[62] The personal names do not relate to any known Scandinavian name-forms while the use of the Norse word for 'daughter' could suggest that

Figure 60 (far left and left). The Bressay Stone (Royal Museum of Scotland).
This cross-slab (height 1.20m) was found at a church site at Cullingsburgh, Bressay, an island off east Shetland: it has some similar features to stones found at Papil, Burra, an island off west Shetland (an important ecclesiastical centre in pre-Norse Shetland). The hooded clerics depicted on both faces of the Bressay Stone, holding croziers and with book satchels slung over their shoulders can be interpreted as representations of the *papar*: they were remembered in later Norse sources as having had books, bells and croziers associated with them (see p. 211 below).

Figure 61 (right and far right). Ogam inscription on both sides of the Bressay Stone (Royal Museum of Scotland).
From the bottom up, the inscription reads:
CRROSCC : NAHHTVVDDADDS :
DATTRR : ANN BENNISES :
MEQQDDRROANN
The Gaelic words 'cross' and 'mac' (= son of) can be recognized, while *dattr* is the Norse word for daughter. The other words are Pictish and untranslatable (perhaps personal names). Further evidence of a very mixed linguistic situation is seen in the placing of two dots between words (a practice evidently borrowed from Norse runic inscriptions) and doubled consonants, which are found in Irish ogams.

some surviving members of the native population had been sufficiently influenced by Scandinavian speech to adopt a Norse term into their language (rather than being a memorial to a converted Norse settler).[63] It certainly implies that *one* Christian stone sculptor had survived in Shetland and was continuing to practise his art and use his language.

The Bressay stone has been regarded as something of an oddity in the corpus of little-understood Pictish ogam inscriptions as a whole and the contemporaneity of carvings and inscriptions are not incontrovertible.[64] However, the most recent study of Christian sculpture in Shetland suggests that it does not stand alone but that there are other sculptured stones which can be dated well into the period of Norse raids and settlement.[65] This interpretation leads to the conclusion that some places continued to function as Christian centres where the Christian dead were buried and had monuments raised over them through the ninth and perhaps even into the tenth century. The art-forms on stones from these sites are interpreted as showing that contacts between Shetland and the Picts of eastern Scotland were maintained until the mid-ninth century when they were replaced by more far-reaching links with Iona and Anglo-Scandinavian Northumbria.[66] If this interpretation proves acceptable, a significant new element is added to the whole circumstances of the Norse impact on the Northern Isles. It suggests that the native population of Shetland must have survived to some degree and that they continued to practise their religion, at any rate in south and west Shetland, perhaps to the extent of influencing some of the pagan Norsemen who settled in Shetland in the ninth century. Without the immediate political direction which the earls certainly exercised in Orkney, it may have been easier for influence to be transmitted between surviving natives and Norse incomers; a situation which could help to explain the dearth of pagan graves throughout Shetland (except for the northernmost island of Unst).

Another dramatic piece of archaeological evidence has to be taken into consideration concerning the situation of the Celtic church in Shetland: the St Ninian's Isle treasure. This hoard of Pictish silver objects was discovered in a box buried in the chancel of the ruined church on St Ninian's Isle, apparently just below the floor level of an earlier church.[67] It has been dated to c.800, and like most hoards is likely to have been deposited because of disturbed political conditions, which meant that the owner did not survive to recover his possessions. The conclusion has always been that the Vikings were the cause of those disturbed conditions. But considering the well-known predilection of the Vikings for plundering churches it seems rather strange that a local landowner should consider taking his family valuables to a church for safe-keeping (for the treasure is generally accepted to have been secular property even though some of the objects appear to have been made for an ecclesiastical purpose).[68] The owner of the treasure himself cannot have survived. One is left wondering if the fear of an attack on his own house and lands was greater than any threat against the local church, which he regarded as a safe place in which to deposit his family treasure.

Pagan and Christian sculpture: Scotland

Evidence of the contact between native culture and new Scandinavian tradi-

tions from surviving stone monuments elsewhere in Scotland is scattered and
difficult to analyse; in total, however, there is a rich corpus of source material.
The production of any Christian carving in Orkney ceases, although some may
have been produced in Caithness, from one or two undistinguished examples.[69] The two areas of Scandinavian Scotland where a lively sculptural
tradition developed in the tenth and eleventh centuries are in the south-west
and in Man. In the former, the influence appears to come from Cumbria to the
south,[70] and the important Anglian stone-carving tradition of north-west
England forms one element of the mixed styles which developed. The links
would appear to have been sea-borne, and such links reach up the Clyde coast
to Govan, where there must have been an important monastic centre; the
surviving sculpture of this school shows influences from many directions,
including possibly a pagan one.[71]

The importance of sea-borne contacts – which, as stressed in chapter 1, are
all too easily forgotten or under-emphasized – are also reflected in the Scottish
distribution of the strange tombstones known as hogbacks. These house-
shaped tomb-covers with a curved roof-ridge appear to derive from a
Scandinavian longhouse shape, although there are several theories as to the
origin of this style of monumental carving.[72] But they quite clearly are
associated with Scandinavian areas of settlement in England, for the main
centres of production were in the northern Danelaw; they may have developed
in the early tenth century in Norwegian or Gaelic-Norse settlement areas of
north-west England and spread eastwards to the Tees valley and dales of north
Yorkshire.[73] It has been suggested that in origin they represent the warrior's
house in death, and the carving of warrior scenes on some of them certainly
supports the theory that they are to be associated with a pagan concept of the
afterlife.[74] Other depictions of pagan mythology on the earliest of them, even
though they are located in Christian churchyards, give further evidence of 'the
cultural interaction between Christian and pagan societies in tenth-century
Northumbria'.[75] The Scottish examples are mostly rather later in date and give
no evidence of pagan association but their distribution suggests a layer of
Anglo-Scandinavian influence in parts of the Lowlands which relates to the
Scandinavian place-names of south-east Scotland. They are concentrated
along the east coast between the Tweed and Brechin with an inland cluster on
the River Teviot, and there is a group associated with Govan on the west coast,
but none in the Hebrides or Man (see fig. 41). A late collection in Orkney and
Shetland testifies to links between the Northern Isles and south-east Scotland
in the period of church organization in the north in the eleventh and twelfth
centuries.[76] The two earliest Scottish examples, at Govan on the Clyde and on
the island of Inchcolm in the Firth of Forth (see fig. 62) (dated to the mid-tenth
century) have been seen as proof in stone of the theory that the Forth–Clyde
route was the main means of communication between the kingdoms of York
and Dublin. Their siting in Christian burial grounds may indeed point towards
their commissioning by 'local Scandinavian settlers rather than for vikings on
the move',[77] although if so this does not really prove that they are necessarily
on a trade route. The general inference can probably be drawn that these
monuments scattered along the coastal parts of south-east Scotland and the
Clyde testify to pockets of settlers who have been influenced by Scandinavian
communities further south, and who were probably of mixed origin. If they can

Figure 62. Hogback tombstone on the island of Inchcolm in the Firth of Forth (photographs: author).

This tombstone (length 161.5cm) is probably the earliest of its type in Scotland (mid-tenth century). It is located in a very Christian environment (*a*) and was at one time associated with a standing cross. It is closely linked to the northern English prototype with tegulated roof and inward-facing end-beasts with muzzles (much worn). In the centre of the west face can be seen the figure of a man with raised hands – or holding weapons (*b*); on the other side is a cross.

be linked up with the place-name evidence for Scandinavian-speaking communities in the Lothians, Berwickshire and Fife,[78] then they point to further Scandinavian imprint around the Forth and the Tay estuaries.

It is very remarkable how the Scandinavian settlement of certain areas of north Britain produced a flowering of stone sculpture when the settlers themselves came from an environment where there was little stone sculpture at this time. The craftsmanship was evidently local and indigenous; the stimulus was brought in by these settlers who had the power and wealth as patrons to engender this development. It is unlikely that this wealth was derived from farming alone in marginal parts of north-western Britain. The crosses and hogbacks of Cumbria and the memorial stones of Man have been linked to a 'warrior aristocracy who were involved in the Odinn cult and who were actively engaged in warfare'.[79] They probably supplemented their income by raiding or joining the armies of the kings of Dublin as they pursued their ambitions in north England in the first half of the tenth century. 'Involvement in the Odinn cult' may actually have been on the wane, but at least these settlers liked to see representations of the old myths on their grave monuments. The depiction of these myths on such famous crosses as Gosforth, Cumbria and Kirk Andreas, Isle of Man, tells us that concepts of the afterworld derived from pagan tradition survived along with an adoption of Christian beliefs – as can be seen also on church portals in Norway. Scenes from the legend of Sigurd the Dragon-Slayer[80] are found on different kinds of grave monuments right across the area of northern England which came under the control of the kings of Dublin and York, and the cult of Odin figures prominently in this legend. Although these at first appear 'alien to Christian sentiment'[81] it has been argued that the tales of some of the Norse heroes can be equated with Christian teaching and the sculptor is perhaps comparing pagan myth and Christian doctrine when carving scenes from both worlds on one stone.[82] These carved stones are found in association with churches and were apparently erected by an Anglo-Scandinavian class of tolerant patrons who liked to remember the old traditions of their forefathers regarding the world of the gods, although pious enough to commission Christian monuments as a testimonial to their own firm beliefs. Perhaps rather surprisingly, there is only one stone possibly displaying pagan mythology in the areas which received the greatest number of Scandinavian settlers – the Northern and Western Isles and the north Scottish mainland (see below, p. 178).

Man and the Hebrides

The development of the Isle of Man as an important Norse settlement in the Irish Sea produced a flowering of its stone sculptural tradition. The remarkable series of pagan graves in Man is striking evidence that a warrior aristocracy had settled in the island during the ninth century. It is possible that they did not bring their own women with them, and if not, there must have been a rapid amalgamation with the native population and a mixed Norse-Celtic culture is certainly in evidence by the time that the cross series were being carved in the tenth century.[83] The Gaelic element on Man may have derived from Scotland and the Hebrides.[84] Certainly one of the sculptors of the early crosses was

Figure 63 (left). Gaut's cross-slab, Michael, Isle of Man; height 1.83m (photograph by courtesy of The Manx Museum and National Trust).

One of the most famous of the Manx cross-slabs, this illustrates the mingling of Celtic art tradition and Scandinavian interlace design, with the distinctive 'ring-chain' pattern on the shaft of the cross. A long inscription in runes runs up both sides, continuing above the cross-head (as can be seen). It reads, 'Melbrigdi, son of Athakan the smith, erected this cross for his sin ... soul, but Gaut made it and all in Man'. Melbrigdi and his father both had Celtic names; Gaut and his father (Bjarn from Coll) had Norse ones. Gaut was producing his masterpieces in the mid-tenth century.

Figure 64 (centre and right). Cross-slab from Kilbar, Barra, Outer Hebrides (Royal Museum of Scotland).

Certain similarities between this stone (height 1.65m) and the Manx crosses suggest close cultural links between the northern Hebrides and Man in the tenth or early eleventh centuries. The runic inscription on the back (*right*) reads: 'after Thorgerth, Steinar's daughter, this cross was raised'.

called Gaut whose father Bjarn was from Coll (an island in the Inner Hebrides) as we know from two of the runic inscriptions on the crosses – a remarkable feature of the Manx series and providing the largest corpus of early runic inscriptions in the British Isles (see fig. 63).[85] It is as yet not completely clear where all the influences seen in the Manx crosses derive from, for apart from Scandinavian ornament an Irish and Scottish element can be defined,[86] as well

Figure 65. Cross-slab from Iona (Abbey Museum no. 49; Royal Commission on Ancient Monuments, Scotland: Crown Copyright reserved).

The lower part of a much-damaged shaft of a free-standing cross or narrow cross-slab, this is the only carved stone from the whole collection at Iona which bears any resemblance to the Manx cross-slabs, and incorporates traditions other than the purely Christian. This face is covered with 'irregular and poorly-executed double-beaded plaitwork', with a dragonesque creature at left bottom. These features are certainly Scandinavian in character.

as a northern English one,[87] Man being equally open to influences from all these areas. The flourishing of a Norse-Celtic culture in the island to which these cross-slabs testify is paralleled by the occurrence at just the same period of the silver hoards.[88] These also signify the sudden importance of Man in the economic trading nexus around the Irish Sea and provide tangible evidence of the silver in circulation and thus of the wealth which must certainly have existed for such memorial slabs to be commissioned.

This school of carving seems to have had some influence in the Hebrides generally, although the number of sculptured stones from this period in the islands is remarkably small compared with Man itself. This can hardly be due to the late conversion of the Norse, for as we have seen, some of the settlers were strongly influenced by Christianity in the ninth century, and the great monastic centre at Iona ultimately survived, despite its exposure to the Viking raiding bands.[89] Perhaps significantly, all of the runic inscriptions on memorial stones in the Western Isles are unmistakably Christian, whereas those from the Northern Isles could derive from either a heathen or a Christian background.[90] A tenth- or early eleventh-century stone slab with a runic inscription from Kilbar, Barra, is derived from a Manx prototype (fig. 64)[91] and the possibility exists that it may have been carved by the sculptor whose family came from Coll – which lies to the south-east of Barra – and who is so well known from the Manx series.[92] Some of the collection of crosses at Iona resemble Norse slabs on the Isle of Man, and one cross-shaft in particular

Figure 66. Ship-scene on Iona cross-slab (Abbey Museum no. 49; Royal Commission on Ancient Monuments, Scotland: Crown Copyright reserved).
   This scene appears on the other face of the cross-slab shown in fig. 65 (see also fig. 5). The numbers relate to identification in RCAHMS, *Argyll Inventory*, IV, no. 95. The figures in the boat (2–8) appear to be wielding spears and swords, while figure 9 can be identified as a smith from the collection of tools (10–15). The animal (16) may be an otter.

closely resembles Manx products in its general design and in the material used (figs. 65 and 5). However, the most recent assessment says that the figure of a smith which appears to be carved on one face can perhaps be paralleled in Yorkshire rather than on the Isle of Man (fig. 66).[93]. If this carving does depict the legend of Sigurd, on a stone set up in the Christian environment of Iona, it testifies to a strong retention of interest in the old Norse traditions, as in Man. Two other stones from the Iona collection show the difficulty of defining what is Norse or Celtic in inspiration in a mixed cultural environment as existed in the Hebrides of the tenth and eleventh centuries. The decoration of one (no. 41) is simply 'Common in Scandinavian-influenced sculpture ... in the British Isles';[94] the other (no. 42) is a crude copy of an early Christian cross-slab with knotted terminals (fig. 67) but with a runic inscription down one side which appears to be original. The inscription says that the stone was laid 'by Kali Olvirsson over his brother Fugl'[95] – Norsemen whose names suggest a family connexion with well-known people in the *Jarls' Saga* of a later date.[96] This grave-slab is thought to date from the late tenth century, the period when Olaf Cuaran, king of Dublin, had retired to Iona (980), by which time the monastery would appear to have become a spiritual centre for converted Norsemen of the Western and perhaps the Northern Isles.[97] These stones are clear evidence of a Scandinavian element in the mixed cultural society of the Hebrides in the period. They are, however, something of a contrast with the glories of the earlier Celtic crosses of the pre-Viking Age.

CHURCHES AND ECCLESIASTICAL ORGANIZATION

Although there is some evidence of 'continuity of resort' in regard to earlier Christian sites when the converted Norse started to build their own churches during the eleventh century, this phase of their religious development is likely to have been influenced by wider contacts with the Christian church in other north European countries. The first burst of church-building would have been marked by the founding of private chapels by Norse landowners on their estates.[98] This is a notable feature of the Icelandic church where all the original chapels belonged to individual farmers, except for the church at Thingvellir. The situation in Norway differed, however, for most churches there were public in the sense that they were built either by the king or the community and were related to the administrative structure.[99] In the Norse colonies around Scotland, a mixture of the two models, varying according to different political circumstances, may have been adopted. The earliest historical evidence about the building or use of churches is of Earl Thorfinn's construction of his 'fine minster' at Birsay which became the first seat of the bishop in the mid-eleventh century.[100] The establishment of a resident bishop provided the political direction which was necessary for the creation of an ecclesiastical network.

Thorfinn's bishop was a Norseman from his name (Thorolf); he had been preceded in the islands by an English missionary bishop appointed from the archiepiscopal see of York.[101] This earlier appointment was not necessarily purely nominal, but without the support of the lay authorities such a bishop would not have effected much change in his diocese. The archbishops of York

Figure 67. Grave-stone with runic inscription from Iona (Abbey Museum no. 42; Royal Commission on Ancient Monuments, Scotland: Crown Copyright reserved).

The inscription reads: 'Kali the son of Ölvir laid this stone over his brother Fugl' (RCAHMS, *Argyll Inventory*, IV, no. 68). When complete, the stone measured 1.11m × c.0.77m.

strove hard later in the eleventh century to see that their bishops succeeded in establishing themselves in the islands in opposition to those consecrated by the archbishops of Hamburg. Episcopal appointments in the Hebrides were also being made at this period and the centre of the bishop's diocese was becoming fixed in Man, probably at Peel, rather than Iona.[102] Earl Thorfinn's direction and protection may have been very relevant here, too. The main effect of this introduction of bishops and the creation of a territorial diocesan system would have been to strengthen the Roman, European aspect of the Christian religion in the islands. Earl Thorfinn's pilgrimage to Rome is symptomatic of this development, just as MacBeth's pilgrimage at about the same time (1050) strengthened Scotland's place within the Roman and Latin ecclesiastical sphere.[103]

Chapels and problems of dating

Archaeological evidence suggests that, in imitation of the earl's example, there was a great burst of private chapel-building by individual families in all the areas of Norse settlement in Scotland; presumably after localities had become thoroughly converted by established missionizing priests who were under the direction of the bishop and the protection of the secular authority. It is possible that the Kirbister (ON *kirkja-bólstaðr* = church farm) place-names of Orkney are evidence of this phase of church-building rather than of an earlier period,[104] the name indicating that these chapels were distinctive in some way. A parochial system developed later, probably during the twelfth century when certain chapels were elevated to parochial status and had their own priest, or were grouped into 'priests' districts' (ON *prestegjelder*).[105]

A well-known and significant fact about the private chapels of Orkney and Man is that they relate to the ounceland and treen divisions which were the territorial basis of a tax assessment and naval levy system.[106] The close relationship of these administrative divisions and the sites of chapels strongly suggests that the chapels must have been founded according to some central direction. Who dictated their distribution? It must have been either the church or the secular ruler; knowing the earl's close concern with the organization of the early church in Orkney it seems likely that he was responsible there, possibly at the time of the formal institution of a resident bishop in the mid-eleventh century.[107] Alternatively, the whole system may rest on a Celtic pattern, which the Norse basically adapted with even the later parish divisions being based on much older territorial groupings; it is possible that this may have been the situation in Man and the Isles. But in Orkney it is most unlikely that all the ounceland chapels – amounting to 140 – replaced previous Celtic places of worship;[108] although a supposed chapel site on Sanday is called the 'Kill o' Howe', suggesting the continued use of the Celtic word for church (cf. Manx 'keill').[109]

The number of small chapels in the island of Sanday (possibly 29) is exceptional even by Orkney standards just as the number surviving on the island of Islay is exceptional by Hebridean standards.[110] In Shetland the relationship seems to lie between chapel sites and the 'scattald' districts (not the ounceland divisions). The name 'scattald' (perhaps ON *skatt-völlr* = 'field/

enclosed land for which tax was paid') suggests that it also had been in origin a taxable unit.[111] There were about 200 of them in Shetland, and they varied very much in size. In some places there is an exact correlation between scattalds and chapels, as in the island of Fetlar where each scattald has a chapel site (fig. 68).[112] The scattald was the important unit of social organization in Shetland, for although ouncelands were imposed they were never as basic to the administration as they were in Orkney. Moreover the scattalds do not relate to the parish boundaries, which is another contrast with Orkney, and the conclusion has been reached that they may be much older than the institution of the parishes.[113] There are obviously significant differences here between the social and territorial organization of Orkney and Shetland and the imprint of political direction is much weaker in the latter. There is a possibility that the scattald districts in Shetland had their origin in a pre-Norse settlement pattern, and that some of the scattald chapel sites had a continued existence from the Celtic Christian period. It is certainly remarkable that the two Papils, in Burra and Fetlar, continued to feature prominently in the organization of the medieval Norwegian church in Shetland.[114] But, as in Orkney, it does not seem likely that the majority of small chapels were located on earlier Celtic church sites.

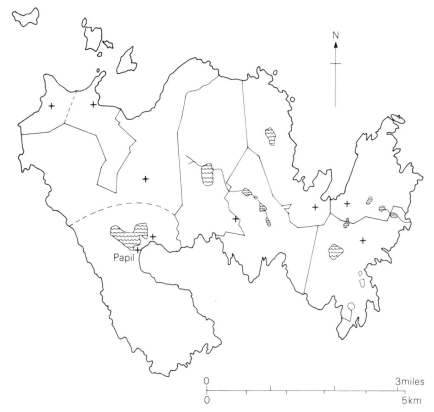

Figure 68. Scattalds and chapel sites on the island of Fetlar, Shetland (based on work done by Lindsay MacGregor).

Figure 69. Comparative plans of chapels in the Northern and Western Isles
(*a, d, e, f, g* and *h* reproduced by kind permission of the Royal Commission
on Ancient Monuments, Scotland, from *Inventories of Ancient Monuments;*
b after C.D. Morris, 'The survey and excavations of Keeill Vael, Druidale, in
their context', in *The Viking Age in the Isle of Man, Ninth Viking Congress,*
1983; *c* after C.D. Morris, 'Viking Orkney: a survey', in *The Prehistory of
Orkney,* ed. C. Renfrew, Edinburgh University Press, 1985, fig. 10; Crown
Copyright reserved).

A The chapel and burial ground at Marwick, Orkney   B Keeill Vael, Isle of Man

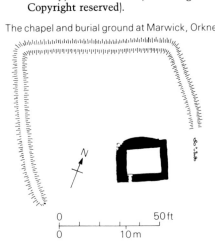 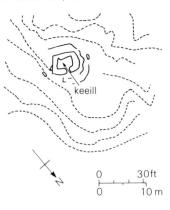

C The Brough of Deerness, Orkney

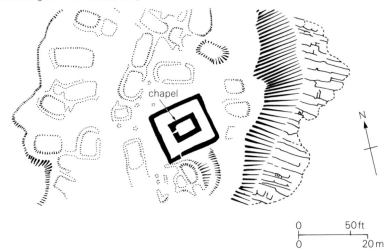

D Cross-Kirk, Tuquoy, Orkney   E St Magnus Church, Egilsay, Orkney

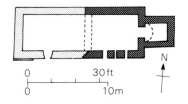 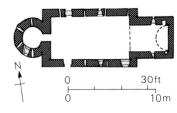

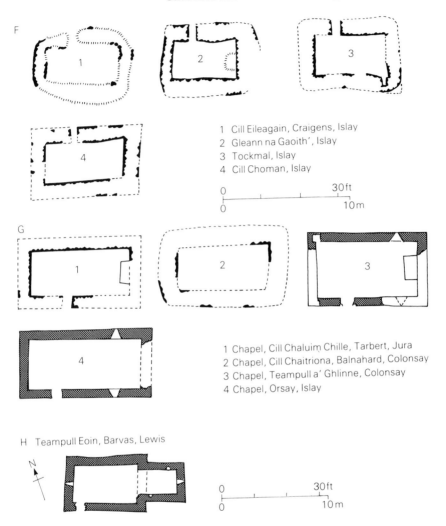

F

1 Cill Eileagain, Craigens, Islay
2 Gleann na Gaoith', Islay
3 Tockmal, Islay
4 Cill Choman, Islay

0   30 ft

0   10 m

G

1 Chapel, Cill Chaluim Chille, Tarbert, Jura
2 Chapel, Cill Chaitriona, Balnahard, Colonsay
3 Chapel, Teampull a' Ghlinne, Colonsay
4 Chapel, Orsay, Islay

H   Teampull Eoin, Barvas, Lewis

0   30 ft

0   10 m

Although there have been attempts to date the early chapel ruins, it is very difficult indeed from the simple architectural styles concerned to postulate any kind of chronology. The simplest, and most probably the earliest, are rectangular cells, such as the chapel at Marwick in Birsay parish, comparable with the earliest Hebridean ecclesiastical structures. It measures 5.18m × 3.66m internally (fig. 69a).[115] Even excavation does not necessarily help to prove whether these date from the Celtic period or from the Norse, as at Keill Vael in the Isle of Man (fig. 69b) where excavation proved nothing.[116] Sometimes the layout of the religious site is indicative of the period from which it dates, so that Lag-Ny-Keilley, on the Isle of Man, with its chapel or oratory inside the enclosed cemetery, its living-cell just outside it and the attached plot, all point towards a Celtic religious site.[117] Oval, ovoid or near-circular enclosures are understood to indicate a site of Celtic origin, whereas rectangular enclosures are taken as a sign of Norse influence. On the Brough of Birsay the rectangular line of the Norse cemetery enclosure overlies what has been interpreted as the curvilinear *vallum* wall of an earlier religious site.[118]

Recent work on presumed early monastic sites on promontories in the Northern Isles has suggested that some of these sites – those with buildings of a rectangular nature – may be of later date than previously thought; perhaps a Norse continuation of the earlier Celtic tradition of placing hermitages in such wild and remote spots.[119] The great difficulty of excavating and dating these establishments has already been seen in the case of the Brough of Deerness (see above, p. 166). Although there was some slight evidence of an earlier structure underneath, the church site as it stands today (see fig. 69c) could be early medieval and surrounded by secular and domestic buildings – as at the Brough of Birsay – rather than Dark Age and eremitic.[120]

An example of an original ounceland chapel which became a parish church and which has retained clear features of its earliest structural period can be seen at Cross-Kirk, in the Westside district of Westray (fig. 69d). Now remote from any farm, it was once close to a large and important residence, currently being excavated,[121] and probably the seat of the chieftain Kugi of Westray who appears in the twelfth-century section of the *Jarls' Saga*. The original chapel was composed of a nave measuring 4.2m × 5.7m internally, and a small chancel where the priest would have officiated, measuring about 2.8m × 2m. This is a developed example from the small rectangular plan, and the increased sophistication can also be seen in the chancel archway and round-headed window.[122] At some later point, but exactly when it is not at all easy to determine, the nave was lengthened to 14.2m.

The difficulty of dating even elaborate ecclesiastical structures is well illustrated by the variations in the date which have been put on the well-preserved remains of St Magnus's church on the island of Egilsay, Orkney (fig. 69e), where St Magnus was murdered in the early part of the twelfth century (c.1117). It has been sometimes assigned to a much earlier period, but also to the period after St Magnus's death, that is as a commemorative church. Its planning and details have much in common with Irish buildings of the eleventh century,[123] although links with north German churches with round towers have recently been postulated.[124]

Earl Thorfinn's Christ Church

The Brough of Birsay provides all the elements which make a study of the Norse period in Scotland so exciting: it is a dramatic archaeological site (see fig. 70) which has been associated with dramatic historical information. There is little doubt that the name Birsay is the same as the place mentioned in saga and historical sources as being the site of Earl Thorfinn's Christ Church, the first seat of the bishops in the Orkneys,[125] but there are problems in identifying the actual location of his church in the area known today as Birsay. Two medieval churches still exist: one on the Brough (ruined), and the other in the village, the present-day parish church of St Magnus (rebuilt) (see figs. 70 and 71). Which one is on the site of the first episcopal church, founded by the earl? Both these locations have provided evidence of intensive settlement. The

Figure 70. Brough of Birsay, Orkney: aerial view of the secular and ecclesiastical structures (photograph: Gunnie Moberg).
Figure 71. Birsay Bay, Orkney (photograph: Gunnie Moberg).
  This aerial view shows the present-day village grouped around the parish church of St Magnus with its graveyard. The ruined palace of the Stewart earls (sixteenth-century) is in the right foreground, the Brough of Birsay, with its archaeological site, in the background.

impressive remains of high-status Norse dwellings on the Brough have, as discussed, been associated with Earl Thorfinn and his father, and the nearby ruined church has been identified as Thorfinn's Christ Church.[126] The village location with St Magnus's Church has been a centre of settlement since at least the late Norse period, from preliminary excavation undertaken to the west of the burn,[127] and was probably the site of the bishop's palace in the late Middle Ages, and certainly the residence of the sixteenth-century Stewart earls (fig. 71).

One thing is certain: when Earl Thorfinn built his Christ Church he would have built it near his own residence, for bishops' churches in the Scandinavian north in the eleventh century were proprietorial establishments, functioning as private chapels of the rulers who instituted bishoprics.[128] At the present time the only secular buildings of eleventh-century date excavated at Birsay are the remarkable structures lying to the east of the church on the Brough.[129] As no buildings of comparable date and similar secular status have yet been found near the village church, the Brough site does appear to be the more likely location of Earl Thorfinn's *dýrligt musteri* ('fine minister' or 'magnificent church') – in close association with the truncated remains of what was possibly the earl's residence.[130]

The surviving structures of the church on the Brough are not very large, but they indicate expert construction and a certain degree of sophistication: consisting of a nave (9.5m × 4.7m internally), a small chancel (3m × 3m) with

Figure 72. Apse of the church on the Brough of Birsay (photograph: author). The re-used runic memorial stone was found in the north chancel wall (*right of photograph*).

an apse (see fig. 72), and evidence at the west end that a tower was intended, although probably never built (see fig. 73). A mid-eleventh century date has been suggested, from the style of building, the plan and the shape of one window;[131] however, the sophistication of the plan would point to a later time-scale in most circumstances of northern Scotland and opinion is tending to revert towards the original idea of a twelfth-century date.[132] The discovery of a re-used runic memorial stone in the north wall raises tantalizing questions about the date of the original inscription (perhaps pre-Christian) and about the addition by a presumed Christian called Philip. The dating of this memorial stone requires careful elucidation, as it might help to determine the actual building date of the church.[133] It has also to be noted that there is some evidence of an earlier church underneath the present structure: the chronological relationship of the two buildings has not yet been examined. To the north side of the church a range of buildings round a courtyard have been interpreted as the episcopal residence, although it could equally have formed a monastic establishment of slightly later date.[134] A grave found in front of the altar in the place of honour can perhaps be regarded as the founder's tomb.[135] The two side altars flanking the entrance to the choir suggest that the church was served by a community of monks or canons; the altars may, however, be secondary insertions. All these features mark this church out as a completely exceptional building which has, unusually, not been extended or rebuilt at a later date. The parish church in the village, on the other hand, has been

Figure 73. View of the church on the Brough of Birsay from the west (photograph: author).
   The foundation of the tower can be clearly seen in the ground which, along with the projecting stones either side of the door, suggest that it would have been a substantial structure.

A

B

Figure 74. St Magnus's Church, Birsay (photographs: author).
   (*a*) Reconstructed many times, the parish church lies on medieval
foundations and may incorporate medieval fabric. A re-inserted lancet
window can be seen in the middle of the south wall. (*b*) Part of an earlier
building phase can be seen projecting from the east gable wall during
excavation. This may be the remains of a chancel wall; it incorporates
fashioned red sandstone which does not feature in the church on the Brough.

reconstructed on many occasions, although probably on the alignment of the original medieval building (see fig. 74a). Recent excavations at the east end have shown several early building phases, the most sophisticated with a moulded plinth in red sandstone of probable twelfth-century date (fig. 74b).[136] The dedication to St Magnus must certainly post-date the cult of the martyred earl which developed in the 1120s and 1130s.

Two factors make the morphology of the Norse settlements at Birsay particularly complex, one political and the other geological. The first involves the move of the bishops from Birsay to Kirkwall in 1137, when Thorfinn's Christ Church lost its pre-eminence as the main seat of the bishops in the islands. In similar circumstances in West Norway when the bishops moved from the inconvenient off-shore island of Selja to Bergen, in the second half of the twelfth century, the site at Selja was occupied by Benedictine monks from St Albans.[137] It is quite likely that a parallel change would have taken place at Birsay and this could have provided the occasion when the church on the Brough became monastic, and the buildings round the courtyard were established to house a community of monks. The geological factor is even less well recorded, but the strong possibility exists that the Brough may, in the early Norse period, have been joined to the Orkney Mainland (see fig. 75) by a narrow isthmus or tombolo beach (as at St Ninian's Isle in Shetland). Due to drastic erosion both on the Brough and the adjoining Mainland coast the islet has certainly become more isolated and difficult of access than it would have been in the Norse period. A tombolo can be breached and destroyed by a severe storm or series of storms at any time, as is well known in the Northern Isles.[138]

Figure 75. Wave-cut platform between the Brough of Birsay and the Point of Buckquoy (Royal Commission on Ancient Monuments, Scotland; Crown Copyright reserved).
    This aerial view graphically illustrates the extent of the erosion which has separated the Brough from the Mainland of Orkney.

The exposed position of this part of the Orkney Mainland makes it very vulnerable to deteriorating climatic factors and an increase in Atlantic gales, such as occurred in the later Middle Ages when parts of Orkney suffered from sand-blow.[139] Increasing difficulties of access to the Brough may therefore have contributed to the political decision to move the seat of the bishopric to Kirkwall.[140] Such a development could also explain the local shift of bishop's residence from the Brough to the present village locality, for the late medieval bishops' palace lay somewhere near the present parish church of St Magnus and was succeeded by the Stewart earls' palace in the late sixteenth century. The whole of Birsay was given to the bishops by the earls as a pious gift at some date after the founding of the bishopric and it remained a valuable part of the bishopric estate until the Stewart earls acquired it in the sixteenth century.[141]

Until further excavation produces more decisive evidence the interpretation of the church on the Brough must remain an open question. Excavation round Birsay Bay has already revealed a totally unexpected density of settlement of the whole area in the Pictish and Norse periods. The pattern of settlement probably changed many times and the difficulty of trying to pinpoint the exact location of a building at one period in time may appear a fruitless exercise. It provides a dramatic example of the problems of attempting to relate historical and archaeological evidence. Despite these problems, the ruined church on the Brough of Birsay remains a fine memorial to the piety of the converted Norse earls – for it can hardly have been constructed by anyone else. It is the oldest and most impressive church ruin of its date in northern or western Scotland, and can be viewed on a par with St Rule's Church in St Andrews, built probably in the late eleventh century for Scotland's premier bishop. Even without the historical information about the earl who may have built the church on the Brough and established there the first resident bishop in the islands, it would furnish proof in stone of the stature and cultural contacts of the Norse rulers of the Orkneys.

7 The Literary Framework: Norse Society in the Settlements

When an attempt is made to add flesh and blood to the bare bones of the historical and archaeological framework it is the literary sources which provide fullest enlightenment about life and society in Scandinavian Scotland (primarily that of the earldom of Orkney). Despite the caution needed when using these sources which were written down long after the events portrayed,[1] they provide nonetheless a vivid picture of a society and a way of life which is a most valuable addition to our body of evidence.

AN HEROIC SOCIETY

The most striking impression gained from these sources is the heroic nature of the society portrayed. The sagas emphasize this aspect deliberately for their purpose was to record the heroic deeds of the family concerned, and in the case of the *Jarls' Saga*, of the individual earls, while the skaldic verses laud the victories and slaughters of the powerful military leaders. All early medieval society was 'heroic' in that economic and political power rested on military might, and great emphasis was laid on the practising of the martial arts, prowess in battle and the effective use of weapons. The Picts and the Scots were probably just as heroically-minded, but we do not have the quantity of verse or saga telling us so (although Pictish art gives us some vivid visual impressions of the value this people laid on horsemanship). The deeds of the rulers of the province of Moray are in fact more fully recorded in the Icelandic sagas than in any other source.

Earls and kings

Different titles were used by the Norse rulers of Orkney and the overlords of the Western Isles. As the *Historia Norwegiae* later described them: 'These [the islands west of Norway settled by Vikings], occupied by different inhabitants, are now divided into two dominions; the southern islands are elevated to [being ruled by] kinglets, while the northern are adorned by the protection of earls; and both pay large tribute to the Kings of Norway.'[2] In origin the title of king (ON *konungr*) and earl (ON *jarl*) in Norway were not dissimilar in that both were titles of dignity borne by a particular family and any male member of the family had the right to claim the title. In Viking-Age Norway there appears to have been little difference between those families who held the title of king and those who were earls. Once Harald Finehair had introduced the idea of an over-king, when he conquered the chieftains of the west coast, the concept of a kingdom of Norway began to gain ground.[3] But for a century after his time Norway was divided between the royal dynasty of Vestfold and the comital dynasty of Lade, who as earls of a stretch of western Norway from Trondheim northwards were just as powerful as the kings in the south. In the twelfth-century Lawcodes the earl's position is clearly below that of the king, and his legal worth was by then exactly half that of a king. But an earl's position could be a threat to the king, and although the title lasted longer in Norway than elsewhere in Scandinavia the number of earls was much reduced until eventually the only continuous line was the dynasty of the Møre family in Orkney, *the* earls 'par excellence'. Although *Jarls' Saga* very carefully says that the first earls were given their title over the islands by King Harald in the late ninth century, we have seen that these are hardly details of which we can be certain, for the problem of whether the earls conquered the islands on their own account, or whether they were given their authority in them by the king, is not at all clear.[4] Certainly it was not long before the earls were supposed to visit the king in order to be given a grant of their title. But there continued to be doubts over the official or hereditary nature of the earls' position in the islands. However, there are no doubts about the need for the earl to prove to his followers that he was a successful and energetic warrior, and when Earl Hallad, first son of Earl Rognvald of Møre to hold the title of earl in Orkney, showed himself unable to keep the earldom clear of pirates 'he grew tired of his high position'[5] and gave up the earldom, taking the rank of 'hold', and sailed to Norway, which, we are told, made him a 'laughing-stock'.[6]

The title of 'king' in the Hebrides seems likely to have been adopted through close contact with the Irish situation.[7] Most petty rulers in Ireland in the ninth century were entitled King (OI *rí*),[8] and once the Vikings had established themselves in some sort of political authority in Ireland they too adopted – or were given – the title of king. When Thorstein the Red, son of Olaf the White, king of Dublin, was attempting to conquer North Scotland he is said to have been 'king' over the lands he conquered,[9] although none of the earls of Orkney ever took the title of king over their lands in the north of Scotland. This entitlement to the dignity of king must have stemmed from Thorstein's father's assumption of the title when he conquered Dublin, and which was then considered to be a family title like that of earl. Similarly, when Halfdan Long-Legs subdued the Orkney islands 'he made himself king over them',[10] a title which he was able to assume because of his father's status in Norway. The title 'king of the Isles' (that is, of the Hebrides and Man) appears about the middle of the tenth century, and although it is not clear where the dynasty came from, it was probably a branch of the Dublin family or else of the royal line of Limerick, another Norse trading city, on the west coast.[11] By the time that the kings of Norway were able to assert political control in the west (late eleventh century), the usage was so well established that they were unable to prevent the use of the royal title, even if they had wanted to.

The earl's hird

All war leaders survived only by attracting and retaining a military following and we have plenty of evidence that the Orkney earls, conquerors in the

Northern and Western Isles and further afield in Scotland, Ireland and England, had a large retinue of warriors – their hird (ON *hird*). Successful earls, unlike Earl Hallad, were the ones who kept predators at bay from their own lands but who preyed on the wealth and riches of other communities, with the proceeds of which they maintained their following.[12] A description of Earl Sigurd Hlodversson rewarding his followers with booty after the battle of Dungal's peak comes into *Njal's Saga*:

> The earl made there a great banquet [back in the Mainland of Orkney] and at this banquet the earl gave Kari a good sword, and a gilded spear; and to Helgio, a gold ring, and a cloak; and to Grim, a shield, and a sword. After that he made Helgi and Grim his bodyguardsmen, and thanked them for their good courage. They were with the earl that winter.[13]

Sigurd's son, Thorfinn, was also remembered as a great lord who 'furnished all his body-guard and many other men of rank both with meat and ale the whole winter through, so that men had no need to go to the ale-house, just as it is the custom of Kings and earls in other countries to frequently entertain their bodyguards at Yule.'[14] Thorfinn should have known, for according to tradition he spent some time as leader of the king's bodyguard (*þingamannalid*) in England.[15] This is not unlikely after the Danish conquest (1016) when a royal bodyguard was instituted who were known as housecarls (ON = *húskarlar*), which survived until the Norman Conquest.[16] Unfortunately the scant documentary sources of this period do not furnish corroborating evidence for Thorfinn's service at the Anglo-Scandinavian royal court. The importance of hospitality and the significance of the corporate feasting and drinking which helped to maintain the bonds between the lord and his close followers can be glimpsed in the literary sources. Thorfinn's skald, Arnor, boasts of the times he sat in the lower high-seat, as drinking companion of the earl when he was with him in the Orkneys.[17] A scene in *Njal's Saga* describes how Earl Sigurd was visited by King Sitric (Sigtrygg) of Dublin who was seeking support from the Orkney earldom: he was received at one of the earl's residences:

> The hall was so arranged that King Sigtrygg sat on the centre high-seat with the earls on either side of him. The followers of King Sigtrygg and Earl Gilli sat on one side, and on Earl Sigurd's side sat Flosi and Thorstein Hallsson. Every seat in the hall was occupied.[18]

The significance of seating arrangements round the table for honoured guests and the members of their following is symbolic of the hierarchical nature of such heroic societies.[19]

Although there is no evidence from the Hebrides of this aspect of Norse/Gaelic heroic society this is simply due to an absence of saga and skaldic verse associated with the kings of the Isles. As mentioned in the passage quoted above, King Sitric of Dublin and Earl Gilli of Coll had their followings, and Earl Gilli gave Flosi 'a load of silver' after they heard the news of the battle of Clontarf and the death of his lord, Earl Sigurd (see p. 133 above). Archaeological evidence bears witness to the existence of a rich aristocratic class of pagan Norsemen in the Isles whose graves contain the remains of different kinds of weapons and who would undoubtedly have raided and conquered in warrior bands and cultivated the martial arts.[20] The graves of the Orkney earls have never been discovered, and were probably looted long ago: we do not, therefore, possess any tangible evidence of their military equipment. One passage in *Jarls' Saga* describes Earl Thorfinn fighting at the battle of Torfness accoutred with sword and great spear and with a gilded helmet on his head.[21] We know from Anglo-Saxon sources that gilded weapons and armour were worn as a status symbol by royal and princely leaders,[22] so there seems no reason to question such a description of an eleventh-century earl of Orkney.

The importance of both the earl's following and the possession of weapons in Orkney society is borne out by the survival of the names Hirdmanstein (ON *hirðmanna-stefna* = assembly of hirdmen) and Wappinstein (ON *vapna-stefna* = weapon-assembly, 'muster') for two courts in late medieval Orkney.[23] The Hirdmanstein was 'the first heid court eftyr Yeuill', Yule or mid-winter being the traditional time of assembly of hirdmen at their lord's residence. The Wappinstein also probably had its origins in the Norse age, for there was a provision in the old Norwegian laws that every free man should attend a weapon 'thing' with the necessary weapons: sword, axe, spear and shield.[24] The link between the bearing of weapons and the possession of legal rights is a fundamental one throughout the Germanic world in the early Middle Ages and law-courts were often the same occasions as assemblies of war.[25] In these two courts, the late medieval earldom of Orkney seems to have preserved institutions of some antiquity, even though they did not survive for long thereafter – as the remarkable annual gathering at the Manx Tynwald has done.[26]

The earl's hirdmen thus formed a court around him in peacetime as well as a bodyguard in war and they would have been bound by a strict oath of loyalty to their lord. We have thirteenth-century evidence for the organization of the Norwegian king's hird when those 'handgangne menn' (those who had 'gone to the hand') are said to have submitted to the king's will and bound themselves to him by oaths of fealty.[27] What seems to be an older form of submission is described in *Jarls' Saga* when Thorkell came to Earl Thorfinn after King Olaf's arbitration on the matter of compensation for Earl Einar's murder: 'One day the Earl was drinking on board ready to sail when Thorkell Amundsen suddenly appeared before him, placed his head on the earl's knee, and said he could do whatever he liked with him'.[28] This act was symbolic of total submission to the earl's will, and Thorkell explains why he did it: the king may have awarded him the right to his lands in Orkney, and the right to live there, in the arbitration, but he knew it was impossible for him to go to the Isles unless he was on good terms with the earl and had reached his own settlement with him in compensation for the killing of the earl's brother Einar. So much for royal intervention in this matter. This scene redresses the picture sometimes given in the saga of strong royal control over events in the islands, and illustrates the way in which the earls made their own terms with their hirdmen, and the authority which they exercised over them. Earl Thorfinn stated that Thorkell would have to stay with him under his control, and never leave him without his permission. His obligations were to defend the land and devote his life to the earl's service. Thorkell then 'gave a solemn undertaking to do whatever the Earl asked of him'; and confirmed their agreement with an oath. He fulfilled his obligations to his lord in the later struggle between the two earls, Thorfinn and Rognvald Brusisson, killing Rognvald on Papa Stronsay because, it was said, no one else would do it. The saga writer adds, 'but

then, he had sworn to do any thing Thorfinn believed would add to his power.'
The earl must have rewarded him well.

When Arnor Jarlaskald eulogizes his earl and patron we glimpse the depth of
the personal bond existing between the hirdman and his lord, which formed
the basis of all social and political life in the heroic world of the Norse settlers.

> Bjǫrt verđr sól at svartri,
> søkkr fold í mar døkkvan,
> brestr erfiđi Austra,
> allr glymr sae á fjǫllum,
>
> ađr at Eyjum friđri
> – inndróttar – þorfinni
> – þeim hjalpi god geymi –
> goeđingr myni foeđask.

[The bright sun will turn black, the earth sink into the dark sea, the burden of
the dwarf Austri (the sky) will break, all the ocean will roar upon the
mountains, before a chieftain finer than þorfinnr shall be born in the Orkney
Isles – may God help that keeper of the bodyguard.' – B. Fidjestol, 'Arnórr
þórđarsson, Skald of the Orkney Jarls' in *Northern and Western Isles*, 243]

Pagan beliefs and the cult of Odin

The pagan element of early Norse society does not emerge strongly in the
written sources. This is hardly surprising as the sagas were written down in a
fully Christian milieu and by men who were aware of the Church's disapproval
of such matters. Nonetheless those who suffered from the Viking raids –
whether Irish, English, Frankish or even Muslim – consistently refer to the
raiders as 'heathen', 'pagans' or 'gentiles'.[29] This usage in the Irish Annals
continues until the second half of the ninth century. But the raiding phase of
Viking activity and the attacks on the churches of Celtic Scotland and Ireland
were not motivated primarily by heathen antagonism to the Christian God.
The religion of the Scandinavian pagans was not a personal faith which
directed a way of life or wished to convert others. It was closely bound up with
the family group and was maintained by social occasions such as sacrifices and
feasting. The disruption to communities and families caused by the movement overseas was probably disruptive to their religion also.[30] There is no
evidence of powerful priests who kept the faith alive or helped to transfer it to
the new settlements. Temples have never been unequivocally identified at any
excavated sites in the Atlantic settlements; the likelihood of their destruction
and replacement by churches on conversion is very high.[31]

By the Viking Age many gods in the pagan pantheon were rapidly losing their
importance, and worship centred around Thor, the most powerful of the gods,
Frey and his sister Freyja who stood for fertility and powers of increase, and
Odin.[32] Odin is the one god whose influence can be dimly perceived as having
retained some vitality among the Scandinavian settlers in Britain. He was the
god of battle, the lord of the dead, and the Valkyries were his servants; but he

was a fickle god and did not always grant victory to the valiant.[33] It is probable that his cult spread along with the expansion of Norse influence in western Europe for he provided a suitable religious patronage to the warrior kings and their retinues, and an inspiration for the heroic ethos cultivated by the skalds. It is not surprising then if echoes of his role are heard in the sources which have survived, because they were devoted to keeping alive the memory of the warrior kings and earls. The poem in honour of Erik Bloodaxe, *Eiriksmál* (probably composed in Orkney soon after his death), is concerned with Odin's reception of him into Valhall, the hall of the slain warriors, despite the fact that Erik was nominally a Christian.[34]

There also survives an account in *Jarls' Saga* of the famous ritual murder called 'blood-eagling' which is associated with the cult of Odin. This was carried out on the occasion of Earl Torf-Einar's murder of the son of Harald Finehair, Halfdan Long-Legs, who had conquered the islands. After a naval battle Halfdan had fled to North Ronaldsay:

> There they found Halfdan Long-Legs. Earl Einar carved the bloody eagle on his back by laying his sword in the hollow at the backbone and hacking all the ribs from the back-bone down to the loins and drawing out the lungs; and he gave him to Odin as an offering for his victory.[35]

It has been argued that this form of ritual slaying is a potent symbol of Viking threat to the peaceful Christian kingdoms of the west and a kind of pagan exultation in victory.[36] In the case of Halfdan's murder the deed was perpetrated against a fellow-Norseman and pagan, but the purpose of the act would appear to have been one of exultation by Torf-Einar in the final killing of a rival to his position in the Isles, and a member of the royal Vestfold house who had been responsible for the death of his father. The circumstances of the vengeance are strongly supported by Torf-Einar's own verses written on the occasion, but they do not actually describe the method of killing employed. Doubts about the veracity of the revolting details of dismemberment used in the blood-eagling ritual on other victims of Viking atrocity suggest possible elaboration by the later saga writers who misunderstood the elliptical phrases of early skaldic verse.[37] Included in one of Torf-Einar's verses is a very generalized reference to his victim being 'torn by the eagle's talon'. Is the prose description of the bloody ritual a later elaboration by the saga writer wishing to add graphic details to his story about a former age? Torf-Einar was a ruthless man and a pagan, bent on revenge and conquest of the Isles against a formidable foe. He may well indeed have given his victim to Odin as an offering for his victory; he certainly says that he piled a cairn over him[38] in the traditional manner of pagan burial. But the rite of 'blood-eagling' is not an essential detail making the incident more or less likely.

Later in the saga, a powerful earl's success or death in battle is associated with the image of the raven, the bird of Odin. This is the story of the banner woven for Sigurd the Stout by his mother, Eithne: 'very cleverly embroidered with the figure of a raven, and when the banner fluttered in the breeze, the raven seemed to be flying ahead'.[39] Eithne endowed it with magic qualities that 'will bring victory to the man it's carried before, but death to the one who carries it'. This was fulfilled when the earl lost three standard bearers in the ensuing battle of Skitten Myre but was victorious; there was a fateful twist at the battle of Clontarf when no-one would carry the raven banner 'so the Earl had to do it himself and he was killed'.[40] Despite the official conversion of Earl Sigurd, his association with the pagan image of Odin's bird suggests that it was considered to be as supernatural an element as it had always been. How reliable can we assume that a story of this kind is likely to be? To what extent can conclusions be based on it about the beliefs in Odin and the efficacy of his symbol? It is very interesting that a similar legend about a Viking raven banner is recorded in a later medieval English source; the actual existence of this banner is nonetheless authenticated by contemporary record. It was the banner 'which they called the raven' captured by the West Saxons from a raiding force led by the brother of the two famous Vikings Ivarr and Halfdan in an attack on North Devon in 878.[41] From this description in the contemporary *Anglo-Saxon Chronicle* it is clear that this was considered to be a real trophy, and it is not surprising, therefore, that the same banner is mentioned in a much later source as endowed with magical properties, for the fluttering of the raven image is then said to have been a forecast of victory and its drooping a presage of defeat.[42] Moreover, it had been woven, according to legend, by the three daughters of Ragnar Lothbrok, the father of the leaders of the invasion. Other famous banners are known in northern history.[43] Despite the accumulation of myth around them, raven banners were not, however, later inventions. They were potent symbols of pagan military prowess, and there is no reason to doubt the existence of Sigurd's raven banner; indeed the Old Norse poem *Darraðarliod* is early evidence for its significance (see below). Given such evidence of the significance attached to a symbol of pagan militarism, it may well have been the case that 'paganism and the cult of Odin held out into the eleventh century on Orkney'[44] – at any rate in the circle of the earl and his hirdmen.

The numbers of Orcadian place-names which have been shown to include the name of Odin suggest that he was a popular god in the earldom during the

Figure 76. Early nineteenth-century representation of the Stone of Odin at Stenness, Orkney (*right*), which was destroyed in 1814 (Royal Commission on Ancient Monuments, Scotland; Crown Copyright reserved).

Much folklore and superstition were attached to this stone and the hole was used for curative and contractual purposes.

Western Gable of the Stones of Stennis

pagan period. Two 'Stones of Odin' are known: one giving its name to the farm of Odinstone in Shapinsay,[45] the other originally forming part of the collection of prehistoric standing stones at the famous site of Stenness on Mainland (see fig. 76).[46] Memories of old myths relating to Odin have also been collected in Orkney. Place-names elsewhere in Scandinavian Scotland should also provide some evidence for pagan worship and cult sites as they do in Scandinavia and Iceland,[47] although little work has been done in collecting such names. Those with the Old Norse element *hof* (= temple, such as Hoove in Shetland) are thought to indicate a 'vestige of paganism'.[48] The well-known name of Thurso in Caithness has occasioned a great deal of discussion among linguists as to whether it derives from the god's name 'Thor' or from ON *þjór* (= 'bull').[49] Further fascinating possibilities are raised by the theory that place-names in Iceland and Norway with the element *saurr* (= 'wet land, excrement, semen, mud') are to be associated with the worship of Frey and Freyja, and thus may have been centres of a fertility cult.[50] In the combination Sowerby/Sorbie (*saur-býr*) this is a most widespread place-name throughout areas of Scandinavian settlement in Britain, including the Western Isles (but not, strangely, Orkney or Shetland). However, in this respect as in regard to all apparent evidence for pagan worship, 'caution is obviously called for'.[51]

THE ORKNEY BONDER

What do we know of the less heroic classes of Norse society, below the rank of earl or king? In the early Viking Age the broad mass of farmers were divided into two classes, the 'bonder' (ON *bóndi*, best translated as 'farmer') and the superior rank of 'hold' (ON *hauldr*), a class known in Danish England;[52] the term is used in *Jarls' Saga* with reference to only a very few powerful individuals.[53] It may be that in the first few centuries in the north the earls towered above the rest of Orcadian society, who were all covered by the general term of 'bonder', and that it was not until the time of Earl Thorfinn that a powerful intermediate class of chieftains was established in the islands, who were all related to the earls.[54] This class of men were given grants of earldom estates (ON *veizla*) in the outlying islands in order to raise the earl's naval levies and collect in his skatts. There they became the founders of semi-independent houses, foreshadowing the class of 'gödings' (ON *goeðingar*), a term particularly associated with the Orkney landowners, which appears in the twelfth-century section of the saga, and meaning that this class were endowed with 'goods'.[55] The trouble with this interpretation of Orcadian society, however, is that it may underestimate the power and wealth of the 'bonder' in the earlier centuries. They appear from the saga account to have played an important role in society, for when they acted in concert they had some ability to negotiate with the earl. They were free in legal terms, having an atonement value or 'wergild', and they had the right to attend the law courts. However, the question of the tenure of their estates was one which was not easily established and about which there were evidently tensions with the earls from time to time. These were not men who held earldom lands for rent and military service, but who probably considered that they held their family lands by prescriptive right, or according to original conquest and settlement –

although we have no evidence about how the land had been acquired, or how they thought it had been acquired.

'Odal' land tenure

There are some problematical passages in *Jarls' Saga* where the earls are described as having acquired the 'odal/udal' rights of the farmers and as having granted these back again when wanting to bargain with the bonder. It is not at all clear what actually happened on these occasions, for by the time of the sagas 'feudal' ideas of lordship and land tenure were permeating the Scandinavian world and we cannot be certain whether the writer had any clear knowledge of transactions which had taken place many centuries earlier. Similarly in Norway King Harald Finehair is said to have acquired the 'odal/udal' property of the Norwegian farmers, for according to Snorri: 'King Harald made this law over all the lands he conquered, that all the udal property should belong to him; and that the bonder, both great and small, should pay him land dues for their possession.'[56] This is part and parcel of the strong tradition about King Harald's conquest of all the parts of Norway and his unification of all the different petty kingdoms into one realm; Hakon the Good is later credited with having relaxed the heavy burdens laid on the people. Also in the Isle of Man there was a tradition of some similar claim to complete ownership of the lands by Godred Crovan who conquered the island in 1079 and granted lands to the islanders 'on condition that none of them should presume to claim any of the land by hereditary right. Hence it arises that up to the present day [i.e. the thirteenth century] the whole island belongs to the king alone, and that all its revenues are his.'[57] Although there is no mention here of the concept of 'odal' rights – which did not exist in the Isle of Man at any time as far as is known – the legendary theme is the same, that a famous conqueror had established his dynasty's superior right over the farmers from very early times. Similar traditions existed in many countries where kingdoms or lordships had been founded by conquest.[58]

In both Orkney and Norway that tradition involved the loss or deprivation of 'odal/udal' (ON *oðal*) rights. These were inalienable rights over family lands (lands not held in corporate ownership, but individually), and these rights were closely associated in origin with the pagan elements of ancestor worship.[59] The term is restricted to Norway, Sweden and some of the Norse colonies, although the concept of inalienable family lands is known in some other societies and in other parts of North Europe in the Middle Ages under the name of 'alod' (which may or may not derive from the same origin as 'odal'). Such lands were hedged about with various rules and could not be sold out of the possession of the family who had the right of 'first refusal'.[60] It is a 'primitive' concept which stems from an age before states and kings developed overriding authority and it survived in the Scandinavian milieu – where royal power was slower to develop – longer than in most other parts of northern Europe, for it is the antithesis of the idea basic to 'feudal' monarchies of the twelfth century and later that kings had an underlying right to all land, which was only granted out to the holders on a life-rent basis.

In the case of thirteenth-century accounts of Harald Finehair's appropriation of all the odal lands of Norway we can see later writers attempting to justify the growth of royal power in terms of an ancient appropriation of private possessions. Norwegian historians have agonized over the passage quoted above from *Heimskringla*, and how it should be interpreted. There may be a kernel of historical truth in the matter, that Harald did indeed appropriate the lands of his opponents whom he conquered – particularly in the west and in Trøndelag.[61] But to the medieval writers, familiar with a national skatt and royal estates all over Norway, it may have appeared that he had been attempting to acquire a comprehensive 'odal-right' (sovereignty over the whole land). There is evidently a rationalizing element of some sort in these later accounts, which may also be trying to explain the loss of freedom in Norway during the centuries since the Viking Age.[62]

The struggle over 'odal' rights

Attempts to rationalize are probably also present in the traditions regarding the odal lands in Orkney, which are scattered through *Jarls' Saga*. There were evidently two versions of the theory of how the earls got possession of the odal rights in the first place. In *Harald Fine Hair's Saga* and *Jarls' Saga*, we are told that when King Harald came to Orkney to avenge the murder of his son Halfdan Long-Legs he imposed a fine of 60 gold marks on the Isles, which Earl Einar offered to pay on condition that the odal rights of all landowners were made over to him; and the bonders' agreement to this condition is rationalized thus: 'for the rich ones expected to be able to buy back their rights; and the poor ones had no money to pay the fine.'[63] It is added that the earls held the odal rights ('*áttu óðul ǫll*') for a long time afterwards, until Earl Sigurd Hlodversson gave them back to the farmers. However, in *St Olaf's Saga*, Snorri gives a different interpretation which attributes the acquisition of all odal properties in the islands to King Harald who made the people 'hold them under oath from him' and who then handed over the islands to the earl as a fief after he had made his peace with the king. Although the earl had to pay a fine of 60 marks, it was expressly said that he was to pay no tribute ('scatt or feu duty') for the islands as they were much plundered by Vikings at that time.[64] This would appear to be a greater refinement on the other version and the same theory is repeated later by King Olaf to Earl Brusi that his ancestor Harald Finehair had appropriated to himself all odal rights in Orkney and the earls had held the country as a fief since then, not as their own odal property.[65] We may suspect that this is the official version, which gave the kings overriding control of the acquisition of the 'odal' in the first place, thus helping to establish their superiority over the earls.

The fine of 60 marks which appears in both versions may be the kernel of historical truth which has survived, surrounded by varying explanations. There seems no particular reason to doubt the idea of Harald Finehair exacting a fine in retribution for the murder of his son, for this accords better with what is known about royal rights in the early period than the acquisition of superiority over land. The older parts of the Norwegian law-codes are concerned with the laws of retribution and the payments exacted by avenging members of a kindred according to the status of the individual killed.

However, it is not clear why in the case of Halfdan Long-Legs' murder this retribution should have been demanded from all the farmers in the islands, and this may be a later addition to help explain how the earls came to have so much control over the islands. The process of conquest and settlement was no doubt quite obscure to the thirteenth-century writers. They may therefore have felt obliged to devise a theory accounting for the ordinary farmers' loss of family rights over their lands. We certainly cannot use this saga material as evidence to prove that Orkney had been settled before even the late eighth century (as has been done) on the basis that the settlers' lands could not be counted as 'odal' unless they had been held by the family for ten generations; and that therefore the Orkney farmers at the time of King Harald in the later ninth century had been in possession of their lands for 200 years![66]

There are further occasions in *Jarls' Saga* when negotiations are reputed to have taken place between the earl and the bonder over the legal status of the latter's lands, which suggest that there was continuing tension between the earls and the farmers over the burdens which were incumbent on their lands. According to the account of Sigurd the Stout's battle with Earl Finnlaech at Skitten Myre, the earl 'gave the Orkneymen their odal rights in return for war-service'.[67] This was certainly remembered as being a reversion to a previous situation, for the comment is included at the end of the account of the battle: 'and the Orkneymen got back their odal rights.'[68] So on this occasion the earl was evidently relaxing some imposition on the farmers' lands – probably an inheritance tax – in return for getting them to agree to fight against Earl Finnlaech in Caithness, and probably to accept the idea of permanent war-service. If this passage can be relied on as an accurate record of some transaction which took place between Earl Sigurd and the Orkneymen, then it would appear to be a significant piece of evidence for the imposition of military service on the farmers' lands in the late tenth century which would have been fitted into the ounceland system.[69] It may, of course, relate particularly to the fact that the farmers were agreeing to fight in Caithness and therefore be an extension of any military obligation that they had within the islands.

Finally the earl tried to manipulate the status of the farmers' lands in the twelfth century and as this was not long before the saga was written down the incident is certainly likely to have been accurately remembered. When Earl Rognvald II was building his great votive church in Kirkwall to the memory of his murdered uncle, St Magnus, about the year 1137, he attempted to recover the cost by introducing the concept of a feudal 'relief' for the farmers by 'declaring that the Earls should be considered to have inherited all the odal possessions of the owners, but that they were to be redeemable by the heirs'.[70] However, 'This was considered a great hardship',[71] and at an assembly the earl proposed that the bonder should 'purchase the odal possessions'[72] to avoid the imposition of any redemption fee. This was agreed to at the rate of one mark for every 'plough's land'.[73] What, in fact, may have happened was that a tax or levy was laid on all the cultivated land in the earldom to help finance the ambitious plans for the cathedral in Kirkwall, which was agreed to by the farmers under threat of the imposition of an entry fee on the inheritance of their family estates which were held according to odal custom. This suggests that they had not paid such an entrance fee before; it also suggests that the earls would have liked to have instituted such a concept if they could, and further it tells us that the farmers were able to prevent its imposition, although having to agree to a land tax for the building of the cathedral, which in a curious way was treated as a redemption sum for their odal possessions. The earl probably had to promise not to raise the question of inheritance fees again in the future. In the final analysis it was a successful ruse on the part of the earl to raise cash by threatening the farmers' traditional freedom of inheritance of their family lands.

The impression given by the core of these traditional accounts is that the Orkney farmers were a body of men determined to preserve independent control of their family estates in the face of a powerful earl who for reasons of state would like to have had overriding authority, and perhaps on occasion managed to get it, according to his individual situation. The farmers' freedom of inheritance is expressed as their 'odal' in a rather mystical way by the saga writer. The author, an Icelander, would not be particularly familiar with the workings of 'odal' land tenure in Orkney which differed from that of Iceland.[74] But the Orkney farmers' wish to maintain their independence emerges clearly enough from the saga narrative. The reason why this system of land-ownership became rooted in Orkney and Shetland (and perhaps Caithness) but not in the Faroes, Iceland or the Isle of Man is a historical problem whose explanation must lie in the particular political situation in each group of islands. It may reflect the need of the bonder in the Northern Isles to preserve their independence from their powerful local ruler – a situation which did not exist in Iceland or the Faroes. Presumably, then, the king of Man was so powerful that the concept failed to take root in that island.[75] Paradoxically, the geographical conditions which made the establishment of a powerful earldom possible in the Orkney archipelago also fostered the growth of a firmly entrenched body of farmers whose political strength has perhaps not been sufficiently appreciated. Surviving documentary evidence attests to their continued existence throughout the Middle Ages.[76]

The struggle over military service

The most vivid story in the early part of *Jarls' Saga* of the tension between the Orkney bonder and the earl is contained in the account of Earl Einar Sigurds-son's efforts to raise a naval levy from his part of the isles (post–1014) in an attempt to maintain his father's conquests in the west: 'Einar was the most overbearing of men, and brought an exceedingly bad harvest in his realm through the enforced service of the bonder.'[77] The farmers found a spokesman, Thorkell Amundsson, to present their case to the earl at the spring Lawthing, which suggests that these assemblies could be a forum for the expression of discontent by the farmers. Indeed Einar agreed on the first occasion to reduce the levy from his share of the islands from six ships to three. Thorkell earned the earl's displeasure, however, when he repeated the demands the next year and became the chief opponent of the earl, and eventually his murderer – smashing his axe into Einar's head as the earl sat beside the fire in Thorkell's own hall in Sandwick at the end of October 1020.[78] We are given a very vivid impression from this account of the power of rich farmers like Thorkell to exercise some restraint on the ambitions of overbearing earls like Einar, even if it did in the end mean murdering him. Thorkell based his own power entirely on his family position and odal estates, although he did look to Einar's half-brother Thorfinn as his protector when he had to flee Orkney.[79]

The rule of their 'protectors' was evidently becoming irksome to the Orkney bonder by the late tenth and eleventh centuries. The military demands of ambitious warriors, striving to maintain authority outside the Orkney islands, would appear to have been unwelcome to men whose lands and agricultural interests were by then more significant than the call of plunder and booty or the harrying life which was still the earls' main occupation. Trouble arose over Earl Einar's demands for war service because he was attempting to maintain the extent of his father's conquests on one-third of the revenue, for he had to share the earldom with his two brothers. The division of the islands between brothers was always a source of political weakness. Once Earl Thorfinn had gained the whole of the earldom lands (in the 1040s) he was able to be as successful as his father – and as popular, for his demands on the farmers did not then exceed what was considered customary and reasonable for skatt and service. But when the earls made extra military demands the farmers could resist them: as when Earl Sigurd gave back the land-holding rights, and Earl Einar reduced his levy. Both these earls needed extra service in order to pursue their military ambitions further south in Scotland.

Kindred and lordship

The relationship between the earls and powerful individuals such as Thorkell Amundssen provides one of the main themes of the saga narrative. It is likely, however, that in Scandinavian Scotland the family was the most fundamental social unit. Certainly in Norway the early law-codes – crucial sources for understanding Norse society – suggest that the family was the protector of the peace and the avenger of violence against any of its members. However, it has been questioned whether we can rely on the twelfth-century law-codes as an accurate reflection of the family's role in an earlier age, and particularly whether the complicated lists of compensatory payments of which the law-codes are full correspond to any historical reality.[80] It is, nonetheless, likely that a man's status and worth in society were determined by his family, and that according to his rank he had a value which would be demanded as compensation in case of slaying or injury. In the feud of Thorkell Amundssen and Earl Einar, King Olaf awarded compensation to the value of three 'lendirmen' (ON *lendr maðr* = a man endowed with royal lands) for the murder of the earl, although one-third was remitted because of Earl Einar's own murder of Eyvind Urushorn, a close follower of the king.[81] Apparently adjustments to the rigid compensation scale were made in individual instances, and where the individuals were earls and members of his hird the king would adjudicate; but for the majority of the population the matter would be decided in the local courts. Vengeance was an essential sanction and a regular part of this primitive judicial structure, although compensatory payments (ON *mansbót*) to buy off the feud became the more usual form of settling disputes. However, in the early years of the earldom the vengeance remembered as having been taken by Torf-Einar against Halfdan Long-Legs, who had been responsible for the murder of his father Earl Rognvald, is characteristic of the feud, and highly probable. The theme of vengeance is clearly stated in Torf-

204 Chapter 7 The Literary Framework

Einar's own poem – as well as expressions of scorn for his brothers Rolf, Hrollaug and Thore in Møre who had done nothing to avenge their father's death:

> Not from Hrolf's hand
> nor Hrollaug's, the hurled shaft,
> no death-dart. Our
> duty is to the dead,
> our father; here the fight
> grows fierce, while at Møre
> what says the ale-swilling earl?
> Nought of the sword-swing.[82]

The family's feud had been carried across the North Sea and continued in the new settlements. In general, however, it is more likely that family bonds were much weakened by the disruption to kindred structures caused by the movements of people overseas and the mobility of the Viking Age. Most of the settlers must have left large numbers of kindred behind, for it cannot have been common for whole families to abandon their ancestral lands and move overseas. A rigid kinship structure would have been loosened therefore in the colonizing period, although it could have been built up again in a few generations. The account of Aud the Deep-Minded, moving north from Scotland and seeking out her brothers in Iceland, tells us of the maintenance of family links in very remarkable – and probably unusual – circumstances. Even so, her brother Helgi's ideas of family solidarity only extended to putting up half Aud's following which she thought a 'poor offer'.[83] Where they existed family links were important: but in a violent and mobile society the bond of lordship and the protection of powerful war-leaders must also have played a vital role in the lives of the settlers. Indeed, lords or chieftains may always have been more important in all Scandinavian society than has been recognized, just as they obviously were in Iceland and in Ireland.[84]

LAW AND SOCIETY

It is significant that Thorkell Amundssen's first clash with Earl Einar took place in the public assembly, the Thing (ON *þing* = law court). The earl flew into a rage with Thorkell and said that 'another spring they would not both be at the Thing safe and sound',[85] which suggests that such meetings were held regularly at that time of the year, and as one of the important items for discussion was the levy required by the earl for the summer's war-cruise, this was probably the meeting later known as the 'Wappinstein'.[86] There is little additional information in the saga about the early legal structure in the Orkney earldom; it has been assumed that because the earls themselves presided over the judicial assemblies, as well as making laws, the Things in the Northern Isles would not have had the independence which they enjoyed in other parts of the Norse world.[87] Yet despite the power of the earls it is undoubted that a legal structure must have been established in the islands from the earliest days of settlement, for it was an integral part of the organization of society in Norway.

Courts and judicial divisions

We know from Icelandic and Norwegian example that the Norsemen at home and in the Atlantic settlements employed the most remarkable system of administrative divisions based on judicial districts.[88] There were assemblies at every level, from the *bygdeting* (= community court) which was attended by all freemen in a locality to the *lagting* (= law court) which was attended by representatives from the whole law province and which altered or created new laws as needed. There were four legal provinces throughout Norway and it seems likely that Orkney and Shetland (evidence for the Hebrides does not exist) followed the legal customs of the Gulathing district which covered all western Norway south of Trondheim. The Norwegian law-codes date from the twelfth or thirteenth centuries but incorporate older customary practice. At a later date there was a whole hierarchy of courts; the *fylkesting* (= shire court), *heradsting* (= hundred court), and in some places even a *tredingsting, fjerding-sting* or *attungsting*, implying the division of larger districts into thirds, quarters and eighths. The clearest picture of some similar form of judicial administrative order in Scandinavian Scotland comes from the Isle of Man which, apart from the central assembly site at Tynwald (ON *þing-völlr* = assembly field or enclosure), had 2 courts for the Northside and Southside divisions of the island, 6 smaller courts for the 'sheading' divisions (ON *séttungr* = a sixth part) (fig. 23) and 16 to 17 parochial courts.[89] Later evidence suggests that the Hebrides were administratively linked in with the island of Man itself in the constitution of the kingdom, and the northern Isles (Lewis, Harris and Skye) sent eight representatives to Tynwald. It is assumed that the southern Hebrides at one time also sent eight, for the number from Man itself was 16.[90] Late sixteenth-century evidence says that the 'whole Isles of Scotland' were formerly divided into four parts, based on the large islands of Lewis, Skye, Mull and Islay, which may have been a continuation of Norse administrative arrangements.[91] Such organization is likely to have been developed by the kings of Man and the Isles in the period after their emergence in the tenth century as sole rulers in the area.

A similar quartering of Orkney into four judicial/administrative divisions (*fjórðungr*), which included Caithness, has been worked out from late medieval evidence. Each quarter sent nine 'roithmen' (ON *raðmenn* = councillors) to the Lawthing who made up the 'logretta' (ON *lögrétta* = body of judges), and 'the commons' are referred to in documents as being present.[92] This assembly was presided over by the Lawman, a powerful figure in Orcadian history, who eventually became a paid crown servant. However, the situation in the Northern Isles in the sixteenth century was very different from the early Norse age, and it is not easy to get back to that period through the customary accretions of the centuries and the subtle alteration of Old Norse names into a terminology peculiarly adapted to the Orcadian situation. There was, for instance, a close association of the parish divisions and judicial representation, and it has been suggested that the parish divisions are in origin much older than the period of parochial organization in the twelfth century[93] and that they were originally associated with the temple districts of the heathen religion, used also for the representation of chieftains at the Icelandic *Alþing*.

Thing-sites in north and west

The structure of legal provinces and the existence of a hierarchy of law courts is seen by many Norwegian historians to represent a healthy democratic element in early Norse society, until eroded by royal power and church pretensions through the Middle Ages. The importance of the *Alþing* in the Icelandic Commonwealth was basic to the existence of that community, although lordship also played an important role there too. It seems very likely that as the power of the earls of Orkney grew the courts in the islands came under his control, and the main assembly became the earl's court. Tingwall in Rendall (ON *þing-völlr* = assembly field or enclosure) must certainly have been the site of an assembly at an early period, but Kirkwall was undoubtedly the more usual place of meeting after it became the earls' main residence in the later twelfth century. The name Dingieshowe in the eastern Mainland (ON *þing-haugr* = assembly-mound) also points to a meeting place of early courts,[94] as does the name Thingswa (ON *þing-svað* = assembly-slope) in Caithness, two miles west of Thurso.[95] But the limited number of such place-names in Orkney and Caithness and the lack of evidence for the regular 'thing' structure that one does find in Shetland suggests that the earl's overriding authority in judicial matters prevented fixed local assemblies from thriving in the joint earldom. There is nothing in Orkney to compare with the impressive site at Tingwall in Shetland, with its strong traditions as the meeting-place of the annual Lawthing (see fig. 77). The Law Ting Holm juts out into an inland loch and there are still traces of an encircling stone enclosure and stone causeway which leads straight from the Holm towards the parish church a few hundred yards away and where the Shetland Lawthing met to arbitrate in a case recorded in 1307.[96] This conjunction of church and state is reminiscent of the assembly site at Thingvellir in Iceland and witnesses the church's growing interest in these legal assemblies, in oath-taking and in the full range of offences under ecclesiastical law. The Law Ting Holm at Tingwall in Shetland was still being used for legal transactions as late as the sixteenth century and the evidence for a large number of other 'thing' sites in Shetland, the names of some of which survive today as parish names (such as Delting, Sandsting and Aithsting), tells us that local judicial assemblies continued to have a very important place in the organization of society there. It is likely that this situation developed in the period after 1195 when Shetland was taken away from the earls and put directly under control of the Norwegian kings, making it more comparable with the Faroe Islands to the north.

Elsewhere in Scotland, the names of Dingwall at the head of the Cromarty Firth and of Tinwald in Dumfriesshire gave strong indications of flourishing communities of Scandinavian settlers, who were dominant enough in these localities to be able to organize their own legal assembly for the running of their own affairs according to their own laws and customs. The most famous is the stepped hillock at Tynwald in the Isle of Man, still the site of the annual assembly on St John's Day of the island parliament where the new laws are read out and petitions heard (see fig. 78). Its importance as a place for the convening of peace meetings between the various contenders to the throne of Man is well illustrated in the *Chronicle of Man* during the late Norse period.[97] It is not unlikely that Irish customs were involved in the inauguration

Figure 77. Views of Tingwall, Shetland (photographs: author).

(*above*) The Law Ting Holm, former site of the annual judicial assembly of the Shetland islands, can be seen jutting out into the loch. The parish church (the white building) is on the extreme right. Tingwall was in the possession of the Archdeacon of Shetland in the medieval period: he was the most important church official in the islands.

(*below*) The remains of a substantial causeway, leading across marshy ground to the Law Ting Holm.

Figure 78. Tynwald, Isle of Man (photograph: R.M.M. Crawford).
The processional way, lined with flags, leads from the assembly mound to St John's Church.

ceremonies of the kings of Man and the kings of Dublin which took place at Tynwald and at the Thingmote in Dublin respectively;[98] and it would not be surprising if there was strong Celtic influence in matters of social organization in parts of the Hebrides. At a later date the Council of the Isles met on Eilean na Comhairle (= 'council isle') at Finlaggan in Islay (fig. 79) where the Lords of the Isles were installed and had a residence.[99] The situation has similarities with the Law Ting Holm in Shetland (fig. 77) and is likely to have been an ancient assembly site.[100] There were probably many other lesser assembly sites in the Hebrides, but they are barely remembered and their names not easily recognized. The name Hinnisdal (Tinwhill) in North Skye has been interpreted as a *þingvǫllr* name and not far away is Cnoc an Eirachd (OI *airecht* = assembly) near Duntulm (called the Hill of Pleas by Pennant in 1772).[101] This is a field of research where place-names and archaeology are of equal importance and remains on the ground like a 'doom-ring' (ON *dóm hring* = 'judgment circle') said to exist at Scalabreck on Bernera and on Papa Stour, Shetland,[102] may be the only surviving testimony to former legal organization at a very local level.

This scattered and unresearched evidence points attention towards an important aspect of Scandinavian Scotland, and reaches back to a most significant element of Norse society. The 'thing' place names give us evidence of the social and judicial organization of the communities of Scandinavian speakers established in different parts of Scotland, even though we lack any documentary or historical evidence of such organization in many of the areas where these names occur. They are a permanent record of the fact that the Scandinavian invaders were prepared 'to settle down and lead their lives in a society governed by law',[103] which is not an aspect usually associated with the Viking way of life. Such assemblies must have provided a forum for the peaceful settlement of feuds and disputes, as a possible alternative to violence and bloodshed.[104] Their concern with the processes of law was one of the most valuable contributions made by the Norwegians and Danes to the cultures of the countries they settled in, and it is likely that Scotland was no exception in benefitting from these peoples' flair for judicial organization.[105] They appear to

Figure 79. Aerial view of Finlaggan, Islay, Southern Hebrides (Royal Commission on Ancient Monuments, Scotland; Crown Copyright reserved).
    These two islands lie in an inland loch, about 4.5km from the sea. Eilean Mor ('the great isle'), the larger of the two, is traditionally the site of the residence of the Lords of the Isles. It was formerly joined by a causeway to the smaller Eilean na Comhairle ('council isle') where in the late Middle Ages the Council of the Isles met – an assembly of lords from the main Hebridean islands and a probable successor to the earlier Norse 'Thing'.

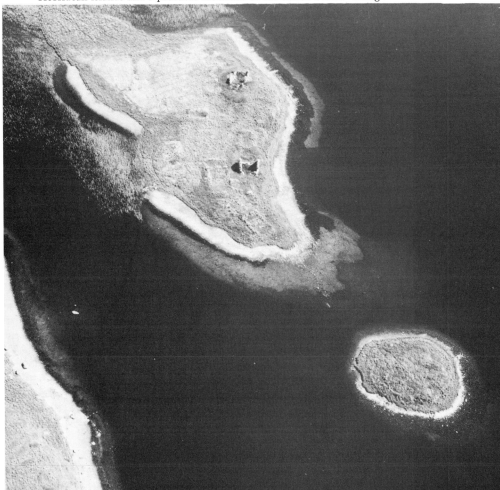

have imposed their legal structures wherever they settled and these must have been a vital element in helping the colonists to maintain their cultural cohesion, before being absorbed into the feudal administration of the Scottish kingdom in the twelfth and thirteenth centuries.

SLAVERY AND CELTIC SURVIVAL

Leaving the free members of Norse society and turning to those who enjoyed no legal rights – the unfree – we are able to glean little direct information about the class of thralls (ON *þraell*) in Scandinavian Scotland. The unfree played an important role in Norwegian and Icelandic society until the twelfth century.[106] The slave trade was basic to the success of the Viking raids around the Irish and Scottish coasts, and Icelandic evidence for the existence of a servile class derived from the Celtic parts of Britain is too substantial to be ignored.[107]

The enslavement of the Celtic population

Evidence from the Icelandic *Book of Settlements* supplies us with a vivid example of what happened to one Celtic family who had the misfortune to be swept up by the Norsemen in their slave-raiding and conquering phase. Several remarkable passages tell of the descendants of Erp, whose father, Earl Melduin of Argyll, had been killed by Earl Sigurd 'the Mighty' of Orkney and whose mother, Muirgeal (daughter of King Giljomal of Ireland), was taken into captivity to become the handmaid of Earl Sigurd's wife whom she 'served faithfully'.[108] Muirgeal was then bought 'for a high price' by Aud the Deep-minded (*djúpúdga*), one of the famous figures in saga literature and a founding mother of the Icelandic settlement. Muirgeal and her son Erp were among the many slaves who went with Aud to Iceland on her famous journey; most of them are said to have been freed during the early years of the settlement of Iceland and they became the founders of several important families. It was traditionally remembered that Aud said of Erp: 'It has never been my wish that a man of such high birth should be called a slave.'[109]

The Icelandic sources repeatedly refer to men and women being 'from the Hebrides' (*Suðreyskr* or *Suðreyingr*) or Irish in origin.[110] But there is never any mention of slaves from the Orkneys, which all adds to the general picture of uncertainty as to what happened to the native population in the Northern Isles during the Norse invasions.[111] Very few settlers of Iceland are said to have come from Orkney or Shetland either, and the reason probably lies in the greater stability of the Norse settlement there, whereas there was some form of pressure on the settlers in the Western Isles in the late ninth century which impelled so many of them to move out, with their slaves, to other areas of colonization.[112] The Norse farmers in Orkney are likely to have worked their lands with the aid of the indigenous population which had either been enslaved or very much depressed in the social scale. Conversion should have meant the end of a slave-based society, for it was incumbent on all Christians to free their servile dependants,[113] but we have no evidence of a class of *leysingar* (= freedmen) from either the early or post-conversion period in the

Scottish settlements. The only reference in *Jarls' Saga* is of a servile group who had apparently continued to exist in the service of the earls into the eleventh century. When Earl Thorfinn was attacked and his homestead on the Mainland (at Birsay?) set on fire c.1046, the women and thralls (*ófriálsum karlmǫnnum*) were allowed to leave the buildings.[114] This suggests that the earls' estates may still have been worked by a servile class in the Christian period, unless the later saga writer was using anachronistic terminology for the details of this famous event.

Survival: Picts and *papar*

Enslavement does not, of course, mean the demise of a people, even though their identity may be unrecognizable in the archaeological record and their language doomed to non-survival in the long run.[115] The persistence of elements of Celtic culture traceable in folklore motifs or other unquantifiable and 'unhistorical' aspects of later island culture indicates that a Celtic strata of society did survive in the north. By the twelfth century, however, the former native population in Orkney had been invested with supernatural qualities, to judge from a highly interesting passage in *Historia Norvegiae*[116] which describes them as dwarves who lived in underground houses. The place-names in Shetland in which the element 'petta' (= Picts) occurs suggest that the previous inhabitants very soon came to be regarded more or less as trolls who inhabited certain lonely places.[117] Part of the process of supernaturalization was the belief (expressed in the *Historia Norvegiae*) that the Picts lost all their strength in the middle of the day, which it has been suggested is an element of Celtic folklore.[118] Similar elements appear in a story retold by the eleventh-century Hamburg cleric, Adam of Bremen, about some Frisian sailors who were shipwrecked on an island in the northern seas where men similarly lurked in underground hollows at midday.[119] These are two versions of a common myth about the native inhabitants of northern islands which circulated in different parts of Scandinavia in the eleventh and twelfth centuries.

Residual memory of the *papar* (the Celtic priests, whose name is permanently enshrined in the 'Papay' and 'Papil' place-names of the islands of the west and north[120]) was rather less weird. The *Historia Norvegiae* records that they wore white robes like priests and that they had written books associated with them; this is reminiscent of the details given by Ari the Icelander about the *papar* who were found by the first settlers of Iceland and who left behind them bells, croziers and books from which it was known they were Irish.[121] The writer of *Historia Norvegiae* adds, however, that they were 'Africans, adhering to Judaism', possibly deduced from the Middle Eastern and North African derivation of Irish monasticism.[122]

Survival: literary and linguistic

The Orkney earldom is increasingly being seen as a probable centre of transmission of Gaelic culture from Scotland and Ireland to Scandinavia, and

Iceland in particular.[123] The persistent attempts of the earls to dominate the Hebrides, Ireland and mainland Scotland show that political links with the Gaelic south and west were maintained and these, of course, would have led to social links. There are several instances of intermarriage between the earldom family and Celts; tenth- and eleventh-century earls had Pictish, Irish, and Scottish wives, while Icelandic tradition remembered that the sister of Sigurd the Stout was married to Earl Gilli of the Hebrides,[124] who bore a Gaelic name.

The example of Celtic influence which is most relevant to the period covered here is the story in *Jarls' Saga* of Sigurd the Mighty's death, which was caused by a wound to his leg from a tooth projecting from the severed head of Earl Maelbrigte of Moray which he had cut off and attached to his saddle.[125] It was traditional Celtic practice to cut off the head of your enemy and it is recorded, moreover, that among the Continental Celts as well as in Ireland severed heads were hung as trophies on the victor's horse.[126] Along with this goes the idea of the head of the slain man avenging the former bearer of the head (Sigurd's death was caused by a scratch from the tooth sticking out of Melbrigte's jaw) for this is a motif which appears in Old Irish literature. These legendary accretions which grew up about the story of the death of Sigurd the Mighty are therefore highly flavoured with Celtic ideas and strong evidence of Irish or Scottish influence which was either transmitted to Iceland in the settlement period and eventually written down in the twelfth century or passed on from Orkney to Iceland at a later date. Individuals like the Irish slave Muirgeal (discussed above), who served Earl Sigurd's wife so faithfully, would be very well informed about the fate of the earl. A strange detail about her relationship with Earl Sigurd's wife hints at the authenticity of the whole tradition of her place in the earldom household: she was remembered as being 'a clever woman' who was involved in saving one of the earl's children when her mistress 'was taking her bath'.[127] As mentioned above, Muirgeal eventually went to Iceland with Aud and any tales about the death of Earl Sigurd embellished with Gaelic myths would not be forgotten by her six grandchildren who all founded families in Iceland.[128]

The mainland half of the Orkney earl's dominion, the province of Caithness, was bitterly fought over by earls and Celtic chieftains and it was here that Celtic and Scandinavian traditions met, and the two cultures mingled.[129] A native dynasty survived into the tenth century at Duncansby and a Celticized aristocracy in Caithness emerges from the pages of *Jarls' Saga* in the twelfth century.[130] It would not be surprising, therefore, if an occasional Celtic element cropped up in Old Norse sources relating to places and circumstances in Caithness. One example is the possible occurrence of the Gaelic term 'conveth' in one version of the twelfth-century section of the saga. This was a well-known hospitality rent paid to the king of Scotland north of the Forth in the Middle Ages (Gael. *commaid*).[131] The Norse equivalent was 'wattle' (ON *veizla*) which was paid to the earl in Orkney, but the Gaelic term was possibly familiar in Caithness, for it is said that when the earl boarded out his men in Caithness 'the men of Caithness said that the Earl was on *commaid*' (*á kunnmiđum*). There may have been an intended pun on an ON phrase 'to be on familiar fishing grounds' (*at vera á kunnmiđum*),[132] but since the phrase is attributed to 'the men of Caithness', it was probably a local usage, with which the saga writer was unfamiliar. If it is indeed the Gaelic word 'conveth' which was still used in Caithness this would appear to be an example of a continuation of a pre-Norse usage (or at least dating from the days of the native dynasty in the tenth century) which retained its Celtic term for some time after the founding of the Orkney earldom. Interestingly, there is one instance of the same term being used in the Isle of Man, where it occurs in a land-grant of Godred II (1153–1187).[133]

Another remarkable example of a continued Celtic institution is the use of the Gaelic word *airigh* for a shieling, which was adopted by many Scandinavian communities around the British Isles, as well as in the Faroes.[134] It is probable that it spread to Orkney and Caithness from the west at some stage in the process which took it north to the Faroes. An early documented form for it exists in *Jarls' Saga* in the name 'Asgrim's erg' which lay in Caithness (probably Assery),[135] and there is particular interest in the fact that the sixteenth-century translation of the saga has a gloss on the word 'erg', adding 'or *setr* as we call them',[136] although it is not certain at what stage in the transmission of the text this gloss was added. Both these Gaelic words, 'conveth' and the place-name element 'erg', are included in the saga in connection with Caithness, although they probably had entirely different origins; the former perhaps pre-dating and surviving the Norse conquest, the latter being adopted later as the usage of the word spread at some time after the Norse phase of settlement.

Many Gaelic traditions which entered Norse literature may have derived from the Western Isles,[137] but there is one which is strongly linked with Caithness, namely the remarkable 'Song of Dorrud' (*Darraðarlioð*). Of all the portents and visions seen on both sides during the battle of Clontarf[138] that seen by Dorrud in Caithness is the best known. The account of what he saw and the poem which he composed perhaps soon after the battle is recorded in *Njal's Saga*, and it is a powerful mixture of Celtic and Old Norse imagery.[139] A Caithness man, Dorrud, saw 12 women riding together to a certain 'bower' and when he followed them and looked in at a window he saw them inside weaving their web of fate. The weavers – Nordic Valkyries from their names – were directing the course of the battle; the idea that such action as weaving could have magical properties is itself of Celtic inspiration as well as the gruesome imagery for the parts of the loom and weaving equipment. The story of Dorrud's vision may therefore have been composed in a milieu where Norse and Celtic cultures mingled, very probably in Caithness where Dorrud's vision is located. His name is thought to derive from the *ON* word for a banner, and the *vefr darraðar* of the poem's refrain to be a battle standard connected with Odin the god of war. Of course, Earl Sigurd's magic raven banner was very well known throughout the northern world[140] and the part it played in the battle of Clontarf may have provided an inspiration for the composer of *Darraðarlioð*; if so, the poem provides us with early evidence of the banner's significance in the battle.

A colonial society

The process of colonizing anciently settled territory and of having to come to terms with a native population and its culture – even if subjected – must inevitably have made the Norse society of Scandinavian Scotland different both from Norwegian society as it developed at home and from the communities that flourished in the empty lands of the North Atlantic, in the Faroes, Iceland and Greenland. For a start it is likely to have made that society more warlike; both in the Hebrides where the *Gall-Gaedhil* acquired a warlike reputation[141] and in the Northern Isles the kings and earls were occupied with conquest and the establishment of their authority throughout this period. It must have been a prime requirement of any administrative system set up by the earls that their territory supply them with men and resources for the pursuing of a military life-style. At the date when the sagas were written down, it was clearly believed that the earls originally held the islands as a grant from the king of Norway for the purpose of protecting them against pirates (including possibly attack by Scots, although this is nowhere stated).[142] Certainly, not long after, Rollo (traditionally believed to have been Rolf, son of Rognvald of Møre and brother of Torf-Einar) was given land in North Frankia, the nucleus of the later Normandy, by Charles the Simple 'for the defence of the kingdom' (*pro tutela regni*).[143]

The Norse settlers of Scandinavian Scotland were also very much more open to influences from the kingdoms and societies in the south than their cousins in Norway or the North Atlantic. They were not only familiar with the political and cultural situation in Scotland and Ireland, but also mobile enough to be well-informed about the Anglo-Saxon and Frankish kingdoms. Earl Thorfinn, most notably of the rulers of the Norse settlements, was brought up at the Scottish court, served in the royal bodyguard at the English court and visited the imperial and papal courts. The possible results of such wide-ranging links may be visible on the ground in the remarkable remains still surviving on the Brough of Birsay.[144] The Romanesque cathedral of St Magnus in Kirkwall is the most startling result of the twelfth-century earls' links with a more southern culture.

Influence from the Celtic world is also evident in less tangible spheres, such as the literary and linguistic respects noted above. Several examples of Gaelic loan-words of agricultural origin which have passed into the dialects of the Northern Isles, the Faroes and sometimes Iceland have been collected together.[145] It is rarely possible to prove as satisfactorily as in the case of *airigh/ airge* that this occurred in the Norse period. Influence is only to be expected, for the Norse immigrants were settling along the fringes of a vigorous and culturally rich Celtic world. Unfortunately, it is very difficult to pin down. Archaeological evidence of such influence is strong in the period when grave-goods supply a wealth of evidence. The adoption by the Norse of Celtic brooches provides dramatic material proof of transactions at a trading level,[146] and the numbers of fragments of Irish and Scottish metalwork in Norwegian graves tell of numerous encounters between Viking and Celt throughout north Britain.[147] The 'Copenhagen' reliquary is the most perfect – and one of the most puzzling – of these objects which found their way into Viking hands, in its case most probably from a Pictish monastery.[148] We cannot know whether the Norwegian lady who owned it (Ranvaig), and whose name is incised on it in a runic inscription, appreciated it for its beauty alone or whether it continued to serve its purpose as a shrine – to which function it reverted in a Norwegian church in the late Middle Ages (see fig. 80).

Figure 80. Ranvaig's shrine (National Museum, Copenhagen).
   This reliquary of oak, covered in bronze and copper, was preserved
(probably in a church) in Norway. Possibly of Pictish workmanship, and
dated to the eighth century, it must have been acquired as Viking loot, but
was not broken up, and indeed became the proud possession of Ranvaig, who
had inscribed on the underside in runes: 'Ranvaik a kistu thasa' (Ranvaig
owns this casket).

   The written source to which we turn when attempting to analyse society in
the Norse settlements – *Jarls' Saga* – may be particularly misleading in respect
of the cultural mixture of society in Orkney. Written in Iceland, the product of
a classically Scandinavian colony, it presents the history of the earls as the
most famous Norse dynasty ruling over a Norse society. But the number of
Gaelic personal names recorded in the saga is sufficient indication of the racial
mix in that society[149] whose culture must to some degree have been a hybrid
one. Even more so was this the case in Man, much nearer to the heartland of
Celtic culture (Ireland) and in close contact with the kings of Dublin.[150]
Historical sources from our period about the culture and society of Man barely
exist, and it is not until the conquest of Godred Crovan in 1079 that the
Chronicle of Man begins its laconic and pedestrian account of the political
struggles within the kingdom. However, the sculptured stones and runic
inscriptions tell their own tale of the mixed society that was developing in the
tenth century.[151]

Recently, stress has been laid on the similarities between Norse and Celtic societies,[152] perhaps most convincingly in the sphere of social customs like multiple marriage, concubinage and fosterage. It is also said, quite rightly, that 'these similarities should occasion no surprise'. Societies in a similar stage of development will, of course, develop similar social features as responses to certain needs. The practice of fosterage 'formed an integral part of the Gaelic system of education',[153] yet it was well known in Iceland,[154] features in Orkney society where Thorkell Amundsson fostered Earl Thorfinn 'and was thence called Thorkel Fostri',[155] and was practised in the family of Harald Finehair, whose son Hakon was brought up by King Athelstan of England and became known as 'Aethelstan's foster son'.[156]

Multiple marriage or polygamy was also a feature of both Norse and Irish society; it persisted in Iceland right through the Middle Ages and in the Gaelic West into the modern historical period.[157] It is highly likely that the sons of the earliest earls were by many different women; we have for instance no knowledge of the mothers of four of Earl Sigurd the Stout's sons, apart from Thorfinn. All the sons of an earl had an equal right to claim his lands, far into the Christian period when distinctions between regular and irregular unions were beginning to be recognized. Earl Thorfinn appears to have differed from his predecessors, having been brought up in a Christian environment, for there is no mention in any Icelandic source that he had any children apart from his two sons by Ingebjorg 'Earls' mother'. The one passage in *Jarls' Saga* giving any hint of an intimate relationship between a man and a woman relates to Thorfinn and Ingebjorg escaping from the blazing homestead set on fire by Rognvald Brusisson, when the earl broke through a wooden dividing wall and leapt out carrying his wife in his arms.[158]

THE STATUS OF WOMEN

The practice of concubinage does not appear from Icelandic sources to have detracted from the high status enjoyed by women during the Viking Age.[159] It was probably the mobility of the age which gave women an opportunity to be freer and more independent than in a society where women were tied to the farm and the home. Colonial situations generally have allowed women the chance to exercise their judgment and to organize the lives of their families to a greater degree than in long-settled societies. Although we have very little historical evidence of any Norse women in the Scottish colonies, the many female graves found throughout the area of Norse settlement (except in the Isle of Man) give us some indication of the importance of women in a heathen community – as is well known in the home countries.[160] Even after conversion, women continued to be buried with status symbols: not the forbidden grave-goods, but memorial stones above the grave. Those with runic inscriptions tell us specifically of named individuals, and the Kilbar Cross is a particularly fine memorial to a woman who must have been of some standing on the island of Barra in the tenth century, Thorgerd Steinar's daughter (see fig. 64). She had a purely Scandinavian name as do two other women recorded on memorial stones in Man.[161]

The most famous independent matriarch and founder of an Icelandic dynasty came from the Hebrides, namely, Aud the Deep-Minded. Aud was a woman of great wealth and power in a society where traditional structures had broken down in the fluidity of a colonial situation. Daughter of Ketil Flatneb, conqueror of the Hebrides in the mid-ninth century, she was married to Olaf the White, probably identical with the king of Dublin who ruled the Norse communities in Ireland from 853 to 871.[162] By birth and marriage she was therefore a part of the most powerful layer of conquering Viking society in the west. But it was as a widow, after the death of her father and her husband, that she is said to have started to lead the life of an independent matriarch. She then accompanied her son Thorstein to Caithness; but on his death the situation evidently became too risky, for 'she realised that she had no further prospects there',[163] and tradition remembered that 'she had a ship built secretly in a forest' in which she sailed to Orkney,[164] probably because of the period of native resurgence in Caithness on the death of Thorstein and Sigurd the Mighty. Her remarkable survival in difficult circumstances was well known:

> It is generally thought that it would be hard to find another example of a woman escaping from such hazards with so much wealth and such a large retinue. From this it can be seen what a paragon amongst women she was.[165]

Then began her progress through the Norse colonies with a programme of marriage alliances for her grand-daughters, no doubt funded by the large amount of treasure she seems to have amassed. One grand-daughter, Groa, was married in Orkney (although one source says that her husband was Dungadr the native chief from Duncansby[166]); Olof was married to the most powerful family in the Faroes; and Aud then moved on to Iceland with a large body of followers, some high-born and some slaves. She there married other grand-daughters to settlers and established some of the most important families in the Commonwealth. A remarkable story.[167] But it stands alone; and the reason for her success can be seen to be command of her own resources. Aud lived off her liquid capital, for once her father, husband and son were dead she could not remain in the Hebrides, Ireland or Caithness, but had to keep moving, paying her way to maintain her following, acquire her slaves and marry off her grand-daughters. It is as much an example of the weakness of a woman without male relatives in a violent society as it is of the freedom of women to lead an independent life without male domination. Only in Iceland could Aud take land on her own account without having to fight for it; and that is probably the reason why she left Scandinavian Scotland and went north.

The numbers of farm-names which have a woman's name as the specific first element is remarkably high in Iceland compared with Norway,[168] which certainly suggests that women were more easily able to own, if not found, their own farm in the new settlement. The sagas provide many examples of women being settlers on their own account and the *Book of Settlements* gives details for the different procedure to be followed for the hallowing of a land-claim by women as well as by men.[169] It may have been more difficult for women to found farms in the Norse settlements of northern and western Scotland where indigenous populations existed, and, although feminine name elements *are* found, they are possibly attached to secondary settlements (and certainly to field-names) as is also the case in the Viking settlement areas of northern and eastern England.[170] However, the name Girlsta in Shetland (= *Geirhildar-staðir*) is certainly derived from the feminine personal name Geirhild. She may even ha·e been the historical Geirhild, daughter of Raven-Floki, one of the first discoverers of Iceland, and who is remembered in the *Book of Settlements* as having drowned in *Geirhildarvatn* in Shetland, possibly the Loch of Girlsta.[171]

In Orkney, a woman's role appears to have been more traditional – or at least the only women portrayed in *Jarls' Saga* are playing a very stereotyped role,[172] and it is quite clear they are only mentioned because of their contribution to the dramatic incidents being recounted. Ragnhild, the daughter of Erik Blood-axe and Gunnhild, was a scheming woman who caused strife between relatives of the earls and was the downfall of several of them. She is said to have been married first to Arnfinn Thorfinnsson, whom she had 'done to death at Murkle in Caithness',[173] giving herself in marriage to his brother, Havard. She then urged Havard's nephew, Einar 'Buttered-Bread', to aspire to the earldom, and he killed Havard in battle at Stenness. She then urged another nephew, Einar 'Hard-chaps', to avenge the dead earl, and when this was done and the first Einar killed, she sent for another son of Thorfinn 'Skull-Splitter', Liot, and married him, whereupon he 'took over the Earldom and became a mighty chief'. This stereotyped saga-woman knew every trick of the trade:[174] she used flattery, she urged men to dastardly deeds by encouraging their ambitions, she made false promises, and then acted high-mindedly in wanting the dead Earl Einar avenged. Surprisingly enough Ragnhild did not get her deserts in the end but appears to have lived happily ever after with her third husband. The only thing this chapter of the saga tells us is that the saga writer knew well what a thirteenth-century audience liked to hear about the female sex. The other female stereotype in this section of the *Jarls' Saga* is Eithne, the mother of Sigurd the Stout, who urged her son on to take up the challenge given to him by Finnlaech the Scots earl to a pitched battle on Skitten Myre, although Sigurd told her 'that the odds must be no less than seven to one'.[175] Like many other women in the Icelandic sagas, she goads her son on with talk of fate and honour, and then weaves him the magic banner with its fateful curse that will bring victory to the side for whom it is borne and death to him who bears it. More gripping stuff for the medieval audience, but hardly the material of which history can be made – even though the existence of Sigurd's banner is not much in doubt.

Well-established tradition about a notable female settler in Iceland is one thing, but changing attitudes and the conventions of saga writing make the literary sources suspect when it comes to looking for evidence of the role of women in early Norse society. Conversion to Christianity, the ending of a slave-based society, the decline of opportunity for raiding and colonial expansion into new lands all contributed towards changing the status of women in Norse society, and we cannot be sure that this change was for the better.[176]

Epilogue

With the death of Thorfinn the Mighty c.1065, we reach a date conveniently close to that taken as marking the end of the Viking Age in most areas of Europe.[1] The Norman invasion of Anglo-Saxon England in the following year was carried out by a powerful ruler of a militarized duchy who shared a common ancestor with the earl of Orkney; this event effectively closed the door on the aspirations of Scandinavian claimants to the throne of Cnut, although their attempts continued during the following decades. The new earls of Orkney, sons of Thorfinn, were closely involved in the dramatic events of 1066, fighting on the side of Harald Hardrada at the battle of Stamford Bridge, just as other earls of Orkney had been involved in the many political and military adventures undertaken by Scandinavian warriors in the British Isles in the period covered by this book. But the opportunities for such military enterprises were rapidly declining in the northern world, with the development of kingship and the stabilization of national boundaries.

The wider network woven by Viking raiders, traders and settlers in the British Isles and Ireland in the ninth and tenth centuries was breaking up by the mid-eleventh century. The settlements and trading bases had not existed in isolation, but had formed links in the chain of Scandinavian influence encircling these islands, with Orkney's nodal position providing a key link in that chain. The end of the Viking Age meant that the links in the chain parted – not snapped, more eased apart – as the different Scandinavian settlements became absorbed into the societies and the constituent cultures of the countries they had imposed themselves upon, in England, Ireland, southern Wales and Scotland. At this point, interpretations differ greatly, as historians and archaeologists reach very different conclusions about the extent of the Scandinavian influence which is seen as a very variable factor, entirely dependent on the individual circumstances and different elements in the social and political picture.[2] In general, 'belief in continuity has become much more prevalent',[3] and rapid assimilation into local society which itself was not so very much changed by the Danish element is the most recent interpretation of Viking settlement in the East Midlands of England.[4] They are seen there more as a factor accelerating already changing patterns in society, but it is hardly possible to make any such conclusions about the impact of the Vikings in Scotland, primarily because of the absence of historical evidence about the existing society, but also because the density of settlement was probably rather different from eastern England. In southern Scotland, the impact was sporadic and transitory with very few permanent Scandinavian communities establishing themselves on the land, and in northern Scotland, the settlement was so overwhelming that local social and administrative structures are unlikely to have survived.

The end of the Viking Age was marked in Scandinavia by many other aspects of a changing social order;[5] the growth of monarchy – which, as has been seen, was a significant element in the history of the Scandinavian settlements in Scotland; the demise of the freebooting Viking chieftain, replaced by an aristocracy more supportive of the institution of monarchy and a united national kingdom; the end of slavery, which probably had more significant effects on Viking society than it will ever be possible to define; and above all, the adoption of Christianity, which made Scandinavia and the settlements overseas part of a European culture, erasing those individual remnants of an earlier form of social structure which had lasted longer in Scandinavia than anywhere else. The end of the Viking Age involved many changes in many directions.

The Vikings affected most countries of northern Europe and a vivid image of them is deeply ingrained in the popular imagination. But that image is an unremittingly negative one, boosted by the legends enshrined in written sources that they were opposed by the valiant efforts of patriotic kings, such as Alfred the Great or Brian Boru, who saved their people and their culture from the depredations of the pagan invaders. In Scotland also, the Vikings have been regarded as the 'enemies of social progress'[6] whose ravages precipitated two centuries of resistance which welded the various peoples of Lowland Scotland together into a national unit. Indeed, Constantine II appears to be the king set to fill the role of preserver of national independence in this struggle.[7] Despite the scarcity of evidence, it is very probable that the Vikings influenced the political development of Lowland Scotland during these formative centuries. If we look to Ireland, the remarkable and full accounts of the *Annals of Ulster* provide some insight into how closely involved the Norse invaders were in the internal affairs of the numerous small kingdoms. This not only lends support to the theories that Kenneth MacAlpin's political career may have benefitted from alliance with the Norse,[8] but it also tells us that the Norse themselves had political aspirations which, because of their mastery of the waterways, they attempted to implement on an international scale. These political aspirations also had commercial undertones, of which the elucidation of the complex history of the kings of York and Dublin and their attempts to run a commercial and political empire from the mid-ninth to the mid-tenth century has made us more aware.[9] Somewhere in this scheme of things fitted the waterways of southern Scotland and the wealth of the Picto-Scottish kingdom. Does this make the Vikings the enemies of social progress or the enlightened practitioners of maritime commercial principles?

For such ambitious and far-reaching enterprises, it has truly been said that 'the Vikings were too few for the many and varied causes they bore in hand'.[10] Should the 'eventual eclipse of their sea-based pirate empire'[11] be regarded as failure? Should it not rather be cause for admiration that they established the colonies that they did, and succeeded in impressing their identity on so many different parts of the British Isles and Ireland and in so many different ways? Considering the paucity of the historical sources from northern Britain in the ninth to the eleventh centuries, it is remarkable that these people are recorded in them at all. Considering the fragile and transitory nature of most archaeological objects, we should be grateful that so many finds and hoards from all over Scotland have been found to tell us of the movement of Viking raiders, traders or armies, and that the graves equipped with so many objects of interest have survived gales and storms and been found on remote beaches and headlands in the far islands of the Atlantic. Moreover, the excavated settlement site of Jarlshof has no parallel in the rest of Scotland, just as the saga of the earls of Orkney has no parallel in the social and literary record of Scotland. As has been seen in chapter 4, the place-name maps of northern and western Scotland are a permanent memorial to the thousands of nameless men and women who moved into these areas from across the North Sea and made the oceanic fringes of Scotland their own domain. The diversity of evidence about the Vikings in Scotland is what this book has been concerned with; that diversity provides an impressive witness to these peoples and to their distinctive contribution to the ethnic and cultural mix in the medieval kingdom of Scotland.

By the mid-eleventh century, the Scandinavian imprint on Scotland was probably at its most marked, and the Norse settlement as firmly implanted a feature of North Britain as the Danish settlement had been in South Britain. The earl of Orkney dominated the maritime parts of Scotland north of the Great Glen. The Western Isles were part of the same Scandinavian sphere, although as yet without the framework established by the powerful dynasty which imposed itself on Man later in the century. Both these political units were the most enduring and impressive survivals of the Viking Age in North Britain; the settlement in the Isles, the maritime contacts and the commercial wealth created vigorous communities with a distinctive and flourishing culture which would probably not have developed without the stimulus of the Scandinavian settlement. The Western Isles were no longer 'the appendages of an essentially land-based Dalriadan kingdom but home of a race of vigorous and independent chieftains, who could choose the master they wished to serve'.[12] The same could be said of the Northern Isles, and it was dominance of the waterways and continuing contacts with the home country of Norway which gave them the mastery which their Pictish predecessors could never have attained. The creation of the new political axis stretching north and west round the Scottish coasts remained an important element of Scotland's geography for centuries after the Viking Age, and only gradually and very painfully were these insular communities drawn into the medieval Scottish kingdom, turning, in the process, into a remote fringe zone.[13] In the 1060s, the medieval kingdom of Scotland was only just in the making; the king of Norway could, in theory, have claimed some form of overlordship over parts of the north and west mainland; and the re-establishment of Gaelic speech in the Western Isles had probably only just begun.

The sea culture of the Western Isles has been pinpointed as a significant legacy of the Viking Age in the west[14] and, because of the Scottish dynasty's Gaelic and western origins, this became part of the kingdom's cultural heritage. Other elements attributable to a Scandinavian legacy are difficult to pin down and their origins impossible to ascertain, such as the Gaelic legal term rannsaich, 'to search' or 'scrutinize' which is a loan from Old Norse *rannsaka*,[15] and a term in Scottish burgh law 'kirseth' which was the period of grace in which a settler had to pay no rent, deriving from Old Norse *kyrrseta*, 'to sit quietly'.[16] How the influence was exercised which ensured the adoption of such terms is a process of which we have no knowledge, nor do we know whether it came directly across the North Sea or from the Scandinavian communities to the south of Scotland or from communities within the country. But such survivals give a hint of a social significance in the legal sphere which was more long-lasting than the Viking Age itself, and which has parallels in England, where Old Norse terms entered into legal terminology, and where the later jury system may possibly derive from a Scandinavian example.[17] Given evidence of this kind – which has yet to be properly collected and studied – it is surely unfair to claim that 'the principal Scandinavian contribution to Scots society was negative'.[18]

Abbreviations

Note Places of publication are given only for works published outside the United Kingdom. In abbreviating less frequently cited periodicals the commonly accepted usage of *Soc.* for *Society, J.* for *Journal, Trans.* for *Transactions* has been followed. Other abbreviations are listed below.

APS	*The Acts of the Parliament of Scotland*, ed. T. Thomson and C. Innes (Edinburgh, 1814–75)
Andersen, *Samlingen av Norge*	P. S. Andersen, *Samlingen av Norge og Kristningen av Landet* (Oslo, 1977)
BAR	British Archaeological Reports (British series unless otherwise indicated)
Birsay (1983)	*Birsay: A Centre of Political and Ecclesiastical Power: Orkney Heritage*, 2 (1983)
Chronicle of Man	*Chronicle of Man and the Sudreys*, trans. the Rt Revd Dr Goss, with notes by P. A. Munch (Manx Society, 1874)
DN	*Diplomatarium Norvegicum*, I–XXI (Christiania/Oslo, 1849–1976)
Duncan, *Scotland*	A. A. M. Duncan, *Scotland: the Making of a Kingdom* (1975)
EHD	*English Historical Documents*, I, ed. D. Whitelock (2nd edn, 1979); II, ed. D. C. Douglas and G. Greenaway (2nd edn, 1981)
EHR	*English Historical Review*
ES	*Early Sources of Scottish History*, AD *500–1286*, I, ed. A. O. Anderson (1922)
Farrell, *Vikings*	R. T. Farrell (ed.), *The Vikings* (Chichester, USA, 1982)
Fellows-Jensen, 'Northern and Western Isles'	G. Fellows-Jensen, 'Viking settlement in the Northern and Western Isles', in *The Northern and Western Isles in the Viking World*, ed. A. Fenton and H. Palsson (1984), 148–68
Fenton and Palsson, *Northern and Western Isles*	A. Fenton and H. Palsson (eds.), *The Northern and Western Isles in the Viking World* (1984)
Hacon's Saga	Icelandic Sagas and Other Historical Documents relating to the settlements and descents of the Northmen in the British Isles, IV, *The Saga of Hacon*, trans. Sir G. Dasent, Rolls Series, 88.iv (1894)
Hms (Laing)	*Heimskringla* by Snorri Sturlason, pt i, *The Olaf Sagas*, 2 vols, trans. Samuel Laing, revised with an intro. and notes by J. Simpson (1984); pt ii, *Sagas of the Norse Kings*, trans. Samuel Laing, revised with an intro. and notes by P. Foote (1961)
G	Gaelic
I	Irish
Icelandic Dic.	*An Icelandic-English Dictionary*, initiated by R. Cleasby, revised, enlarged and completed by G. Vigfusson (2nd edn, 1957)
JMM	*The Journal of the Manx Museum*
Jones, *History*	G. Jones, *A History of the Vikings* (1968)
KL	*Kulturhistorisk Leksikon for Nordisk Middelalder*, I–XXII (Copenhagen, 1956–78)

Marwick, *Farm-Names*	H. Marwick, *Orkney Farm-Names* (1952)
Med. Arch.	*Medieval Archaeology*
Med. Scand.	*Mediaeval Scandinavia*
B. R. S. and E. M. Megaw, 'Norse heritage'	B. R. S. and E. M. Megaw, 'The Norse heritage in the Isle of Man', in *The Early Christian Cultures of North-West Europe*, ed. B. Dickens and C. Fox (1950), 143–70
Morris, 'Viking Orkney'	C. D. Morris, 'Viking Orkney: a survey', in *The Prehistory of Orkney*, ed. C. Renfrew (1985), 210–42
NBL	*Norsk Biografisk Leksikon*, I–XIX (Christiania/Oslo, 1923–83)
Nicolaisen, *Scottish Place-Names*	W. F. H. Nicolaisen, *Scottish Place-Names* (1976)
O'Corrain, *Ireland*	D. O'Corrain, *Ireland before the Vikings* (Dublin, 1972)
ON	Old Norse
OS Anderson	*The Orkneyinga Saga*, trans. from the Icelandic by J. A. Hjaltalin and G. Goudie, ed. with notes and intro. by J. Anderson (1873, rep. 1973)
OS Dasent	*Orkneyinga Saga*, ed. G. Vigfusson, trans. Sir G. W. Dasent, Rolls Series, 88.i (1887) and iii (1894)
OS Guthmundsson	*Orkneyinga Saga*, ed. F. Guthmundsson, Islensk Fornrit, XXXIV (Reykavik, 1965)
OS P & E	*Orkneyinga Saga. The History of the Earls of Orkney*, trans. and with an intro. by H. Palsson and P. Edwards (1978)
OS Taylor	*The Orkneyinga Saga*, a new trans. with intro. and notes by A. B. Taylor (1938)
POAS	*Proceedings of the Orkney Antiquarian Society*
PPS	*Proceedings of the Prehistoric Society*
PSAS	*Proceedings of the Society of Antiquaries of Scotland*
RCAHMS	Royal Commission on the Ancient and Historical Monuments of Scotland
RCAMS	Royal Commission on the Ancient Monuments of Scotland
REO	*Records of the Earldom of Orkney, 1299–1614*, ed. with intro. and notes by J. Storer Clouston, Scottish History Society, 2nd series, 7 (1914)
SAF	*Scottish Archaeological Forum*
Saga-Book	*Saga-Book of the Viking Society*
Sawyer, *Kings*	P.H. Sawyer, *Kings and Vikings* (1982)
Scot. Stud.	*Scottish Studies*
SHR	*Scottish Historical Review*
Smyth, *Scandinavian Kings*	A. P. Smyth, *Scandinavian Kings in the British Isles 850–880* (1977)
Smyth, *Warlords*	A. P. Smyth, *Warlords and Holy Men* (1984)
Smyth, *York and Dublin*	A. P. Smyth, *Scandinavian York and Dublin* (2 vols, New Jersey and Dublin, 1975 and 1979)
TGSI	*Transactions of the Gaelic Society of Inverness*
TRHS	*Transactions of the Royal Historical Society*
Viking Antiquities	*Viking Antiquities in Great Britain and Ireland*, ed. H. Shetelig, I–V (Oslo, 1940), VI (1954)
First Viking Congress	*The Viking Congress 1950*, ed. W. D. Simpson (1954)
Second Viking Congress	*Annen Viking Congress 1953*, ed. K. Falck (Bergen, 1955)
Third Viking Congress	*Priðji Vikingafundur 1956*, ed. K. Eldjarn (Reykjavík, 1958)
Fourth Viking Congress	*The Fourth Viking Congress, 1961*, ed. A. Small (1965)
Fifth Viking Congress	*The Fifth Viking Congress, 1965*, ed. B. Niclasen (Torshavn, 1968)
Sixth Viking Congress	*Proceedings of the Sixth Viking Congress, 1969*, ed. P. Foote and D. Strömbäck (1971)

Seventh Viking Congress	*Proceedings of the Seventh Viking Congress, 1973*, ed. B. Almqvist and D. Green (Dublin, 1976)
Eighth Viking Congress	*Proceedings of the Eighth Viking Congress, 1977*, ed. H. Bekker-Nielsen, P. Foote and O. Olsen (Odense, 1981)
Ninth Viking Congress	*The Viking Age in the Isle of Man; select papers from the Ninth Viking Congress, 1981*, ed. C. Fell, P. Foote, J. Graham-Campbell and R. Thomson (1983)
Tenth Viking Congress	In press
Wainwright, *Northern Isles*	F. T. Wainwright, *The Northern Isles* (1962)

Notes

Introduction

1. Apparently first used by nineteenth-century historians such as E. W. Robertson, *Scotland under her Early Kings*, I (1862), 22.
2. See Duncan, *Scotland*, esp. 547–51, 577–83; R. Nicholson, *Scotland: The Later Middle Ages* (1974), esp. 413–18; G. W. S. Barrow, *Kingship and Unity* (1981), esp. ch. 6; B. E. Crawford, 'Foreign relations: Scandinavia', in *Scottish Society in the Fifteenth Century*, ed. J. M. Brown (1977), esp. 86–90.
3. Jones, *History*, 76, n.1.
4. J. Brønsted, *The Vikings* (1960), 36–7.
5. K. Eldjarn, 'The Viking myth', in Farrell, *Vikings*, 266.
6. *Ibid.*
7. O'Corrain, *Ireland*, 96.
8. See ch. 2 below.
9. Smyth, *Scandinavian Kings*, 87–8.
10. Morris, 'Viking Orkney', 210.
11. Sawyer, *Kings*, 29–33.
12. P. H. Sawyer, *The Age of the Vikings* (2nd edn, 1971), 31.
13. *The Annals of Ulster* (to AD 1131), I, ed. S. MacAirt and G. MacNiocaill (1983), ix and refs. there cited. O'Corrain, *Ireland*, 91.
14. G. Turville-Petre, *Origins of Icelandic Literature* (1953), 174–5.
15. See chs. 2, 6 and 7 below.
16. *The Book of Settlements*, trans. H. Palsson and P. Edwards (1972).
17. See Morris, 'Viking Orkney', 211.
18. L. J. Alcock, 'The archaeology of Celtic Britain, fifth to twelfth centuries AD', in *Twenty-Five Years of Mediaeval Archaeology*, ed. D. A. Hinton (1983), 57.
19. F. T. Wainwright, *Archaeology and Place-Names and History* (1962); *idem* (ed.), *The Northern Isles* (1962); and the collection of many of his articles in *Scandinavian England* (1975).
20. D. M. Wilson, 'Scandinavian settlement in the north and west of the British Isles – an archaeological point of view', *TRHS*, XXVI (1976), 99.
21. See ch. 5 below and particularly n.90.
22. See ch. 5 below, pp. 118–19.
23. Morris, 'Viking Orkney', 239–40 and references there cited.
24. See ch. 5, pp. 128–34 below.
25. Morris, 'Viking Orkney', 226–29, and see below, ch. 5, p. 151.
26. See ch. 5 below, n.99.
27. L. and E. Alcock, 'Scandinavian settlement in the Inner Hebrides: recent research on place-names and in the field', in *Settlement in Scotland 1000 BC – AD 1000*, ed. L. M. Thoms, *SAF*, X (1980), 66–8.
28. Wainwright, *Archaeology and Place-Names*, 9, 25.
29. Sawyer, *Kings*, 37; P. Stafford, *The East Midlands in the Early Middle Ages* (1985), 69–73.
30. M. Gelling, *Signposts to the Past* (1978), 12.
31. See ch. 4, p. 94 below.
32. See ch. 4, p. 105 below.
33. Postgraduate theses being written under the direction of Dr P. S. Andersen in the Historisk Institutt, University of Oslo, are studying the history of Norse settlement in different locations in the Scottish islands with a multidisciplinary approach, as (for example) N. P. Thuesen, 'Norrøn Bosetning pa Orknøyene' (thesis, University of Oslo, 1978), and D. Olson, 'Norse settlement in the Hebrides, an interdisciplinary study' (thesis, University of Oslo, 1983). See also Lindsay J. MacGregor, 'Sources for a study of Norse settlement in Shetland and Faroe', in *Essays in Shetland History*, ed. B. E. Crawford (1984), 1–18.
34. M. Oftedal, 'Norse place-names in Celtic Scotland', in *Proceedings of the International Congress of Celtic Studies, 1959* (Dublin, 1962), 47.

35. Stafford, *East Midlands*, 69.
36. The whole compilation (including chs. 4–32, called *Jarlasögur* by Snorri Sturlasson, who used it for his own History of the Kings of Norway, and later material about the twelfth-century earls) is known by the name of *Orkneyinga Saga*. The different translations and editions are referred to in the notes as *OS* followed by the translator's name (see list of abbreviations). These are used promiscuously, according to the suitability of the particular translation, meaningfulness of the verses, or usefulness of the historical information in the footnotes.
37. Duncan, *Scotland*, 191–2.
38. Andersen, *Samlingen av Norge*, 25.
39. P. G. Foote, 'Some account of the present state of saga-research', *Scandinavica*, 3–4 (1964–5), 115–16.
40. The edition used is Samuel Laing's translation (1844) printed in the Everyman's Library (1930), revised with an introduction and footnotes by P. G. Foote (1961) and J. Simpson (1964); referred to as *Hms* (Laing).
41. Turville-Petre, *Origins*, 224.
42. *Hms* (Laing), 4.
43. *OS* P. and E., Introduction, 14.
44. Lee M. Hollander, *The Skalds* (New York, 1945), 178; B. Fidjestøl, 'Arnórr þórðarsson: Skald of the Orkney Jarls', in *Northern and Western Isles*, 239.
45. *OS*, ch. 26, trans. by Hollander, *Skalds*, 178.
46. Turville-Petre, *Origins*, 148; Fidjestøl, 'Arnorr Thordarson', 240.
47. Andersen, *Samlingen av Norge*, 215. The first critical studies of saga literature were by the Swedish historians L. Weibull, *Kritiska Undersökningar i Nordens historia omkring år 1000* (1911) and H. Koht, 'Sagaernes opfatning av vor gamle historie', *Historisk Tidsskrift*, 5 (1914). More recent studies include S. Ellehøj, *Studier over den aeldste norrøne historieskrivning* (Copenhagen, 1965).
48. See S. Rafnsson, *Studier i Landnamabok* (Lund, 1974); J. Benediktsson, 'Landnamabok: some remarks on its value as a historical source', *Saga-Book*, XVII (1969);

idem, 'Some problems in the history of the settlement of Iceland', in *The Vikings*, ed. T. Andersson and K. L. Sandred (Uppsala, 1978).
49. Jones, *History*, 10.
50. K. Liestøl, *The Origin of the Icelandic Family Sagas* (Oslo, 1930), 247.
51. P. Wormald, 'Viking studies, whence and whither?', in Farrell, *Vikings*, 130–1.
52. Wainright, *Archaeology and Place-Names*, 8.
53. R. I. Page, 'A tale of two cities', *Peritia*, I (1982), 351.
54. Gelling, *Signposts*, 12.

1 The Geographical Framework

1. See Epilogue below.
2. E. G. Bowen, 'Britain and the British sea', in *The Irish Sea Province in Archaeology and History*, ed. D. Moore (1970), 13.
3. T. Nyberg, 'Continental Europe and the North Sea and Baltic area in the early Middle Ages', in *Rapports* II. Chronologie (1980), 200.
4. *Ibid.*, 193–4.
5. G. Donaldson, 'Viking tracks in Scotland', in *Procs. of the Conference on Scottish Studies*, no. 3 (1976), 3; J. Leirfall, *West Over Sea* (1979), 11.
6. *OS* P. and E., 120–1.
7. A. Binns, *Viking Voyagers: Then and Now* (1980), 69–77.
8. P. G. Foote and D. M. Wilson, *The Viking Achievement* (1970), 256.
9. F. Brandt, 'On the navigation of the Vikings', in *The World of the Vikings* (Stockholm, 1972), 16.
10. Donaldson, 'Viking tracks', 3; S. McGrail, 'Ships, shipwrights and seamen', in *The Viking World*, ed. J. Graham-Campbell (1980), 62.
11. Binns, *Voyagers*, 84.
12. McGrail, 'Ships', 38–58; A. W. Brøgger and H. Shetelig, *The Viking Ships* (Oslo, 1951), 104–6.
13. N. Lund, 'The settlers: where do we get them from – and do we need them?', in *Eighth Viking Congress*, 153.
14. P. H. Sawyer, 'The causes of the Viking Age', in Farrell, *Vikings*, 5; Sawyer, *Kings*, 75–6.
15. D. Ellmers, 'The ships of the Vik-

ings', in *The World of the Vikings* (Stockholm, 1972), 13; McGrail, 'Ships', 44–5.

16. Donaldson, 'Viking tracks', 5.

17. W. J. Watson, *History of the Celtic Place-Names of Scotland* (1926), 45.

18. J. Stewart, 'Shetland farm names', in *Fourth Viking Congress*, 262; Foote and Wilson, *Viking Achievement*, 236.

19. R. Lamb, *Papa Westray and Westray: an Archaeological Survey* (1983), 21.

20. A. E. Christensen, 'Boats and boat-building in western Norway and the Islands' in *Northern and Western Isles*, 86.

21. G. Bersu and D. M. Wilson, *Three Viking Graves in the Isle of Man* (1966), 4, 92.

22. S. H. H. Kaland, 'Westnessut-gravingene på Rousay, Orknøyene', *Viking* (1973), fig. 8; Lamb, *Papa Westray and Westray*, 9, 19–21, 39.

23. C. L. Curle, *Pictish and Norse Finds from the Brough of Birsay 1934–74* (1982), 54.

24. Brøgger and Sketelig, *Viking Ships*, 62; Christensen, 'Boats and boat-building', 87–8.

25. S. Grieg, 'Viking antiquities in Scotland', *Viking Antiquities*, II, 179.

26. J. Graham-Campbell, *Viking Artefacts* (1980), no. 278; McGrail, 'Ships', 46 and pp. 44, 54 for excellent illustrations on the way strakes were fastened to the stem pieces.

27. J. R. C. Hamilton, *Excavations at Jarlshof, Shetland* (1956), 114–15.

28. RCAHMS, *Argyll, An Inventory of the Monuments*, IV (*Iona*) (1982), no. 95.

29. G. Henderson, *The Norse Influence on Celtic Scotland* (1910), 136–49; M. Oftedal, 'On the frequency of Norse loan words in Scottish Gaelic', *Scottish Gaelic Studies*, IX (1961–2), 122.

30. OS P. and E., 172.

31. *Hacon's Saga*, 267–8.

32. A. Small, 'The Viking Highlands – a geographical view', in *The Dark Ages in the Highlands* (Inverness Field Club, 1971), 75.

33. B. E. Crawford, 'The earldom of Caithness and the kingdom of Scotland 1150–1266', *Northern Scotland*, II.2 (1976–7), 97.

34. A. Sommerfelt, 'On the Norse form of the name of the Picts and the date of the first Norse raids on Scotland', *Lochlann*, I (1958), 218–19.

35. *ES*, I, 331.

36. *Hms* (Laing), 343.

37. *Hacon's Saga*, 364.

38. G. W. S. Barrow, *Kingship and Unity* (1981), 105; Sir Lindsay Scott, 'The colonisation of Scotland in the second mill. BC', *PPS* (1951), 34.

39. L. Alcock *et al.*, *Excavations at Urquhart and Dunnottar Castles: Interim Report* (Dept of Archaeology, University of Glasgow, 1985), 2.

40. *ES*, I, 51, 59.

41. Scott, 'Colonisation', 34.

42. See ch. 2, p. 57, ch. 3, p. 67 below.

43. Watson, *Celtic Place-Names*, 505; H. Cheape, 'Recounting tradition: a critical view of medieval reportage', in Fenton and Palsson, *Northern and Western Isles*, 210–11.

44. J. Jakobsen, *The Place-Names of Shetland* (1936), 36.

45. Donaldson, 'Viking tracks', 6.

46. H. Marwick, *Orkney* (1952), 100, 174.

47. W. J. Watson, *The Place-Names of Ross and Cromarty* (1904), 42.

48. A. MacBain, 'The Norse element in the topography of the Highlands and Isles', *TGSI*, XIX (1893–4), 225.

49. *OS* Guthmundsson, 98; Cheape, 'Recounting tradition', 212–15.

50. *OS* P. and E., 81.

51. *Hacon's Saga*, 354.

52. Smyth, *York and Dublin*, II, 32–3.

53. *OS* P. and E., 80–1.

54. Barrow, *Kingship*, 106.

55. Duncan, *Scotland*, 547.

56. *APS*, I, 110.

57. A. A. M. Duncan and A. L. Brown, 'Argyll and the Isles in the earlier Middle Ages', *PSAS*, XC (1956–7), 195–6; Barrow, *Kingship*, 109.

58. Sir Lindsay Scott, 'The Norse in the Hebrides', *First Viking Congress*, 214.

59. See ch. 3, p. 66 below.

60. Smyth, *Scandinavian Kings*, 74.

61. Scott, 'Colonisation', 32.

62. Smyth, *York and Dublin*, I, 22; see map of 'The Irish Sea in the Viking

Age' in *Historical Atlas of Britain*, ed. J. Gillingham (1981), 49.
63. Scott, 'Colonisation', 35.
64. See ch. 2, p. 51 below.
65. See ch. 3, p. 86 below.
66. E. G. Bowen, *Britain and the Western Seaways* (1972), 94.
67. *Chronicle of Man*, 82–3.
68. *OS P. and E.*, 81.
69. A. Ritchie, 'The first settlers', in *The Prehistory of Orkney*, ed. C. Renfrew (1985), 38–9, 50.
70. Morris, 'Viking Orkney', 227; see below, ch. 5, p. 151.
71. *OS P. and E.*, 67.
72. D. A. Davidson and R. L. Jones, 'The environment of Orkney', in *The Prehistory of Orkney*, ed. C. Renfrew (1985), 35.
73. H. H. Lamb, *Climate, History and the Modern World* (1982), 163, 168–70; J. R. Hunter, 'Recent excavations on the Brough of Birsay', in *Birsay* (1983), 152.
74. A. Fenton, *The Northern Isles: Orkney and Shetland* (1978), 142.
75. B. E. Crawford, 'The Biggins, Papa Stour: a multi-disciplinary investigation', in *Shetland Archaeology*, ed. B. Smith (1985), 147.
76. F. Shaw, *The Northern and Western Isles of Scotland* (1980), 118.
77. *DN*, VII, 10.
78. Shaw, *The Northern and Western Isles of Scotland*, 108.
79. G. Fellows-Jensen, 'Viking settlement in the Northern and Western Isles: the place-name evidence as seen from Denmark and the Danelaw' in Fenton and Palsson, *Northern and Western Isles*, 149.
80. See ch. 4, p. 100 below.
81. See ch. 2, pp. 57–8 below.
82. See ch. 2, p. 59 below.
83. Scott, 'Colonisation', 34.
84. Small, 'Viking Highlands', 83.
85. G. Fellows-Jensen, 'Scandinavian settlement in the Isle of Man and north-west England: the place-name evidence', in *Ninth Viking Congress*, 46, 48; see ch. 4, p. 111ff below.

2 The Chronological Framework: Part 1 c.800–954

1. P. H. Sawyer, *The Age of the Vikings* (1971), 202–3, and discussion by P. Wormald, 'Viking studies: whence and whither?', in Farrell, *Vikings*, 129–31.
2. A. Binns, *Viking Voyagers: Then and Now* (1980), 13.
3. *Ibid.*, 14.
4. *EHD*, no. 193.
5. Sawyer, *Kings*, 79.
6. P. H. Sawyer, 'The two Viking Ages of Britain: a discussion', *Med. Scand.*, ii (1969), 163; and A. Thorsteinsson, *ibid.*, 202.
7. *ES*, I, 255; *Annals of Ulster*, 251.
8. *Ibid.*, 255, 257.
9. O'Corrain, *Ireland*, 81.
10. *ES*, I, 256–7.
11. O'Corrain, *Ireland*, 82.
12. *Ibid.*, 81.
13. *ES*, I, 324, 392.
14. Wormald, 'Viking studies', 132; Smyth, *Warlords*, 146.
15. *ES*, I, 281 n.6; O'Corrain, *Ireland*, 296–7; Duncan, *Scotland*, 79; Smyth, *Scandinavian Kings*, 88, n.17.
16. R. H. M. Dolley, *The Hiberno-Norse coins in the British Museum* (1966), 18–19; P. H. Sawyer, 'The Vikings and the Irish Sea', in *The Irish Sea Province in Archaeology and History*, ed. D. Moore (1970), 89; Duncan, *Scotland*, 84.
17. D. Greene, 'The influence of Scandinavian on Irish', in *Seventh Viking Congress*, 76–7; *idem*, 'The evidence of language and place-names in Ireland', in *The Vikings*, ed. T. Andersson and K. Sandred (Uppsala, 1978), 120, 123.
18. A. Small, 'The Viking Highlands', in *The Dark Ages in the Highlands* (1971), 71.
19. A. W. Brøgger, *Ancient Emigrants* (1929), 20.
20. Jones, *History*, 197.
21. Wormald, 'Viking studies', 146–7.
22. Sawyer, *Kings*, 70–3; *idem*, 'The causes of the Viking Age', in Farrell, *Vikings*, 5–6, and consideration of these ideas by Wormald in the same volume, pp. 146–7.
23. J. Graham-Campbell, *The Viking World* (1980), 87–99.
24. Jones, *History*, 159, 162.
25. Sawyer, *Kings*, 77.
26. See ch. 1, p. 14 above.
27. Sawyer, *Age of the Vikings*, 31.
28. J. Petersen, 'British antiquities of the Viking period found in Norway', *Viking Antiquities*, V (Oslo, 1940), 15–79; P. S. Andersen, *Vik-*

ings of the West (Oslo, 1971; repr. 1985), 27–8; J. Graham-Campbell and D. Kidd, *The Vikings* (1980), 34.

29. Wormald, 'Viking studies', 133.
30. *ES*, I, 263–5; *Annals of Ulster*, 283.
31. *Ibid.*, 264–5.
32. W. F. Skene, *Celtic Scotland* (1877), II, 302.
33. Binns, *Voyagers*, 17.
34. *ES*, I, 255.
35. Wormald, 'Viking studies', 134.
36. N. Lund, 'The settlers', in *Eighth Viking Congress*, 148.
37. O'Corrain, *Ireland*, 89; Smyth, *Scandinavian Kings*, 167.
38. *ES*, I, 265.
39. Smyth, *Scandinavian Kings*, 154–6.
40. J. Brøndsted, *The Vikings* (1965), 38–9.
41. Jones, *History*, 211; Andersen, *Vikings*, 77.
42. Jones, *History*, 232 n.2.
43. L. de Paor, 'The Viking towns of Ireland', in *Seventh Viking Congress*, 30–1.
44. Sir L. Scott, 'The Norse in the Hebrides', *First Viking Congress*, 203, 212.
45. See ch. 5 below.
46. Brøgger, *Emigrants*, 65; see ch. 5, p. 148 below.
47. J. S. Clouston, *A History of Orkney* (1932), 19–20, where, however, the 'ness-taking' is thought to have taken place *after* the original Norse settlement.
48. *ES*, I, 392; *Hms* (Laing), I, 218.
49. *ES*, I, 267.
50. W. D. H. Sellar, 'The origins and ancestry of Somerled', *SHR*, XLV (1966), 135.
51. Although Skene, *Celtic Scotland*, I, 311–12, seems to think that Galloway was so called because of the Anglian rule in the area over the Gaels. See Duncan, *Scotland*, p. 89, for discussion of the problems concerning the identity of Galloway; also ch. 4, p. 100 below.
52. Jones, *History*, 206 n.1. C. Marstrander, 'Bidrag til det Norske Sprogs' Historie i Irland', *Videnskapsselskapets Skrifter*, II H.-F. Klasse (1915), no. 5, 6–8, sees a clear distinction between the Irish *Gall-Gaedhil* of the ninth century and the later Scots who settled in and gave the name to Galloway. O'Corrain refers to

them as 'half-Irish, half-Norse', *Ireland*, 70, and as 'a racial mix of Vikings and Gaelic Scots' in 'High Kings, Vikings and other Kings', *Irish Historical Studies*, XXI (1978–9), 301.
53. Smyth, *Scandinavian Kings*, 115. See Duncan, *Scotland*, 89, for supporting evidence; Smyth, *Warlords*, 157.
54. A point made by Marstrander, 'Bidrag', 6.
55. Smyth, *Scandinavian Kings*, 124; idem, *Warlords*, 156.
56. *Ibid.*, 162–3.
57. Sellar, *Origins*, 135.
58. *ES*, I, 267.
59. Smyth, *Warlords*, 176, 180, 189.
60. Duncan, *Scotland*, 57, 86.
61. M. O. Anderson, 'Dalriada and the creation of the Kingdom of the Scots', in *Ireland in Early Mediaeval Europe*, ed. D. Whitelock, R. MacKitterick and D. Dumville (1982), 106.
62. *ES*, I, 268.
63. *Ibid.*, I, 271.
64. Smyth, *Warlords*, 185.
65. *ES*, I, 277.
66. *ES*, I, 281. See Smyth, *Warlords*, 159–60, for the identification of this Olaf.
67. N. K. Chadwick, 'The Vikings and the Western world', in *Procs. International Congress of Celtic Studies, 1959* (1962), 25; see map, p. 49, in *Historical Atlas of Britain*, ed. M. Falkus and J. Gillingham (1981).
68. Smyth, *Scandinavian Kings*, 146; idem, *Warlords*, 156.
69. *ES*, I, 288.
70. *ES*, I, 296; corroborated by a French source (Prudentius of Troyes, *Annales*) written about the middle of the ninth century which says that the islands of the Scots were taken by Northmen who 'dwelt there' (*ES*, I, 277).
71. *Ibid.*, I, 292; Smyth, *Scandinavian Kings*, 148.
72. *ES*, I, 301–2.
73. Smyth, *Scandinavian Kings*, 154; idem, *Warlords*, 192.
74. *Idem, Scandinavian Kings*, 151; idem, *Warlords*, 192.
75. *Idem, York and Dublin*, I, 22.
76. *Idem, Scandinavian Kings*, passim, although see trenchant criticism by O'Corrain, 'High-kings', 314–19.

77. Smyth, *Scandinavian Kings*, 159–65.
78. *ES*, I, 305.
79. O'Corrain, *Ireland*, 96.
80. *Hms* (Laing), II, 65.
81. *Ibid.*, 66.
82. D. W. Hunter Marshall, *The Sudreys in Early Viking Times* (1929), 32.
83. H. Shetelig, 'An introduction to the Viking history of Western Europe', in *Viking Antiquities*, I (Oslo, 1940), 24.
84. See Introduction above.
85. Smyth, *Scandinavian Kings*, 72, 121–2; *idem, Warlords*, 152, 156. Also see Sawyer, *Kings*, 13, for suggestion that Harald's career was modelled by saga writers on that of Magnus Barelegs.
86. *ES*, I, 334; *Hms* (Laing), II, 67; *OS* P. and E., 30.
87. Andersen, *Samlingen av Norge*, 85.
88. *Hms* (Laing), II, 58, 67.
89. *ES*, I, lii.
90. *Ibid.*, I, 292; Shetelig, 'Viking history', 26.
91. Smyth, *Scandinavian Kings*, 62–7, but see consideration of the problem by R. W. McTurk, 'Ragnarr Lothbrok in the Irish Annals', *Seventh Viking Congress*, 106–11.
92. Shetelig, 'Viking history', 26; H. Marwick, *Orkney* (1951), 39.
93. H. Koht, *NBL* sub Ragnvald Mørejarl.
94. *ES*, I, 331.
95. *Ibid.*, I, 388–90; *OS* P. and E., 33; see ch. 7, p. 196 below.
96. *The Book of Settlements*, trans. H. Palsson and P. Edwards (1972), 15.
97. *Hms* (Laing), II, 65.
98. Andersen, *Samlingen av Norge*, 83.
99. *ES*, I, 396, 393n.
100. *Ibid.*, I, 324 n.1.
101. Wormald, 'Viking studies', 147.
102. *ES*, I, 331; see ch. 7, p. 211 below.
103. Smyth, *Warlords*, 160.
104. E. J. Cowan, 'Caithness in the Sagas', in *Caithness: A Cultural Cross-roads*, ed. J. R. Baldwin (1982), 28.
105. *ES*, I, 378; *The Book of Settlements* (1972), 51.
106. *ES*, I, 395.
107. *Ibid.*, I, 378; *Book of Settlements*, trans. Palsson and Edwards, 51.
108. *Hms* (Laing), II, 67.
109. See ch. 4, p. 96 below.
110. *OS* P. and E., 30; *OS* Taylor, 352; R. W. Feachem, 'Fortifications', in *The Problem of the Picts*, ed. F. T. Wainwright (1955, repr. 1980), 70; L. Laing, *Archaeology of Late Celtic Britain and Ireland* (1975), 68–9.
111. Duncan, *Scotland*, 111.
112. See ch. 3, p. 64 below.
113. *OS* P. and E., 30.
114. *OS* Anderson, 107 n.2; *OS* Taylor, 353.
115. *ES*, I, 371.
116. *OS* P. and E., 31.
117. Smyth, *York and Dublin*, I, 62, 78.
118. *ES*, I, 399.
119. *Ibid.*, I, 398.
120. Smyth, *Warlords*, 208.
121. *ES*, I, 402; F. T. Wainwright, *Scandinavian England* (1975), 178.
122. *ES*, I, 406–7.
123. Duncan, *Scotland*, 92; Wainwright, *Scandinavian England*, 172–3; Smyth, *Warlords*, 197–8.
124. Wainwright, *Scandinavian England*, 338–42.
125. Smyth, *York and Dublin*, II, 64, 67–8.
126. *ES*, I, 426.
127. Smyth, *York and Dublin*, II, 41–55; M. Wood, 'Brunanburh revisited', *Saga-Book*, xx (1978–9), 200–17.
128. Smyth, *York and Dublin*, II, 79; *idem, Warlords*, 192.
129. *ES*, I, 475; Smyth, *Warlords*, 210.
130. *Ibid.*, 194–5, 198.
131. See ch. 1, p. 21 above.
132. Smyth, *York and Dublin*, II, 177–8.
133. *ES*, I, 455; *OS* Taylor, 144.
134. *ES*, I, 459; *Hms* (Laing), II, 86.
135. *Anglo-Saxon Chronicle*, in *ES*, I, 460 n.2.
136. W. G. Collingwood, *Scandinavian Britain* (1908), 142; but see A. Seeberg, 'Five kings', *Saga-Book*, xx (1978–79), 106–14; M. Wood, *In Search of the Dark Ages* (1981), 175–6.
137. *ES*, I, 461–2.
138. Although see *ES*, I, 462 n.2.
139. Smyth, *York and Dublin*, II, 181–2.
140. Wormald, 'Viking studies', 141; Smyth, *Warlords*, 207–8.
141. D. P. Kirby, 'The evolution of the frontier c. 400–1018' in *An Historical Atlas of Scotland*, ed. P. MacNeill and R. Nicholson (1975), 25–6.

3 The Chronological Framework: Part 2 c.975–1065

1. Jones, *History*, 354–60; P. H. Sawyer, *The Age of the Vikings* (1971), 131.
2. Smyth, *York and Dublin*, II, 77–8.
3. *OS* P. and E., 36; see ch. 7, p. 218 below.
4. *OS* P. and E., 37.
5. A. B. Taylor, 'Karl Hundason, "King of Scots"', *PSAS*, LXXI (1936–7), 338; D. P. Kirby, 'Moray prior to *c.* 1110' in *An Historical Atlas of Scotland*, ed. P. MacNeill and R. Nicholson (1975), 20.
6. See ch. 2, p. 57 above.
7. *ES*, I, 495 n.6.
8. *OS* Taylor, 413.
9. *Ibid.*, 148; *OS* P. and E., 37–8.
10. *Ibid.*.
11. Duncan, *Scotland*, 100.
12. *OS* Taylor, 361; Taylor, 'Karl Hundason', 340; Kirby, 'Evolution of the frontier', 21.
13. *OS* Taylor, 148; *OS* P. and E., 38.
14. H. Shetelig, 'An introduction to the Viking history of Western Europe', in *Viking Antiquities*, I (Oslo, 1940), 30.
15. *OS* Taylor, 413.
16. *NBL*, sub Sigurd Digre.
17. *ES*, I, 499.
18. W. F. Skene, *Celtic Scotland* (1876), I, 375–6; Smyth, *Warlords*, 150.
19. *OS* Taylor, 401.
20. *Ibid.*, 147.
21. *OS* Anderson, xxvi.
22. W. F. H. Nicolaisen, 'Scandinavians and Celts in Caithness: the place-name evidence', in *Caithness: a Cultural Crossroads*, ed. J. Baldwin (1982), 76–7.
23. Skene, *Celtic Scotland*, I, 378.
24. *ES*, I, 499.
25. *ES*, I, 489, 494.
26. *Ibid.*, 500, 502.
27. *Ibid.*, 528.
28. *Ibid.*, 503; *Chronicle of Man*, 136–7.
29. *ES*, I, 485–6; B. R. S. and E. M. Megaw, 'Norse heritage', 157.
30. R. L. Bremner, 'Some notes on the Norsemen in Argyllshire and on the Clyde', *Saga-Book*, III (1901–3), 352; A. O. Johnsen, 'The payments from the Hebrides and the Isle of Man to the crown of Norway, 1152–1263', *SHR*, XLVII (1969), 20.
31. Kirby, 'Moray prior to *c.* 1100', 21; see chs. 1 and 2.
32. *OS* P. and E., 38.
33. *ES*, I, 534.
34. *Ibid.*.
35. *Ibid.*, 536.
36. Jones, *History*, 397–7; O'Corrain, *Ireland*, 130; see ch. 7, p. 213 below.
37. *ES*, I, 538–9; see discussion of the significance of the raven banner in ch. 7, pp. 196–7 below.
38. M. Chesnutt, 'An unsolved problem in Old Norse-Icelandic literary history', *Med. Scand.*, I (1968), 122.
39. *OS* Anderson, xxviii, quoting Dasent.
40. See ch. 6, p. 168 below.
41. Andersen, *Samlingen av Norge*, 178.
42. Adam of Bremen, *History of the Archbishops of Hamburgh-Bremen*, trans. F. T. Tschan (New York, 1959), 211.
43. Smyth, *Scandinavian Kings*, 221–2; P. Wormald, 'Viking studies: whence and whither?', in Farrell, *Vikings*, 139–41.
44. Jones, *History*, 133.
45. Sawyer, *Kings*, 15.
46. Quoted by Jones, *History*, 134.
47. *ES*, I, 507–11.
48. Jones, *History*, 133.
49. *ES*, I, 509.
50. *Ibid.*
51. *OS* Taylor, 150.
52. Wainwright, *Northern Isles*, 159.
53. See ch. 6, p. 168 below.
54. *ES*, I, 509.
55. *OS* P. and E., 40.
56. J. S. Clouston, 'Two features of the Orkney earldom', *SHR*, XVI (1918–19), 15.
57. *OS* P. and E., 42.
58. Taylor, 'Karl Hundason', 338; see pp. 58, 65 above.
59. Skene, *Celtic Scotland*, I, 410; J. S. Clouston, *A History of Orkney* (1932), 40.
60. Taylor, 'Karl Hundason', 336.
61. *Ibid.*, 334–41 where, however, Taylor does not make any reference to this possibility.
62. *ES*, I, 578.
63. *Ibid.*, 579; E. J. Cowan, 'Caithness in the sagas', in *Caithness: a Cultural Crossroads*, ed. J. Baldwin (1982), 33.
64. See Introduction, p. 8 above.
65. *OS* Taylor, 167.
66. *OS* P. and E., 53; Taylor, 167;

Broadfirth (*Breiðafjörðr*) is usually translated as Moray Firth, but could possibly apply to the Dornoch Firth.

67. *OS* P. and E., 53.
68. *Ibid.*, 71.
69. *Ibid.*, 72; G. W. S. Barrow, *Kingship and Unity* (1981), 27; Duncan, *Scotland*, 100, 118.
70. *OS* P. and E., 57.
71. G. V. C. Young, *The History of the Isle of Man under the Norse* (1981), 48.
72. *OS* P. and E., 53, 54.
73. *Ibid.*, 58.
74. Perhaps Waterford in Ireland, where there was an internal power struggle in 1037: O'Corrain, *Ireland*, 133.
75. *OS* P. and E., 60.
76. See ch. 5 below, n.67.
77. *OS* P. and E., 60.
78. See ch. 7, p. 193 below.
79. *OS* P. and E., 71.
80. *OS* Taylor, 175; *OS* P. and E., 60.
81. *OS* Anderson, 44.
82. *Ibid.*, 44 n.1; *OS* Taylor, 368. A Tusker Rock also exists off the coast of South Wales.
83. *Hacon's Saga*, ch. 265; *OS* Guthmundsson, 82, also suggests a location off Shetland and possibly the Out Skerries.
84. *NBL*, sub Thorfinn Sigurdsson.
85. J. Jakobsen, *The Place-Names of Shetland* (1936), 168.
86. The probable trans. of 'Tussasker' is 'Giants' Skerries' (*OS* P. and E., 71) and there are legends of the activities of the giants Sigger, Saxie and Herman in the Burrafirth area of N. Unst, off which lie the Muckle Flugga group of rocks (J. Saxby, *Shetland Traditional Lore*, 1932, 133).
87. *OS* Taylor, 162.
88. *Ibid.*, 178, 181; *OS* P. and E., 64.
89. *Hms* (Laing), *St Olaf's Saga*, 230.
90. See ch. 2, p. 53 above.
91. Andersen, *Samlingen av Norge*, 134.
92. *OS* Taylor, 155–63; *OS* P. and E., 43–49.
93. *ES*, I, 554; *Islandske Annaler*, ed. G. Storm (1888), 106, 316.
94. Andersen, *Samlingen av Norge*, 120.
95. *Ibid.*, 121.
96. *OS* Taylor, 169–72.
97. Andersen, *Samlingen av Norge*, 143–4.

98. *OS* Taylor, 176.
99. *OS* P. and E., 63, 64.
100. Andersen, *Samlingen av Norge*, 152.
101. *OS* Taylor, 185–7; *OS* P. and E., 68–9.
102. *Ibid.*, 106; *Hms* (Laing), *St Olaf's Saga*, 230.
103. *OS* Taylor, 159.
104. B. E. Crawford, 'Weland of Stiklaw: a Scottish royal servant at the Norwegian Court', *Historisk Tidsskrift* (1973), 334–5.
105. *OS* P. and E., 71.
106. R. Radford, 'Art and architecture: Celtic and Norse', in Wainwright, *Northern Isles*, 164; B. E. Crawford, 'Birsay and the early earls and bishops of Orkney', in *Birsay* (1983), 100.
107. P. Foote and D. M. Wilson, *The Viking Achievement* (1970), 415.
108. Smyth, *Warlords*, 171–2.
109. See ch. 6, p. 168 below.
110. *Hms* (Laing), *St Olaf's Saga*, 159.
111. Crawford, 'Earls and bishops', 105.
112. *OS* P. and E., 71.
113. Adam of Bremen, *History*, 180.
114. *Ibid.*, 216.
115. *Ibid.*, and see my detailed discussion of the problems associated with the interpretation of this name, Crawford, 'Earls and bishops', n.13.
116. J. Johannesson, *Islendinga Saga* (Manitoba, 1974), 141.
117. C. Halliday, *The Scandinavian Kingdom of Dublin* (1884), 92; A. Walsh, *Scandinavian Relations with Ireland during the Viking Period* (1922), 54–5; J. Watt, *The Church in Medieval Ireland* (1972), 2.
118. Andersen, *Samlingen av Norge*, 329.
119. As also probably in Dublin: Smyth, *York and Dublin*, II, 200.
120. Clouston, *History*, 150.
121. B. E. Crawford, 'The earldom of Caithness and the kingdom of Scotland', *Northern Scotland*, II.2 (1976–7), 99–100.
122. *Chronicle of Man*, 114.
123. Young, *History of the Isle of Man*, 57.
124. *ES*, I, 96; B. E. Crawford, 'Diocese of Orkney', in *Series Episcoporum Ecclesiae Catholicae Occidentalis ab Initio ad Annum 1198*, ed. O. Engels and S. Weinfurter (in press).

125. Andersen, *Samlingen av Norge*, 113.
126. *OS* P. and E., 71.
127. *Ibid.*, 65.
128. Clouston, *History*, 32, 152–3.
129. Marwick, *Farm-Names*, 192.
130. Andersen, *Samlingen av Norge*, 64–5.
131. A. Steinnes, 'The huseby system in Orkney', *SHR*, xxxviii (1959), 45.
132. A. McKerral, 'Ancient denominations of agricultural Land in Scotland', *PSAS*, lxxvii (1943–4), 57.
133. Jakobsen, *Place-Names*, 126.
134. W. C. MacKenzie, *Scottish Place-Names* (1931), 136.
135. Clouston, *History*, 163.
136. B. R. S. Megaw, 'Norseman and native in the Kingdom of the Isles', *Scot. Stud.*, xx (1976), 26.
137. A. M. Cubbon and M. Dolley, 'The 1972 Kirkmichael Treasure Trove', *JMM*, viii (1980), 19.
138. F. M. Stenton, *Anglo-Saxon England* (1971), 587.
139. B. Dickens, 'An Orkney raid on Wales', *POAS*, viii (1929–30), 47; W. Davies, *Wales in the Early Middle Ages* (1982), 67.
140. Walsh, *Scandinavian Relations*, 39; Andersen, *Samlingen av Norge*, 264.
141. H. Marwick, 'Leidang in the West', *POAS*, xiii (1934–5), 15–16.
142. Andersen, *Samlingen av Norge*, 262, 268–70.
143. Marwick, *Farm-Names*, 210.
144. *Idem*, 'Naval defence in north Scotland', *SHR*, xxxviii (1949); Barrow, *Kingship*, 174.
145. C. Marstrander, 'Treen og Keeill', *Norsk Tidsskrift for Sprogvidenskap*, viii (1937), 424; Marwick, *Farm-Names*, 209.
146. *Ibid.*, 207; G. Hafström, 'Atlantic and Baltic earldoms', *Sixth Viking Congress*, 62.
147. J. MacQueen, 'Pennyland and davoch in south-west Scotland; a preliminary note', *Scot. Stud.*, xxiii (1979), 69.
148. W. D. Lamont, '"House" and "pennyland" in the Highlands and Isles', *Scot. Stud.*, xxv (1981), 72.
149. Marwick, *Farm-Names*, 212.
150. Hafström, 'Earldoms', 63.
151. *Ibid.*; see ch. 5, p. 154 below.
152. Marwick, *Farm-Names*, 208.
153. M. Bangor-Jones, 'Land assessments and settlement history', in *The Firthlands*, ed. J. Baldwin (1986), 157.
154. Sawyer, *Kings*, 110.
155. Andersen, *Samlingen av Norge*, 231–2.
156. Megaw, 'Norseman and native', 19.
157. See ch. 5, p. 128 below.
158. J. Bannerman, *Studies in the History of Dalriada* (1974), 140–1; B. R. S. Megaw, 'Note on pennyland and davoch in south-western Scotland', *Scot. Stud.*, xxiii (1979), 75; A. Easson, 'Ouncelands and pennylands in the West Highlands and Islands of Scotland' (in press).
159. Lamont, '"House" and "pennyland"', 68.
160. Lamont, '"House" and "pennyland"', 72.
161. See ch. 1, p. 25 above.
162. O'Corrain, *Ireland*, 107.
163. MacQueen, 'Pennyland and davoch', 75.
164. Hafström, 'Earldoms', 63.
165. See ch. 4, p. 102 below.
166. K. Helle, *Norge Blir en Stat* (1974), 96.
167. See ch. 5, p. 135 below.

4 The Linguistic Framework: Place-Names and Settlement

1. W. F. H. Nicolaisen, 'Scandinavian place-names in Scotland as a source of knowledge', *Northern Studies*, vii/viii (1976), 23, has a long list of the major fields of knowledge for which place-names are an important source.
2. Nicolaisen, 'Source of knowledge' (1976), 16, and *idem*, *Scottish Place-Names*, 85, puts the Northern and Western Isles together as forming one linguistic province.
3. For a study of the whole controversy and the arguments involved, see G. Fellows-Jensen, 'The Vikings in England; a review', *Anglo-Saxon England*, iv, ed. P. Clemoes (1975), 181–207; a more recent assessment is in P. Stafford, *The East Midlands in the Early Middle Ages* (1985), 115–21.
4. See G. Fellows-Jensen, 'The Manx place-name debate', in *Man and the Environment in the Isle of Man*, ed. P. Davey, BAR 54 (ii) (1978), 315–18 and papers there

cited. Also papers in *The Vikings*, ed. T. Andersson and K. L. Sandred (Uppsala, 1978); P. Gelling, 'Celtic continuity in the Isle of Man', in *Studies in Celtic Survival*, ed. L. Laing, BAR 37 (1977).

5. Wainwright, *Northern Isles*, 105–6, discusses Marwick's and Jakobsen's supposedly pre-Norse names in the Northern Isles; also see W. F. H. Nicolaisen, 'Early Scandinavian naming in the Western and Northern Isles', *Northern Scotland*, III (1979–80), 109 n.6.

6. See Wainwright's discussion of Brøgger and Shetelig's theories, *Northern Isles*, 101–2; and a more recent analysis by I. A. Crawford, 'War or peace: Viking colonisation in the Northern and Western Isles of Scotland reviewed', *Eighth Viking Congress*, 261–2.

7. Nicolaisen, *Scottish Place-Names*, 138.

8. *Idem*, 'Scandinavians and Celts in Caithness: the place-name evidence', in *Caithness: a Cultural Crossroads*, ed. J. Baldwin (1982), 79.

9. See chs. 2, p. 57, and 3, p. 72 above, and ch. 7, p. 206 below.

10. W. J. Watson, *Place-Names of Ross and Cromarty* (1904), xviii; B. E. Crawford, 'The making of a frontier: the firthlands from 9th–12th centuries', in *The Firthlands of Ross and Sutherland*, ed. J. Baldwin (1986), 43.

11. Nicolaisen, 'Early Scandinavian naming' (1979–80), 109; G. Fellows-Jensen, 'Northern and Western Isles', 151.

12. M. Oftedal, 'Norse place-names in the Hebrides', *Second Viking Congress*, 111.

13. *Ibid.*, 112.

14. M. Oftedal, 'On the frequency of Norse loan-words in Scottish Gaelic', *Scottish Gaelic Studies*, IX (1961–2), 119.

15. Despite Sir Lindsay Scott's belief that the island was of no significance to the Orkneymen; 'The Norse in the Hebrides', *First Viking Congress*, 213.

16. Nicolaisen, *Scottish Place-Names*, 141 and map 15.

17. I. Fraser, 'Gaelic and Norse elements in coastal place-names in the Western Isles', *TGSI*, L (1976–8), 254.

18. A. B. Taylor, 'British and Irish place-names in Old Norse literature', *Second Viking Congress*, 121 n.2; M. Oftedal, 'Norse place-names in Celtic Scotland', in *Procs. of the International Congress of Celtic Studies, 1959* (1962), 46.

19. Oftedal, 'Place-names in the Hebrides', 107. The maps of percentages of Norse place-names in Scott, 'Norse in the Hebrides', 190, must be understood as providing only very rough estimates. But see also Nicolaisen, *Scottish Place-Names*, maps 14 and 15.

20. Fellows-Jensen, 'Northern and Western Isles', 151.

21. Nicolaisen, *Scottish Place-Names*, 138.

22. P. S. Andersen, 'To what extent did *balley/balla (baile)* names in the Isle of Man supplant place-names of Norse origin?', *Ninth Viking Congress*, 167 and particularly n.14.

23. Nicolaisen, *Scottish Place-Names*, 94; Duncan, *Scotland*, 85.

24. This distinction was first made by Nicolaisen in 'Norse Settlement in the Northern and Western Isles', *Scottish Historical Rev.*, XLVIII (1969), 16, repeated in 'Scandinavian place-names' in *An Historical Atlas of Scotland*, ed. P. MacNeill and R. Nicolson (1975), 7; in Nicolaisen, *Scottish Place-Names*, 94–5, and in 'The Viking settlement of Scotland: the evidence of place-names', in Farrell, *Vikings*, 108.

25. See comments by I. Fraser, 'The Norse elements in Sutherland place-names', *Scottish Literary J.* (1978), 25; and Smyth, *Warlords*, 149–50.

26. R. L. Bremner, *The Norsemen in Alban* (1923), 281.

27. See ch. 1, p. 25 above.

28. See ch. 6, p. 172 below.

29. Nicolaisen, *Scottish Place-Names*, maps 9 and 10; G. Fellows-Jensen, 'Anthroponymical specifics in place-names in *-by* in the British Isles', *Studia Anthroponymica Scandinavica*, I (1983), 49; also *idem*, 'Scandinavian settlement in Cumbria and Dumfriesshire. The

place-name evidence', in *The Scandinavians in Cumbria*, ed. J. R. Baldwin and I. D. Whyte (1985), 67.

30. See ch. 2, p. 47 above; Smyth, *Warlords*, 157; G. W. S. Barrow, *Kingship and Unity* (1981), 107; Duncan, *Scotland*, 89.

31. Nicolaisen, *Scottish Place-Names*, map 10.

32. Smyth, *York and Dublin*, I, 197; Nicolaisen, *Scottish Place-Names*, 108–12.

33. D. Brooke, 'Kirk-compound place-names in Galloway and Carrick', *Trans. Dumfriesshire and Galloway Natural History and Antiquarian Soc.*, LVIII (1983), 58.

34. *Ibid.*

35. Nicolaisen, *Scottish Place-Names*, maps 2 and 3.

36. *Ibid.*, 115.

37. See ch. 6, p. 172 below.

38. I. A. Crawford, 'War or peace', 264.

39. A. Small, 'The Norse building tradition in Shetland', in *Vestnordisk Byggeskikk Gjennom to tusen Ar*, ed. B. Myrhe *et al.* (1982), 244–6. See below, pp. 113–14 and ch. 5.

40. Nicolaisen, 'Viking settlement' (1982), 96.

41. H. Marwick, *The Orkney Norn* (1929), xv; *idem*, *Farm-Names*, 3–5, 43; R. Lamb, *Sanday and North Ronaldsay* (1980), 9.

42. See ch. 2, p. 47 above.

43. Fellows-Jensen, 'Northern and Western Isles', 152.

44. M. Oftedal, 'Names of lakes on the Isle of Lewis in the Outer Hebrides', *Eighth Viking Congress*, 187. A similar conclusion was made by I. Fraser, 'The place-names of Lewis', *Northern Studies*, IV (1974), 18.

45. A. Small, 'Norse Settlement in Skye', in *Les Vikings et Leur Civilisation*, ed. R. Boyer (1976), 36.

46. See references in n.4 above.

47. M. Dolley, 'The palimpsest of Viking settlement on Man', *Eighth Viking Congress*, 177–8.

48. *Ibid.*, 177.

49. See ch. 7, p. 214 below.

50. See G. Fellows-Jensen, 'A Gaelic-Scandinavian loan word in English place-names', *J. English Place-Name Soc.*, x (1977–8) for other references and discussion of the whole problem, and also a recent assessment by the same author: 'Northern and Western Isles' (1984), 163.

51. Nicolaisen, 'Early Scandinavian naming' (1979–80), 116–19.

52. Wainwright, *Northern Isles*, 133–5; Fellows-Jensen, 'Northern and Western Isles', 153–4.

53. Oftedal, 'Place-names in the Hebrides', 111; Taylor, 'British and Irish place-names', 119; Nicolaisen, 'Early Scandinavian naming' (1979–80), 109 and references there cited; W. B. Lockwood, 'On the early history and origin of the names Orkney and Shetland', *Namn og Bygd* (1980), 31–4.

54. M. Olsen, *Farms and Fanes of Ancient Norway* (1928), 27.

55. A. Small, 'The distribution of settlement in Shetland and Faeroe in Viking times', *Saga-Book*, XVII (1967–8), 149; L. MacGregor, 'Sources for a study of Norse settlement in Shetland and Faeroe', in *Essays in Shetland History*, ed. B. E. Crawford (1984), 3; D. Olson, 'Norse settlement in the Hebrides: an interdisciplinary study' (thesis, University of Oslo, 1983), 34; also see ch. 5, p. 149 below.

56. M. Gelling, *Signposts to the Past* (1978), 118, 123, 126.

57. Fellows-Jensen, 'Northern and Western Isles', 154–5.

58. D. Olson, 'Norse settlement', 35.

59. The main research done in this field by H. Marwick in Orkney (*Farm-Names*, 227–51) was based on the pioneering place-name studies of O. Rygh, *Norske Gaardnavne* (*Norwegian Farm-Names*), in particular *Forord og Indledning* (1898), and Olsen, *Farms and Fanes*. It was extended by W. F. H. Nicolaisen to Shetland and the Western Isles ('Norse settlement', 1969), repeated in 'Scandinavian place-names' (1975) and *Scottish Place-Names* (1976) and 'Viking settlement' (1982).

60. Marwick, *Farm-Names*, 249.

61. Nicolaisen, *Scottish Place-Names*, 86.

62. Nicolaisen, 'Norse settlement' (1969), map 1; *idem*, 'Scandinavian place-names' (1975), map 6a; *idem*,

Scottish Place-Names, map 5; and *idem*, 'Viking settlement' (1982), fig. 1. Distribution is based on 1″ O.S. maps (Nicolaisen, *Scottish Place-Names*, 87).

63. Nicolaisen, 'Norse settlement' (1969), map 2; *idem*, 'Scandinavian place-names' (1975), map 6b; *idem*, *Scottish Place-Names*, map 6; *idem*, 'Viking settlement' (1982), fig. 2.

64. Fraser, 'Sutherland place-names'.

65. Nicolaisen, *Scottish Place-Names*, 90.

66. Nicolaisen, 'Norse settlement' (1969), map 3; *idem*, 'Scandinavian place-names' (1975), map 6c; *idem*, *Scottish Place-Names* (1976), map 7; *idem*, 'Viking settlement' (1982), fig. 3.

67. Nicolaisen, *Scottish Place-Names*, 92.

68. Nicolaisen, 'Norse settlement' (1969), 11; *idem*, *Scottish Place-Names*, 90.

69. *Ibid.*

70. Fellows-Jensen, 'Northern and Western Isles', 158.

71. Nicolaisen, 'Norse settlement' (1969), 12; *idem*, *Scottish Place-Names*, 91; *idem*, 'Viking settlement' (1982), 100 (where there is no reference to the settlement of Iceland).

72. Fellows-Jensen, 'Scandinavian settlement in the Isle of Man and north-west England: the place-name evidence', in *Ninth Viking Congress*, 38.

73. Fellows-Jensen, 'Northern and Western Isles', 162.

74. Morris, 'Viking Orkney', 231.

75. J. Jakobsen, *The Place-Names of Shetland* (1936), 94–5.

76. J. Stewart, 'Shetland farm-names', *Fourth Viking Congress*, 251.

77. Duncan, *Scotland*, 81.

78. A. W. Brøgger, *Ancient Emigrants* (1929), 73, although see Jakobsen, *Place-Names*, 157.

79. A. O'Dell, *The Historical Geography of the Shetland Isles* (1939), 238.

80. Fellows-Jensen, 'Northern and Western Isles', 162.

81. Stewart, 'Farm-names', 250.

82. Small, 'Settlement in Skye', 34 and fig. II.

83. D. Olson, 'Norse settlement', 110–12.

84. *Ibid.*, 225.

85. M. Nieke, 'Settlement patterns in the first millennium AD: a case study of the island of Islay', in *Settlement in North Britain 1000 BC–AD 1000*, ed. J. C. Chapman and H. C. Mytum, BAR 118 (1983), 313.

86. Olsen, *Farms and Fanes*, 56; Nicolaisen, *Scottish Place-Names*, 92, where, however, doubts are expressed as to whether it signifies division in the new Norwegian settlements.

87. Fellows-Jensen, 'Northern and Western Isles', 160.

88. N. P. Thuesen, 'Norrøn Bosetning pa Orknøyene' (University of Oslo thesis, 1978), 116; Marwick, *Farm-Names*, 233.

89. Stewart, 'Farm-names', 251.

90. Marwick, *Farm-Names*, 92, 184; see ch. 3 for explanation of the term 'urisland'.

91. B. E. Crawford, 'Settlement, continuity and change in one Shetland island', in Fenton and Palsson, *Northern and Western Isles*, 46.

92. M. Gelling, *Place-Names in the Landscape* (1984), 6.

93. Fellows-Jensen, 'Northern and Western Isles', 154.

94. Marwick, *Farm-Names*, 248; although he did not include them in his scheme of place-names because of difficulty in dating them.

95. Fellows-Jensen, 'Northern and Western Isles', 155.

96. See ch. 3, p. 83 above.

97. Fellows-Jensen, 'Northern and Western Isles', 155.

98. Marwick, *Farm-Names*, sub *Everby*, 29.

99. *DN*, VI, no. 651.

100. Information from Brian Smith, Archivist, Shetland Islands Council.

101. Marwick, *Farm-Names*, 249–50.

102. Fellows-Jensen, 'Northern and Western Isles', 156.

103. See ch. 3, p. 70 above.

104. H. Marwick, 'Orkney farm-name studies', *POAS*, IX (1930–1), 31–2.

105. Marwick, *Farm-Names*, 233–4; see reservations expressed by R. G. Cant, 'Settlement, society and church organisation in the Northern Isles', in Fenton and Palsson,

Northern and Western Isles, 176;
see ch. 6, p. 180 below.

106. L. Hellberg, *Ortnamn och den Svenska bosettningen på Åland*, 2 (1980), 168, cited by Fellows-Jensen, 'Northern and Western Isles', 157.

107. Fellows-Jensen, 'Scandinavian settlement' (1983), 41–2, 46.

108. L. Hellberg, 'Kumlabygdens ortnamn och aldre bebyggelse', in *Kumlabygden*, III (1967), 282–4, cited by Fellows-Jensen, 'Northern and Western Isles', 157.

109. J. S. Clouston, *A History of Orkney* (1932), 32–3.

110. Small, 'Norse building traditions', 243–4.

111. Jakobsen, *Place-Names*, 28.

112. See ch. 5, p. 180 below.

113. Nicolaisen, 'Source of knowledge' (1976), 21.

114. Smyth, *Warlords*, 152–3.

115. Wainwright, *Northern Isles*, 142–3; Fellows-Jensen, 'Northern and Western Isles', 149.

116. Nicolaisen, 'Early Scandinavian naming' (1979–80), 108.

117. Brøgger, *Emigrants*, 85.

118. J. Jakobsen, *An Etymological Dictionary of the Norn Language in Shetland* (1928–32), I, XXXI; M. Haegstad, 'Hildinakvadet', *Videnselskapsskrifter*, II, H-F Klasse (1900).

119. Wainwright, *Northern Isles*, 144.

5 The Archaeological Framework: Part 1 Settlement and Economy

1. See review of recent excavations by L. Alcock, 'Populi Bestiales Pictorum Feroci Animo: a survey of Pictish settlement archaeology', in *Roman Frontier Studies 1979*, ed. W. S. Hanson and L. J. F. Keppie, *BAR* International ser. 71 (1980), compared with F. T. Wainwright (ed.), *The Problem of the Picts* (1955 and 1980).

2. A. Ritchie, 'Orkney in the Pictish kingdom', in *The Prehistory of Orkney*, ed. C. Renfrew (1985), 183–204.

3. Alcock, 'Pictish settlement archaeology', 62; J. N. G. Ritchie and M. Harman, *Exploring Scotland's Heritage. Argyll and the Western Isles* (1985), 13.

4. The only full studies of Norse grave material in Scotland remain Grieg, 'Viking antiquities' and Shetelig, 'Viking graves'; with a valuable analysis of burials in part of Argyll in *RCAHMS Argyll: An Inventory of the Monuments*, V (Islay, Jura, Colonsay and Oronsay) (1984), 29–32, nos. 292–302.

5. B. E. Crawford, 'Viking graves', in *An Historical Atlas of Scotland*, ed. P. MacNeill and R. Nicholson (1975), 16.

6. See Introduction, p. 6 above.

7. Grieg, 'Viking antiquities', 13–14; J. G. Scott, 'A note on Viking settlement in Galloway', *Trans. Dumfriesshire and Galloway Natural History and Antiquarian Soc.*, LVIII (1983), 52–3.

8. See ch. 2, p. 48 above.

9. See ch. 4, p. 98 above.

10. Grieg, 'Viking antiquities', 103–5; Wainwright, *Northern Isles*, 148.

11. S. Kaland, 'Westnessutgravningene pa Rousay, Orknøyene', *Viking*, (1973), 77–101; A. Thorsteinsson, 'The Viking burial place at Pierowall, Westray, Orkney', *Fifth Viking Congress*, 150–73.

12. See Introduction above and ch. 6, p. 169 below.

13. Shetelig, 'Viking graves', 72; see ch. 4, p. 100 above.

14. Wainwright, *Northern Isles*, 126; see ch. 2, pp. 46–7 above.

15. R. B. K. Stevenson, 'The brooch from Westness, Orkney', *Fifth Viking Congress*, 30.

16. A. Liestøl, 'Runes', in *Northern and Western Isles*, 232–3.

17. A. Brøgger, *Ancient Emigrants* (1929), 122, 131.

18. Grieg, 'Viking antiquities', 27.

19. L. Laing, *The Archaeology of Late Celtic Britain and Ireland* (1975), 184.

20. A. Ritchie, 'Excavation of Pictish and Viking-Age farmsteads at Buckquoy', *PSAS*, CVIII (1976–7), 190.

21. Compare D. M. Wilson, 'The Norsemen', in *Who are the Scots?*, ed. G. Menzies (1971), 107, with *idem*, 'Scandinavian settlement in the north and west of the British Isles – an archaeological point of view', *TRHS*, XXVI (1976), 100, 107.

22. J. N. G. Ritchie, 'Excavations at Machrins, Colonsay', *PSAS*, 111

(1981), 268; *Argyll Inventory*, V, 153, no. 300.

23. Wilson, 'Scandinavian settlement', 99.

24. J. Graham-Campbell, *Viking Artefacts* (1980), 27–8.

25. Grieg, 'Viking antiquities', 75–7; Stevenson, 'The brooch from Westness', 30.

26. Shetelig, 'Viking graves', 97–9.

27. D. J. Freke, *Peel Castle Excavations: Interim Report 1984* (1985), 15.

28. G. Bersu and D. M. Wilson, *Three Viking Graves in the Isle of Man* (1966), D. M. Wilson, *The Viking Age in the Isle of Man* (Odense, 1974), 18–29; J. Anderson, *Scotland in Pagan Times* (1883), 48–55.

29. See ch. 2, pp. 40–1 above.

30. Shetelig, 'Viking graves', 100.

31. R. Reece, *Iona, Its History and Archaeology* (pamphlet); *RCAHMS, Argyll, an Inventory of the Monuments (Iona)*, IV (1982), 19.

32. Wainwright, *Northern Isles*, 154.

33. A. B. Taylor, 'The Norsemen in St Kilda', *Saga-Book*, XVII (1967–8), 124–9; A. Small (ed.), *A St Kilda Handbook* (1979), 62.

34. Shetelig, 'Viking graves', 101.

35. Brøgger, *Emigrants*, 66, 126–7, but see I. A. Crawford, 'War or peace – Viking colonisation in the Northern and Western Isles of Scotland reviewed', *Eighth Viking Congress*, 262–3.

36. K. Eldjarn, 'Graves and grave goods: survey and evaluation', in Fenton and Palsson, *Northern and Western Isles*, 7–8.

37. See p. 148 below; C. Blindheim, 'Trade problems in the Viking age: some reflections on insular metalwork found in Norwegian graves of the Viking age', in *The Vikings*, ed. T. Andersson and K. J. Sandred (1978), 173.

38. S. Kaland, 'Some economic aspects of the Orkneys in the Viking period', *Norwegian Archaeological Rev.*, XV (1982), 92 (if my understanding of the English is correct); Graham-Campbell, *Artefacts*, 85–6; E. Wamers, 'Some ecclesiastical and secular insular metalwork found in Norwegian Viking graves', *Peritia*, II (1983), 277–306.

39. Graham-Campbell, *Artefacts*, no. 306.

40. P. Foote and D. M. Wilson, *The Viking Achievement* (1970), 196–7; Grieg, 'Viking antiquities', 54–5; Duncan, *Scotland*, 83; *Argyll Inventory*, V, 30, no. 298.

41. P. Wormald, 'Viking studies: whence and whither?', in Farrell, *Vikings*, 132.

42. Laing, *Archaeology*, 201.

43. See ch. 2, p. 47 above.

44. Smyth, *Warlords*, 160–5.

45. *OS* P. and E., 191.

46. J. Graham-Campbell, 'The Viking-Age silver and gold hoards of Scandinavian character from Scotland', *PSAS*, CVII (1975–6), 114–35, and list of references there cited, 133–5; idem, 'The Viking-Age silver hoards of Ireland', *Seventh Viking Congress*, 39–74; idem, 'The Viking-Age silver hoards of the Isle of Man', *Ninth Viking Congress* (1983), 53–81.

47. Wilson, 'Scandinavian settlement', 101; A. M. Cubbon, 'The 1972 Kirk Michael Viking treasure trove', *JMM*, VIII (1980), 10.

48. J. Graham-Campbell, 'Viking silver hoards: an introduction', in Farrell, *Vikings*, 36; Sawyer, *Kings*, 35.

49. See ch. 6, p. 171 below.

50. Grieg, 'Viking antiquities', 119–33; Graham-Campbell, 'Hoards from Scotland' (1975–6), 119–21.

51. Anderson, *Pagan Times*, 92–102; J. Graham-Campbell, 'Some Viking-Age pennanular brooches from Scotland and the origins of the 'Thistle Brooch', in *From the Stone-Age to the 'Forty-Five*, ed. A. O'Connor and D. V. Clarke (1983), 310.

52. Graham-Campbell, 'Hoards from Scotland' (1975–6), 127.

53. N. P. Brooks and J. Graham-Campbell, 'Reflections on the Viking-Age silver hoard from Croydon, Surrey', in *Anglo-Saxon Monetary History*, ed. M. A. S. Blackburn (1986), 105.

54. Graham-Campbell, 'Hoards from Scotland' (1975–6), 115; see ch. 2.

55. D. M. Wilson, 'The brooches', in *St Ninian's Isle and its Treasure*, I, ed. A. Small, C. Thomas and D. M. Wilson (1973), 81–2.

56. J. Anderson, *Scotland in Early Christian Times* (1881), 1–6; M. Olsen, 'Runic inscriptions etc.', in *Viking Antiquities*, VI (Oslo, 1954),

169–71; A. Liestøl, 'Runes', in Fenton and Palsson, *Northern and Western Isles*, 231–2.

57. Anderson, *Early Christian Times*, 45–7; Olsen, 'Runic inscriptions', 178–9; Liestøl, 'Runes', 232.
58. Graham-Campbell, 'Hoards from Scotland' (1975–6), 118.
59. *Ibid.*, 117, fig. 2.
60. Wilson, *Viking Age*, 39; Graham-Campbell, 'Silver hoards of the Isle of Man' (1983), 55.
61. Cubbon and Dolley, 'Viking treasure trove', 12, fig. i.
62. Graham-Campbell, 'Silver hoards of the Isle of Man' (1983), 61.
63. *Njal's Saga*, trans. M. Magnusson and H. Palsson (1960), 352.
64. R. B. K. Stevenson, 'A hoard of Anglo-Saxon coins found at Iona Abbey', *PSAS*, lxxxv (1950–1), 172; *Argyll Inventory* IV (Iona) (1982), 20–1.
65. *OS* Taylor, 152; see ch. 7, p. 202 below.
66. J. S. Clouston, *A History of Orkney* (1932), 36.
67. Graham-Campbell, 'Silver hoards of the Isle of Man' (1983), 55, fig. 3.
68. See ch. 3, p. 74 above.
69. Wilson, *Viking Age*, 39.
70. Graham-Campbell, 'Hoards from Scotland' (1975–6), 125; R. Warner, 'Scottish silver arm-rings: an analysis of weights', *PSAS*, cvii (1975–6), 141.
71. Graham-Campbell, 'Hoards from Scotland' (1975–6), 126.
72. Graham-Campbell, 'Silver hoards of the Isle of Man' (1983), 63.
73. See ch. 3, p. 88 above.
74. Graham-Campbell, 'Hoards from Scotland' (1975–6), 127.
75. *Idem*, 'Viking silver hoards' (1982), 63.
76. Graham-Campbell, 'Hoards of Ireland' (1976), 51–3; Brooks and Graham-Campbell, 'Viking-Age silver hoard from Croydon', 98.
77. Graham-Campbell, 'Hoards from Scotland' (1975–6), 127.
78. Wilson, 'Scandinavian settlement', 110.
79. P. S. Andersen, *Vikings of the West* (1971), 56.
80. B. O'Riordain, 'The High Street excavations', *Seventh Viking Congress*, 135–40; Smyth, *York and Dublin*, II, 201–9.
81. *OS* Taylor, 183.

82. Brøgger, *Emigrants*, 121; A. R. Lewis, *The Northern Seas* (1958), 339, although see Small's comments in 'Viking highlands', 86.
83. Shetelig, 'Viking graves', 70.
84. Wilson, 'Scandinavian settlement', 110–11; Kaland, 'Economic aspects', 91–2.
85. *Islendinga Saga*, trans. J. Simon; 'Snorri Sturlason: his life and times', *Parergon*, xv (1976), 3.
86. *KL* sub *Kornhandel*.
87. C. D. Morris, 'The Vikings in the British Isles', in Farrell, *Vikings*, 89.
88. Quoted by B. R. S. and E. M. Megaw, 'Norse heritage', 161.
89. T. D. Kendrick, *A History of the Vikings* (1930, 1968), 15.
90. R. J. C. Hamilton, *Excavations at Jarlshof* (1956); idem, *Jarlshof Shetland* (HMSO Guidebook, 1953); idem, 'Jarlshof', in *Recent Archaeological Excavations in Britain*, ed. R. Bruce Mitford (1956), 197–222; A. Curle, 'A dwelling of the Viking period at "Jarlshof", Sumburgh, Shetland', in *Viking Antiquities*, vi (Oslo, 1954), 11–30.
91. A. Small, 'Excavations at Underhoull, Unst, Shetland', *PSAS*, xcviii (1964–6); idem, 'A Viking longhouse in Unst, Shetland', *Fifth Viking Congress*, 62–71.
92. G. F. Bigelow, 'Sandwick, Unst and the Norse Shetland economy', in *Shetland Archaeology*, ed. B. Smith (1985), 95–127.
93. B. E. Crawford, 'Progress report on excavations at "Da Biggins", Papa Stour, Shetland, 1977', *Northern Studies*, xi (1978), 25–9, and xiii (1979), 37–41; idem, 'The Biggins, Papa Stour – a multi-disciplinary investigation', in *Shetland Archaeology*, ed. B. Smith, 128–58.
94. R. Radford, *The Early Christian and Norse Settlements at Birsay, Orkney* (HMSO Guidebook, 1959); S. Cruden, 'Excavations at Birsay, Orkney', *Fourth Viking Congress*, 22–30.
95. Annual Archaeological Reports issued by the Dept of Archaeology, University of Durham, 1978–82; Interim Reports published by C. D. Morris and J. Hunter, *Northern Studies*, vii/viii (1976); J. R. Hunter, ix (1977); C. D. Morris, x (1977), xi (1978), xiii (1979), and xvi (1980); J. R. Hunter and C. D.

Morris, 'Recent excavations at the Brough of Birsay, Orkney', *Eighth Viking Congress*, 245–58; C. D. Morris, 'Excavations around the Bay of Birsay', and J. R. Hunter, 'Recent excavations on the Brough of Birsay', in *Birsay* (1983), 119–70; J. W. Hedges, 'Trial excavations on Pictish and Viking settlements at Saevar Howe, Birsay, Orkney', *Glasgow Archaeological J.*, x (1983), 73–124; Morris, 'Viking Orkney', 216–21.

96. A. Ritchie, 'Pict and Norseman in northern Scotland', *SAF*, vi (1974), 23–36; *idem*, 'Buckquoy', 174–227; *idem*, 'Orkney in the Pictish kingdom', in *The Prehistory of Orkney*, ed. C. Renfrew (1985), 193, 196.

97. P. Gelling, 'The Norse buildings at Skaill, Deerness, Orkney and their immediate predecessor', in Fenton and Palsson, *Northern and Western Isles*, 12–39; *idem*, 'Excavations at Skaill, Deerness', in *The Prehistory of Orkney*, ed. C. Renfrew (1985), 176–82; O. Owen, 'Interim report on the rescue project at Tuquoy, Westray, Orkney', Dept of Archaeology, University of Durham (1982); J. R. Hunter, *Archaeology Extra* no. 2 (Newssheet from Dept of Archaeology, University of Bradford).

98. A. Curle, 'A Viking settlement at Freswick', *PSAS*, lxxiii (1939), 71–109; V. G. Childe, 'Another late Viking house at Freswick, Caithness', *PSAS*, lxvii (1942–3), 5–17; A. Curle, 'A Viking settlement at Freswick, Caithness', in *Viking Antiquities*, vi (Oslo, 1954), 31–63; C. E. Batey *et al.*, 'Freswick, Caithness' Summary Report (Dept of Archaeology, University of Durham, 1981, 1983); C. D. Morris, 'The Vikings in the British Isles', in Farrell, *Vikings*, 75–7.

99. I. A. Crawford, 'Scot, Norseman and Gael', *SAF*, vi (1974), 1–17; *idem*, 'War or peace', 259–69.

100. A. MacLaren, 'A Norse house on Drimore Machair, S. Uist', *Glasgow Archaeological J.*, iii (1974), 9–18; D. N. Marshall, 'Report on excavations at Little Dunagoil', *Trans. Buteshire Natural History Soc.*, xvi (1964), 30–69; L. and E. Alcock, 'Scandinavian settlement in the Inner Hebrides: recent research on place-names and in the field', *SAF*, x (1980), 61–72.

101. Most conveniently summarized by Wilson, *Viking Age*, 13–14; Morris, 'Vikings in the British Isles', 83, and A. M. Cubbon, 'Viking archaeology in Man' in *Ninth Viking Congress*, 18–19.

102. Wilson, *Viking Age*, 14–15.

103. G. Bersu, 'A promontory fort on the shore of Ramsay Bay, Isle of Man', *Antiquaries J.*, xxix (1949), 62–79; *idem*, 'The Vikings in the Isle of Man', *JMM*, vii (1968), 84–5; Morris, 'Vikings in the British Isles', 84.

104. Wilson, 'Scandinavian settlement', 102.

105. L. Alcock, 'Early historic fortifications of Scotland', *Current Archaeology* (Oct. 1981), vii no. 8.

106. *Idem*, 'A multi-disciplinary chronology for Alt Clut, Castle Rock, Dumbarton', *PSAS*, cvii (1975–6), 111; see ch. 2, p. 50 above.

107. I. A. Crawford, 'War or peace', 267.

108. A. and G. Ritchie, *The Ancient Monuments of Orkney* (1978), 64–5; E. Talbot, 'Scandinavian fortifications in the British Isles', *SAF*, vi (1974), 39–40.

109. *OS* Taylor, 139, and see ch. 2, p. 57 above.

110. See references in n.35 above and particularly I. A. Crawford, 'War or peace', 259–63.

111. Jones, *History*, 247–8, for convenient summary of relevant references.

112. See ch. 4, p. 94 above.

113. O'Corrain, *Ireland*, 82–96 and references cited in Bibliography.

114. Hamilton, *Jarlshof*, 129; A. Small, 'The Norse building tradition in Shetland', in *Vestnordisk Byggeskikk gjennom To Tusen Ar*, ed. B. Myhre, B. Stoklund and P. Gjerder (Stavanger, 1982), 241.

115. Small, 'Underhoull', 235; *idem*, 'Norse building tradition', 241.

116. Morris, 'Viking Orkney', 217–21; J. R. Hunter, 'Recent excavations' (1983), 160; *idem*, *Rescue Excavations on the Brough of Birsay* (1986), 102–3, 110–13.

117. Gelling, 'Norse buildings at Skaill', 38; *idem*, 'Excavations at Skaill', 179.

118. A. Ritchie, 'Pict and Norseman', 29; *idem*, 'Orkney in the Pictish kingdom', 194.
119. I. A. Crawford, 'War or peace', 267.
120. A. Ritchie, 'Buckquoy', 189; *idem*, 'Birsay around AD 800', *Birsay* (1983), 58.
121. See ch. 4, p. 114 above.
122. A. Ritchie, 'Pict and Norseman', fig. 1.
123. P. S. Gelling, 'The Braaid Site, a re-excavation of one of the structures', *JMM*, VI (1964), 204; Wilson, *Viking Age*, 12; Cubbon, 'Vikings in the Isle of Man', 18.
124. A. Ritchie, 'Pict and Norseman', 32; Alcock, 'Pictish settlement archaeology', 74; Small, 'Norse building tradition', 241; Gelling, 'Norse buildings at Skaill', 38; N. Fojut, 'Some thoughts on the Shetland Iron Age', in *Shetland Archaeology*, ed. B. Smith (1985), 60–2.
125. A. Ritchie, 'Buckquoy', 182; *idem*, 'Orkney in the Pictish Kingdom', 196–7.
126. A. Ritchie, 'Buckquoy', 183.
127. Alcock, 'Pictish settlement archaeology', 74; A. Ritchie, 'Orkney in the Pictish kingdom', 196.
128. Wilson, 'Scandinavian settlement', 122; I. A. Crawford, 'War or peace', 265.
129. B. Myhre, 'Synspunkter på huskonstruksjon i sørvestnorske gårdshus fra jernalder og middelalder' ('Views on the building techniques of farm houses from the Iron Age and early Middle Ages in South-West Norway'), in *Vestnordiske Byggeskikk gjennom To Tusen Ar*, ed. B. Myhre, B. Stoklund and P. Gjaerder (Stavanger, 1982), 108.
130. A. Thorsteinsson, 'The testimony of ancient architecture', *Faeroe Isles Review*, I (1976), 13; *idem*, 'Faerøske huskonstruktioner fra vikingetid til 1800–arene' ('Faeroese house constructions from the Viking period until the 19th century'), in *Vestnordisk Byggeskikk gjennom To Tusen Ar*, ed. B. Myhre, B. Stoklund and P. Gjaerder (1982), 149–53.
131. B. E. Crawford, 'The Biggins, Papa Stour', 142–3. C14 estimations made since that report was written.
132. A. Ritchie, 'Buckquoy', 183.
133. Thorsteinsson, 'Faerøske huskonstruktioner', 149.
134. A. Ritchie, 'Pict and Norseman', 33; Small, 'Norse building tradition', 248; Morris, 'Vikings in the British Isles', 83.
135. Cubbon, 'Vikings in the Isle of Man', 18.
136. A. Roussell, 'Det nordiske hus i vikingetid', in *Forntida Gardar i Island*, ed. M. Stenberger (Copenhagen, 1943), 201–14.
137. L. Laing, 'The Norse house' in *Settlement-Types in Post-Roman Scotland*, BAR 13 (1975), 21; A. Fenton, 'The longhouse in northern Scotland', in *Vestnordisk Byggeskikk gjennom To Tusan Ar*, ed. B. Myhre, B. Stoklund and P. Gjaerder (1982), 231.
138. *Ibid.*, 231; Small, 'Norse building tradition', 248, suggests a mid-ninth century date; A. Ritchie, 'Buckquoy', 189, a late-eleventh or early twelfth-century date; see G. Bigelow, 'Sandwick, Unst' (1985), 112, for most recent discussion.
139. Hamilton, *Jarlshof*, 109.
140. B. Stoklund, 'Building traditions in the northern world', in Fenton and Palsson, *Northern and Western Isles*, 98.
141. *Ibid.*, 101; B. E. Crawford, 'The Biggins, Papa Stour', 131.
142. A. Ritchie, 'Buckquoy', 192; *idem*, 'Orkney in the Pictish kingdom', 200; and comments by Morris, 'Viking Orkney', 216.
143. C. Curle, 'The finds from the Brough of Birsay', *Birsay*, 78; *idem*, *Pictish and Norse Finds from the Brough of Birsay, 1934–74* (1982), 101; see Hunter, *Rescue Excavations*, 113.
144. Hedges, 'Saevar Howe', 120.
145. I. A. Crawford, 'War or peace', 267; a contrast is also seen at Skaill: Gelling, 'Norse buildings at Skaill', 38.
146. A. Ritchie, 'Buckquoy', Appendix 8; T. Fanning, 'Some aspects of the bronze ringed pin in Scotland', in *From the Stone Age to the 'Forty-Five*, ed. A. O'Connor and D. V. Clarke (1983), 330.
147. Graham-Campbell, 'Viking-Age pennanular brooches' (1983), 319.
148. C. Curle, *Pictish and Norse Finds*, 101.
149. See ch. 4, p. 101 above.
150. Gelling, 'Norse buildings at Skaill', 38.

151. J. Hunter, *Archaeology Extra no. 2* (1985).
152. Gelling, 'Norse buildings at Skaill', 38.
153. See ch. 1, p. 27 above.
154. A. Small, 'The distribution of settlement in Shetland and Faroe in Viking times', *Saga-Book*, XVII (1967–8), 149; D. Olson, 'Norse settlement in the Hebrides: an interdisciplinary study' (thesis, University of Oslo, 1983), 34.
155. Morris, 'Vikings in the British Isles' (1982), 78; *idem*, 'Viking Orkney', 215.
156. *Ibid.*, 232.
157. A. Fenton, *The Northern Isles* (1978), 13; Small, 'Norse building tradition', 246; A. Ritchie, 'Orkney in the Pictish kingdom', 200–1.
158. Fenton, *Northern Isles*, 49–50; W. P. Thomson, *The Little General and the Rousay Crofters* (1981), fig. 6.
159. Fenton, *Northern Isles*, 33; B. Smith, 'What is a scattald? Rural communities in Shetland, 1400–1900', in *Essays in Shetland History*, ed. B. E. Crawford (1984), 104–6.
160. L. J. MacGregor, 'Sources for a study of Norse settlement in Shetland and Faroe', in *Essays in Shetland History*, ed. B. E. Crawford (1984), 5.
161. See ch. 4 above.
162. Smith, 'What is a scattald?', 102–3.
163. Fenton, *Northern Isles*, 23; Small, 'Norse building tradition', 248.
164. Small, 'Norse building tradition', 245; Morris, 'Vikings in the British Isles', 78; *idem*, 'Viking Orkney', 215.
165. Small, 'Underhoull', 247.
166. B. E. Crawford, 'The Biggins, Papa Stour', 136; MacGregor, 'Norse settlement', 3.
167. J. S. Clouston, 'The Orkney townships', *SHR*, XVII (1919–20), 16–45; 'The Orkney lands', *POAS*, II (1923–4), 61–8; 'The Orkney "bus"', *POAS*, V (1926–7), 41–50; A. C. O'Dell, *The Historical Geography of the Shetland Islands* (1939); W. P. Thomson, 'Funzie, Fetlar: a Shetland runrig township in the nineteenth century', *Scottish Geographical Mag.*, LXXXVI (1970), 170–85.
168. I. A. Crawford, 'The present state of settlement history in the West Highlands and Islands', in *From the Stone Age to the 'Forty-Five*, ed. A. O'Connor and D. V. Clarke (1983), 350–67 and references there cited.
169. Small, 'Viking highlands', 78; *idem*, 'The historical geography of the Norse Viking colonization of the Scottish Highlands', *Norsk Geografisk Tidsskrift*, XXII (1968), 9.
170. See ch. 1, p. 84 above.
171. A. Ritchie, 'Buckquoy', 191; *idem*, 'Orkney in the Pictish Kingdom', 198, but see discussion of these percentages in Morris, 'Viking Orkney', 227–8.
172. Small, 'Viking highlands', 78; Morris, 'Viking Orkney', 228.
173. *OS* P. and E., 186.
174. Small, 'Historical geography', 11.
175. A. Ritchie, 'Buckquoy', 205.
176. Fenton, *Northern Isles*, 510–23; A. M. Donaldson, C. D. Morris and D. J. Rackham, 'The Birsay Bay project', in *Environmental Aspects of Coasts and Islands*, ed. B. Brothwell and G. Dimbleby, *BAR* International ser. 94 (1981), 76; Kaland, 'Economic aspects', 89–91.
177. C. Dickson, in Hedges, 'Saevar Howe', 114; J. R. Hunter, *Archaeology Extra no. 2*.
178. Anderson, *Pagan Times*, 36–7; Grieg, 'Viking antiquities', figs. 20, 81.
179. Hamilton, *Jarlshof*, 206–10; R. Ritchie, 'Soapstone quarrying in Viking Lands', in Fenton and Palsson, *Northern and Western Isles*, fig. 24; S. Buttler, *Preliminary Report on Excavations at Cross Geos, Clibberswick, Unst, Shetland* (typescript); A. Ritchie, *Exploring Scotland's Heritage: Orkney and Shetland* (1985), no. 56.
180. Gelling, 'Norse buildings at Skaill', 19.
181. R. Hall (ed.), 'Viking-Age York and the North', *CBA Research Report*, no. 27 (1978), 39.
182. C. Curle, 'Finds from the Brough', 71; A. Ritchie, 'Orkney in the Pictish kingdom', 193.
183. Morris, 'Viking Orkney', 223 and references there cited.
184. *OS* Taylor, 141.
185. B. E. Crawford, 'Report on the

renewed excavations at The Biggins, Papa Stour, Shetland, 1982' (xerox, 1983).
186. C. Curle, 'Finds from the Brough', 77 and pl. 1a.
187. Hamilton, *Jarlshof*, 109.
188. Morris, 'Viking Orkney', 219–21.
189. Gelling, 'Norse buildings at Skaill', fig. 1, p. 13.
190. Morris, 'Viking Orkney', 231.
191. B. E. Crawford, 'Birsay and the early earls and bishops of Orkney', *Birsay* (1983), 100; see ch. 3, p. 79 above.
192. Radford, *Early Christian and Norse Settlements at Birsay*, 6, 7, 20.
193. See ch. 6, pp. 184–9 below.
194. A. and G. Ritchie, *The Ancient Monuments of Orkney* (HMSO Guide, 1978), 62–3.
195. A. Ritchie, *Orkney and Shetland*, 115.
196. Hunter, *Rescue Excavations*, 110–13.
197. Cruden, 'Excavations at Birsay', 28–9.
198. C. Curle, *Pictish and Norse Finds*, 54.
199. Radford, *Early Christian and Norse Settlements at Birsay*, 20.
200. KL sub *Bastu*; Icelandic *Dic* sub *bað-stofa*; I. Talve, *Bastu och Torkhus i Nord Europa* (Stockholm, 1960), 366–7.
201. A. Curle, 'A Viking settlement', 77–8; Hamilton, *Jarlshof*, 110; Gelling, 'Norse buildings at Skaill', 32–5.

6 **The Archaeological Framework: Part 2 Conversion and the Organization of Christianity**

1. C. Thomas, 'The early Christian Church', in *Who are the Scots*, ed. G. Menzies (1971), 95.
2. C. Thomas, 'Sculptured stones and crosses', in *St Ninian's Isle and its Treasure*, I, ed. A. Small, C. Thomas and D. M. Wilson (1973), 21.
3. H. Shetelig, 'The Viking graves', in *Viking Antiquities*, VI (1954), 88; P. Foote and D. M. Wilson, *The Viking Achievement* (1970), 407; K. Eldjarn, 'Graves and grave-goods: survey and evaluation', in Fenton and Palsson, *Northern and Western Isles*, 8.
4. Foote and Wilson, *Viking Achievement*, 407; M. Magnusson, *Hammer of the North* (1976), 96.
5. Sawyer, *Kings*, 133.
6. H. Shetelig, 'Ship-burials', *Saga-Book*, IV (1904–5), 331–59; A. W. Brøgger and H. Shetelig, *The Viking Ships* (1951), 104–66.
7. RCAHMS: *Argyll, An Inventory of the Monuments*, V (Islay, etc.) (1984), 29–30; Eldjarn, 'Graves', 8.
8. Shetelig, 'Viking graves', 95; L. Laing, *The Archaeology of late Celtic Britain and Ireland* (1975), 184, 201; Morris, 'Viking Orkney', 240; but note caution expressed by L. Alcock, 'The supposed Viking burials on the Islands of Canna and Sanday', in *From the Stone Age to the 'Forty-Five*, ed. A. O'Connor and D. V. Clarke (1983), 294.
9. G. Bersu and D. M. Wilson, *Three Viking Graves in the Isle of Man* (1966), 10, 51.
10. *Ibid.*, 7, 51.
11. *Argyll Inventory*, V, 29; Morris, 'Viking Orkney', 240.
12. Shetelig, 'Viking graves', 91.
13. See ch. 7, p. 199 below.
14. B. R. S. and E. M. Megaw, 'Norse heritage, 146; B. Megaw, 'Norseman and native in the Kingdom of the Isles', *Scottish Studies*, xx (1976), 21, 26.
15. A. Thorsteinsson, 'The Viking burial place at Pierowall, Westray, Orkney', in *Fifth Viking Congress*, 150; C. E. Batey, 'Viking and late Norse Caithness: the archaeological evidence', in *Tenth Viking Congress* (in press).
16. Shetelig, 'Viking graves', 97.
17. *Book of Settlements*, ed. H. Palsson and P. Edwards (1972), 55.
18. Bersu and Wilson, *Three Viking Graves*, 87.
19. A. Brøgger, *Ancient Emigrants* (1929), 130; D. M. Wilson, 'The Norsemen', in *Who are the Scots*, ed. G. Menzies (1971), 107; Eldjarn, 'Graves', 8; Morris, 'Viking Orkney', 239.
20. H. Shetelig, 'Ship-burial at Kiloran Bay, Colonsay, Scotland', *Saga-Book*, v (1906–7), 172–4; J. Anderson, 'Notice of bronze brooches and personal ornaments from a ship-burial of the Viking time in Colonsay', *PSAS*, XLI (1906), 443; S. Grieg, 'Viking antiquities in Scotland', *Viking Antiquities*, II (1940), 59; *Argyll Inventory*, V, no. 298.

21. Grieg, 'Viking antiquities', 58–9; J. Graham-Campbell, *Viking Artefacts* (1980), no. 307; *Argyll Inventory*, V (1984), 31.
22. See ch. 2, p. 48 above.
23. See Introduction and ch. 5, p. 121 above.
24. Shetelig, 'Viking graves', 95; D. M. Wilson, 'Scandinavian settlement in the north and west of the British Isles', *TRHS*, xxvi (1976), 99.
25. B. R. S. and E. Megaw, 'Norse heritage', 146–7; Bersu and Wilson, *Three Viking Graves*, xiii–xiv.
26. *Ibid.*, 13, and comments on p. xiv.
27. B. R. S. and E. M. Megaw, 'Norse heritage', 146 n.2.
28. D. J. Freke, *Peel Castle Excavations. Interim Report* (1984), 15–16.
29. Grieg, 'Viking antiquities', 13; J. G. Scott, 'A note on Viking settlement in Galloway', *Trans. Dumfriesshire and Galloway Natural History and Archaeology Soc.*, lviii (1983), 52–3.
30. Shetelig, 'Viking graves', 69.
31. Wainwright, *Northern Isles*, 160.
32. G. J. Marcus, *The Conquest of the North Atlantic* (1980), 22; Smyth, *Warlords*, 168.
33. *Book of Settlements*, 15.
34. A. MacDonald, 'On "papar" names in N. and W. Scotland', *Northern Studies*, ix (1977), 25–7, also printed in BAR 37 (1977); Smyth, *Warlords*, 169; see ch. 4, p. 112 above.
35. MacDonald, '"Papar" names', 29.
36. R. W. Munro, 'Profusion of Pabbays', *Notes and Queries of the Society of West Highland and Island Historical Research*, xvi (1981), 18; A. Morrison, 'Early Harris estate papers', *TGSI*, li (1978–80), 90.
37. B. E. Crawford, 'The Biggins, Papa Stour: a multi-disciplinary investigation', in *Shetland Archaeology*, ed. B. Smith (1985), 135.
38. R. Radford, 'Birsay and the spread of Christianity to the north', *Birsay* (1983), 20.
39. *Historia Norvegiae*, trans. in *ES*, I, 331.
40. H. Marwick, 'Antiquarian notes on Papa Westray', *POAS*, iii (1924–5), 36. But see comments made in ch. 4, p. 111 above.
41. C. Thomas, 'Sculptured stones', 13.
42. Radford, 'Spread of Christianity', 20; Morris, 'Viking Orkney', 217.
43. C. D. Morris, 'The Brough of Deerness, Orkney: a new survey', *Archaeologia Atlantica*, ii (1977), 70; idem, 'Viking Orkney', 235–6; C. Thomas, *The Early Christian Archaeology of North Britain* (1971), 34–5.
44. C. Thomas, 'Sculptured stones', 13.
45. *Book of Settlements*, 123; J. Johannesson, *Islendinga Saga* (Manitoba, 1974), 123.
46. C. Thomas, 'Sculptured stones', 14; Wainwright, *Northern Isles*, 113.
47. H. Marwick, *Orkney* (1951), 106–7; R. Radford, 'Art and architecture: Celtic and Norse', in Wainwright, *Northern Isles*, 172, 164.
48. R. G. Cant, 'Norse influence in the organisation of the mediaeval church in the Western Isles', *Northern Studies*, xxi (1984), 3–4.
49. C. J. S. Marstrander, 'Treen og Keeil', *Norsk Tidsskrift for Sprogvidenskap*, vii (1937), 420; see ch. 3, p. 88 above.
50. See assessment of the problem by C. R. Lowe, 'The problems of keeills and treens', Appendix I to C. D. Morris, 'The survey and excavations at Keeill Vael, Druidale, in their context', in *Ninth Viking Congress*, 124.
51. B. R. S. and E. M. Megaw, 'Norse heritage', 15.
52. R. G. Cant, 'Settlement, society and church organisation in the Northern Isles', in Fenton and Palsson, *Northern and Western Isles*, 175.
53. Smyth, *Warlords*, 210.
54. *Ibid.*, 211.
55. *Historia Norvegiae*, trans. in *ES*, I, 331; see ch. 7, p. 211 below.
56. See ch. 3, p. 70 above.
57. Wainwright, *Northern Isles*, 160; Wilson, 'Norsemen', 107.
58. Morris, 'Viking Orkney', 240.
59. J. W. Hedges, 'Trial excavations on Pictish and Viking settlements at Saevar Howe, Birsay, Orkney', *Glasgow Archaeological J.*, x (1983), 116–17; Morris, 'Viking Orkney', 239.
60. Wainwright, *Northern Isles*, 161.
61. R. B. K. Stevenson, 'Pictish art', in *The Problem of the Picts* (1955),

128; Wainwright, *Northern Isles*, 159.
62. J. Romilly Allen, *The Early Christian Monuments of Scotland* (1903), 9–10; Wainwright, *Northern Isles*, 114; J. Close-Brooks and R. B. K. Stevenson, *Dark Age Sculpture* (1982), 35.
63. Wainwright, *Northern Isles*, 159.
64. See comments in Morris, 'Viking Orkney', 238.
65. R. B. K. Stevenson, 'Christian sculpture in Norse Shetland', in *Heiđurscrit til Sverra Dahl, Frođskaparrit*, 28/29 (1981), 285–7.
66. *Ibid.*, 289.
67. C. Thomas, 'Sculptured stones', 13.
68. D. MacRoberts, 'The ecclesiastical character of the St Ninian's Isle treasure', *Fourth Viking Congress*, 224–46.
69. Stevenson, 'Christian sculpture', 288.
70. R. Bailey, *Viking-Age Sculpture* (1980), 227.
71. *Ibid.*, 122, 229; Smyth, *York and Dublin*, II, 272.
72. Bailey, *Sculpture*, 92–6; Smyth, *York and Dublin*, II, 273.
73. Bailey, *Sculpture*, 96; J. T. Lang, 'The Hogback: a Viking colonial monument', *Anglo-Saxon Studies in Archaeology and History*, III (1984), 89.
74. Smyth, *York and Dublin*, II, 275.
75. *Ibid.*, 273.
76. J. T. Lang, 'Hogback monuments in Scotland', *PSAS*, cv (1972–4), 206–35.
77. Smyth, *York and Dublin*, II, 78.
78. See ch. 4, p. 100 above.
79. Smyth, *York and Dublin*, II, 283.
80. C. Fell, 'The Sigurd legend', in *The Viking World*, ed. J. Graham-Campbell (1980), 184.
81. Smyth, *York and Dublin*, II, 271.
82. Bailey, *Sculpture*, 124–31.
83. D. M. Wilson, 'Manx memorial stones of the Viking period', *Saga-Book*, xviii (1970–1); idem, *The Viking Age in the Isle of Man* (1974), 31–3; idem, 'The art of the Manx crosses', in *Ninth Viking Congress*, 178.
84. Smyth, *York and Dublin*, II, 272.
85. R. I. Page, 'The Manx rune-stones', in *Ninth Viking Congress*, 133–46.
86. B. R. S. and E. M. Megaw, 'Norse heritage', 151.
87. Laing, *Archaeology*, 215–16.
88. See ch. 5, p. 133 above.
89. Wilson, 'Scandinavian settlement', 102; Smyth, *Warlords*, 210–11.
90. A. Liestøl, 'Runes', in *Northern and Western Isles*, 228.
91. H. Shetelig, 'The Norse style of ornamentation in the Viking settlements', in *Viking Antiquities*, VI, 123–5; Close-Brooks and Stevenson, *Dark-Age Sculpture*, 43; Wilson, 'Manx crosses', 183.
92. Liestøl, 'Runes', 228–9.
93. W. G. Collingwood, 'Viking-Age cross at Iona', *Saga-Book*, III pt iii (1904), 305; *RCAHMS Argyll. An Inventory of the Monuments*, IV (Iona) (1982), 21, 213.
94. *Ibid.*, 191.
95. *Ibid.*, 190.
96. A. Liestøl, 'An Iona rune stone and the world of Man and the Isles', in *Ninth Viking Congress*, 87.
97. Smyth, *Warlords*, 212; *Argyll Inventory*, IV, 21.
98. Marwick, *Farm-Names*, 214.
99. Johannesson, *Islendinga Saga*, 167; Andersen, *Samlingen av Norge*, 319.
100. See ch. 3, p. 81 above.
101. B. E. Crawford, 'Birsay and the early earls and bishops of Orkney', *Birsay* (1983), 105.
102. D. E. R. Watt, 'Diocese of the Isles', in *Series Episcoporum Ecclesiae Catholicae Occidentalis ab Initio ad Annum 1198*, ed. O. Engels and S. Weinferter (in press).
103. I. B. Cowan, 'Early ecclesiastical foundations', in *An Historical Atlas of Scotland*, ed. P. MacNeil and R. Nicholson (1975), 19.
104. See ch. 4, p. 112 above.
105. J. S. Clouston, *The History of Orkney* (1932), 142–3; R. G. Cant, *The Mediaeval Churches and Chapels of Shetland* (1975), 11; idem, 'Norse influence', 7–12.
106. Marwick, *Orkney*, 113; Lowe, 'Keeills and treens', 124; see ch. 3, pp. 86–8 above.
107. Marwick, *Farm-Names*, 214–15.
108. Cant, 'Settlement', 175.
109. R. G. Lamb, *Sanday and North Ronaldsay: an Archaeological Survey of the North Isles of Orkney* (1980), 8.
110. *Ibid.*, 25–8; Cant, 'Settlement', 175; *Argyll Inventory*, V, 27.
111. B. Smith, 'What is a scattald?

Rural communities in Shetland, 1400–1900', in *Essays in Shetland History*, ed. B. E. Crawford (1984), 99; see ch. 5, pp. 149–50 above.

112. J. Stewart, 'Place-names of Fetlar', *Fifth Viking Congress*, 176.

113. Smith, 'What is a scattald?', 105.

114. Cant, 'Settlement', 174–5.

115. *RCAMS 12th Report with an Inventory of the Ancient Monuments of Orkney and Shetland*, II, *Inventory of Orkney* (1946), fig. 64; Radford, 'Art and architecture', 180.

116. Morris, 'Keeill Vael, Druidale', 121–4.

117. C. Thomas, *Christian Archaeology*, 82.

118. Radford, 'Art and architecture', 168, 180; C. Thomas, *Christian Archaeology*, 37; Radford, 'Spread of Christianity', 20.

119. R. G. Lamb, 'Coastal settlements of the North', *SAF*, v (1973), 76–98; *idem*, 'The Burri Stacks of Culswick, Shetland', *PSAS*, cvii (1975–6), 149.

120. See references cited in n.43 above.

121. See ch. 5, p. 138 above.

122. *Inventory of Orkney* (1946), no. 1032; A. and G. Ritchie, *The Ancient Monuments of Orkney* (1978), 73.

123. Radford, 'Art and architecture', 182–3; *idem*, 'Spread of Christianity', 27.

124. Lecture given by Professor E. Fernie to the Society of Antiquaries of Scotland.

125. See chs. 3 and 5 above.

126. R. Radford, *The Early Christian and Norse Settlements at Birsay, Orkney* (HMSO Guidebook, 1959), 11, 20; *idem*, 'Art and architecture', 176–7; *idem*, 'Spread of Christianity', 23, 32; see ch. 5, p. 156 above.

127. C. D. Morris, 'Birsay "small sites" excavation and survey, 1978', *Northern Studies*, xiii (1979), 3–8; *idem*, 'Excavations', 142–7. For evidence regarding the site of the village church, see R. G. Lamb, 'The Cathedral of Christchurch and the monastery of Birsay', *PSAS*, cv (1972–4), 200–5; *idem*, 'The cathedral and the monastery', *Birsay* (1983), 36–45.

128. B. E. Crawford, 'Earls and bishops', 104; see ch. 3, pp. 81–2 above.

129. See ch. 5, p. 156 above.

130. *OS* Guthmundsson, 80; *OS* Taylor, 189; *OS* P. and E., 71.

131. Radford, *Early Christian and Norse Settlements at Birsay*, 7; *idem*, 'Art and architecture', 176; A. and G. Ritchie, *Ancient Monuments of Orkney*, 62–3.

132. *Inventory of Orkney* (1946), 3; R. Fawcett, *Scottish Mediaeval Churches* (1985), no. 29, p. 27; A. Ritchie, *Exploring Scotland's Heritage: Orkney and Shetland* (1985), 113.

133. H. Marwick, 'A rune-inscribed stone from Birsay, Orkney', *PSAS*, lvi (1921–2), 68; *Inventory of Orkney* (1946), no. 120; M. Olsen, 'Runic inscriptions', in *Viking Antiquities*, VI (Oslo, 1954), 63–4; Liestøl, 'Runes', 225–6. I am grateful to Professor R. Page for help over the interpretation of the 'Philippus' inscription.

134. Lamb, 'Cathedral and monastery', 40; B. E. Crawford, 'Earls and bishops', 115.

135. Radford, *Early Christian and Norse Settlements at Birsay*, 15; *idem*, 'Art and architecture', 177.

136. J. Barber, No. 199 in list of excavated sites in *Mediaeval Archaeology*, xxvii (1983), 223. See brief references to the excavation by R. G. Cant, 'Introduction' to *Birsay* (1983), 8–9; and Lamb, *ibid.* 41.

137. R. Djupedal, *Klosteret pa Selja* (1977), 32; B. E. Crawford, 'Earls and bishops', 115.

138. I am grateful to Dr Alan Werritty of the Department of Geography, University of St Andrews, and Professor Ronald Miller of Stromness for information on this point.

139. W. P. Thomson, 'Fifteenth-century depression in Orkney', in *Essays in Shetland History*, ed. B. E. Crawford (1984), 130.

140. B. E. Crawford, 'The cult of St Magnus in Shetland', in *Essays in Shetland History*, ed. B. E. Crawford (1984), 71–2.

141. P. D. Anderson, 'Birsay in the sixteenth century', *Birsay* (1983), 84.

7 The Literary Framework: Norse Society in the Settlements

1. See Introduction above.
2. *ES*, I, 330.
3. Andersen, *Samlingen av Norge*, 276.
4. See ch. 2, p. 53 above.
5. *OS* Taylor, 140.
6. *OS* P. and E., 31.
7. B. R. S. and E. M. Megaw, 'Norse heritage', 169 n.1; G. W. S. Barrow, *Kingship and Unity* (1981), 107.
8. D. O'Corrain, 'High Kings, Vikings and other kings', *Irish Historical Studies*, xxi (1978–9), 301.
9. See ch. 2, p. 57 above.
10. *OS* Taylor, 142; Smyth, *Scandinavian Kings*, 192.
11. B. R. S. and E. M. Megaw, 'Norse heritage', 156; *Chronicle of Man*, 134.
12. Sawyer, *Kings*, 144.
13. *ES*, I, 500.
14. *OS* Taylor, 169.
15. *OS* P. and E., 70; *OS* Guthmundsson, 79; L. M. Larson, *The King's Household in England before the Norman Conquest* (1904), 153–4.
16. J. Brønsted, *The Vikings* (1960), 98; F. Stenton, *Anglo-Saxon England* (3rd edn, 1971), 412.
17. *ES*, I, 543.
18. *Njal's Saga*, trans. M. Magnusson and H. Palsson (1964), 342.
19. P. Foote and D. M. Wilson, *The Viking Achievement* (1970), 102.
20. See ch. 5, p. 125 above.
21. *OS* Taylor, 167; see description of King Hakon at the battle of Fitjar also with a gilded helmet (*Hms* [Laing], 105).
22. N. P. Brooks, 'Arms, status and warfare in late-Saxon England', in *Aethelred the Unready*, ed. D. Hill, *BAR* 59 (1978), 82–7.
23. *REO*, lxxxvi; H. Marwick, *Orkney* (1951), 80.
24. P. S. Andersen, *Vikings of the West* (1971), 39; *Icelandic Dic.*, sub *vapna-tak*.
25. Brooks, 'Arms, status and warfare', 83; cf. Scots Wapinschaw and English Wapentake.
26. B. R. S. and E. M. Megaw, 'Norse heritage', 169.
27. K. Helle, *Norge Blir en Stat 1130–1319* (Oslo, 1974), 201.
28. *OS* P. and E., 48.
29. Smyth, *Scandinavian Kings*, 222; P. Wormald, 'Viking studies: whence and whither', in Farrell, *Vikings*, 139.
30. L. Musset, 'La pénétration Chrétienne dans l'Europe du nord', *Settimane di Studio*, xiv (1967), 266.
31. J. R. C. Hamilton, *Excavations at Jarlshof, Shetland* (1956), 110; O. Olsen, *Hørg, Hov og Kirke* (Copenhagen, 1966), 284–85.
32. Foote and Wilson, *Viking Achievement*, 389–90.
33. *Ibid.*, 390–1.
34. *Ibid.*; Smyth, *York and Dublin*, II, 274–5.
35. *OS* Taylor, 142.
36. Smyth, *Scandinavian Kings*, 277; Wormald, 'Viking studies', 140.
37. R. Frank, 'Viking atrocity and skaldic verse, the rite of the Blood-Eagle', *EHR*, xcix (1984), 332–41.
38. *OS* Taylor, 143.
39. *OS* P. and E., 38.
40. *Ibid.*, 39; and see ch. 2, p. 68 above.
41. *Alfred the Great*, ed. S. Keynes and M. Lapidge (1984), 248 n.99.
42. Smyth, *Scandinavian Kings*, 269.
43. A. Holtsmark, 'Vefr Darrradar', *Maal og Minne* (1939), 94.
44. Smyth, *Warlords*, 210.
45. W. Irvine, *The Isle of Shapinsay* (1977), 29.
46. E. Marwick, 'The Stone of Odin', *PSAS*, cvii (1975–6), 33.
47. M. Olsen, *Farms and Fanes of Ancient Norway* (1928), 263–98.
48. O. Olsen, *Hørg*, 280; J. Jakobsen, *The Place-Names of Shetland* (1936), 59.
49. See postscript to W. F. Nicolaisen, 'Scandinavians and Celts in Caithness: the place-name evidence', in *Caithness: a Cultural Cross-Roads*, ed. J. Baldwin (1982), 84–5, for all references to this controversy.
50. B. Guthmundsson, *The Origin of the Icelanders* (1967), 41, 46–8.
51. Nicolaisen, *Scottish Place-Names*, 101–2.
52. Sawyer, *Kings*, 43.
53. *OS* Taylor, 353; J. S. Clouston, *A History of Orkney* (1932), 191.
54. *Ibid.*, 59–60.
55. Foote and Wilson, *Viking Achievement*, 131; J. S. Clouston, 'Two features of the Orkney Earldom', *SHR*, xvi (1918–19), 39; *REO*, xl; Clouston, *History*, 158.

56. *Hms* (Laing), 54.

57. *Chronicle of Man*, 53.

58. *Ibid.*, 147.

59. *KL* sub *odalsrett*; *Icelandic Dic.*, sub *odal*.

60. A. Brøgger, *Ancient Emigrants* (1929), 135–42; Foote and Wilson, *Viking Achievement*, 82.

61. Andersen, *Samlingen av Norge*, 87, 89.

62. Jones, *History*, 91; Sawyer, *Kings*, 41.

63. *OS* Taylor, 144; *Hms* (Laing), II, 74.

64. *Hms* (Laing), I, 218–19.

65. *OS* Taylor, 157.

66. Clouston, *History*, 11.

67. *OS* Taylor, 149.

68. *Ibid.*

69. See ch. 3, p. 88 above.

70. *OS* Anderson, 112; similarly trans. by P. and E., 128, but see *OS* Taylor, 260, where the law is interpreted as a retrospective one, as also by Clouston, *History*, 33, 178.

71. *OS* Anderson, 112.

72. *Ibid.*, trans. 'the chance to buy their estates', P. and E., 128.

73. Clouston, *History*, ch. viii, n.3.

74. *KL* sub *odalsrett*: J. Johannesson, *Islendinga Saga* (Manitoba, 1974), 345.

75. Although see B. R. W. and E. M. Megaw, 'Norse heritage', 170 n.1.

76. *REO*, *passim*.

77. *OS* Taylor, 151.

78. *Ibid.*, 156.

79. *Ibid.*, 152.

80. Sawyer, *Kings*, 42–6.

81. *OS* P. and E., 48.

82. *Ibid.*, 33; see fig. 19.

83. *The Book of Settlements*, trans. H. Palsson and P. Edwards (1972), 52.

84. Sawyer, *Kings*, 46; *idem*, 'The Vikings in Ireland', in *Ireland in Early Mediaeval Europe*, ed. D. Whitelock, R. McKitterick and D. Dumville (1982), 358; O'Corrain, *Ireland*, 42–3.

85. *OS* Taylor, 152.

86. See above, p. 194.

87. Marwick, *Orkney*, 79–80.

88. Andersen, *Samlingen av Norge*, 249–261; Johannesson, *Islendinga Saga*, 35, 49, 66, 74.

89. C. Marstrander, 'Om Tingsteder pa Man', *Norsk Tidskrift for Sprog Videnskap*, x (1938), 384–93.

90. *REO*, lxxviii; B. R. S. and E. M. Megaw, 'Norse heritage', 167–8.

91. R. W. and J. M. Munro, 'The Lordship of the Isles', in *An Historical Atlas of Scotland* (1975), 67.

92. *REO*, lxxviii–lxxxviii.

93. Marwick, *Farm-Names*, 214.

94. Marwick, *Orkney*, 79.

95. P. Thorson, 'Ancient Thurso, a religious and judicial centre', *Fifth Viking Congress*, 75.

96. *REO*, xxix, p. 69; B. E. Crawford, 'The Shetland Lawthing seal', *New Shetlander*, cxxvii (1979), 24.

97. *Chronicle of Man*, 93.

98. B. R. S. and E. M. Megaw, 'Norse Heritage', 169, n.1.

99. *RCAHMS*, *Argyll Inventory*, V, no. 404.

100. R. W. Munro (ed.), *Monro's Western Isles of Scotland and Genealogies of the Clans* (1961), 99.

101. B. Gordon, 'Some Norse placenames in Trotternish', *Scottish Gaelic Studies*, x (1963–5), 90; G. W. S. Barrow, 'Popular courts in early mediaeval Scotland: some place-name evidence', *Scot. Stud.*, xxv (1981), 21.

102. A. Morrison, 'Early Harris estate papers', in *TGSI*, li (1978–80), 102; B. E. Crawford, 'Papa Stour: survival, continuity and change in one Shetland Island', in Fenton and Palsson, *Northern and Western Isles*, 48.

103. Nicolaisen, *Scottish Place-Names*, 119–20.

104. Andersen, *Samlingen av Norge*, 66.

105. See Epilogue below; Duncan, *Scotland*, 349–50.

106. Foote and Wilson, *Viking Achievement*, 66–7; Andersen, *Samlingen av Norge*, 197–9; Sawyer, *Kings*, 39.

107. Smyth, *Warlords*, 163–72; see ch. 2 above.

108. *Book of Settlements*, 51.

109. *Laxdaela Saga*, trans. M. Magnusson and H. Palsson (1969), 54.

110. Johannesson, *Islendinga Saga*, 17.

111. See ch. 5, p. 140ff.

112. See ch. 2, p. 48.

113. Sawyer, *Kings*, 40.

114. *OS* Taylor, 183; *OS* Guthmundsson, 72.

115. See ch. 5, p. 139ff.

116. *ES*, I, 331.

117. Brøgger, *Emigrants*, 60–1.

118. B. Almqvist, 'Scandinavian and Celtic folklore contacts in the

Earldom of Orkney', *Saga-Book*, xx (1978–9), 87.

119. *History of the Archbishops of Hamburg-Bremen*, trans. F. T. Tschan (New York, 1959), 22.

120. See ch. 4, p. 112, and fuller discussion of the *papar* in ch. 6, p. 165ff.

121. *ES*, I, 331, 340.

122. *Ibid.*; I. B. Cowan, 'Early ecclesiastical foundations', in *An Historical Atlas of Scotland c. 400 – c. 1600* (1975), 17.

123. M. Chesnutt, 'An unsolved problem in Old-Norse Icelandic literary history', *Med. Scand.*, I (1968), 129; Almqvist, 'Scandinavian and Celtic folklore contacts', 81–5.

124. See ch. 3, p. 66 above.

125. *OS* Taylor, 139; see ch. 2, p. 58 above.

126. Almqvist, 'Scandinavian and Celtic folklore contacts', 98.

127. *Book of Settlements*, 51.

128. *Ibid.*, 53.

129. E. J. Cowan, 'Caithness in the sagas', in *Caithness: a Cultural Cross-Roads*, ed. J. Baldwin (1982), 25.

130. *Ibid.*, 30–1.

131. Duncan, *Scotland*, 154.

132. *OS* Guthmundsson, 243; A. W. Johnston, 'Orkney and Shetland folk', *Saga-Book*, IX (1908), 402.

133. B. R. S. Megaw, 'Norsemen and native in the kingdom of the Isles', *Scot. Stud.*, xx (1976), 20.

134. See ch. 4, pp. 102–3 above.

135. *OS* Taylor, 337.

136. *Ibid.*, 333; *OS* Guthmundsson, 276 n.3.

137. Chesnutt, 'An unsolved problem', 128.

138. A. K. Goedheer, *Irish and Norse Traditions about the Battle of Clontarf* (1928); O'Corrain, *Ireland*, 130–1; Jones, *History*, 396–7.

139. *KL* sub *Darraðarlioð*; Holtsmark, 'Vefr Darraðar', 95–6.

140. See above, pp. 106–7.

141. See ch. 2, p. 47.

142. See above, pp. 192, 200.

143. Jones, *History*, 229; D. Logan, *The Vikings in History* (1983), 134.

144. See ch. 6, p. 184ff above.

145. A. Fenton, 'Northern links', *Northern Studies*, xvi (1980), 9–12; *idem*, 'Northern links: continuity and change', in Fenton and Palsson,

Northern and Western Isles, 137–43.

146. See ch. 5, p. 148 above.

147. J. Petersen, 'British antiquities of the Viking period found in Norway', in *Viking Antiquities*, V (Oslo, 1940), 15–79; E. Wamers, 'Some ecclesiastical and secular Insular metalwork found in Norwegian Viking graves', *Peritia*, II (1983), 277–306.

148. Petersen, 'British antiquities', 79; J. Graham-Campbell, *Viking Artefacts* (1980), no. 314; J. Graham-Campbell and D. Kidd, *The Vikings* (1980), 34; D. M. Wilson, 'Scandinavian settlement in the north and west of the British Isles', *TRHS*, xxvi (1976), 100.

149. Almqvist, 'Scandinavian and Celtic folklore contacts', 85.

150. For a convincing assessment of 'continuity' in the Isle of Man, based mostly on evidence from a later period, see Megaw, 'Norseman and native', 1–44.

151. See ch. 6, p. 174ff above.

152. Sawyer, 'Vikings in Ireland', 345, 361

153. Barrow, *Kingship*, 107.

154. *KL* sub *fostr*; Sawyer, 'Vikings in Ireland', 358.

155. *OS* Taylor, 152.

156. *Hms* (Laing), 81.

157. W. D. H. Sellar, 'Marriage, divorce and concubinage in Gaelic Scotland', *TGSI*, LI (1978–80), 464–93; B. E. Crawford, 'Marriage and the status of women in Norse society', in *Marriage and Property*, ed. E. M. Craik (1984), 76–7.

158. *OS* Taylor, 183.

159. B. E. Crawford, 'Status of women', 73–4.

160. E. Roesdahl, *Viking-Age Denmark* (1982), 27.

161. C. Fell, *Women in Anglo-Saxon England* (1984), 142–3.

162. See ch. 2, p. 48 above.

163. *Laxdaela Saga*, trans. Magnusson and Edwards, 51.

164. *Ibid.*; *Book of Settlements*, 51.

165. *Laxdaela Saga*, trans. Magnusson and Edwards, 52.

166. *OS* Anderson, 2.

167. B. E. Crawford, 'Status of women', 81–2.

168. *Ibid.*, 80; Guthmundsson, *Origin*, 39–40.

169. *Ibid.*, 31–2.

170. Fell, *Women*, 132.

171. *Book of Settlements*, 17; Jakobsen, *Place-Names*, 150.
172. Fell, *Women*, 141.
173. OS Taylor, 145; see ch. 3, p. 63 and fig. 19.
174. Cowan, 'Caithness in the sagas', 29.
175. OS Taylor, 148.
176. B. E. Crawford, 'Status of women', 82–3.

Epilogue

1. Jones, *History*, 387.
2. For a general assessment relating to all these areas, see H. R. Loyn, *The Vikings in Britain* (1977), ch. 7.
3. M. Gelling, *Signposts to the Past* (1978), 223.
4. P. Stafford, *The East Midlands in the Early Middle Ages* (1985), 192.
5. Jones, *History*, 390–2.
6. J. Foster, 'Scottish nationality and the origins of capitalism', in *Scottish Capitalism*, ed. T. Dickson (1980), 36.
7. See ch. 3, p. 59 above.
8. See ch. 2, p. 49 above.
9. Smyth, *York and Dublin*, I and II, *passim*.
10. Jones, *History*, 394.
11. Foster, 'Scottish nationality', 36.
12. Duncan, *Scotland*, 86.
13. G. W. S. Barrow, *Kingship and Unity* (1981), 105.
14. Duncan, *Scotland*, 86.
15. G. W. S. Barrow, *The Anglo-Norman Era in Scottish History* (1980), 159 n.81.
16. W. Croft Dickinson, 'Some Scandinavian influences in Scottish legal procedure', *Arv*, xv (1959), 156; Duncan, *Scotland*, 349–50; see ch. 7, pp. 209–10 above.
17. Loyn, *Vikings*, 127–8.
18. Foster, 'Scottish nationality', 36.

Bibliography

Adam of Bremen, *History of the Archbishops of Hamburg-Bremen*, trans. with an intro. and notes by F. T. Tschan (New York, 1959).

Alcock, L., 'A multi-disciplinary chronology for Alt Clut, Castle Rock, Dumbarton', *PSAS*, CVII (1975–6), 103–13.

—'*Populi Bestiales Pictorum Feroci Animo*: a survey of Pictish settlement archaeology', in *Roman Frontier Studies*, papers presented to the 12th International Congress of Roman Frontier Studies, ed. W. S. Hanson and L. J. F. Keppie (BAR International Ser. 71, 1980), 61–95.

—'The archaeology of Celtic Britain, fifth to twelfth centuries AD', in *Twenty-Five Years of Medieval Archaeology*, ed. D. A. Hinton (1983), 48–66.

—'The supposed Viking burials on the islands of Canna and Sanday', in *From the Stone Age to the 'Forty-Five*, ed. A. O'Connor and D. V. Clarke (1983), 292–309.

—and Alcock, E., 'Scandinavian settlement in the Inner Hebrides: recent research on place-names and in the field', in *Settlements in Scotland 1000 BC–AD 1000*, ed. L. M. Thoms, *SAF*, x (1980), 61–73.

—Foster, S. M. and Driscoll, S. T., *Excavations at Urquhart and Dunnottar Castles, 1983 and 1984: Interim Reports*, Dept of Archaeology, University of Glasgow (1985).

Allen, J. Romilly, *The Early Christian Monuments of Scotland* (1903).

Almqvist, B., 'Scandinavian and Celtic folklore contacts in the earldom of Orkney', *Saga-Book*, xx (1978–9), 80–105.

Anderson, J., *Scotland in Early Christian Times* (second series, 1881).

—*Scotland in Pagan Times. The Iron Age* (1883).

—'Notice of bronze brooches and personal ornaments from a ship burial of the Vikingtime in Colonsay', *PSAS*, XLI (1906), 437–49.

Anderson, M. O., 'Dalriada and the creation of the kingdom of the Scots', in *Ireland in Early Mediaeval Europe*, ed. D. Whitelock, R. MacKitterick and D. Dumville (1982), 106–32.

Andersen, P. S., *Vikings of the West* (Oslo, 1971, repr. 1985).

—*Samlingen av Norge og Kristningen av Landet* (Oslo, 1977).

—'To what extent did the *balley-/balla (baile)* names in the Isle of Man supplant place-names of Norse origin?', in *Ninth Viking Congress*, 147–68.

Anderson, P. D., 'Birsay in the sixteenth century', in *Birsay: A Centre of Political and Ecclesiastical Power*, Orkney Heritage, 2 (1983), 82–97.

Andersson, T. and Sandred, K. L., ed., *The Vikings. Proceedings of the Symposium of the Faculty of Arts of Uppsala University* (Uppsala, 1978).

The Annals of Ulster (to AD 1131), I, ed. S. MacAirt and G. MacNiocaill (Dublin, 1983).

Bailey, R. N., *Viking-Age Sculpture in Northern England* (1980).

Bangor-Jones, M., 'Land assessment and settlement history', in *The Firthlands of Ross and Sutherland*, ed. J. Baldwin (1986), 153–67.

Bannerman, J., *Studies in the History of Dalriada* (1974).

Barrow, G. W. S., *The Anglo-Norman Era in Scottish History* (1980).

—'MacBeth and other mormaers of Moray', in *Inverness: The Hub of the Highlands* (1975).

—'Popular courts in early mediaeval Scotland: some suggested place-name evidence', *Scot. Stud.* xxv (1981), 1–24.

—*Kingship and Unity* (1981).

Batey, C. E., et al., *Freswick, Caithness; Excavations and Survey at Freswick Links and Freswick Castle, 1979–80. Summary Report* (University of Durham, Dept of Archaeology, 1981).

—'The late Norse site of Freswick', in *Caithness: A Cultural Crossroads*, ed. J. Baldwin (1982), 43–60.
—*Freswick, Caithness; Excavations and Survey at Freswick Links, 1981–2. Summary Report* (University of Durham, Dept of Archaeology, 1983.
—'Viking and late Norse Caithness: the archaeological evidence', in *Tenth Viking Congress* (in press).
Benediktsson, J., 'Landnámabók: some remarks on its value as a historical source', *Saga-Book*, XVII (1966–9), 275–92.
—'Some problems in the history of the settlement of Iceland', in *The Vikings*, ed. T. Andersson and K. L. Sandred (Uppsala, 1978), 161–5.
Bersu, G., 'A promontory fort on the shore of Ramsay Bay, Isle of Man', *Antiquaries J.*, xxix (1949), 62–79.
—'The Vikings in the Isle of Man', *JMM*, VII (1968), 83–8.
—and Wilson, D. M., *Three Viking Graves in the Isle of Man* (Soc. for Medieval Archaeology monograph series no. I, 1966).
Bigelow, G., 'Sandwick, Unst and the late Norse Shetland economy', in *Shetland Archaeology*, ed. B. Smith (1985), 95–127.
Binns, A., *Viking Voyagers. Then and Now* (1980).
Birsay: A Centre of Political and Ecclesiastical Power: Orkney Heritage, 2 (1983).
Blindheim, C., 'Trade problems in the Viking Age. Some reflections on Insular metalwork found in Norwegian graves of the Viking Age', in *The Vikings*, ed. T. Andersson and K. J. Sandred (Uppsala, 1978), 166–76.
Book of Settlements (Landnámabók, trans. with intro. and notes by H. Palsson and P. Edwards (University of Manitoba Icelandic Studies I, 1972).
Bowen, E. G., 'Britain and the British seas', in *The Irish Sea Province in Archaeology and History*, ed. D. Moore (1970), 13–28.
Brandt, F., 'On the navigation of the Vikings', in the *World of the Vikings*; catalogue of an Exhibition mounted by the Statens Historiska Museum, Stockholm, in co-operation with the National Maritime Museum, Greenwich (Stockholm, 1972), 14–26.
Bremner, R. L., 'Some notes on the Norsemen in Argyllshire and on the Clyde', *Saga-Book*, III (1904), 338–80.
—*The Norsemen in Alban* (1923).
Brøgger, A. W., *Ancient Emigrants* (1929).
—*Den Norske Bosetningen på Shetland-Orknøyene. Studier og Resulter.* Skrifter utgitt av Det Norske Videnskaps-Akademi i Oslo, II Hist-Filos. Klasse no. 3 (Oslo, 1930.
—and H. Shetelig, *The Viking Ships* (Oslo, 1951, repr. 1971).
Brøndsted, J., *The Vikings* (1965).
Brook, D., 'Kirk-compound place-names in Galloway and Carrick', *Trans. Dumfriesshire and Galloway Natural History and Antiquarian Soc.*, LVIII (1983), 56–71.
Brooks, N. P., 'Arms, status and warfare in late-Saxon England', in *Aethelred the Unready*, ed. D. Hill (BAR 59, 1978), 81–104.
—and J. Graham-Campbell, 'Reflections on the Viking-age silver hoard from Croydon, Surrey', in *Anglo-Saxon Monetary History*, ed. M. A. S. Blackburn (1986), 91–110.
Buttler, S., 'Preliminary report on excavations at Cross Geos, Clibberswick, Unst, Shetland in July and August, 1983' (University of Liverpool, the Jane Herdman Laboratories of Geology).
Cant, R. G., *The Mediaeval Churches and Chapels of Shetland* (1975.
—'Introduction', in *Birsay. A Centre of Political and Ecclesiastical Power, Orkney Heritage*, 2 (1983), 7–11.
—'Norse influence in the organisation of the mediaeval church in the Western Isles', *Northern Studies*, XXI (1984), 1–14.
—'Settlement, society and church organisation in the Northern Isles', in *Northern and Western Isles*, 169–79.
Chadwick, N. K., 'The Vikings and the western world', in *Procs. International Congress of Celtic Studies, 1959* (1962), 13–42.
Cheape, H., 'Recounting tradition: a critical view of medieval reportage', in Fenton and Palsson, *Northern and Western Isles*, 197–222.

254 *Scandinavian Scotland*

Chesnutt, M., 'An unsolved problem in Old-Norse Icelandic literary history', *Med. Scand.*, I (1968), 122–34.

Childe, V. G., 'Another late Viking house at Freswick, Caithness', *PSAS*, LXXVII (1942–3), 5–17.

Christensen, A. E., 'Boats and boatbuilding in Western Norway and the Islands', in *Northern and Western Isles*, 85–95.

Chronicle of Man and the Sudreys, trans. the Rt Revd Dr Goss, with notes by P. A. Munch (Manx Soc., 1874).

Close-Brooks, J. and Stevenson, R. B. K., *Dark-Age Sculpture* (1982).

Clouston, J. S., 'Two features of the Orkney earldom', *SHR*, XVI (1918–19), 15–28.

—'The Orkney townships', *SHR*, XVII (1919–20), 16–45.

—'The Orkney lands', *POAS*, II (1923–4), 61–8.

—'The Orkney "Bus"', *POAS*, V (1926–7), 41–50.

—*A History of Orkney* (1932).

Collingwood, W. G., 'Viking-Age Cross at Iona', *Saga-Book*, III (1904), 304–6.

—*Scandinavian Britain* (1908).

Cowan, E. J., 'Caithness in the sagas', in *Caithness: A Cultural Crossroads*, ed. J. R. Baldwin (1982), 25–44.

Cowan, I. B., 'Early ecclesiastical foundations' in *An Historical Atlas of Scotland*, ed. P. MacNeill and R. Nicholson (1975), 17–19.

Crawford, B. E., 'Weland of Stiklaw: a Scottish royal servant at the Norwegian court', *Historisk Tidsskrift* (norsk), IV (1973), 329–39.

—'Viking graves', in *An Historical Atlas of Scotland*, ed. P. MacNeill and R. Nicholson (1975), 16–17.

—'The earldom of Caithness and the kingdom of Scotland, 1150–1266', *Northern Scotland*, II (1976–7), 97–117; repr. with some additions in *Essays on the Nobility of Mediaeval Scotland*, ed. K. M. Stringer (1985), 25–43.

—'Foreign relations: Scandinavia', in *Scottish Society in the Fifteenth Century*, ed. J. M. Brown (1977), 85–100.

—'The Shetland Lawthing seal', *New Shetlander*, CXXVII (1979), 22–4.

—'Progress report on excavations at "Da Biggins", Papa Stour, Shetland, 1977', *Northern Studies*, XI (1978), 25–9; XIII (1979), 37–41.

—'Report on the renewed excavations at The Biggins, Papa Stour, Shetland, 1982' (Dept of Mediaeval History, University of St Andrews).

—'Birsay and the early earls and bishops of Orkney', in *Birsay: A Centre of Political and Ecclesiastical Power. Orkney Heritage*, 2 (1983), 97–118.

—'Papa Stour: survival, continuity and change in one Shetland island', in *Northern and Western Isles*, 40–58.

—'The cult of St Magnus in Shetland', in *Essays in Shetland History*, ed. B. E. Crawford (1984), 65–81.

—'Marriage and the status of women in Norse society', in *Marriage and Property*, ed. E. M. Craik (1984), 71–88.

—'The Biggins, Papa Stour: a multi-disciplinary investigation', in *Shetland Archaeology*, ed. B. Smith (1985), 128–58.

—'Diocese of Orkney', in *Series Episcoporum Ecclesiae Catholicae Occidentalis Ab Initio Usque ad Annum 1198*, ed. O. Engels and S. Weinfurter (in press).

—'The making of a frontier: the Firthlands from 9th–12th centuries', in *The Firthlands of Ross and Sutherland*, ed. J. Baldwin (1986), 38–46.

Crawford, I. A., 'Scot? Norseman and Gael', *SAF*, VI (1974), 1–16.

—'War or peace – Viking colonisation in the Northern and Western Isles of Scotland reviewed', *Eighth Viking Congress*, 259–70.

—'The present state of settlement history in the West Highlands and Islands', in *From the Stone Age to the 'Forty-Five*, ed. A. O'Connor and D. V. Clarke (1983), 350–67.

Cruden, S., 'Earl Thorfinn the Mighty and the Brough of Birsay', *Third Viking Congress*, 156–62.

—'Excavations at Birsay, Orkney,' *Fourth Viking Congress*, 22–31.

Cubbon, A. M. and Dolley, M., 'The Kirk Michael Viking treasure trove', *JMM*, VIII (1980), 5–20.

—'The archaeology of the Vikings in the Isle of Man', *Ninth Viking Congress*, 13–26.

Curle, A., 'A Viking settlement at Freswick, Caithness', *PSAS*, LXXIII (1939), 71–109.
—'A dwelling of the Viking period at "Jarlshof", Sumburgh, Shetland', *Viking Anti-quities*, VI (1954), 11–30.
—'A Viking settlement at Freswick, Caithness', *Viking Antiquities*, VI (1954), 31–63.
Curle, C. L., *Pictish and Norse Finds from the Brough of Birsay, 1934–74* (Soc. of Antiquaries of Scotland monograph series no. 1, 1982).
—'The finds from the Brough of Birsay, 1934–74', in *Birsay: A Centre of Political and Ecclesiastical Power. Orkney Heritage* 2 (1983), 67–81.
Davidson, D. A. and Jones, R. L., 'The environment of Orkney' in *The Prehistory of Orkney*, ed. C. Renfrew (1985), 10–35.
Davies, W., *Wales in the Early Middle Ages* (1982).
Dickens, B., 'Orkney raid on Wales', *POAS*, viii (1929–30), 47–8.
Dickinson, 'Some Scandinavian influences in Scottish legal procedure?' *Arv*, 15 (1959), 155–59.
Dolley, R. H. M., *The Hiberno-Norse Coins in the British Museum* (Sylloge of Coins in the British Isles, 1966).
—'The palimpsest of Viking settlement on Man', *Eighth Viking Congress* (1981), 173–82.
Donaldson, A. M., Morris, C. D. and Rackham, F. J., 'The Birsay Bay project', in *Environmental Aspects of Coasts and Islands*, ed. D. Brothwell and G. Dimbleby (BAR International Ser. 94, 1981), 65–85.
Donaldson, G., 'Viking tracks in Scotland', *Proceedings of the Conference on Scottish Studies*, Old Dominion University, Norfolk, Va, 3 (1976), 3–10.
Duncan, A. A. M., *Scotland: the Making of a Kingdom* (1975).
—and A. L. Brown, 'Argyll and the Isles in the earlier Middle Ages', *PSAS*, XC (1956–7), 192–220.
Djupedal, R., *Klosteret på Selja*. Selje Tourist Office (Bergen, 1977).
Easson, A., 'Ouncelands and pennylands in the West Highlands and Islands of Scotland' (in press).
Eldjarn, K., 'The Viking myth', in *The Vikings*, ed. R. T. Farrell (1982), 262–73.
—'Graves and grave-goods: survey and evaluation', in *Northern and Western Isles*, 2–11.
Ellehoj, S., *Studier over den aeldste norøne historieskrivning* (Copenhagen, 1965).
Ellmers, D., 'The ships of the Vikings', in *The World of the Vikings*; catalogue of an Exhibition mounted by the Statens Historiska Museum, Stockholm, in co-operation with the National Maritime Museum, Greenwich (Stockholm, 1972), 13–14.
Fanning, T., 'Some aspects of the bronze ringed pin in Scotland', in *From the Stone Age to the 'Forty-Five*, ed. A. O'Connor and D. V. Clarke (1983), 324–42.
Farrell, R. T. (ed.), *The Vikings* (1982).
Fawcett, R., *Scottish Mediaeval Churches. An Introduction to the Ecclesiastical Architecture of the 12th to the 16th centuries in the care of the Secretary of State for Scotland* (1985).
Feachem, R. W., 'Fortifications', in *The Problem of the Picts*, ed. F. T. Wainwright (1955; repr. 1980), 66–86.
Fell, C., 'The Sigurd legend', in *The Viking World*, ed. J. Graham-Campbell (1980), 184–6.
—*Women in Anglo-Saxon England* (1984).
Fellows-Jensen, G., 'The Vikings in England: a review', *Anglo-Saxon England*, IV (1975), 181–206.
—'A Gaelic-Scandinavian loan-word in English place-names', *J. English Place-Name Soc.*, x (1977–8), 18–25.
—'The Manx place-name debate', in *Man and Environment in the Isle of Man*, ed. P. Davey, BAR 54 (ii) (1978), 315–18.
—'Scandinavian settlement in the Isle of Man and north-west England: the place-name evidence', in *Ninth Viking Congress*, 37–52.
—'Anthroponymical specifics in place-names in *by* in the British Isles', *Studia Anthroponimica Scandinavica*, I (1983), 45–60.
—'Viking settlement in the Northern and Western Isles; the place-name evidence as seen from Denmark and the Danelaw', in Fenton and Palsson, *Northern and Western Isles*, 148–68.

—'Scandinavian settlement in Cumbria and Dumfriesshire; the place-name evidence', in *The Scandinavians in Cumbria*, ed. J. Baldwin and I. D. Whyte (1985), 65–82.

Fenton, A., *The Northern Isles: Orkney and Shetland* (1978).

—'Northern links', *Northern Studies*, xvi (1980), 5–16.

—'The longhouse in northern Scotland', in *Vestnordisk Byggeskikk gjennom to tusen år*, ed. B. Myhre, B. Stoklund and P. Gjaerder (Arkeologisk museum i Stavanger, Skrifter no. 7, 1982), 231–40.

—'Northern links: continuity and change', in *Northern and Western Isles*, 129–45.

Fenton, A. and Palsson, H. (eds.), *The Northern and Western Isles in the Viking World* (1984).

Fidjestøl, B., 'Arnor Thordarson: skald of the Orkney Jarls', in *Northern and Western Isles*, 239–57.

Fojut, N., 'Towards a geography of Shetland brochs', *Glasgow Archaeological J.*, ix (1982), 38–59.

—'Some thoughts on the Shetland Iron Age', in *Shetland Archaeology*, ed. B. Smith (1985), 47–84.

Foote, P. G., 'Some account of the present state of saga-research', *Scandinavica* iii–iv (1964–5), 115–26.

—and Wilson, D. M., *The Viking Achievement* (1970).

Foster, J., 'Scottish nationality and the origins of capitalism', in *Scottish Capitalism*, ed. T. Dickson (1980), 19–62.

Frank, R., 'Viking atrocity and skaldic verse: the rite of the blood-eagle', *EHR*, xcix (1984), 332–43.

Fraser, I., 'The place-names of Lewis, the Norse evidence', *Northern Studies*, iv (1974), 11–21.

—'Gaelic and Norse elements in coastal place-names in the Western Isles', *TGSI*, l (1976–8), 237–55.

—'The Norse element in Sutherland place-names', *Scottish Literary J.* Language Supplement no. 9 (1978), 17–27.

Freke, D. J., *Peel Castle Excavations: Interim Report 1984* (St Patrick's Isle (I.O.M.) Archaeological Trust, 1985).

Gelling, M., 'Norse and Gaelic in medieval Man; the place-name evidence', in *The Vikings*, ed. T. Andersson and K. Sandred (1978), 107–18.

—*Signposts to the Past* (1978).

—*Place-Names in the Landscape* (1984).

Gelling, P.S., 'The Braaid site; a re-excavation of one of the structures', *JMM*, vi (1964), 201–5.

—'Celtic continuity in the Isle of Man', in *Studies in Celtic Survival*, ed. L. Laing (BAR 37, 1977), 77–82.

—'The Norse buildings at Skaill, Deerness, Orkney and their immediate predecessors', in *Northern and Western Isles*, 12–38.

—'Excavations at Skaill, Deerness', in *The Prehistory of Orkney*, ed. C. Renfrew (1985), 176–82.

Gillingham, J. and Falkus, M. (eds.), *Historical Atlas of Britain* (1981).

Goedheer, A. K., *Irish and Norse Traditions about the Battle of Clontarf* (1928).

Gordon, B., 'Some Norse place-names in Trotternish', *Scottish Gaelic Studies*, x (1963–5), 82–112.

Graham Campbell, J., 'The Viking-age silver and gold hoards of Scandinavian character from Scotland', *PSAS*, cvii (1975–6), 114–35.

—'The Viking-age silver hoards of Ireland', *Seventh Viking Congress* (1976), 39–74.

—*Viking Artefacts. A Select Catalogue* (1980).

—and Kidd, D., *The Vikings* (1980).

—(ed.), *The Viking World* (1980).

—'Viking silver hoards; an introduction', in *The Vikings*, ed. R. T. Farrell (1982), 32–41.

—'Some Viking-age pennanular brooches from Scotland and the origins of the "Thistle brooch"', in *From the Stone Age to the 'Forty-Five*, ed. A. O'Connor and D. V. Clarke (1983), 310–23.

—'The Viking-age silver hoards of the Isle of Man', *Ninth Viking Congress*, 53–80.

Greene, D., 'The influence of Scandinavian on Irish', *Seventh Viking Congress*, 75–82.
—'The evidence of language and place-names in Ireland', in *The Vikings*, ed. T. Andersson and K. Sandred (1978), 119–23.
Grieg, S., 'Viking antiquities in Scotland', *Viking Antiquities*, II (Oslo, 1940).
Guthmundsson, B., *The Origin of the Icelanders* (Lincoln, Nebr., 1967).
Haegstad, M., 'Kildinakvadet', *Videnskapsselskapsskrifter*, II, Hist.-Filos. Klasse, 1900.
Hafström, G., 'Atlantic and Baltic earldoms', *Sixth Viking Congress*, 51–8.
Hall, R. (ed.), *Viking-Age York and the North* (CBA Res. Rep. no. 27, 1978).
Halliday, C., *The Scandinavian Kingdom of Dublin* (1884).
Hamilton, J. R. C., *Jarlshof, Shetland* (1953).
—'Jarlshof, a prehistoric and Viking settlement site in Shetland', in *Recent Archaeological Excavations in Britain*, ed. R. Bruce Mitford (1956), 197–222.
—*Excavations at Jarlshof, Shetland* (1956).
Hedges, J. W., 'Trial excavation on Pictish and Viking settlements at Saevar Howe, Birsay, Orkney', *Glasgow Archaeological J.*, x (1983), 73–124.
Hellberg, L., 'Kumlabygdens ortnamn och äldre bebyggelse', *Kumlabygden*, III (1967).
—*Ortnamn och den Svenska bosättningen på Aland. Ortnamn och samhalle.2* (1980).
Helle, K., *Norge Blir en Stat* (Oslo, 1974).
Henderson, G., *The Norse Influence on Celtic Scotland* (1910).
Historia Norvegiae, in *Monumenta Historica Norvegiae*, ed. G. Storm (Christiania, 1880), 71–124.
Hollander, L. M., *The Skalds* (New York, 1945).
Holtsmark, A., 'Vefr Darradar', *Maal og Minne* (1939), 74–96.
Hunter, J. R., 'Excavations at the Brough of Birsay, Orkney', *Northern Studies*, IX (1977), 44–7; XI (1978), 23–4.
—'Recent excavations on the Brough of Birsay', in *Birsay: A Centre of Political and Ecclesiastical Power. Orkney Heritage*, 2 (1983), 152–70.
—*Archaeology Extra*, nos. 1 and 2 (Newsheet from Univ. of Bradford, Dept of Archaeology, 1984, 1985).
—*Rescue Excavations on the Brough of Birsay 1974–82* (Soc. of Antiquaries of Scotland monograph series no. 4, 1986).
—and Morris, C. D., 'Recent excavations at the Brough of Birsay', *Eighth Viking Congress*, 245–58.
Hunter Marshall, D. W., *The Sudreys in Early Viking TImes* (1929).
Irvine, W., *The Isle of Shapinsay* (1977).
Islandske Annaler indtil 1578, ed. G. Storm (Christiania, 1888).
Jakobsen, J., *An Etymological Dictionary of the Norn Language in Shetland* (2 vols., 1928 and 1932, repr. 1985).
—*The Place-Names of Shetland* (1936).
Johannesson, J., *Islendinga Saga. A History of the Old Icelandic Commonwealth* (Manitoba, 1974).
Johnsen, A. O., 'The payments from the Hebrides and Isle of Man to the crown of Norway, 1152–1263', *SHR*, XLVIII (1969), 18–34.
Johnston, A. W., 'Orkney and Shetland folk, 880–1350', *Saga-Book*, IX (1914–18), 372–407.
Jones, G., *A History of the Vikings* (1968).
Kaland, S. H. H., 'Westnessutgravningene på Rousay, Orknøyene', *Viking* (1973), 77–102.
—'Some economic aspects of the Orkneys in the Viking period', *Norwegian Archaeological Rev.*, xv (1982), 85–95.
Kendrick, T. D., *A History of the Vikings* (1930, repr. 1968).
Keynes, S. and Lapidge, M. (eds.), *Alfred the Great* (1984).
Kirby, D. P., 'The evolution of the frontier, c.400–1018', in *An Historical Atlas of Scotland*, ed. P. MacNeill and R. Nicholson (1975), 24–6.
—'Moray prior to 1100', in *An Historical Atlas of Scotland*, ed. P. MacNeill and R. Nicholson (1975), 20–1.

Koht, H., 'Sagaernes opfatning av vor gamle historie', *Historisk Tidsskrift* (norsk), 5, raekke II (1914); also printed in *Rikssamling og Kristendom. Norske Historikere i Utvalg*, I, ed. A. Holmsen and J. Simensen (Oslo, 1967), 41–55.

Laing, L., 'The Norse house', in *Settlement-Types in post-Roman Scotland* (BAR 13, 1975), 21–2.

—*The Archaeology of Late Celtic Britain and Ireland* (1975).

Lamb, H. H., *Climate, History and the Modern World* (1982).

Lamb, R. G., 'The cathedral of Christchurch and the monastery of Birsay', *PSAS*, cv (1972–4), 200–5.

—'Coastal settlements of the north', *SAF*, v (1973).

—'The Burri stacks of Culswick, Shetland and other paired-stack settlements', *PSAS*, cvii (1975–6), 144–54.

—*Sanday and North Ronaldsay. An Archaeological Survey of the North Isles of Orkney* (1980).

—*Rousay, Egilsay and Wyre (with adjacent small islands). An Archaeological Survey* (RCAHMS, The Archaeological Sites and Monuments of Scotland, 16, 1982).

—*Papa Westray and Westray (with adjacent small islands). An Archaeological Survey* (RCAHMS, The Archaeological Sites and Monuments of Scotland, 19, 1983).

—'The Cathedral and the monastery', in *Birsay: A Centre of Political and Ecclesiastical Power. Orkney Heritage*, 2 (1983), 36–45.

—'The Orkney Trebs', in *Settlement in North Britain, 1000 BC–AD 1000*, ed. J. C. Chapman and H. C. Mytum (BAR 118, 1983), 175–84.

Lamont, W. D., '"House" and "pennyland" in the Highlands and Isles', *Scot. Stud.*, xxv (1981), 65–77.

Lang, J. T., 'Hogback monuments in Scotland', *PSAS*, cv (1972–4), 206–35.

—'The Hogback: A Viking colonial monument', *Anglo-Saxon Studies in Archaeology and History*, iii (1984), 85–176.

Larson, L. M., *The King's Household in England before the Norman Conquest* (Bull. Univ. Wisconsin, no. 100, Madison, 1904).

Laxdaela Saga, trans. M. Magnusson and H. Palsson (1969).

Leirfall, J., *West Over Sea* (1979).

Lewis, A. R., *The Northern Seas* (1958).

Liestøl, A., 'An Iona rune stone and the world of Man and the Isles', in *Ninth Viking Congress*, 85–94.

—'Runes', in *Northern and Western Isles*, 224–38.

Liestøl, K., *The Origins of the Icelandica Family Sagas* (Oslo, 1930).

Lockwood, W. B., 'On the early history and origin of the names Orkney and Shetland', *Namn og Bygd* (1980), 19–35.

Logan, D., *The Vikings in History* (1983).

Lowe, C. R., 'The problem of keeills and treens'; appendix I to 'The survey and excavations at Keeill Vael, Druidale in their context', by C. D. Morris, *Ninth Viking Congress*, 124–6.

Loyn, H. R., *The Vikings in Britain* (1977).

Lund, N., 'The settlers: where do we get them from and do we need them?', *Eighth Viking Congress*, 147–72.

MacBain, A., 'The Norse element in the topography of the Highlands and Isles', *TGSI*, xix (1893–4), 217–45.

MacDonald, A., 'On "papar" names in N. and W. Scotland', *Northern Studies*, ix (1977), 25–30. Also printed in BAR 37 (1977), 107–11.

MacDonald, D. A., 'The Vikings in Gaelic oral traditions', in *Northern and Western Isles*, 265–79.

McGrail, S., 'Ships, shipwrights and seamen', in *The Viking World*, ed. J. Graham-Campbell (1980).

MacGregor, L. J., 'Sources for a study of Norse settlement in Shetland and Faroe', in *Essays in Shetland History*, ed. B. E. Crawford (1984), 1–17.

MacKenzie, W. C., *Scottish Place-Names* (1931).

McKerral, A., 'Ancient denominations of agricultural land in Scotland', *PSAS*, lxxviii (1943–4), 39–79.

MacLaren, A., 'A Norse house on Drimore Machair, S. Uist', *Glasgow Archaeological J.*, III (1974), 9–18.

MacQueen, J., 'Pennyland and davoch in south-west Scotland; a preliminary note', *Scottish Studies*, XXIII (1979), 69–74.

MacRoberts, D., 'The ecclesiastical character of the St Ninian's Isle Treasure', *Fourth Viking Congress*, 224–46.

McTurk, R. W., 'Ragnar Lothbrok in the Irish Annals, *Seventh Viking Congress*, 93–124.

Magnusson, M., *Hammar of the North: Myths and Heroes of the Viking Age* (1976).

Marcus, G. J., *The Conquest of the North Atlantic* (1980).

Marshall, D. M., 'Report on the excavation at Little Dunagoil', *Trans. Buteshire Natural History Soc.*, XVI (1964), 30–69.

Marstrander, C., *Bidrag til det Norske Sprogs' Historie i Ireland*. Videnskapsselskaps Skrifter, II, Hist.-Filos. Klasse (1915), no. 5.

—'Treen og keill. Et førnorsk jorddelingsprinsipp på de Britiske øyene', *Norsk Tidsskrift for Sprogvidenskap*, VIII (1937), 287–442.

—'Om tingsteder pa Man', *Norsk Tidsskrift for Sprogvidenskap*, X (1938), 384–93.

Marwick, E., 'The stone of Odin', *PSAS*, CVII (1975–6), 28–34.

Marwick, H., 'A rune-inscribed stone from Birsay, Orkney', *PSAS*, LVI (1921–2), 67–71.

—'Antiquarian notes on Papa Westray', *POAS*, III (1924–5), 31–48.

—*The Orkney Norn* (1929).

—'Orkney farm-name studies', *POAS*, IX (1930–1), 25–34.

—'Leidang in the west', *POAS*, XIII (1934–5), 15–30.

—'Naval defence in north Scotland', *SHR*, XXVIII (1949), 1–11.

—*Orkney* (1951).

—*Orkney Farm-Names* (1952).

Megaw, B. R. S. and E. M., 'The Norse heritage in the Isle of Man', in *The Early Christian Cultures of North-West Europe*, ed. B. Dickens and C. Fox (1950), 143–70.

—'Norseman and native in the Kingdom of the Isles', *Scottish Studies*, XX (1976), 1–44.

—'Note on "Pennyland and davoch in south-western Scotland"', *Scottish Studies*, XXIII (1979), 75–7.

Megaw, E. M. and Cowin, W. S., 'Odin's bird: notes on the raven past and present', *JMM*, V (1943), 105–6.

Morris, C. D. and Hunter, J., 'Brough of Birsay excavation and survey 1974, 1975, Interim Reports', *Northern Studies*, VII/VIII (1976), 24–33; X (1977), 28–31; XI (1978), 19–25.

—'Birsay "small sites" excavations and survey', *Northern Studies*, XIII (1979), 3–19.

—'Brough of Birsay, Orkney', *Northern Studies*, XVI (1980), 17–28.

—'The Brough of Deerness, Orkney: a new survey', *Archaeologia Atlantica*, II (1977), 65–74.

—'The Vikings in the British Isles', in *The Vikings*, ed. R. T. Farrell (1982), 70–90.

—'Excavations around the Bay of Birsay', *Birsay: A Centre of Political and Ecclesiastical Power. Orkney Heritage*, 2 (1983), 119–51.

—'The survey and excavations at Keeill Vael, Druidale, in their context', *Ninth Viking Congress*, 107–33.

—'Viking Orkney: a survey', in *The Prehistory of Orkney*, ed. C. Renfrew (1985), 210–42.

Morrison, A., 'Early Harris estate papers, 1679–1703', *TGSI*, LI (1978–80), 71–72.

Munro, R. W. (ed.), *Monro's Western Isles of Scotland and Genealogies of the Clans 1549* (1961).

Munro, R. W. and J. M., 'The Lordship of the Isles', in *An Historical Atlas of Scotland*, ed. P. MacNeill and R. Nicholson (1975), 65–7.

—'Profusion of Pabbays', *Notes and Queries of the Soc. of West Highland and Island Historical Research*, XVI (Sept. 1981), 17–19.

Musset, L., 'La pénétration chrétienne dans l'Europe du nord et son influence sur la civilisation Scandinave', in *La Conversione al Christianesimo nell'Europa dell'Alto Medioevo. Settimane di Studio*, XIV (1967), 263–325.

Myhre, B., 'Synspunkter pa huskonstruksion i sørvestnorske gårdshus fra jernalder og middelalder' (Views on the building technique of farm-houses from the Iron Age and early Middle Ages in S-W Norway', in *Vestnordisk byggeskikk gjennom to tusen år*, ed. B. Myhre, B. Stoklund and P. Gjaerder, Arkeologisk museum i Stavanger, Skrifter no. 7 (1982), 98–118.

Nicholson, R., *Scotland: The Later Middle Ages* (1974).

Nicolaisen, W. F. H., 'Norse settlement in the Northern and Western Isles', *SHR*, XLVIII (1969), 6–17.

—'Scandinavian place-names', in *An Historical Atlas of Scotland*, ed. P. MacNeill and R. Nicholson (1975), 6–7.

—'Scandinavian place-names in Scotland as a source of knowledge', *Northern Studies*, VII/VIII (1976), 14–23.

—*Scottish Place-Names* (1976).

—'Early Scandinavian naming in the Western and Northern Isles', *Northern Scotland*, III (1979–80), 105–22.

—'Scandinavians and Celts in Caithness: the place-name evidence', in *Caithness: A Cultural Crossroads*, ed. J. Baldwin (1982), 75–85.

—'The Viking settlement of Scotland: the evidence of place-names', in *The Vikings*, ed. R. T. Farrell (1982), 95–115.

Nieke, M., 'Settlement patterns in the 1st millenium AD: a case study of the island of Islay', in *Settlement in North Britain 1000 BC–AD 1000*, ed. J. C. Chapman and H. C. Mytum (BAR 118, 1983), 299–326.

Njal's Saga, trans. M. Magnusson and H. Palsson (1964).

Nyberg, T., 'Continental Europe and the North Sea and Baltic area in the early Middle Ages', *Rapports* II. Chronologie (Comité International des Sciences Historiques: XV Congrès International des Sciences Historiques) (1980), 193–201.

O'Corrain, D., *Ireland Before the Normans* (Dublin, 1972).

—'High-kings, Vikings and other kings', *Irish Historical Studies*, XXI (1978–9), 283–323.

O'Dell, A. C., *The Historical Geography of the Shetland Isles* (1939).

Oftedal, M., 'Norse place-names in the Hebrides', *Second Viking Congress*, 107–12.

—'On the frequency of Norse loan-words in Scottish Gaelic', *Scottish Gaelic Studies*, IX (1961–2), 116–27.

—'Norse place-names in Celtic Scotland', *Procs. International Congress of Celtic Studies, 1959* (Dublin, 1962), 43–50.

—'Names of lakes on the Isle of Lewis in the Outer Hebrides', *Eighth Viking Congress*, 183–8.

Olsen, M., *Farms and Fanes of Ancient Norway* (Instituttet for Sammenlignende Kulturforskning, ser. A: Forelesninger, IX, Oslo, 1928.

—'Runic inscriptions in Great Britain, Ireland and the Isle of Man', *Viking Antiquities*, VI (Oslo, 1954), 151–34.

Olsen, O., *Hørg, Hov og Kirke* (Copenhagen, 1966).

Olson, D., 'Norse settlement in the Hebrides, an Interdisciplinary study' (thesis, University of Oslo, 1983).

O'Riordain, B., 'The High St excavations', *Seventh Viking Congress*, 135–40.

Owen, O., *Interim Report* on the Rescue Project at Tuquoy, Westray, Orkney (Dept of Archaeology, University of Durham, 1982).

—*An Interim Report* on the second season of the archaeological rescue project at Tuquoy, Westray, Orkney (Dept of Archaeology, University of Durham, 1983).

R. I. Page, 'A tale of two cities', *Peritia*, I (1982), 335–51.

—'The Manx rune-stones', *Ninth Viking Congress*, 133–46.

de Paor, L., 'The Viking towns of Ireland', *Seventh Viking Congress*, 29–38.

Petersen, J., 'British antiquities of the Viking period found in Norway', *Viking Antiquities*, V (Oslo, 1940).

Radford, C. A. R., *The Early Christian and Norse Settlements at Birsay, Orkney* (1959).

—'Art and architecture, Celtic and Norse', in *The Northern Isles*, ed. F. T. Wainwright (1962), 163–87.

—'Birsay and the spread of Christianity to the north', in *Birsay: A Centre of Political and Ecclesiastical Power. Orkney Heritage*, 2 (1983), 13–35.

Rafnsson, S., *Studier i Landnamabok* (Lund, 1974).

RCAMS, 12th Report with an Inventory of the Ancient Monuments of Orkney and Shetland, II, *Inventory of Orkney* (1946).

RCAHMS, *Argyll, An Inventory of the Monuments*, IV (Iona) (1982).

—V (Islay, Jura, Colonsay and Oronsay) (1984).

—*9th Report with Inventory of Monuments and Constructions in the Outer Hebrides, Skye and the Small Isles* (1928).

Reece, R., *Iona. Its History and Archaeology* (pamphlet, n.d.).

Ritchie, A., 'Pict and Norseman in Northern Scotland', *SAF*, VI (1974), 23–36.

—'Excavation of Pictish and Viking-age farmsteads at Buckquoy, Orkney', *PSAS*, CVIII (1976–7), 174–227.

—'Birsay around AD 800', in *Birsay: A Centre of Political and Ecclesiastical Power. Orkney Heritage*, 2 (1983), 46–66.

—'The first settlers', in *The Prehistory of Orkney*, ed. C. Renfrew (1985), 36–53.

—'Orkney in the Pictish kingdom', in *The Prehistory of Orkney*, ed. C. Renfrew (1985), 183–204.

—*Exploring Scotland's Heritage: Orkney and Shetland* (1985).

—and Ritchie, J. N. G., *The Ancient Monuments of Orkney* (1978).

Ritchie, J. N. G., 'Excavations at Machrins, Colonsay', *PSAS*, CXI (1981), 263–81.

—and Harman, M., *Exploring Scotland's Heritage. Argyll and the Western Isles* (1985).

Ritchie, P. R., 'Soapstone quarrying in Viking lands', in *Northern and Western Isles* (1984), 59–84.

Robertson, E. W., *Scotland under her Early Kings* (2 vols., 1862).

Roesdahl, E., *Viking-Age Denmark* (1982).

Roussell, A., 'Det nordiske hus i vikingetid', in *Forntida Gardar i Island*, ed. M. Stenberger (Copenhagen, 1943), 193–200.

Rygh, O., *Norsk Gaardnavne, Forord og Indledning* (Kristiania, 1898).

Sawyer, P. H., 'The two Viking Ages of Britain; a discussion', *Med. Scand.*, II (1969).

—'The Vikings and the Irish Sea', in *The Irish Sea Province in Archaeology and History*, ed. D. Moore (1970), 86–92.

—*The Age of the Vikings* (2nd edn, 1971).

—*Kings and Vikings* (1982).

—'The causes of the Viking Age', in *The Vikings*, ed. R. T. Farrell (1982), 1–7.

—'The Vikings in Ireland', in *Ireland in Early Mediaeval Europe*, ed. D. Whitelock, R. McKitterick and D. Dumville (1982), 345–61.

Saxby, J., *Shetland Traditional Lore* (1932).

Scott, J. G., 'A note on Viking settlement in Galloway', *Trans. Dumfriess and Galloway Natural History and Antiquarian Soc.*, LVIII (1983).

Scott, Sir L., 'The colonisation of Scotland in the second millennium BC', *PPS*, n.s.XVII (1951), 16–82.

—'The Norse in the Hebrides', *First Viking Congress*, 189–215.

Seeberg, A., 'Five kings', *Saga-Book*, XX (1978–9), 106–13.

Sellar, W. D. H., 'The origins and ancestry of Somerled', *SHR*, XLV (1966), 123–42.

—'Marriage, divorce and concubinage in Gaelic Scotland', *TGSI*, LI (1978–80), 464–93.

Shaw, F., *The Northern and Western Isles of Scotland: their Economy and Society in the Seventeenth Century* (1980).

Shetelig, H., 'Ship-burials', *Saga-Book*, IV (1904–5), 326–63.

—'Ship-burial at Kiloran Bay, Colonsay, Scotland', *Saga-Book*, V (1906–7), 172–4.

—'An introduction to the Viking history of Western Europe', *Viking Antiquities*, I (Oslo, 1940).

—'The Viking graves', *Viking Antiquities*, VI (Oslo, 1954), 65–112.

—'The Norse style of ornamentation in the Viking settlements', *Viking Antiquities*, VI (Oslo, 1954), 115–49.

Simon, J., 'Snorri Sturlason: his life and times', *Parergon. Bulletin of the Australian and New Zealand Assoc. for Medieval and Renaissance Studies*, XV (Canberra, 1956), 3–15.

Skene, W. F., *Celtic Scotland* (2 vols., 1st edn, 1877, 2nd edn, 1886).

Small, A., 'Excavations at Underhoull, Unst, Shetland', *PSAS*, XCVIII (1964–6), 225–48.

—'The distribution of settlement in Shetland and Faroe in Viking times', *Saga-Book*, XVII (1967–8), 145–55.

—'A Viking longhouse in Unst, Shetland', *Fifth Viking Congress* (1968), 62–70.

—'The historical geography of the Norse Viking colonisation of the Scottish Highlands', *Norsk Geografisk Tidsskrift*, XXII (1968), 1–16.

—'The Viking Highlands – a geographical view', in *The Dark Ages in the Highlands*, 95th Anniversary Conference of the Inverness Field Club (1971), 69–90.

—'Norse settlement in Skye', in 'Les Vikings et leur civilisation: problèmes actuels', ed. R. Boyer in *Bibliothèque Arctique et Antartique*, V (1976), 29–37.

—(ed.), *A St Kilda Handbook* (1979).

—'The Norse building tradition in Shetland', in *Vestnordisk Byggeskikk gjennom to tusen år*, ed. B. Myhre, B. Stoklund and P. Gjaerder, Arkeologisk museum i Stavanger, Skrifter no. 7.

—, Thomas, C., and Wilson, D. M. (ed.), *St Ninian's Isle and its Treasure* (2 vols., 1973).

Smith, B., 'What is a scattald? Rural communities in Shetland, 1400–1900', in *Essays in Shetland History*, ed. B. E. Crawford (1984), 99–124.

Smyth, A. P., *Scandinavian York and Dublin* (2 vols., New Jersey and Dublin, 1975 and 1979).

—*Scandinavian Kings in the British Isles, 850–880* (1977).

—*Warlords and Holy Men* (1984).

Sommerfelt, A., 'On the Norse form of the name of the Picts and the date of the first Norse raids on Scotland', *Lochlann*, I (1958), 218–22.

Stafford, P., *The East Midlands in the Early Middle Ages* (1985).

Steinnes, A., 'The "Huseby" system in Orkney', *SHR*, XXXVIII (1959), 36–46.

Stenton, F. M., *Anglo-Saxon England* (2nd edn, 1971).

Stevenson, R. B. K., 'A hoard of Anglo-Saxon coins found at Iona Abbey', *PSAS*, LXXXV (1950–1), 170–4.

—'Pictish art', in *The Problem of the Picts*, ed. F. T. Wainwright (1955; repr. 1980), 97–128.

—'The brooch from Westness, Orkney', *Fifth Viking Congress*, 25–31.

—'Christian sculpture in Norse Shetland', in *Heidursrit til Sverra Dahl, Frodskaparrit*, XXVIII–XXIX (1981), 283–92.

Stewart, J., 'Shetland farm names', in *Fourth Viking Congress*, 247–66.

—'The place-names of Fetlar', *Fifth Viking Congress*, 174–85.

Stoklund, B., 'Building traditions in the northern world', in *Northern and Western Isles* (1984), 96–115.

Talbot, E., 'Scandinavian fortifications in the British Isles', *SAF*, VI (1974), 37–45.

Talve, I., *Bastu och Torkhus i Nord Europa* (Stockholm, 1960).

Taylor, A. B., 'Karl Hundason, "king of Scots"', *PSAS*, LXXI (1936–7), 334–42.

—'British and Irish place-names in Old Norse literature', *Second Viking Congress*, 113–22.

—'The Norsemen on St Kilda', *Saga-Book*, XVII (1967–8), 116–44.

Thomas, C., *The Early Christian Archaeology of North Britain* (1971).

—'The early Christian church', in *Who are the Scots?*, ed. G. Menzies (1971), 90–102.

—'Sculptured stones and crosses from St Ninian's Isle and Papil', in *St Ninian's Isle and Its Treasure*, ed. A. Small, C. Thomas and D. M. Wilson, I (1973), 8–44.

Thomas, F., 'What is a pennyland?', *PSAS*, XVIII (1883–4).

Thomson, W. P., 'Funzie, Fetlar: a Shetland runrig township in the 19th century', *Scottish Geographical Mag.*, LXXXVI (1970), 170–85.

—*The Little General and the Rousay Crofters* (1981).

—'Fifteenth century depression in Orkney: the evidence of Lord Henry Sinclair's Rentals', in *Essays in Shetland History*, ed. B. E. Crawford (1984), 125–42.

Thorson, P., 'Ancient Thurso. A religious and judicial centre', *Fifth Viking Congress* (1968), 71–7.

Thorsteinsson, A., 'The Viking burial place at Pierowall, Westray, Orkney', *Fifth Viking Congress*, 150–73.

—'The testimony of ancient architecture', *Faroe Isles Review*, I (1976), 12–19.

—'Faerøske huskonstruktioner fra vikingetid til 1800-årene' (Faeroese house construction from the Viking period until the nineteenth century), in *Vestnordisk Byggeskikk gjennom to tusen år*, ed. B. Myhre, B. Stoklund and P. Gjaerder, Arkeologisk Museum i Stavanger, Skrifter no. 7 (1982), 149–62.

Thuesen, N. P., 'Norrøn Bosetning på Orknøyene' (thesis, University of Oslo, 1978).

Turville-Petre, G., *Origins of Icelandic Literature* (1953).

Wainwright, F. T. (ed.), *The Problem of the Picts* (1955; repr. 1980).

—*Archaeology and Place-Names and History* (1962).

—(ed.), *The Northern Isles* (1962).

—*Scandinavian England* (1975).

Walsh, A., *Scandinavian Relations with Ireland during the Viking period* (1922).

Wamers, E., 'Some ecclesiastical and secular Insular metalwork found in Norwegian Viking graves', *Peritia*, ii (1983), 277–306.

Warner, 'Scottish silver arm-rings: an analysis of weights', *PSAS*, cvii (1975–6), 136–43.

Watson, W. J., *The Place-Names of Ross and Cromarty* (1904).

—*History of the Celtic Place-Names of Scotland* (1926).

Watt, D. E. R., *Fasti Ecclesiae Scoticanae Medii Aevi ad annum 1638* (1969).

—'Diocese of the Isles', in *Series Episcoporum Ecclesiae Catholicae Occidentalis ab Initio ad Annum 1198*, ed. C. Engels and S. Weinfurter (in press).

Watt, J., *The Church in Medieval Ireland* (1972).

Weibull, L., *Kritiska Undersökningar i Nordens Historia omkring år 1000* (1911).

Wilson, D. M., 'Manx memorial stones of the Viking period', *Saga-Book*, xviii (1970–1), 1–18.

—'The Norsemen', in *Who Are the Scots?*, ed. G. Menzies (1971), 103–13.

—'The treasure' in *St Ninian's Isle and Its Treasure*, ed. A. Small, C. Thomas and D. M. Wilson, I (1973), 45–144.

—*The Viking Age in the Isle of Man* (Odense, 1974).

—'Scandinavian settlement in the north and west of the British Isles – an archaeological point-of-view', *TRHS*, xxvi (1976), 95–113.

—'The art of the Manx crosses', *Ninth Viking Congress*, 175–87.

Wood, M., 'Brunanburh revisited', *Saga-Book*, xx (1978–9), 200–17.

Wormald, P., 'Viking studies: whence and whither?', in *The Vikings*, ed. R. T. Farrell (1982), 128–53.

Young, G. V. C., *The History of the Isle of Man under the Norse* (1981).

Index